*Issues of
the Heart*

"Keep your heart with all diligence,
for out of it are the issues of life."
Proverbs 4:23

Issues of the Heart

Memoirs of an Artilleryman in Vietnam

Howard Olsen

McFarland & Company, Inc., Publishers
Jefferson, North Carolina, and London

British Library Cataloguing-in-Publication data are available

Library of Congress Cataloguing-in-Publication Data

Olsen, Howard, 1947–
    Issues of the heart : memoirs of an artilleryman in Vietnam /
Howard Olsen.
        p.   cm.
    [Includes index.]
    ISBN 0-89950-506-6 (sewn softcover : 50# alk. paper) ∞
    1. Vietnamese Conflict, 1961–1975 – Personal narratives, American.
2. Vietnamese Conflict, 1961–1975 – Regimental histories – United
States.   3. United States. Army. Field Artillery, 8th. Battalion,
1st. "Charlie" Battery – History.   4. Olsen, Howard, 1947–
I. Title.
DS559.5.047   1990
959.704'342 – dc20   89-43662
                                                                CIP

Manufactured in the United States of America

McFarland & Company, Inc., Publishers
  Box 611, Jefferson, North Carolina 28640

To Debbie Winger,
Diane Bretthauer,
Bob Dylan
and to my close friend
Jesus Christ

Foreword

I had always intended to write about my experience in Vietnam, even from the earliest days following my departure in late 1968. In spite of the fact that I destroyed my uniform and every vestige of military gear I was discharged with, in an effort to dissociate myself from military life, I kept my photographs, journal and a tape I had recorded under fire. Periodically, I listened to the tape and reread the journal, somehow enjoying the bitter-sweet memories they evoked. I went from times of forgetting, to remembering, and back to forgetting. Sometimes the wheel turned quickly, sometimes it took years. In 1975, I discarded even my journal and photographs. I guess that had my tape been in my possession at the time, I would have destroyed that too.

For one year following, I successfully put Vietnam out of my mind. For the first time since my discharge, I held a job for more than six months. Then slowly the memories began to return. They were intense, momentary flashes of sight and sound. They appeared with almost mystical insight, sometimes making me laugh but more often making me cry. There was no stopping them; they came to me suddenly and caught me off guard. So, as my past again unfolded, I put pen to paper and began writing notes to myself, capturing those moments of vivid clarity.

Three years later those flashbacks were terrifying nightmares, periodic scenes that not only visited my dreams but stalked my waking moments as well. Viet Cong darted across open fields as I walked in the country. Frenzied moments of bloodcurdling combat shattered my sleep. Recurring nightmares of being trapped back in Vietnam caused me to wake in terror, soaked in the sweat of silent screams. Then came the anger, the rage, the depression and the uncontrolled weeping.

It became clear that I would have to deal with my past thoroughly if I was ever truly to leave it behind. Thus began my arduous journey. I knew in my heart that I had to write my story, if for no other reason than to get it out of my head. A psychologist working with the Veterans Outreach Center in St. Paul, Minnesota, said that Vietnam was like a three-dimensional movie playing over and over in my mind, complete with sounds and smells that kept it alive. I kept it alive because I could not let myself forget. She said that if I wrote it all down, then I wouldn't have to keep a record of it alive in my mind. I wouldn't have to worry about losing it, but could put it up on a shelf and it would be there whenever I needed it.

She was right! As hard as it was for me to embrace my past and all the feelings, as I began to write I also began to experience a healing process. I chose to lay each bitter event on the altar of forgiveness. In the ten years that it took me to write my story, the first four were by far the hardest. It seems only by grace and uncommon loyalty that my wife was able to stick with me during those years.

The interest of the United States in South Vietnam was born in the post–World War II era. Depending on which historian you read, or whom you choose to believe, American interest was motivated purely for the ideological good of all democracies and the free world—or it was motivated by self-serving demands for protection for industrial and economic strongholds developed in Southeast Asia by major American corporations. Even twenty years later, the lessons of Vietnam are still debated, and they remain a source of conflict and impasse for many people. It is frustrating for not just those of us who were directly involved but also for the American public to not be able to come to a consensus. I did not write this memoir to be a political statement. It has more to do with one young man's coming of age during a traumatic, harshly inhumane war, as all wars are, than it has to do with politics.

This book is an expression of the events of "Charlie" Battery, 1st Battalion, 8th Field Artillery, 25th Infantry Division, as seen through the eyes of one individual who served there. It is not intended to be an exhaustive compilation of military or political facts, even though they are historically and accurately interwoven within the framework of this novel.

History will never be understood through the eyes of only one person. This artilleryman's experience, no matter how commonplace or shared by other Veterans, is still his own, and therefore unique. In the sense that it reflects a common vein of experience, however, one that many other Vietnam combat veterans once shared and still are sharing, it will stand as a reminder of troubling words and images echoing across the American continent at the close of the 1980s.

I have taken great pains to insure an accurate, honest portrayal of the times, lives and events occurring in this book. All the dates and places have been confirmed by previously classified documents and materials I obtained from extensive research at the Carlisle Military Institute and from the Department of the Army's archives in Washington, D.C. Some names have been fictionalized while many remain the same. The sequence of events, though secondary in importance, is true. Detailed experiences have been impossible to forget.

Even though I have heard that there were no heroes in Vietnam, I have come to the opinion that every combat veteran who served in Vietnam was a hero— heroes whose sacrifices and loyalty will always go unrecognized and unrewarded.

For the thousands of young men who came of age in Vietnam; for the thousands who gave their lives that others might return; and for the thousands who have since taken their lives in suicide, this book is written.

Contents

Introduction

As 1965 drew to a close, I was just 17. I was in that period of growth that learned persons call the "formative years." Broken relationships with my father and mother had caused me to drift away from my family, and graduation from high school further separated me from my closest friends. I had already become a loner, a rebel standing against most social and fashionable norms. For me and others my age, it was a time of developing self-awareness. I had a deep longing to find myself, my worth, to discover my abilities and to understand my behavior and where I belonged.

But the sixties also had a cutting edge to them. The chimes sounding throughout the land also resonated deep in my own life. As I made the fateful approach to Vietnam, old as well as new sounds vied for my attention. Music, then the life blood of American youth, played an important part.

This was the formative age of rock 'n' roll and of a rich variety of other musical styles all of which had some impact on my emergent self. Such labels as the British invasion, rock-a-billy, psychedelic, and acid-rock were in use. The Beatles had just emerged from the cellars of England and Germany, as had the Stones, the Kinks and the Animals. The music of the time was a penetrating blade.

Folk music, with its collegiate hootenannies and blunt social messages, had catapulted such stars as Bob Dylan, Joan Baez, Judy Collins, Pete Seeger, Peter, Paul and Mary, and Simon and Garfunkel to the forefront of a growing protest movement and I spent long hours agonizing over the meaning behind Dylan's words. In addition, there was an emerging blend of folk and rock which assured a permanent niche in musical history for such groups as the Byrds, Buffalo Springfield and others. The folk sound was enlarging its borders.

Fortunately for me, there were others who had not forgotten the roots of American music and who turned me on to the likes of Woody Guthrie, Cisco Houston, Odetta and other folk singers who were carrying on a tradition that started deep in the South. It was from such "Southern comfort" that I discovered the rich, emotionally provocative sound of the traditional blues of singers like Leadbelly, Jimmy Reed, Blind "Lemon" Jefferson and others. It also opened the way for me to discover their contemporary offspring in jazz, rhythm and blues, and soul.

The sixties were also a time of fear. A time when suddenly the nation, or the media, or the military—I'm not really sure which—was shocked by the launching of a Russian satellite into orbit and *sputnik* became a word whispered in awe or shouted as a curse. The Russians had beaten us into space! The threat of communist superiority was a rising vapor across the land and it permeated the public school system of which I was a part. Fighting communism became synonymous with patriotism, baseball, mom and apple pie. Bomb shelters began to appear, and words like "fallout." It was a time of missile crisis in Cuba, of CONELRAD on the radio and Air Raid Drills in school. True paranoia.

For me, the sixties could best be described as a time of movements and of increasing radical change. As with the Moon pulling the tides, there were movements that I was almost entirely unaware of until they were nearly over and gone. While some hidden forces moved quietly in the sixties, others surfaced with exploding viewpoints that often clashed violently. The civil rights movement, while enacted in the streets of places like Memphis and Montgomery, had its black and white images clashing on my living room television. It was also a period of the raising of social consciousness—and, as my adolescent eyes discovered, a world of injustice and the dreary scramble to keep up with one's cohorts. It didn't take JFK's death for me to suffer disillusionment: I had already learned bitter lessons from my parents, teachers, coaches and the local police.

The sixties were a time when real butter was replaced by margarine and sugar by saccharine and its unpleasant aftertaste. Home cooked meals were replaced by TV dinners and convenience food; blandness had begun to permeate an American lifestyle hellbent on acquisition and comfort.

Gangs were popular alternatives for young men and women alienated from a healthy family life and a materialistic society and I had been a part of one for two or three years. I was an outcast, virtually an outlaw, and a part of me wanted to kick the shit out of anyone who threatened me; I often did, in spite of my size. But, paralleling the change in society, a part of me wanted to withdraw and push my past and everyone associated with it out of my life. It was that part of me that secretly wept after beating up another student and bloodying his face. That part that throughout my life had been gradually squeezed into cramped quarters in the cellar of my identity.

In the middle of it all, I began to slip into a kind of hibernation. I had been kicked out of my house, expelled from school, blackballed in my community; I wasn't quite sure who I was or even where I belonged and in the midst of my search I blundered into the military. It was during the Vietnam years that I was forced to grow up rapidly if I was to ever survive. For my friends and "comrades in arms," it was a time of impressionable growth also, and we faced it together.

It began with a fateful ride to a Portland, Oregon, induction facility.

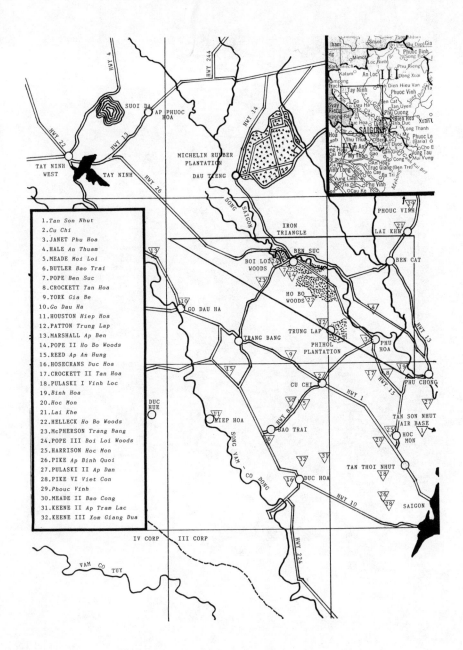

1. Tan Son Nhut
2. Cu Chi
3. JANET Phu Hoa
4. HALE An Thuam
5. MEADE Moi Loi
6. BUTLER Bao Trai
7. POPE Ben Suc
8. CROCKETT Tan Hoa
9. YORK Gia Be
10. Go Dau Ha
11. HOUSTON Hiep Hoa
12. PATTON Trung Lap
13. MARSHALL Ap Ben
14. POPE II Ho Bo Woods
15. REED Ap An Hung
16. HOSECRANS Duc Hoa
17. CROCKETT II Tan Hoa
18. PULASKI I Vinh Loc
19. Binh Hoa
20. Hoc Mon
21. Lai Khe
22. HELLECK Ho Bo Woods
23. McPHERSON Trang Bang
24. POPE III Boi Loi Woods
25. HARRISON Hoc Mon
26. PIKE Ap Binh Quoi
27. PULASKI II Ap Dan
28. PIKE VI Viet Con
29. Phouc Vinh
30. MEADE II Bao Cong
31. KEENE II Ap Tram Lac
32. KEENE III Xom Giang Dua

Charlie Battery—1st Battalion 8th Artillery Fire Support Bases

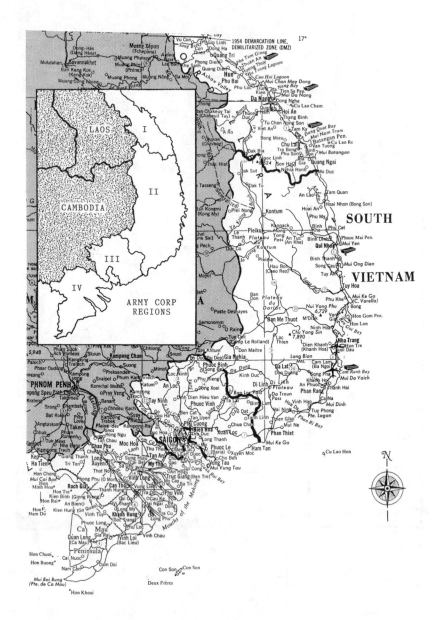

Division of Army Corp Areas; 25th Infantry—III Corp

1 OPERATION BARKING SANDS

1

3 May 1967
Hillsboro, Oregon

"Stop the car!" I gasped, lurching forward and fumbling with the front door knob. "I'm going to be sick."

Mike Finn, a close friend, brought the green '49 Pontiac to a bumpy halt along the edge of an almost deserted road. We were in the country outside of Hillsboro, Oregon. I could feel the nausea rising as I threw my weight against the door, then sprawled into the dirt. Scrambling to my feet, I stumbled through the tall grass that filled the adjoining ditch. My bell bottoms quickly soaked up the dew. Damn! I was always conscious about my appearance, but there was little room for that now. My senses were reeling as it was. I was desperate to reach the fence on the far side of the ditch—I needed something to lean against. At last I threw my weight against a fence post. I could feel the darkness closing in. I jerked like a marionette, my stomach heaving its contents into the grass. I squeezed my eyes and groaned a desperate plea to God. I wanted Him to be real now when I needed Him. I wanted only to be free from the pain. I would try anything. My head continued to spin, even after the retching stopped. Another sure sign that there was no God.

Of course it wasn't just the alcoholic binge that I had been on the last ten hours that affected me. It was the never ending questioning that had me tied up in knots. The sunrise that brought an end to my revelry had also reawakened the fear that I was going to regret what I had just gotten myself into. Today was to be my day of reckoning. We were headed into Portland, to the Army induction center where I had been told to report for my physical.

Had I done the right thing? Doubt plagued me.

Had volunteering for the draft been an act of patriotism or was it really only an act of cowardice? Surely it had been an act of desperation, an attempt to alleviate the boredom and despair that were swallowing my life. Maybe it was just confusion that had prompted me to make such a fateful decision? The consequences of my actions now seemed too heavy to bear.

3

I knew I was running from responsibility but how could I be assured that the path I had chosen would be any less threatening than the life I was trying to avoid? Joining the Army, or rather volunteering for the draft, had seemed very rational at the time. I felt it was time to get it over with—time to quit evading the draft, as I had been doing for the last year or so. It was time to grow up, or so I had told myself. Time to begin acting like a man. Time to quit avoiding my patriotic duty. My duty to God and Country. Now, all those pat answers seemed empty. If they were right, why did I feel such dread, such loss, such conflict? I still hadn't made up my mind that going into the service with the express purpose of killing others, even communists, was right.

Struggling to put it all together, I tried again to think of a course of action that would help me undo what I had done. I needed an act of desperation equal to the one that had gotten me into this predicament.

"Hey c'mon!" Mike yelled, opening his door and peering over the roof of the car. "We're gonna be late!"

"All right . . . all right!" I staggered back to the car. Try as I could, I could not shake the feeling of dread, as revolting as the taste of vomit still stinging my throat.

I slumped down in the seat. I could see the faces of Mike's friends in the rear view mirror. Slack with sleep, they had no idea of the torment I felt. While hardly more than acquaintances, they had elected to accompany me in my final hour of freedom. They were going to give me a rousing farewell. And why not, I thought, they weren't the ones going! They didn't have to worry about the draft. They had all gone from high school straight to college, more anxious to receive their 4-A draft deferment than to start their studies. Already one of them was considering quitting, but was intending to get married so he wouldn't have to worry about getting drafted.

Even if I had wanted to go to college, and I didn't, there was really no way that I could have afforded it. I hadn't been a resident of Oregon long enough to qualify for the cheap tuition that was available to residents at the community college, and attending Portland State was out of the question! College was for rich kids. For those whose parents could easily buy them deferments. And I wouldn't even lay claim to having parents. When my old man booted me out of "his" house over a year ago, I severed all ties with my family. Shit, I wouldn't admit to having parents, much less think about asking them for money to go to school.

One thing was for certain. Nobody was going to take care of me, and no one was going to get me out of this situation, but me.

2

As Hawaii slowly faded the atmosphere inside the Boeing 707 became quiet, almost meditative. The passing hours stood in contrast to our initial boisterous departure. Most of the soldiers around me lay sleeping, or deep in thought. I tried to sleep, but without success. I wished for it. At least there would have been some hope of waking up and finding this was all a dream; a kind of crazy nightmare.

I leaned to my right and looked out the window. Cloud formations filled the sky below, obstructing any view. My future seemed as overcast and as impenetrable. How could I have allowed myself to get into this kind of situation?

I fought to block the flow of questions that assailed my mind, and eventually came sleep and escape.

Somewhere near sleep, I heard a voice speaking to me. It was as distinct as any voice I had ever heard. "You will not die," it said, "until you have finished the purpose for which you were created."

Immediately a vivid picture flashed in my mind, and I saw myself before a multitude eager to hear me speak. I could hear myself telling them about the reality of a living God and about His love for them. As suddenly as it had appeared, the picture faded. Opening my eyes, I found myself still a captive in the plane. Nothing had changed. Still, that picture lingered. I wondered what it meant! More than that, an inner peace had momentarily replaced my anxiety. I had a strong feeling that everything would be all right. The reality of my situation soon left me doubting, however, that this was anything but a fleeting hallucination, a subconscious grasp for hope. A God, I thought, c'mon, there was no such thing.

My thoughts slipped momentarily back to the basement of the Congregational Church I had attended in my youth. I had sung in the choir, attended Bible school, Sunday school, led my youth group, been an altar boy, passed the collection plate, and performed a host of other religious duties, but I had never seen this God they talked about and had seen extremely little godliness in the church-goers. I, of course, was no different. Whatever duty I had performed in church, certainly had not been from my heart. I had lifted money from the collection plate, stolen from the missionary collection glass, made out with the girls in the dimly lit sanctuary, and challenged and taunted others in my group who believed the Christian fables. I could never remember attending church without prodding of some kind from my parents. They had insisted on our attendance (my three brothers and I) in spite of our dogged resistance and complaint—yet never saw the need to go regularly themselves. They, like most people I knew, went mostly at Christmas and Easter. Church, for me, had been nothing more than ritual, an accumulation of checks on an attendance ledger rewarded with pins and bars. Who needed God when pins and bars could buy you recognition and holiness and favor? Church carried the stink of hypocrisy and the burden of guilt. It was nothing more than a circus whose ringmaster was human pride.

Once, in the ninth grade, Mike Finn and I had drunk the tiny goblets of grape juice that were sitting in the church basement following a communion service, pretending it was wine. We were acting like we were getting drunk when the pastor's wife walked in. She had stormed across the kitchen, her face livid with anger, screaming and accusing us of blasphemy, calling us degenerates, heathens and hoods. We had laughed about it afterwards but we had both been stung by the severe tongue-lashing. As we raced out the rear steps I had whispered curses right back at her. Our make-believe had been no different from the pretense and performance they were practicing upstairs! Had our behavior been so worthy of condemnation and theirs not? A God, I questioned; there was no God!

I returned my gaze to the window. The intercom crackled and a pleasant voice stated that the shoreline of Vietnam was now visible. "It will be twenty minutes to arrival," the voice continued. "We will begin our descent in about fifteen minutes. Please pay attention to the no smoking sign, and fasten your seat belts when you are instructed."

As we flew over the coast, my thoughts returned to the dream I had tried to shake. If there was a God, certainly now was the time to believe in Him. Still, only the weak believed in such fairy tales, and I would not be weak! There was no such thing as the supernatural! No Superman. No Santa Claus. No Tonto or Lone Ranger! Yet just remembering the dream brought a kind of comfort. It seemed to temporarily silence the menacing anxiety I felt.

Looking down, my eyes scanned the rising earth. A vibrant green and blue, patchwork-quilted countryside rushed forward to meet our descent. Tiny villages of scattered thatched roofs swept into view like marbles scattered in a player's circle. Centuries-old rice paddy walls outlined each swatch of color, framing the land like a giant Cézanne. A long, blue river wound over the surface, the scrawl of some ancient handwriting. Small canals spread out from its juts and bends, penetrating the surrounding jungle and crop land.

I knew this was the Mekong Delta, the fertile, southern portion of the Republic of Vietnam. Rumor had it that this was also the scene of fierce and bloody fighting.

Its rich soil, abundantly supplied by rain water and industriously cared for by Vietnamese farmers, had made it the rice bowl of the nation, a prize coveted by both the enemy and our allies. As we flew north, we passed over smaller, fertile, strips of rice lands. I knew we would soon reach the Tan Son Nhut military base. Ninety percent of Vietnam's 18 million citizens lived and worked in these lowland areas, and I wondered what they would be like. What kind of reception would we receive?

As we approached the air base, I was both drawn to and repulsed by its unexpected appearance. I was expecting it to look like any other American base—like an American city. But from the air, it looked small and rural. As we continued our descent, I noticed the waterfilled bomb craters which pockmarked the surrounding rice paddies and portions of the runway. Camouflaged anti-aircraft guns poked their snouts up on the perimeter of the landing field, flanked by protruding observation towers.

As the airplane taxied I made note of the massive strands of barbed wire and fencing surrounding the air strip. Rows of wood and metal huts pressed together outside them. Colorful banners covered with huge Oriental letters fluttered in the breeze in a number of areas. Could it be that we had arrived in the middle of some kind of celebration? I pressed my face to the window again for a closer look. Staggered throughout the perimeter were small, sandbagged bunkers with mounted .50 caliber machine guns, and here and there, blurry figures roamed in olive drab fatigues. Off to my right, an Army jeep sped toward the plane, and the plane slowly rolled toward it.

Shortly, we stopped, and two officers entered.

"Welcome to the Republic of Vietnam," one said. "When I give the order to disembark, I want you to walk in single file over to the gates and into the adjoining building. You will be processed 'in country' and given a set of jungle fatigues to replace your khakis. You will exchange any American currency you now have for Military Payment Certificates, MPCs. You will then be taken to a temporary compound for sleeping quarters until your orders have been completely processed and new ones are received. We expect you to be placed in new units within one to three days. Is that understood?"

He paused for a brief moment to give added weight to his statement and then barked, "Disembark!"

Soldiers and blue-green travel bags filled the aisles. I struggled forward with everyone else. I was anxious to get off the plane, to get up and stretch. Outside the hatchway, the heat and humidity exploded in my face. My God, I thought, it's like an oven out here! Within seconds beads of sweat formed on my face. Moments later sweat began to trickle down my crotch.

As soon as roll call was taken and we were all accounted for, we were marched over to a large warehouse. Entering a section which contained concrete floors and wood benches, we were told to stack our baggage and strip. I was only too happy to rid myself of the heavy, starched khakis. They were already wet. We attached ourselves to an already lengthy line of GIs standing before a row of counters running the full length of the building and began the tedious process of collecting jungle gear. As soon as we had made it full circle, we dressed and were immediately herded outside to exchange our money and await transportation to temporary barracks. A money exchange set up in a nearby Quonset hut was collecting American dollars and handing back the unfamiliar MPCs. It looked strangely like Monopoly money. I wasn't sure I should trade in my American money but I had been instructed that only two types of currency existed in the 'Nam, the U.S. Military Payment Certificate and the Vietnamese piasters. Possession of American dollars was illegal, so I decided to play the game by their rules. Some, however, stashed their money. They were going to send it home later, through the mail.

After standing in line for hours, we were finally transported to heavily sand-bagged tin Quonset huts at the perimeter of the air base. By then, I had been issued an M-16 and made to memorize its serial number.

Soon after our arrival, night fell and so did a death-like silence. Glover, Carr, Yuhas and I, friends since A.I.T., regrouped at our bunks as soon as we were officially dismissed. We were looking for some excitement. Yuhas had heard there was a snack bar and an E.M. club somewhere near our barracks and we decided to go look for it. Stumbling over sandbags, we made our way past the outpost bunker and headed toward the center of the compound. It was like trying to find your way in a cave. Night discipline was in effect and all lights had been ex-tinguished. We hadn't a clue as to where we were, or even what direction we were going. Using what little moonlight existed, we negotiated a line of barracks until we came upon a clearing. We stood dumbstruck! It was like a scene from a western movie. Everywhere we looked, people carried rifles or holstered .45's. The buildings were all made of clapboard, with false fronts protruding above their basic framework. Small wood signs were nailed above the entrances to each. Dust rose like an eerie mist wherever people walked. We asked a soldier heading our way where the enlisted men's bar was and he wordlessly pointed without stopping.

The bar, too, was like a scene from another world. The interior, constructed like an old saloon, was filled with smoke and the stench of sweat and booze. Slot machines lined one side of the room. Scattered throughout its center were small groups of soldiers huddled around tables, laughing boisterously or scrutinizing closely held poker hands.

"Hey, let's get a move on!" someone shouted behind us.

We pushed each other forward to get out of the way, slightly embarrassed by the fact that we were all acting like such novices. While the other guys headed toward the bar to get drinks, I shouted my request to Glover and went looking for an empty table.

Shortly after we were seated, a soldier in a sweat-stained bandanna and dirty fatigues approached us.

"Hey, where are you guys from?" he demanded. "Are you new recruits or some-thing? Haven't you been told that you don't go anywhere without your M-16!"

We were taken aback by his hostility.

"We were told that we were to go nowhere without it in the field," I offered defensively.

"Well, I have news for you," he snapped. "This is the field! You don't go anywhere without it, not even to the shitter. And, you'd better learn to sleep with it too if you want to leave here alive. Is that understood?"

Spinning on his heels, he left, not waiting for a reply. We exchanged surprised looks.

"Shit, I wonder who the hell he thinks he was," said Glover.

"Well I sure enough didn't see any stripes on his sleeves," added Carr.

"It looked to me like he was a sergeant," I said. "I think I saw three stripes on his shirt sleeve. It was hard to tell though because they were black, not gold."

"Well I don't care who the fuck he was," said Yuhas. "He had no right to talk to us like that."

"Shit, who cares," I said. "C'mon, let's forget about it."

I tried to shrug it off but I could remember our orientation. It hadn't seemed important then but now it did. The master sergeant issuing weapons had insisted on our memorizing our serial numbers, adding that we wouldn't be allowed to leave the country unless we checked out with the same rifle. I could hardly believe that was true, but it seemed more believable now. Damn, it was hard to make the transition from stateside to a combat zone. It just didn't seem real yet. Especially here—now!

We drank a second round of beers and talked, but quickly grew tired of the loud music and the choking smoke. We decided to split and go find a quiet place to get stoned. Yuhas said he had a couple of joints secretly stashed in the lining of his travel bag, and we left to get them. Groping our way back to the Quonsets, we slipped into a small space between two adjoining barracks and sat and waited for Yuhas to go pick up his weed.

Fifteen minutes slipped by and we began wondering what had happened to Yuhas. We were surprised when he came back accompanied by a stranger.

"Hey guys," he said, "meet Noyse. Man, he's from the same area in the Bronx I am. He says the shit they got over here is dynamite and he's got some for us to try."

"Far out," I said, extending my hand. "My name's Olsen. Glad to meet ya." Glover and Carr introduced themselves and as the night drew to a close, we experienced our first home-grown high.

On the second morning, we hauled our asses out of bed before dawn and after chow assembled at the departure area to wait for shipping orders. Our numbers were steadily decreasing as people began shipping out, but new recruits kept coming in and the staging area never seemed any less full. By 0800 hours it was already 80 degrees in the shade and while waiting impatiently in formation, we grumbled about the "hurry up and wait" policy that was so prevalent in the Army. It made me think that someone in authority always had his head up his ass, but even more disturbing was the subtle but dehumanizing effect it had on each one of us. The Army cared little for individuals—and waiting, especially in vague silence, like every other aspect of training, was designed to destroy any sense of individuality or personal rights. It helped draw us into a place of mindless obedience. The more they treated us like machines the better it was for them. Slowly but surely, they could forge the handcuffs of despair that ultimately left everyone under their control. Shorn of resistance we could be like sheep, led to our own slaughter. This morning's activity had been no different.

As I listened to roll call, shipping orders were handed out. They included all of us. Excitedly, I picked up the papers containing my orders and exchanged information with the others as soon as I could. We were all hoping to be sent together to one place, but no such luck. Yuhas was going north, Glover and Carr were being attached to the 9th Infantry Division in the south, and I was being attached to the 25th.

Disappointment quickly dampened our excitement. We had all grown fairly close and Glover had been like a brother to me. He was like blood. The time we had spent together in Leadership Preparation School, A.I.T. and later on in San Francisco while on leave, had cemented a bond between us. Now that bond was about to be broken and at a time I probably needed him the most. Loneliness and isolation, feelings that had not been strangers in my life, immediately crept into my consciousness. Lucky for me, our separation would come quickly. We were ordered to return to our barracks and pick up our belongings immediately, and to board the deuce-and-a-half ton trucks that were waiting to take us a step further into the unknown.

"What a fuckin' bummer," I said to Glover as we trotted off to pick up our duffel bags. "I'm really gonna miss you, man."

Even though I did my best to hide my emotions, Glover knew how I really felt. More than once I had opened my heart to him. He perhaps knew more of my heart than any other man.

"Hey, brother, it's all right," answered Glover. "We'll be getting together just as soon as we finish this tour. Look, I'm gonna take care of my shit, and you make sure you take care of yours, O.K.? And don't let anything happen to ya."

I avoided his eyes, afraid that he might see the hurt I was feeling, and forced a smile. Packing our gear in silence, we slung our duffel bags on our backs and headed for the trucks. Glover threw his bag up on the first truck and climbed in behind Carr.

"Hey, man, take it easy." I said. "I'll see you twelve months from now, O.K.?"

"Right on," he answered, laughing.

"Carr, be cool!" I shouted.

It tore at my heart to see them go. I forced myself to turn around and head for my own transportation. Yuhas followed. In a matter of minutes it was over. Their trucks, filled to capacity, left. I dropped my duffel bag on the floor of the waiting transport and slumped down on top of it. Laying my M-16 across my lap

I lit up a cigarette, and studied the faces of each stranger that climbed aboard. I wondered what was ahead for me now.

As the convoy motored through the dusty streets of Tan Son Nhut, I wondered where the hell I was going. It never occurred to me during those moments of separation to inquire as to where the 25th Infantry Division was. I turned to one of the soldiers guarding the truck. His fatigues looked like they hadn't been washed for a month. Even the camouflage cover on his helmet was thick with mud. A thick-skinned, brown flak-jacket was draped over his back, and I wondered how he could stand to wear it in this heat. Even though my fatigues were beginning to turn soggy, and a little uncomfortable, his showed obvious signs of discomfort. The back and arms of his shirt were soaked. I noticed a small tan band around his camouflage cover. Written on it were the words "fuck it"; they mirrored both the boredom and detachment that covered his face.

"Where we going?" I asked.

"Cu Chi," he grunted. "It's a base camp set up outside the village of Cu Chi about twenty miles northwest of here. Not far from the Cambodian border."

"What's it like?" I continued even though I felt like I was prying. It seemed like a chore for this guy to divulge any information.

"What's it like!" he repeated. "Well it's like this. It's between a rock and a hard place. I mean it's right between a major VC stronghold in the north and Saigon, the capital. That makes it important to Charlie, and that means he's out to kick ass whenever he can."

His voice was hard, almost bitter. I felt reluctant to continue but my curiosity was greater. "VC?" I asked, "What's that?"

"Viet Cong," he said, half surprised. "That's right," he added, a smile flickering across his face. "You'se is green. Well, we call him Charlie! They're these fuckin' gooks in black pajamas you see during the day but never at night."

I wasn't sure what that meant but I was anxious to learn anything I could. I pressed on. I could see our conversation was getting the attention of other recruits nearby.

"Do you think there'll be any trouble on the way?" I asked.

"Can't tell. I sure as hell hope not, though. We're bound to run into a few mines on the way but we've got Roadrunners up front, and they should find them first."

"What are Roadrunners?" I asked.

"They're specially equipped tanks," he said. "They're mine sweepers that check out the road in front of us. They have mine detection equipment and are built to take the shock of a blast if they miss one. If *we* hit one, we can chalk it up!"

The front of the convoy began clearing the main gate and I leaned over the side. I could see a tank in the lead and an armored personnel carrier behind it. A jeep with an M-60 mounted on it was half visible in a cloud of dust that trailed the tank. One man crouched behind the machine gun. Behind them trailed the deuce-and-a-halfs, each truck throwing long rooster tails of red dust over the occupants behind them. Sliding down behind the cab to avoid as much dust as possible, I pulled my helmet down tight and braced myself for a bumpy ride. Silence fell over the inhabitants of the truck as we slowly rolled through the gate. A short MP with creases in his trousers and spit-shined boots looked up impassively. Both guards in our truck slammed magazines into their M-16s and readied the machine gun atop the cab. I followed suit. In addition, I pulled the recoil mechanism, letting a round slam into the chamber. The guard sitting next to me turned.

"Be sure to keep it on safety," he said. "We don't want any accidents. Listen, we don't fire at nothin' unless we're fired on first. I don't want any of you greenhorns getting spooked and killing anybody you're not supposed to." He laughed.

Kill, I thought, the word sounded foreign, oddly frightening. Yet he had said it so impassively. It sure wasn't the way we had been trained to yell and scream it in Basic Training.

As we crept through Tan Son Nhut I looked down into the upturned faces of Vietnamese women who wandered throughout the compound. Occasionally one would smile, her wide grin revealing brown stained teeth, but most of them seemed unconcerned with our passing. As we slipped by rows of barbed wire and fence outside the perimeter of the base, I noticed the guard sitting next to me slip his M-16 off safety. I did the same.

Our convoy picked up speed. Smaller civilian vehicles we encountered moved aside if there was room, but often as not they drove into the ditch to let us pass. There were very few vehicles on the road and that stuck in my mind. There weren't any cars. Occasionally we passed a bus but even that was nothing more than an oversized golfcart with peasants sandwiched between a canopied roof and stiff, wooden benches. Most people we passed were on foot, or rode bicycles. There were a lot of bicycles! Sometimes ARVN soldiers passed us by, often as not doubled up on motorscooters, but I never saw a car.

Tiny hamlets were scattered every few miles along the rough road, and I studied each with fascination. No training film or officer's lecture had adequately prepared me for my harsh encounter with this Asian reality. No matter what I had expected—this wasn't it! I would have been better prepared watching Tarzan movies. The villages and towns we passed were no more than a collection of primitive bamboo huts, the kind I would expect to find an African running out of, spear in hand. The huts bordered each side of the road, perhaps fifteen to twenty yards out. Each one had a large patch of dirt in front of it, probably worn bare by the trampling of feet. The sides of the huts were made of large grass mats, woven together and fastened to thick bamboo poles in each corner. Long layers of grass, much like sheaves of wheat, covered both the walls and roofs. The long overhang from the roof created a short shaded porch which cast shadows over the face of each building, obscuring the open entrance which faced the road.

Large piles of wood or hay were stacked against the sides of some of the huts or heaped in disarray in what appeared to be their front yards, but for the most part, the villages were barren. There was an occasional oxcart but no other means of transportation, and very few animals, if any. I was immediately struck by the primitiveness, slightly embarrassed and shocked by what seemed to be unabashed poverty. How could people live like this? It was a question I kept repeating.

Although I had been warned to be on the alert when approaching the outskirts of any village, I saw little to frighten me. The only people I saw inside the villages were women and children. The few men I did see were skeleton-like figures whose skin hung on their faces and bodies like layers of wax. They sat crouched in the shadows, their ancient frames clad in loose black pajamas, intent only on observing life with little thought of participating. As the convoy lumbered through these villages the children would run to meet us, crowding alongside the road as we passed. Young girls, who often stood with naked young babies in their arms, hung back, shyly dropping their eyes, or tipping their heads forward so their huge straw hats hid their faces. The older women would come out of the huts and stand in the doorways, their hands on their hips. Amusement crowned their lips.

As we drove past the outstretched, waving arms of children—some bare-bottomed and all of them shoeless—they giggled and laughed. Their innocent, playful greetings sparked my first feelings of compassion. Dressed in rags or loose white shirts, they raised their voices, some pleading, all begging, their eyes bright with anticipation.

"Hey G.I., you numbah one.... Gimme chop chop.... O.K., G.I."

"Hey G.I.... Boom-boom, boom-boom!! My sista, she numbah one. She boom boom O.K., G.I." Their chorus filled the air.

"Fuck you!" the guard would yell back at them in contempt, his face hard.

I was initially startled by his response and wondered why he vented such anger at these innocent kids. They weren't doing anything to hurt him.

The kids would yell and point to the young girls in the background and some of the soldiers would toss candy and C rations to them. Some of them even tossed cigarettes. Before these objects could hit the ground, the children ran for them in a frenzied scramble. It reminded me of the times I too had scrambled for pennies and candy thrown from floats in passing parades. As cigarettes arched into the air the screams from the children increased. Small children abandoned the hands of their even smaller brothers and sisters, hoping to get their share, leaving the toddlers to fall in the dirt. Their wails added to the colorful confusion. The older boys, those who could keep up with the convoy, ran alongside, pleading for more. There was a note of desperation in their voices that was unsettling and it made each playful experience less fun.

Once, the guard drew a can of C's out of his baggy fatigue pocket and crouched to throw it. Hhmm, I had thought, I guess I misjudged him, he's gonna show some kindness to these kids after all. But my expectations were suddenly and quickly crushed.

"Here, you bastard!" he yelled, hurtling the can with injurious force. "Catch this one!"

The can flew through the air, striking one young child in the shoulder, narrowly missing his head. Grabbing his shoulder the child stopped running, hurt and bewilderment on his face. Then I saw hot anger flash as his eyes narrowed and he yelled, "Hey, G.I., you numbah ten—numbah ten G.I."

The guard just spat and quietly sat down.

"Hey, what the hell was that all about?" I finally got up the courage to ask.

"It's these fucking gooks," he replied. "They swarm all over the place whenever we go through a village, begging for food. Chop-chop!! They call you number one if they like you or number ten if they don't. Shit, they'll sell you their sister for two hundred P. You know, piasters. That is if you ever had the chance to screw 'em."

"Is that what "boom-boom" means?" I asked. "Far out!"

"Yeah, but you don't know which one of these "baby-sans" has got VD. They all look dirty to me. I'd just as soon crawl into bed with a snake than to take my chances with them. Besides, you don't know which one of them might be VC and then they'd cut your balls off. Shit, those kids will grab at anything you throw 'em. They bring it back to their mamasans. They're the ones that stand in the doorways. They might look innocent enough, but you can't trust a single one. You don't know when one of those sons-a-bitches is gonna toss a grenade in your lap, so don't get friendly with any of 'em."

That was all he said! It had been a short but meaningful conversation. Once we were back in the countryside, his attention quickly turned to the surrounding fields and business-at-hand.

The guard stayed engrossed in his own thoughts and I in mine. Sitting back against the truck cab I lit another cigarette and watched the passing scenery. Everything was so new, so different. I didn't like the feeling of not being in control of my own life. To make matters worse, I was puzzled by what seemed to be conflicting behavior on the part of our soldiers toward the Vietnamese people. How could the guard feel so much animosity and mistrust for the very people we had come to liberate? I just couldn't figure it out.

Time crept as we made our way to Cu Chi. Sometimes we passed other convoys heading south, and we had to pull over so they could pass, but other than that there was little on the road. Near the larger villages we passed ARVN and American checkmates, roadblocks in unannounced locations checking for VC personnel or supplies being moved by surface transportation. They always created a long line of bikes, buses and peasants, many of whom carried large baskets slung on both ends of a long pole. Once, the convoy had to stop because the point detected a mine in the road. A jeep from the front had swung alongside the convoy to let us know what was happening, alerting us to possible sniper fire. It took nearly twenty minutes to clear the mine and sweep the edges of the road and as we sat under the burning sun the heat baked away what little energy I had. It didn't take long for my fatigues to become soaked. I was grateful to get started again. At least when we were moving the breeze brought a little relief.

The guard had mentioned that until two months ago, this supply route had

14

still been under the control of the Viet Cong and that even now, when the infantry went out to secure the road at nights, they always made contact with the enemy, often losing one or two men. The disturbing thing about it was that whenever the area of contact was reconned after a fight, none of the enemy was ever found. Under the cover of night the Viet Cong crawled away, dragging their dead or wounded with them. He had said the only time you knew for sure you had killed a Cong was when the "grunts" stumbled across a fresh grave on a sweep. Then, they would have to dig it up and count the rotting corpses. As much as we needed more supplies and as much as the Army wanted to run convoys at night, they couldn't. At night, the road was anything but secure. That bit of news did nothing to put me at ease.

By the time we reached Cu Chi and the base camp, which was overwhelmingly larger, I was filthy. It took seven hours to travel only twenty miles, and dust coated my face, hands, fatigues, and M-16. Sweat caked my face. My fatigues remained muddy where soaked with sweat. My pants, shirt and shorts stuck to my skin.

As each vehicle reached the ARVN compound outside Cu Chi it turned and headed toward the main gate of the base camp, penetrating the multiple rows of barbed wire which surrounded it. I thought it peculiar that there was a fence around our base and barbed wire separating it from the ARVN soldiers who secured the village.

As we entered the gates, the tanks and APCs locked their tracks and spun to form a single file on each side of the entrance, creating a huge cloud of dust for us to plow through as we entered. I pulled my fatigue shirt over my face and held my breath as we passed. I couldn't wait to find some place to take a shower.

3

On the morning of November 1, at 0639 hours, I was rousted from a restless sleep. Still exhausted, I forced my legs off the cot, and grabbing my fatigues, I dragged myself to the outside latrines to wash and shave. As soon as we could fall in line we were marched to the mess hall for breakfast and shuttled across Cu Chi for LCTC, the Lightning Combat Training Center located at the west end of the base.

Grinding a cigarette butt under my heel, I joined about a hundred other GIs on a small stand of bleachers surrounded by a thick canopy of trees and bushes and stared solemnly at a blackboard and an instructor. As soon as the bleachers filled, he turned toward us.

He barked, "Sit at attention!" and the postures of 126 men stiffened.

"Men, this is a jungle survival course," he began. "It is mandatory for every incoming recruit, and lasts nine days. Now do you understand what I mean when I say 'survival'? I want you to pay special attention these next nine days because what you learn here may save your life. Vietnam is like no other war we've ever been in. There are no lines here to show you where the enemy is located or which side the enemy is on. There isn't anyone here wearing any other kind of uniform except ours. All these 'gooks' wear are black pajamas, and that's all that Charlie wears too. You can't distinguish who the enemy is unless he's firing at you, and at night you can't even see him. There isn't a safe place in this country except inside your own perimeter. Do ... You ... Understand?"

Every word punctured the air as he spoke.

"The enemy here is a lower form of life. They're cowards and illiterates. Don't associate with any of these gooks unless you're strictly under orders to do so. Don't trust a single gook or you may not walk out of here alive."

His voice rose as he yelled, "Is that understood!"

"Yes, sergeant!" a chorus replied.

I was a little confused. Was he saying that everybody over here was the enemy?

"Now," he continued, "you belong to the 2nd Brigade. Most of you are holdovers, and will be until you finish this school and receive your Division assignment, which will be somewhere within the 25th Infantry Division. This base camp is designated for the 2nd Brigade, and unless you were asleep coming in, you know we are just outside the village of Cu Chi."

He directed our attention to a map now covering the blackboard. "The area around here is flat and dry, except during the rainy season; then it's so muddy that it makes any kind of transportation difficult and often impossible. This area is used primarily for growing cattle, vegetables, and rice farming, and it stands between the Viet Cong and Saigon, the capital, the seat of authority and a prime object of attack. Cu Chi took two months of heavy fighting to pacify. We had to work our way through hundreds of enemy emplacements and thousands of feet of tunnel systems in order to firmly establish a fortified position from which the Division could safely operate.

"Directly northeast of us stands the infamous Ho Bo Woods, a patch of heavy forest perennially used as an enemy hiding place. Just north of us lies War Zone C, a triple canopy jungle reported to be the Viet Cong command center for the whole country. To the south of us is the Oriental River, and to our north, the Saigon River. These carry a steady infiltration of men, supplies and equipment between the Viet Cong bases. Two hundred fifty miles north of us is the 3rd Brigade Task Force at Pleiku. They're fighting to open up Highway 19, which is controlled by the Viet Cong, so we can get equipment and supplies up there and secure that area. South of us is the 1st Brigade area of operations. Their mission is to secure allied base camp areas, to assist the ARVN forces in pacification, and to control resources, particularly food. We are presently involved in seven major operations which have already involved a couple of hundred small unit actions, the majority of which have resulted in some kind of enemy contact. The purpose of these offensive operations is to destroy the VC and North Vietnamese Army installations in this area; to secure lines of communication; to assist local government forces; and to reinforce the Free World Military Assistance Forces and prevent VC rice taxation, harvesting, or transportation.

"We are involved in a relatively small amount of activity at this time, the reason being that two of our battalions are assisting the 3rd Brigade in the neutralization of War Zone C. Also we are experiencing a period of reduced ground mobility because of the rains. But we are expecting a major Viet Cong offensive in this area in the near future and have kept most of our personnel at camp to provide security because of the relative instability at this time. We are presently experiencing a critical shortage of artillerymen, so you can about guess where you'll be going if you have an artillery MOS. In addition, we're experiencing a shortage in certain key maintenance areas and a shortage of NCOs in the engineers. So, don't be surprised to find yourself in a position of authority if you've got that MOS."

The conversation turned to information on the country, and the orientation personnel changed with each new subject. The areas north, west and south of Saigon were crisscrossed with major rivers and an inland waterway system formed by thousands of miles of canals, all of which we were to patrol. Navigation on these canals was made easy by the flat nature of the land, and water transportation provided an efficient and economical method for moving the length and breadth of the Delta region. This was especially true since Vietnam lacked any kind of modern highway system. The U.S. and ARVN military had begun a program to upgrade 2,480 miles of road and bridges only shortly before I arrived.

Within the borders of Vietnam live a wide variety of people: ethnic Vietnamese, Montagnais (Montagnards, or "Mountain Yards" as the word was often pronounced by Americans), Chinese, Chams and Cambodians. But they all looked the same to me. The only distinction I saw was in the way they dressed.

Yearly monsoons brought seasonal rains, and they swept the country on winds coming from the southwest in the summer and the northeast in the winter. Yet there was no winter as I knew it, only summer, one season hotter and dryer than the previous. The year-round temperature barely varied twenty degrees and that was with weather as hot as 115 in the shade.

I spent the first day listening to a hundred different stories, reeling under the glut of information.

Highways continued to be the primary mode of transportation for the resupply of Cu Chi, and convoys left and arrived at an average of two per day, each containing fifty vehicles, and each delivering tons of materials and new recruits. Joint police patrols had been established with the U.S. Military Police, and the ARVN and National Police, to control the population during these convoys and I watched them leave each morning as we passed the main gate on our way to LCTC.

After being briefed the first two days on the history of the school, our involvement in Vietnam, operations and objectives, map reading, navigation and the use of a compass, we began our third day learning the proper way to administer first aid to the wounded. We were then taught the way to call in a "medevac," or what was more commonly called a "dust-off," a reference to the cloud of dust raised when the medical helicopters landed or took off.

Because of the large problem the Division was having with non–combat related medical problems, we received an eight hour block of instruction on field sanitation that covered waste disposal, water purification, insect and rodent control, field hygiene, mess sanitation and insect-borne diseases.

"Avoid drinking local water unless you have purified it," the orientation instructor began, "or it has been boiled for at least twenty minutes. Even then, make sure you add two purifying tablets to the water. If you don't, you're sure-as-hell going to end up with dysentery if not malaria or typhus. The same advice goes for ice; do not use it in your drinks if it has been made from local water!"

He spit out the words, saying it as if it had been said a thousand times and was still going unheeded. Sarcasm and tiredness infected his voice.

"The only kind of water that is safe to drink in this damn country is what we

18

supply," he continued. "Is that understood? Now some of you dumb jackasses are going to forget what I said, or you are just not gonna give a damn because you're hot and thirsty. You're gonna be the ones who are shitting in your pants for three days, or in the hospital with malaria. In addition, don't buy any of the Coke these gooks will try and sell you whenever you're on convoy. The ice they mix in it is nonpotable, and there have been frequent instances where battery acid has been added to the Coke. GIs have died from these drinks, puking up their guts and choking in their own blood.

"Secondly, this area is inhabited by a large variety of bugs and animals, especially poisonous snakes, spiders and scorpions. Now, some of you dumbasses may think they make amusing pets, but remember, many of these animals and especially the rats carry rabies, a disease which is widespread in Southeast Asia. Since it may be transmitted by all types of warm-blooded animals, every bite should be promptly reported and if possible, the animal captured for observation. Now, I doubt that any of you will run into any of the tigers, panthers or wild oxen that inhabit the upland jungles, although occasionally one will be shot on a sweep, but one of the deadliest diseases over here is carried by one of the smallest insects, the mosquito. They carry malaria and encephalitis and account for the major amount of noncombat casualties. You must follow two simple rules to avoid it. Take your antimalaria pill every week without fail and sleep under a mosquito net, no matter how hot or inconvenient it is. Even though the dry season is beginning and water is becoming scarce for the breeding of mosquitos, the Dapsone tablet must be taken daily to protect you from Falciparum Malaria. And, the Chloroquine-Primaquine tablet must be taken weekly to insure your protection against Vivax Malaria. Sleeves should be rolled down at night, and the Tropical Head Net should be used properly. Using both the insect repellant and insecticide sprays will be to your advantage."

After a short break from the morning lectures, we arranged ourselves on the bleachers again and he continued.

"The combination of heat, humidity and dirt will cause infections in small cuts and abrasions within hours unless they are properly cleaned, treated and bandaged. In this manner, leeches are a particular problem since they secrete an anticoagulant which delays blood clotting and leaves an open wound when they are removed. Always clean and bandage such wounds immediately.

"Dermatologic disorders of the feet continue to provide a great number of sick calls and produce considerable noneffectiveness. For protection against fungus infections, take daily baths if possible, change clothing frequently, and use foot and body powder liberally. It will be to your advantage to use a rotational system of stocking drying developed in Korea. Strap an extra pair of socks on top of your steel helmet where they can dry quickly in the sun, and change them as often as your feet get wet. And remember this," he said: "Keep your shot record up to date, both for your own health and protection and because you can't leave the country on R&R without it updated."

The fourth and fifth days were taken up with instruction on various patrol techniques and how they applied to the field; the difference between night and daytime ambushes; and the manner of setting up a night ambush and weaponry employment at the ambush site. For the first time, we were given instruction at night as they demonstrated techniques and mobility. Noise and light discipline were said to be of primary importance when in the field: lights flickering on and off, radios turned higher than necessary, and generator and vehicle engines running were said to play directly into enemy hands. In each of those situations, the enemy could easily detect our position without exposing himself and listening posts (LPs) could not perform their mission of early warning since the only noise generally heard came from our night positions.

Most of the information passed in those two days seemed to apply more toward those with an infantry MOS than that of a person trained in artillery, and since I had never been in the field, I wondered how many of those activities I would be involved in. It sounded frightening to have to take a small platoon out in the middle of the night, especially into enemy territory in unfamiliar terrain. The orientation personnel took no pains to hide from us the rough reality of LPs found in the mornings with every member dead and often mutilated.

The sixth day our attention finally turned toward the application of artillery in the field, and we were taught how to make adjustments for both direct and indirect artillery fire; how to set up a fire support base and tactics for the defense of its perimeter. When discussing the defense system, the instructor had alluded to the necessity of bunker building for protection against mortar and ground attack but had added that the safest place in perimeter battles was, oddly enough, to be fighting from behind a bunker rather than in it. Viet Cong and North Vietnamese human waves had been known to overrun or infiltrate portions of the perimeter and when it came to that, it was safer to be outside, especially during hand-to-hand combat. Shit, the thought of it turned my stomach.

The seventh day proved to be the most unsettling, for we spent the day receiving intensive training and instruction on the handling of explosives, different types of VC booby traps and tunnel warfare. The instructor began the morning session with a unique demonstration, unexpectedly setting off a small, smoky explosion by flicking the wheel of a Zippo cigarette lighter.

"Just as unexpectedly as this," warned the instructor, "you could lose your limbs, or your life. This cigarette lighter is a common type of booby trap and is usually filled with gun powder. The spark sets it off and the explosion blinds you with fragments of iron."

He paused, letting the full impact of his words settle in.

"Ingenious improvisations could well describe most Viet Cong booby traps. Almost all are hard to spot, to disarm, and hard on people. Anything left in the open—any kind of abandoned equipment, camouflaged bunkers, fox holes, tunnels, wire or cords, are to be immediately suspect. Many soldiers picking up discarded weapons have had their hands and arms blown off. Do you hear what I'm saying? This is not the place to be concerned about taking home war souvenirs. That souvenir could leave you permanently crippled. At least half of our casualties are caused by booby traps, and if you don't want to be one of them, you'd better pay special attention to these lectures. Now," he ordered, "fall out, pick up your M-16s and fall in behind one of the instructors stationed behind the bleachers."

I picked up my M-16 and put on my helmet. Jumping off the third pier, I trotted over to where one of the instructors stood. I wasn't sure what was coming next, but I wanted to be as close to the instruction as I could. I didn't want to miss a word. In doing so I had foolishly placed myself at the head of the line that formed. I had forgotten that being first was the same as volunteering, and I hadn't done that since the first day of boot camp. There, I had foolishly volunteered to help in the mess hall kitchen, thinking I would show them that I wanted to be a right helpful kind of guy, and wound up pulling KP all day, laboring behind stacks of dirty pots and pans.

I soon found out that we were going to patrol the jungle area around the training center and that it was set up with the same kinds of booby traps used in the field. I felt a mixture of apprehension and regret as the instructor moved in directly behind me and told me to move out. Shit, I thought, won't I ever learn. Cautiously I stepped onto the dirt path leading into the woods, observing out of the corner of my eye that other groups were doing the same. The instructor continued to explain the kinds of things we should be on the lookout for and prodded me on when I moved too cautiously to suit him.

"Shit," he yelled, "we can't spend all day going through these woods, you asshole. Move it up!"

It wasn't long before I noticed an area in the path where it looked like dirt had been disturbed and I cautiously moved off the path to go around it. I felt a tug and then the release of tension on my boot as I did.

"Hit the dirt!" yelled the instructor. Immediately I fell to my knees and sprawled onto my elbows, pulling my helmet down tight on my head. My heart thumped in panic, anticipating an explosion. I breathed a visible sigh of relief when a cloud of yellow smoke billowed up out of the bushes.

"On your feet!" shouted the instructor.

Embarrassed, I climbed slowly to my feet with the others.

"Olsen," he yelled, "you're a dead man and so might one or two others be behind you. You might not give a fuck about living," he said, "but do you want to be responsible for the loss of your buddy's life, too?"

I cursed him under my breath as he gathered everyone around the booby trap, pointing out the trip wire that had been hidden on both sides of the path. He said it was a favorite trick of the enemy to set up one trap to force people off the trail only to lead them into another one. Before continuing on, he ordered someone else to the point. Relieved, I fell in at the back of the line. With each new booby trap set off came the cursing, and then an explanation. We learned how grenades and unexploded artillery shells could be booby-trapped and set off electrically with just two pieces of tin foil and a battery. When the tin foil was stepped on, the strips made contact and the power of a regular flashlight battery set off the explosives. The tin foil and the batteries, he mentioned, were generally the discards of some unthinking GI which were picked up by the VC or civilians, who then gave them to the enemy. One interesting device was called a foot-breaker cartridge trap. The VC would drive a nail through the bottom of a piece of bamboo, at the joint. Then a hole was made in the ground and a rock or small amount of cement was dropped in to provide a hard backing for the nail. A smaller section of bamboo containing a cartridge was slipped into the larger and the whole contraption was then placed into the hole. With dirt or grass camouflaging the hole, everything was ready for the victim, who when stepping on the bamboo stud would drive the cartridge into the nail, and a bullet into his foot.

As we continued searching the woods, I became more and more amazed at the skill and cunning of the Viet Cong. I slowly began to develop an awe and a respect for this formidable foe. Each new discovery fueled a growing apprehension about being in the field, and I felt no hurry to leave the relatively safe confines of base camp.

There was a seemingly endless chain of booby traps in the woods. The Bouncing Betty, or butterfly bomb, jumped into the air if you stepped on it and it could easily mangle both legs, or tear holes in your abdomen. Another trap was cleverly fastened from a piece of bamboo about three feet long, a steel arrow, a strong rubber band, a catch mechanism and a trip wire. The device was camouflaged and sloped in such a way that the person tripping the wire was struck in the chest by the arrow.

At the end of the trail, we were shown a punji pit, a small camouflaged hole containing sharp bamboo stakes. Often the stakes were coated with human or animal dung which produced a serious infection in the foot. Punji stakes were one of the more popular booby traps: economical and effective. You could step on them while fording streams, crossing river beds, walking trails, or when taking cover in rice paddies or shrub filled ditches. The instructor cautioned us never to dive into a ditch for cover when "walking line" at a road's edge. Charlie generally sprung his ambushes right where he had placed several punji stakes because a GI's first instinct was to dive into the ditch for cover, exactly as we had been trained to do in boot camp.

That angered me. We had been drilled so often to take cover in ditches when ambushed (World War II tactics) that it had become an automatic response.

"How had the Viet Cong known that?" I thought. "If they had learned it by observing our reaction and had time to capitalize on it, why didn't we have time to make the necessary changes in our tactics in Basic Training?"

When the afternoon session started, the topic of conversation turned to explosives and tunnel warfare, and two new instructors entering the area carried with them a number of unfamiliar weapons.

"What you see here is a Projected Charge Demolition Kit MZA1; a Demolition Snake, and an M-1 Line Charge," said the instructor, holding each one separately. "The Snake comes in a kit consisting of a metal casing, explosives, assembly for attachment to a tank, a nose piece to assist in pushing it through entanglements, and various nuts, bolts and firing devices. It was designed to be assembled near an antitank minefield, hooked to a tank, pushed directly forward and detonated. To date, no antitank minefields have been encountered in the 25th Division's Tactical Area of Operations. Thus, the Snake and the Demolition Kit have been tested mainly as a device for clearing hedgerows, jungle, and booby traps. A fifteen foot section of the M2A1 will clear a fifteen meter–wide hedgerow of all trees up to six inches in diameter and will leave a progression of stumps eighteen inches high at the center and forty inches at the edge. A twenty-five foot section placed in the same hedgerow will completely clear the hedgerow of all vegetation and leave a crater three feet deep and four feet wide. Any section of the M2A1 or the Snake will detonate mines and booby traps placed within eight meters of the charge. Although the effectiveness of the M2A1 against hedgerows and mines is impressive, both the bulk and assembly time for the Snake limits its use. Bangalore torpedoes can often do the job more quickly and efficiently."

The instructor paused to hold up another device and then continued.

"The Line Charge consists of six major components. At the head is a small U-shaped rocket, used to propel the line. Attached to the head is 170 feet of nylon covered detonating cable composed of nineteen strands of special detonating cord. There is also a fuse lighter, delay detonator, anchor stake and metal container from which the line is unraveled. The line charge will not clear hedgerows or brush, but it will remove small branches and leaves within one or two meters, greatly improving visibility and ease of travel. The blast will also clear a hedgerow of boody traps strung below or within the branches. However, the line charge will not detonate the firing mechanisms of either antitank or antipersonnel mines or "trip type" booby traps with consistency. Explosives are detonated by sympathetic detonation if within a distance of twelve inches. Although a great concept and possibly useful under certain conditions, it is not recommended for general use in this area."

It was nice to know that the Viet Cong weren't the only ones with the creative capacity for developing weapons. Being able to counteract Charlie's tactics made me feel a little more comfortable.

By midafternoon the topic turned to tunnel warfare, and I was wishing the program would end so I could get out of the insufferable heat. Yet as uncomfortable as I was, I became quickly intrigued. Over the years the enemy had built an intricate system of underground tunnels that sometimes stretched for miles, often large enough to contain hospital beds and printing presses. These tunnel complexes were spread out over the entire area of operations. Just how extensive they were no one really knew. Tunnel entrances were often very difficult to discover and the Viet Cong used them to great advantage, frequently surfacing at ambush sites or from mortar positions and then disappearing into thin air. This was especially common for snipers who fired on infantry units conducting search and destroy missions.

Stepping up to a chart containing a blowup of a tunnel system, the instructor explained the method for destroying them. "During the past quarter, various methods of tunnel destruction have been tested. Of the numerous methods attempted, given sufficient time, personnel and equipment, the following is recommended as an efficient and complete technique for tunnel destruction.

"Two teams are established, one to go into the tunnel, the other to stay above. Both teams are equipped with radios or telephones, both have a compass man and a pacer. Pace is kept by counting knots on a string or by markers placed on a communications wire. The team going into the tunnel has several security personnel, this is to insure adequate protection in case the enemy should be encountered. The team on the surface has a man to unroll engineer tape. Both teams start at the entrance, the compass man in the tunnel dictating the azimuth, or direction of travel, with the man on top following. At sharp turns, new azimuths and distances are called to the surface. At these locations the engineer tape or line is tacked down to allow turns. Every 100 to 150 meters a bulldozer is used to cut a slot perpendicular to the line of the tunnel. This insures that the tunnel rats need never go too far from an exit and that mistakes in tracking are quickly noticed. Eventually, this aids in the rapid destruction of the tunnel by demolitions. After the entire length of the tunnel has been explored, cratering charges are placed, three per open segment, and blown. This method, although time consuming, assures that the entire tunnel, including trap doors and side entrances are discovered and destroyed.

"Now, invariably you will find that you will not have the time or men to engage in this type of operation. Nevertheless, every tunnel complex discovered has to be thoroughly explored for enemy supplies or equipment. In these cases, a volunteer will be selected who is capable in size of entering these tunnels. Since most all of these tunnels are small, built to accommodate the Oriental, they are not easily accessible to everyone. Also, because of their size, there is rarely room for maneuverability. This hinders operation of any M-16s and it is advisable that a .45 caliber pistol be used, accompanied in the other hand by a flashlight. Extreme caution should also be taken when entering these tunnels for they are often booby-trapped and are occasionally the home of cobras and other poisonous snakes."

Jesus, I thought when the session had ended. Will I have to do something like that? I was small, smaller than most, and I would be a most likely candidate for such a search. The thought of entering a tunnel by myself scared me shitless and as I rode the truck over the smelly roads back to the barracks, all I wanted to do was forget what I had just learned and find some place to get drunk.

On the last day of training, we were given a brief history of the customs of the Vietnamese people. Some of the things the instructor talked about stuck in my mind like glue. One was that we would soon be experiencing the coming Tet celebration, a festival which ushered in the new year and was the largest celebration of the year. It would fall between January 21 and February 19. Those were the days, intelligence had reported, that we could expect an all-out offensive by the combined forces of the Viet Cong and the NVA.

Another was his passing remark about religions: that we would probably come into contact with people who believed in Buddhism, Confucianism, Taoism, Catholicism and Animism. Catholicism I had heard of, but what were the others? He gave a brief explanation of each.

"You can also expect that at some time on your patrol you will be invited by the head honcho in some village to partake in a meal with him and his family," he cautioned. "This is a custom of the Vietnamese village in honoring important visitors. Now, one of the main dishes they might serve, along with some kind of rice, will be chicken soup. The custom here is to boil the head of the rooster right along with the rest of the meat. Considered a delicacy, it is always offered to the visitor to show deference and respect. It is considered a dishonor and a slap in the face of the household for you to refuse to eat it. We would like you to be able to honor this custom, but if you can't eat it without puking your guts out, you can try to get out of it by deferring the honor, saying that you yourself are unworthy, and asking that it instead be given to the head of the household as a sign of respect for him, considering him to be even more honorable. But, any of you fuckin' shitheads who do that and bow to a gook ain't worthy of shit in my book," he yelled, "you got that?!"

Fuck you man, I thought to myself. You ain't gonna find me eatin' no chicken heads.

The last lesson was on revolutionary development, civic action programs, and psychological operations (PSYOPS).

Shifting from the bleachers to the inside of the classroom, we noticed three instructors entering the building. I could tell right away they were different. Their uniforms were pressed, starched and cleaned. Two of them wore khakis instead of the familiar green fatigues, and all of them were officers. One sported a major's bright oak leaf cluster on his dress hat, and another, a lieutenant in green fatigues, wore an O.D. baseball cap with a sliver of black thread sewed on to show his rank. All brass. I wondered, what's so important about this?

"One of the methods we are using to pacify this area and wrest it from VC control," the lieutenant began, "is the development of revolutionary development teams. These teams are composed of members of ARVN personnel, mostly regulars, and a combination of other Vietnamese forces. They include the RF/PR, national police, youth and sports personnel, district, village or hamlet officials and 'hoi chanh.' Eighteen such teams are operating in Tay Ninh Province and six are operating in Hau Nghia Province. Each team, as they develop an area, are leaving behind a skeleton detachment in each of the villages to insure that the area does not deteriorate in the team's absence. Our projected goal for 1968 is to have twenty-five teams operating in Tay Ninh Province and five more operating in the Phuoc Hoa District of Binh Duong Province."

Pointing his stick to an area on a free standing map, the lieutenant continued, "This is in the Phu Hoa Dong area. This, the national priority area, has also been enlarged as a part of the 1968 regional development plan and now includes all populated areas in our TAOI." The lieutenant finished his instruction and then moved to the background and stood at parade rest, his stiff posture clashing with the informal stance of his superiors.

A captain dressed in khakis moved in to replace the lieutenant, and the instruction continued. "I'm going to tell you about the civic action program," he said. "Civic action projects were started just recently, and they are being conducted with an emphasis on winning support for the government of Vietnam and goodwill for U.S. forces. Eighty-one projects have been completed this month alone and we are planning on distributing over 2,000 pounds of candy and 15,000 toys to children in the Tri-brigade area over the Christmas and Tet holidays. There have been over 200 MedCaps conducted this month, just fifty short of the number that took place last year during a three month period. MedCaps have been conducted at twenty-six different locations throughout the TAOI, and medical treatment is being given on a regularly scheduled basis at sixteen different locations. An inoculation program has been instituted in association with Med-Caps. Over 1,000 children and 700 adults have received small pox and cholera inoculations this month. MedCaps have already treated over 9,000 people in the beginning of this quarter and we expect to treat close to 60,000 by the end of this month.

"Out of the 200 tons of rice division elements captured this month, eighty tons have been evacuated for distribution in civic action projects. What has not been evacuated has been destroyed. Care in distribution of rice has to be carefully exercised to avoid disruption of the local rice market. A total of three tons of this rice was donated to orphanages in Saigon by division units. Commodities supplied by the Christian Relief Service, the USAIN, and CARE are being distributed to villages and hamlets as part of the Helping Hand Project. Many of these suppliers are nearly exhausted and there are no provisions for replenishments except for private voluntary contributions, civic action funds, and private associations. We are going to have to rely increasingly on the CA/AIK Fund for civic action projects in the future. Now, the only civic action conducted in this area by our Division in the past has been in support of the 25th ARVN Division dependents in Hoc Mon. We hope to change that! Several other units are conducting civic action in this area, and we are awaiting clarification by the 2nd Field Force Command as to our civic responsibilities and our relationship with the units already conducting such activities."

The captain wound down his sermon, and it became the major's turn to address the group. He appeared no less winded than the others and began to talk about the psychological operations being conducted in support of combat operations.

"Our psychological operation here," he began, "consists primarily of air-dropping leaflets, broadcasting messages by aerial loudspeakers or by vehicles, and showing educational propaganda films to the Vietnamese. The 6th PSYOP Battalion has been placed here to support those operations conducted by the 25th Division, and they are responsible for broadcasting and an audiovisual team to show films. This AV team is presently supporting the 2nd Brigade's Operation

26

Saratoga. The Division Cavalry Squadron is responsible for aerial and ground loudspeaker operations.

"This Division has been concentrating its effort on the '*chieu hoi*' program. *Chieu hoi* is Vietnamese for surrender, and those Viet Cong or NVA who turn themselves in and join our side are called '*hoi chanh*'; you might sometimes hear them referred to as Kit Carson Scouts. They make up part of the revolutionary development force explained earlier and are often responsible for the capture of massive amounts of materiel, equipment, and VC supplies. We are presently pushing this program in War Zone C, the source of hardcore VC and NVA units. We have been able to convince twenty-seven *hoi chanhs* to rally to our side since the first of the month and the information they have volunteered concerning future enemy operations planned in this area has proved invaluable.

"Unfortunately, hardcore VC and NVA forces are not easily influenced by the *chieu hoi* program. They prove to be more thoroughly indoctrinated and more ideologically oriented than the local guerrilla. These units usually operate in remote areas, away from civilian and government controlled areas. Many of these individuals don't know where they are or where to go to rally. There is also the physical difficulty of getting to a safe area. Continuous PSYOPS cannot be directed toward a particular unit of this type due to the frequent lack of information on their location or condition. What we are doing is stressing the ideological aspects; exposing the deficiencies of communism as opposed to the benefits of a democratic government. We are especially pointing to the inhumane actions committed by the Viet Cong in the name of liberation and explaining to the NVA that the people of South Vietnam look upon them as conquerors, not as liberators. We have stepped up activities to designate and publicize safe rally points to VC and NVA forces whenever possible and have dropped maps and leaflets to show them those positions. It is important that we learn to react quickly to exploit intelligence gathered which shows the location of these units and their condition."

Knowing that I was playing a vital role in helping to liberate the Vietnamese from communist aggression was reassuring. It was a tool I could use to ward off the doubts I had about being here. What I was doing had heroic implications and I needed that to justify some of the fears and doubts I was having about military life in general. What I was doing was important; it had to be! It was obvious from what this man was saying that communist insurgents, outside forces from North Vietnam, had to be eradicated, and that the local people needed to be protected from the kind of savage brutality committed by the Viet Cong.

It angered me that Viet Cong forces had massacred women and children, even whole villages because they would not support VC forces. I knew in my heart that it was wrong to force your will on anyone—a belief that had been strengthened by the abuse of power I was experiencing in the Army, and if this was what was going on here, I wouldn't have any problem doing whatever was necessary to help free these people. It was encouraging to hear about the gratitude being shown by the South Vietnamese for our help and about the way we were uniting to fight off the enemy.

27

I began to look forward to meeting the Vietnamese and the opportunity to work alongside them in their struggle. As much as I hated being in the service I had been taught all through high school that it was my patriotic duty to fight the evils of communism and here, at last, I could meet the enemy face to face and do my part to help keep the world free. The instructor had begun the day's session by explaining that this particular block of instruction was designed to give each of us a good idea of what we were trying to do in the pacification program, to give us a better understanding of why we were in Vietnam and the ability to verbalize this reason to fellow soldiers. It seemed pretty clear to me.

Riding back to the barracks area that evening, I wondered why the guard on my initial convoy had acted the way he did. Man, there must have been something wrong with him!

II OPERATION ATLANTA

4

Lifting the sandbag I held between my legs, I shook it and set it back down. I was glad it was finally my turn to sit and hold the sandbags while someone else filled them. My body had not made a full adjustment to the heat and I tired easily in spite of the rigorous physical training I had gotten in Basic. I had taken to wearing a sweatband around my forehead, even under my steel helmet, to keep the salty perspiration from burning my eyes. Every little movement seemed to make me sweat.

Filling sandbags was dull, tedious work, but no different than the other jobs I had been assigned while awaiting orders. At least I wasn't burning shit. I had done that yesterday and my clothes still reeked from the stench of fuel oil and burning crap. Just thinking about it caused my nostrils to flare. God, if I had to pull cans out of a latrine and stand in the thick black smoke of burning shit again I would die. The only good thing about it was that no one came around to harass me. I wasn't sure that burning shit was worth it though.

"Shit, man," I said to the corporal in charge of the detail, "how much longer we got to do this anyway?"

"Till we've got four layers on top of this bunker," he answered. "Anyway, don't get in a hurry. Once we've finished with this one they'll only move us to another location until the whole fuckin' area has got four layers on it. Then the brass will probably send down orders to put on five. Either way, they always find something for us to do to keep us busy."

"Yeah, we could always walk around the entire base camp field-stripping cigarettes!" laughed another soldier.

"How long you been here anyway?" asked the soldier filling my bag.

"Eight days," I answered. "How about you?"

"This is my first," he answered.

"Hey, corporal," asked another. "How long do you generally stay in the holdover barracks before shipping out?"

"I've seen 'em here as long as fifteen days," he replied, "but most of 'em are gone in ten."

"Fifteen days!" I exclaimed. "Jesus, I could have that shit detail come around a couple of times by then. I sure hope my orders come down before then."

They all laughed, but I didn't think it was funny.

"Hey, corporal," I asked, "what were those sirens I heard last night? It sounded to me like explosions were taking place somewhere on the base."

"Yeah man!" another soldier said. "I about peed in my pants when I heard them go off!"

I picked up my sandbag and tossed it aside. Grabbing another I shook it open, listening for the corporal's reply.

"Those are warnings for rockets," he said, matter-of-factly. "Whenever there's any incoming they generally go off. They're to alert the camp to take cover. The radar posted around the base provides an early warning. Still, the sirens don't go off until one or two of them have already hit. Mortars are even more difficult to detect. That's why these bunkers are scattered all over the base. They're for cover."

I looked around at the two bunkers we were working on. They were simply culvert halves inverted and covered with sandbags. One of them had a small weathered wooden door supported by a set of rusty hinges. The other had none but the entrance was protected by a wall of sandbags a couple of feet in front of it. The sandbags covering both of them were rotting, spilling their contents. I had heard that rats moved freely in and out of them since they were not in constant use and often made their nests in them. A shudder went through my body just thinking about it. I sure didn't want to have to crawl into one, especially as dark as they were inside.

We had been bagging nearly six hours when I heard the first explosion. I didn't pay much attention to it since it sounded much like outgoing artillery fire. It wasn't until the second or third explosion that the corporal jumped to his feet and grabbed his helmet and rifle.

"Incoming!" he screamed.

Simultaneously, the sirens began blowing and people began to dart out of the Quonset huts in our location, their flak jackets flapping in the air as they struggled to put them on in flight. I was still sitting when the door of the barracks near us burst open and three or four soldiers scrambled out in their underwear. One tripped, sprawling into the dust in front of us. He didn't even hesitate; without as much as a pained expression he simply continued crawling on all fours toward the bunker door. Panic and confusion seemed to be the order of the day. Even though I felt a strong urge to get up and run like everyone else, I wasn't sure as to where or from what. It just didn't register that we were being rocketed, or that I was in any kind of danger.

"Jesus Christ!" the corporal yelled, sticking his head outside the bunker door. "Get in here! Find cover! We're being mortared!"

Suddenly it registered! Panic gripped my insides.

"We're being mortared!" I heard myself yell, wondering what to do first. I shot a quick glance down at my rifle, wondering if I should stop and take it with me. I decided I didn't have time and bolted for the bunker on my hands and knees. I didn't even give a thought to the rats until after I had crawled safely inside.

"What the hell's wrong with you, man!" the corporal hissed.

His words sliced through the stony silence that filled the bunker.

"You could have gotten your shit blown away!" he continued. "You'd better learn to react a whole lot faster than that if you don't want to go home in a body bag. And where the hell is your rifle? What if this was the field and Charlie was coming in right behind a mortar assault? Do you want to be caught without your gun then? That goes for the rest of you guys too! I don't want no greenhorn getting his fool head blown off on my command! Shit!"

I hung my head in embarrassment, grateful for the darkness that hid my face.

So this is what it's like, I thought, still feeling a slight tremble in my legs. I closed my eyes and listened. I couldn't hear anything outside the bunker and wondered if the shelling had stopped. I tried to remember what the explosions had sounded like. I wasn't sure I could. God, help me to remember, I don't want to be caught in a situation unprepared like this again.

It was mid November when I received my assignment. Throwing all my belongings into a duffel bag, I and another recruit, John Vanous, were transported to the headquarters area of "Charlie" Battery, 1st Battalion, 8th Artillery, a unit of 105mm howitzers. It was a desolate location on the northeast perimeter of Cu Chi, mostly empty because everyone but headquarters personnel was in the field.

Although I slept in a common barracks area that night, the next morning I was told to pull my gear and stick it in a bunker that was sleeping quarters for Gun No. 3. I packed my bag again, and carried it across the battery area. Three's bunker was built from stacked ammo boxes surrounded by layers of sandbags and was mostly underground. Open windows stood about shoulder height from the floor but were ground level from the outside. I walked down the wood stairs that led to the entrance and kicked open the door. A rat about the size of a cat scurried out between my legs. A queasy feeling crept into my stomach. I pushed the door open again cautiously, standing back in case there were more. I saw nothing. Peering inside, I noticed that a thick layer of dust covered everything. I tossed my bag onto the wood slats of one of the double bunks, walked over to the window and sat down. Looking out over the perimeter, I waited, although I wasn't sure for what.

I don't know what I expected to see when C Battery rolled in that day, but whatever it was, it in no way touched the reality of their appearance.

The trucks began rolling into the battery area around 1100 hours, backing their howitzers up to the parapets to unload. The trucks rolled past my position, kicking up clouds of dust. The soldiers were filthy, frightening and disgusting. I couldn't imagine what kind of hell had caused these people to look so haggard and disheveled. The thought of being in their shoes was revolting.

I was still sitting by the window when Gun Three pulled up and backed in. A foul-mouthed, red-headed sergeant hanging out the right door of the cab, barked orders to the driver. Soldiers began leaping out the door and back of the truck. A burly, pot-bellied Indian with corporal stripes on his sleeve barged past me and threw his stuff into the corner of the bunker, then quickly disappeared.

"Chief!" the sergeant yelled, "Get that gun unhooked and start laying up ammo on the side. The rest of you guys get the truck unloaded. Bell, get that telephone in and hook it up to the FDC. You!" he yelled to me, "What's your name?"

"Olsen," I yelled, pulling my head inside the bunker and heading outside. "I'm new. I've been assigned to Gun No. 3."

"Great," he yelled. "We really need the help. Help these guys unload the truck. We're really short-handed. I'll talk to you later."

Within twenty minutes the truck had been unloaded, communications established and the gun laid and ready to fire. The crew piled into the bunker to unload their gear and the sergeant introduced them.

Their first order of business was to collect money for beer and select someone to drive over to the E.M. club to pick it up. The sergeant left soon after to attend a meeting at the FDC, to find out how long we would be in base camp and where we would be going next. The remainder of the crew flipped open a portable cooler filled with lukewarm water and beer and began drinking. By the time the sergeant returned most of the crew were asleep. Some were reading or writing letters. I was engaged in conversation with Chief, who was already intoxicated, when the sergeant sat down next to us, grinning. In his arms was a large chunk of ice which he proceeded to break up into the cooler. After emptying the water, he took some of the smaller pieces of ice and filled up a paper cup. Punching a can opener into the top of a can of Ballantine Beer, he filled up the cup and quickly gulped it down, letting the cold beer run out of the corners of his mouth and down his neck.

"Damn!" he said. "There's nothing like an ice cold beer, even when it's a Ballantine."

Chief laughed and handed the sergeant another. Everyone was excited about Sarge's bringing back ice and I wondered why they made such a big deal about it.

About six hours and thirty war stories later the field telephone rang. After answering it the sergeant sullenly informed me that I was to report to the FDC immediately, and to bring my bags.

The Fire Direction Control Center was located in a bunker protruding from the middle of the battery area and as I made my way there, I wondered what was going on. As I approached the bunker I noticed that Vanous was there also, straddling his duffel bag.

"Hey, Vanous," I asked, "what's happening?"

A Spec 5 stepped out of the bunker and addressed us before he had a chance to answer.

"Are you Olsen, from Gun Three?" he asked. "What about you—you Vanous?"

"Yes," we replied in unison.

"Well you can forget about being gun bunnies," he said. "You're being assigned to FDC. C'mon inside and I'll brief you."

The FDC bunker was alive with activity, a deep contrast to the gun bunker. A lieutenant sat slouched in a folding chair pushed against a table made of ammo boxes, a telephone cradled between his shoulder and chin. He was hurriedly shuffling through a stack of paper, a worried look on his face. Someone was hunched over a field radio talking with someone in a code I barely understood, and a corporal was bending over one of two folding tables which had charts fastened to the top. Pushing pins in and out, he relayed information about their placement.

I felt like a foreigner. What the hell's going on, I thought. They can't be serious! I'm not even trained for this. As inept as the Army was, I just couldn't believe that they had just spent over three months training me to operate a howitzer and now they were actually expecting me to fill some kind of combat position for which I was not trained.

What a hell of a place to take on-the-job training! Mistakes here could cost you your life.

A brief round of introductions and a couple of hours of observation did nothing to settle my mind.

That evening, I was told to pack everything I didn't think I would need in the field into a large footlocker that was to be left in the battery's rear area. I was told to keep whatever possessions I had to a bare minimum since storage space in the field was a problem. Sleep did not come easily that night.

"March order!" someone screamed in the door of my barracks.

"March order?" I thought, my mind groggy with sleep. "What the hell does that mean?"

One of the crew sleeping on the cot next to mine kicked off his blanket and swung his feet to the floor.

"Better get your ass going," he mumbled to Vanous and me. "We're moving out."

"Oh, shit," I thought. "Damn, how could this happen so soon?"

I threw my duffel bag on the back of a three-quarter-ton jeep and slipped on my new flak jacket, required on convoy. Shouldering my M-16, I grabbed two full slings of magazines and got ready.

We had been so busy packing I didn't have time to ask many questions about where we were headed, but Lee Scott, the corporal who had been on duty when the mission orders came down, explained.

"We're going on an operation command has code-named Atlanta," he began.

"Apparently command has decided to go back into the Iron Triangle. Intelligence says the Viet Cong are building up their positions in the sanctuary of the Boi Loi Woods, and the discovery of documents and rice in An Thuan and Phu An indicates a transfer of large quantities of rice from the Phu Hoa Dong area. That's why we're going to Phu Hoa."

"We haven't been up in the Boi Loi for months," interrupted Vechione. "I hear they're getting their shit kicked up there!"

"Well, we don't have to worry about it now," said Lee. "The 4th Battalion 23rd Infantry and the 2nd Battalion 12th Infantry are supposed to be airmobiled into that area and the 3rd Brigade is supposed to be coordinating operations with assaults in the southeastern portion of the Trapezoid to support this whole operation. They're going to try to block VC lines of communication from the Triangle."

"We're bound to see some action along the Saigon River then," said Vechione. "I figure that's how the Viet Cong are moving their supplies between the areas."

"Maybe," Lee said, "but they've also got four other infantry elements operating in blocking positions in that sector to prevent ex-filtration from the Triangle, so maybe we won't get up there at all." Leaning over he shouted to the FDC leader who was driving the three-quarter.

"Hey Myers!" he said. "Is it true that we're supposed to be working with those fuckin' ARVNs again?"

The specialist turned around, "The 2nd Battalion 7th ARVN Regiment," he yelled. "We're supposed to help 'em try and expand government control over the villages."

"Hey! Knock off that shit!" came a stern warning from the lieutenant. "We're supposed to be friends here, not enemies. It's up to us to work with government forces whether we think highly of them or not and that kind of attitude don't cut it!"

"Yes, sir!" Lee shot back sarcastically. That ended the conversation.

I wondered if Lee was kidding. His attitude toward the ARVNs didn't seem to jive with what they had said at LCTC. He sounded more like the guard on convoy from Tan Son Nhut. Something just wasn't setting right in my mind. But maybe these were just isolated individuals. After all, the lieutenant seemed to be speaking up for the ARVNs, and he was a lieutenant! I wondered if I shouldn't pay closer attention to what the other guys were saying as well.

I studied Lee's deeply tanned face. His blonde hair hung slightly below the rim of his helmet. A line of freckles made him look boyish but his eyes were those of an older man. If ever he had the look of youthful innocence, it was now gone. I could see a seriousness in his face that I had seen before only in older adults. By his drawl I figured he must be from the South. I wondered where. He seemed like a private sort, keeping to himself or joking only with Vechione. I wondered if he would get uptight if I asked him a lot of questions. There was a lot more I wanted to know. It was slowly dawning on me that this wasn't just a game we were playing. This wasn't child's play or make-believe. Still, I was having trouble adjusting.

A hard jolt snapped my head back as the three-quarter struck a crater in the road, bringing me out of deep thought. I looked around the passing terrain for the enemy. I didn't know if this was going to be a peaceful ride or if the Viet Cong would suddenly appear, raining mortars and machine-gun fire down on us. I didn't know what to expect and it bothered me.

"Hey, Lee," I ventured, "what are we gonna do once we get there? Whatever the name of that place was."

"Phu . . . Hoa . . . Dong. . .," Vechione interjected slowly. "That should be clear enough even for a greenhorn like you."

I felt myself getting angry. Vechione always seemed to have something smart to say and I resented it. I wasn't used to taking crap off anyone, no matter how big they were, and I could sense a confrontation coming on.

"Don't pay no attention to him," Lee said. "He's like that all the time. He just likes to ride people. He's a fuckin' Yankee, that's why . . . and a Wop to boot!"

"Hey! Don't call me no Wop!" snarled Vechione. "I'm Italian an' proud of it," he said, pointing his thumb at his chest. "An' I ain't no hick from the South," he added. Lee just laughed.

It was difficult to know whether Vechione was kidding. He spoke with such vehemence. I didn't like him, and I certainly didn't trust him. I made it a point to watch out for him and not get in his way. I wasn't going to back down from any loud mouth no matter who he was, but I didn't want to get on the bad side of anyone either, particularly since I would have to live with these guys every day. I figured I'd better learn to shrug off what he had to say and not let it bother me, like Lee. At least I could take some comfort in knowing that Lee seemed to know where Vechione was at. They seemed to have a pretty tight relationship.

"What we're gonna do," Lee said, raising his voice to be heard over the din of the convoy, "is set up a fire support base. That means we're gonna dig our asses off and fill sandbags till tomorrow morning. Then we're gonna be firing support for the grunts while they go out and S 'n' D Charlie."

"S 'n' D," I asked, "what's that?"

"That's S for search and D for destroy. You'd better learn the lingo, sonny," snarled Vechione.

"Look," added Lee, "there are only two kinds of tactics we're employing over here. One is to go on an RIF, a reconnaissance-in-force operation which generally only takes place when we're united with a sister battery or a couple of other units from other battalions. Or, we chase Charlie around on search and destroy operations. Most of the time it's a combination of both. If we get word from intelligence that they've spotted, or have reason to believe there's a large body of Viet Cong active somewhere, then they'll put together enough artillery and infantry to go into the area and clear it of any enemy strongholds. It's when we're doing that, that we generally end up working with some gook unit. When we're working Sierra Deltas, we're generally on our own and supporting a company or platoon of grunts who are out trying to find Charlie. We don't always find him, but he seems to have no problem finding us!"

"What do you mean by that?" I asked, puzzled by his expression.

"You'll find out!" laughed Vechione.

Lee just smiled and turned away. "I'm gonna try 'n' get some sleep."

The terrain around Phu Hoa Dong consisted mostly of broad flat plains of rice land with scattered areas of scrub brush. Although some forested areas could be seen from the road, they were often in the distance. Cover for the VC or NVA was limited to the dikes which crisscrossed the now dry rice paddies, or to road embankments, making the trip less dangerous. Concealment in the rice land was poor and the marshes and swamps we occasionally passed weren't much better. The forests and high marsh grass areas which offered the best hiding places were nowhere near the main road and the chance for ambush was slim. What we had to watch for, though, were road mines and snipers. But with the Roadrunners up front, the odds were for a safe journey.

By early afternoon, we pulled off the road northeast of Phu Hoa Dong and followed a small deeply rutted dirt path to an area of scrub brush and thick foliage about 500 meters south of the Saigon River. As the convoy ground to a halt, the lieutenant told Myers to pull out and drive up to the captain's jeep where both officers got out and began going over a set of maps. Within minutes they were joined by an infantry captain whose company had already secured the area. He explained the infantry layout and they quickly coordinated a battery center.

As soon as they had done that the lieutenant took off running across the field, shouting directions. Myers drove the truck after him heading toward a spot the lieutenant was pointing to. As soon as the truck stopped, we began a mad rush to unload the truck and set up. We were now most vulnerable, without cover and in the midst of frantic activity to get the battery laid and ready to fire. I simply did as I was told, not knowing otherwise, but watched closely what others were doing. On the guns, I would have known exactly what to do, but here I knew nothing.

Setting up communications with command headquarters, the guns and the infantry command post, and getting our guns operable, were our first priorities. This involved setting up two portable tables, each containing overlay sheets with grid lines covering charts of our position and the surrounding area; two or three PRC 25 radios, one channel (or push) which was kept open to the infantry unit we supported and one push open to command, and a complete telephone system to each of the six howitzers as well as to the ammo bunker and the captain's quarters. Once this was done, the FDC crew split up, with the lieutenant and two crew members manning the equipment and the rest of us setting up a large canvas tent which served as temporary shelter. Although there was little danger of rain now that we were approaching the dry season, the tent still provided welcome relief from the burning sun and kept out most of the wind and dust being kicked up by the construction going on all around us.

While we were busy setting up our center, the rest of the battery and infantry personnel were hurriedly "lining out" our perimeter. Our base was laid out in a circular pattern, our six howitzers forming a half circle, with the infantry positions forming the remainder. We were near the middle, protected from all sides, as were the captain's bunker and the infantry CP.

Since we were the intelligence gathering headquarters for the base and had the responsibility of coordinating the operations of the base and orchestrating support roles in which the base was involved, it was of extreme importance that we become operable almost immediately and remain so.

While the infantry used heavy explosives to blow holes around the perimeter, cutting and shaping them into hardened defensive positions, we began digging into the earth, filling sandbags. The lieutenant decided that we would simply dig out the interior of the tent, piling sandbags around us for walls, and move the equipment as was necessary. That was fine with me; I could already feel the effects of the blistering sun and had removed my fatigue shirt. Working in the shade of the tent was a welcome relief. We tied up the sides of the tent and went at it. The first sixteen inches of earth yielded quickly to our collapsible shovels but then we struck clay. The remainder of that day and night was spent fighting that sticky substance, forcing chunk after chunk into sandbags and stacking them into walls. We had dug nearly four feet down and had piled walls two layers thick and nearly three feet high before we began sliding perforated steel planking (PSP) over the top of them to form the ceiling. It was morning before we had covered the roof with two layers of sandbags. To make the digging easier we had begun widening the circle around the bunker, digging only down as far as the loose soil went. It looked as though we had set up in the middle of a large bomb crater.

As the sun rose I could feel weariness setting in. I had been working over twenty-four hours, as had the rest of the crew, but, not knowing enough to function in the FDC I had been left to fill bags for three straight shifts. The others, with the exception of Vanous, got a break whenever the shift changed.

I watched and listened attentively to what was happening around me, trying to take it all in. No one had the time to stop and offer any in-depth information. At 0600, my shift was to end, but we weren't allowed to sleep until we had constructed a bunker for sleeping quarters, completion of which was hours away. Since everyone was anxious to get some sleep, Lee said it would be faster if he and I built one single bunker together and shared it. Being on opposite shifts, one of us could sleep in it while the other was on duty. The rest of the crew decided they would follow our example.

By 0800 we were in the middle of a fire mission. Light enemy contact had been established as friendly units were moving in to occupy their blocking positions and the 1st Battalion 27th Infantry had landed in a hot LZ (landing zone) in one of their four airmobile assaults. One helicopter had been shot down and the pilot killed; the rest were under heavy automatic weapons fire.

I worked constructing the bunker while Lee assisted the crew inside. Around 0845 the mission ended and Lee returned to help fill and stack sandbags. We finished the bunker an hour before I was to start duty and since it was near noon, we stopped to open the C rations that had been distributed at the mess tent along with iced tea and hot coffee.

The temperature rose to 93 degrees by noon, and I stripped off any unnecessary clothes. I folded my fatigues up over my knees, letting my combat boots and socks breathe. They stank! By now my chest, arms and legs were covered with dirt and the sweat running down my body left streaks on my skin. Still, I endeavored to pull myself through the shift.

When the personnel bunkers were finally finished I began my period of training and instruction in the operation of the fire direction control center. Vanous and I had both been assigned to the same shift and we were both to be trained as chart operators.

The radio-telephone operator (RTO) for our shift was a portly guy from Texas named Tony Gianettino. Although he looked dark enough to be a Mexican, I assumed with a name like Gianettino that he was Italian, like Vechione. In contrast to Vechione and Lee, Gianettino was very outgoing and friendly, even to the point of being courteous, a characteristic I guessed was a part of his rearing. He readily introduced himself, apologizing for not doing so earlier, and his white teeth flashed a huge grin. His dark curly locks seemed strangely piled on top of his head, in deep contrast to his closely shorn sides, and he wore black horn-rimmed glasses, reminiscent of some photos I had seen of Buddy Holly. I wondered where he got them; they definitely weren't Army issue like mine or Myers'. I was easily drawn to Gianettino, to his good nature and even temperament, and was glad to be assigned to his shift.

Spec 5 Myers was the non-commissioned officer who headed the FDC and although he seemed friendly enough, he didn't volunteer any information about himself but instead got right down to business. As we sat through our shift, both Myers and the lieutenant explained the standard operating procedure (SOP). We were assigned a certain number of infantry elements to give direct fire support to, often as many as three or four different units. These elements would search the area around us daily, maintaining radio contact with us in case of enemy contact. They radioed situation reports to us every thirty minutes to an hour and we in turn radioed "sit reps" to headquarters. We plotted the infantry's position on an hourly basis so that we knew where they were at any given time. The chart operator's responsibility was to plot their position from the coordinates given over the radio. We in turn gave that data to the FDC leader who figured out the data necessary to set and fire the guns. His responsibility was to determine the type of artillery shell used, the type of fuse and setting if it needed to be timed, and the amount of charge necessary to get it there. He also determined the elevation and direction of the howitzers. When that information had been verified by the lieutenant, the guns were set and fired in coordination with the forward observer (FO), who remained in the field with the infantry.

All infantry elements, less the fire support base security forces, generally platoon sized, would move throughout the day, either covering blocking positions or actively pursuing the Viet Cong. During daylight hours, minimum forces secured the Saigon River, allowing extensive S & D operations in the inland Viet Cong base areas. During the night, a maximum number of ambushes would be employed along the river. Control along the river was to be one of our primary responsibilities.

By the time I came on duty most infantry elements had already reported numerous sightings. Two hundred meters north of our position Company B, 2nd of the 27th, had reported finding fourteen pounds of documents, and twenty meters from there, medical supplies, food, clothing, M-16 ammo, VC gas masks and one bicycle. Delta Company found three VC bodies in a tunnel they uncovered.

As the day progressed, supporting gunships patrolling the area came across ten Viet Cong and engaged them. The Viet Cong quickly dispersed into the woods that lined the river and returned fire. So, the gunships withdrew and called upon us to pound the area with artillery. With no infantry in the immediate area it would be impossible to verify body count and that displeased them, but we fired anyway.

Around 1500 hours we received another fire mission. C Company was receiving sniper fire from an unknown location, wounding ten GIs.

Shortly afterwards, Alpha Company made contact with four more Viet Cong twenty meters from C Company's position. Gunships were aiding them in their fight, but again, with unknown results.

Not long after our fire mission ended the radio crackled with a message from headquarters.

"Killer Six Niner, this is Killer Six, over," the message began.

"Killer Six, this is Six Niner, over," replied Gianettino.

"Killer Six Niner, notify your Charlie Oscar that Second of the Twenty-seventh elements have three Whiskey India Alphas from friendly action. These Whiskey Indias are the result of fire from Five Niner's position. All data has checked out but the error could be in the range probable error. Make sure of your data to prevent any more mishaps. Do you read me, over?"

"Killer Six, this is Killer Six Niner. We read you loud and clear. Our Charlie Oscar has been monitoring transmission, over," replied Gianettino.

"This is Killer Six, out," replied headquarters.

Five Niner was the code for B Battery, a sister battery who was also on this mission. Killer Six was the code name for the major who was in command of our unit. He was one stern guy and never sounded friendly.

A short time later D Company reported one more WIA (wounded in action). This time the injury came from a booby trap. A helicopter was called in to evacuate the man.

At 1750, companies A and D came under fire from small arms and rocket propelled grenades (RPGs). We were called immediately, as were supporting gunships, but not before A Company had received one WIA, and D Company, seven. Contact was broken twenty minutes later. Thirty minutes following, gunships reported the enemy resurfacing fifteen meters from the ambush location and engaged them, later reporting two possible Victor Charlies killed.

41

By the time I got off duty, we had fired 328 rounds of ammunition in support of the 1/27th elements and had been credited with destroying one sampan and one machine gun. I was ready for bed.

Dragging myself to the three-quarter, I rummaged around looking for my duffel bag. Finding it squeezed in a corner, I threw it out the back, jumped out and dragged it over to my bunker. Plopping down in the dirt, I drew out my air mattress and began blowing it up. My head felt dizzy from the exertion and I wondered whether I would have enough strength to finish. I just wanted to fall back and sleep right there. I didn't give a shit about overhead cover or anything else. I just wanted to close my eyes and forget about the world around me. Orders were, though, that you had to sleep under cover, so I pushed myself to finish the air mattress and then pushed it into the bunker. Fishing my jungle blanket out of the bag, I threw it on top of the mattress and slipped in behind it. Our bunker was no wider than a coffin and not much deeper. I could barely sit up in it but I didn't care. I passed out as soon as my head hit the ground.

Shortly before midnight I felt someone jerking my camouflaged poncho, whispering that it was time for me to go on duty. I felt like shit! As soon as he left, I fell asleep again. Five minutes later I was rudely awakened again. This time a more demanding voice told me to get up and haul ass into the bunker, that I was supposed to be on duty. Grudgingly, I crawled out, wrapping my poncho around my shoulders to ward off the night chill. Groping my way to the door of the bunker, I slipped inside. Gianettino and Myers were already on duty, although they looked half asleep.

"Want some coffee?" Gianettino asked. "It's hot. I just picked it up from the mess tent."

"No thanks," I said. "I don't drink the stuff."

"Well, if you don't, you probably should," he replied.

I slumped down in a folding chair and pulled the poncho up over my arms.

"You look dead," laughed Gianettino.

"I feel dead," I said. "Where's Vanous?"

"Don't worry. He'll be here in a minute," said Myers. "Vechione left a couple of minutes ago and in less than a pleasant mood."

Myers no sooner finished when in stumbled Vanous, unshaven, looking like death warmed over. I managed a weak laugh. I wondered if that was how I looked.

"Well, we'd better be on the alert," said Myers as he read through the log book. "Looks like the Infantry Command Post took a couple of mortar rounds a few hours ago and C Company's listening post said they threw a hand grenade at a suspected VC who was moving about, but the Cong threw it back in and killed one of ours. I guess headquarters is calling this fire support base Janet," he added before closing the journal.

"Boy, I must have been sound asleep, I didn't hear a thing!" I said. "Hey, Gianettino, how long you been in country?"

"'Bout six months," he answered, "but I still feel like a long-timer. It's Vechione and Lee that are short-timers. They were here before I arrived."

"What about you Myers?" I asked. "How much longer you got to go?"

"Too much time to start counting it now," he replied.

"Don't let 'em fool ya," Gianettino replied. "He's the shortest of us all."

The conversation ended there. We lapsed into silence, everyone simply too tired to talk.

Around 0200, headquarters notified us by radio that air strikes would be pre-empting any movement of ground troops in the morning and that we were to notify the infantry command elements to expect them at 0730 hours, 0939 hours, 1030 hours and again at 1500 hours. I had never seen a B-52 air strike, nor any other air assualt. Gianettino said I would have something to look forward to.

By the time 0600 rolled around, we had experienced an uneventful evening and I had gotten a few more hours of sleep by napping on duty. Gianettino and Myers had taken watch, allowing Vanous and me to sleep, waking us only when necessary. The lieutenant, who had stretched a poncho across the back of the bunker to cut off as much light as possible from his cot, had slept soundly through the night. Even though the shift changed, I remained in the bunker as did most of the crew, waiting for the sun to rise and take the chill out of the morning air.

At 0715 we were notified of the B-52 air strikes that were to be conducted. The 7th Tactical Air Force was flying in support of the 2nd Brigade operations and I was surprised to learn that so were a number of other squadrons. With this much air power amassed against these peasant warriors I had little doubt in my mind as to the outcome of our operations or as to the outcome of the war for that matter.

At exactly 0730, I heard a rumbling in the distance. It grew louder and louder as it approached our area. Within minutes the ground began to shake and then the rumbling ceased.

"What the hell was that?" I asked.

"Those are B-52 strikes," said Gianettino. "Those bombs are dropping more than three thousand meters from our position. Can you imagine how Charlie must feel in those underground tunnels. I betcha he's grabbing his ass right now."

I went outside to see if I could see the explosions. Looking directly northeast of our location I could make out a tiny speck of movement across the horizon. Minutes after it disappeared I could see a large cloud mushrooming in the distance. A few seconds later I began to hear the rumbling again and as it crawled toward our position, growing louder, it shook the ground beneath my feet.

Far out, I thought, I'm sure glad that I'm not Charlie this morning. I could just imagine those tunnels crumbling and caving in under the force of those explosions, the Viet Cong caught inside them suffocating or being crushed to death. I grimaced at the thought. It seemed like a gruesome way to die, even for the Viet Cong.

In the early morning light I surveyed the perimeter of our camp. I noticed for the first time the extent to which the tanks, APCs and explosives had devastated and cleared the thick foliage which had initially surrounded our location. A clear field of fire had now been established all around our perimeter for a distance of at least fifty meters in every direction. You could see the wood line clearly now and the only terrain which offered the enemy any cover was the dikes surrounding the rice paddies to our south.

The infantry platoon which had been left to provide security for our base had already moved out to the edge of our perimeter and were approaching the wood line. GIs with rolled up sleeves and flak jackets sat atop a tank positioned in front of an armored personnel carrier. One soldier on the APC wore neither a flak jacket nor a helmet. Instead, he had draped his body with slings of M-16 ammunition and grenades. He was wearing a baseball type cap backwards, bent over the back of his neck to shade the sun. I watched the brush spring up from under the back of the APC as it crawled into the jungle.

Suddenly overcome with fatigue, I turned and headed for my bunker. I was too dog-shit tired to reflect on what was happening!

I hadn't been asleep more than a half-hour when I felt someone shaking my body.

"Hey, Olsen, get up!" Myers prodded. "The top sergeant came out on this morning's supply chopper and he says that command wants us to have one more layer of sandbags on the roof of the FDC and two more on personnel bunkers before anyone sacks out."

Goddamn, those lousy bastards, I thought as I crawled out of the bunker. They would have to come down with an order like this when I was off duty.

By now Vanous was up too and I watched him walk toward my position. He slumped down beside me and lit up a fag, offering me one. He was less angry than I, feeling more defeated and tired than anything else.

"It's a good thing we caught what sleep we did last night," I said, "or our asses would really be dragging this morning!"

"Fuckin' A," said Vanous.

Before we finished our ciagarettes, Gianettino came waddling over, his large hips and bulging stomach swaying like a bag of potatoes.

"Well, we may as well get started," he said. "The quicker we get at it, the sooner it'll be over."

Neither Vanous or I made a move. We just sat staring at the pile of gray sandbags heaped against the back of the bunker.

"Since it looks like we might be here a few days, we've decided to build one large personnel bunker," he added. "It'll mean less work than trying to cover three or four smaller bunkers." He turned, walked over to the sandbags and picked up a shovel, meeting Myers who was just coming around the corner.

"Hey you guys!" Myers shouted, with some hesitation in his voice. "Let's get started!"

Vanous and I slowly rose in reluctant obedience.

Fifteen minutes later the lieutenant stuck his head out the bunker. Looking in our direction he yelled, "Fire mission!" Myers jumped to his feet, spilling the sandbag he was holding, and sped off for the bunker. Twenty minutes later he returned saying that C Company had been ambushed by some VC who were holed up in a bunker. When it was all over, they had killed one Viet Cong and credited another to artillery fire.

One body count and one bunker, all in a morning's work.

"We've decided to change shifts," he added, looking directly at me. "You, Lee and Gianettino will take one shift, and Vanous, Vechione and I will take the other. So instead of being off this shift, you'll go back on. You'll be off again at noon. O.K.?"

"Sure," I said, "why not." After all, I wasn't getting any sleep filling sandbags, I may as well be pulling duty.

As the sun rose the atmosphere turned hot and muggy, and I stopped shoveling to take off my shirt. My face and arms were already burned, but I didn't figure it would take long for me to get a tan.

"Better watch yourself," warned Myers. "They'll drop an Article 15 on you if you get burned so bad you can't work, and they'll withhold your pay as well. I'd get it a little at a time if I was you. This sun can burn you so bad in one day that you'll be nothing but blisters the same night."

"I got some lotion in my can," said Gianettino. "I'll get it for you. The next time we're in base camp, or if someone else goes in, you should have them pick some up for you."

Around 1030, Vechione came wandering out of the bunker to help. Things were dead inside so they figured he could help while Lee manned the radios.

"Hey," he said with obvious glee, "D Company uncovered a fresh grave a few minutes ago with one dead Viet Cong in it. They said he was killed by artillery fire and they're crediting the kill to us. I'd like to get a hold of just one of those sons-a bitches," he added, "I'd do his head in just like this." Picking up a shovel, he swung it over his head, bringing the edge of the blade down hard against a large chunk of clay, splitting it apart. We all laughed.

At noon I went on duty but nothing was happening inside the bunker so I continued to fill sandbags. By now we had covered the roof of the FDC, built the walls for the personnel bunker and covered it with one layer of sandbags. The personnel bunker looked pretty small for all of us so I opted to keep the small bunker Lee and I had built and asked Vanous if he would help me fill sandbags when we finished.

When we approached my bunker I noticed that my air mattress was completely flat. I dropped to my knees to pull it out.

"Damn, you don't suppose I've put a hole in it already?" I said.

Pulling it out, I picked up my blanket and after shaking off the dirt, folded it neatly and set it atop my duffel bag. I turned the air mattress over, looking for holes.

"Shit, I can't find anything." I crawled into the bunker, looking for a rock or anything else that might have punctured it. "Holy shit!" I cried, banging my head on top of the bunker as I scrambled back out.

45

"Hey, what's the matter?" laughed Vanous. "You nearly knocked the roof off when you hit it."

"Shit, man, there's a huge scorpion in there," I said.

"Hey, no shit? Let me see." Vanous dropped down on his knees and peered inside. "Get a shovel," he said. Sticking the end of the shovel in he dug the scorpion out, keeping it at a distance.

"Hey, it's dead!" laughed Vanous. "I betcha he's what put a hole in your mattress. Ya musta slept on top of it this morning."

"Damn, man," I said, a chill running up my spine, "this place gives me the creeps more each fuckin' day."

Some time later we received a fire mission and I scrambled inside to cover the charts. I still felt a little inadequate even though the chart operation was relatively simple. So, the lieutenant worked alongside me on the other chart, and as I called off the range and direction of fire he yelled "check" if he had the same information and "hold" if he didn't.

D Company was receiving automatic weapons fire and incoming hand grenades about four klicks (kilometers) north of our position and had already sustained heavy casualties by the time our guns responded. The voice of the lieutenant in charge of the platoon was in near panic as he radioed his position to us, but within minutes of receiving clearance a barrage of fire issued from two of our guns. Marking the location of impact, the FO began making adjustments.

"Right 200, drop five zero," he radioed. "Fire for effect, over."

"Right two zero zero, drop five zero, out," repeated Gianettino.

The lieutenant and I moved our pins simultaneously, sticking them in 200 meters to the right and fifty meters down from the previous pin point. Swinging the rule over I called out the azimuth, which remained the same, and the corrected distance. After computing the height and deflection of the guns, Lee picked up the phone he had cradled on his shoulder, spitting out directions.

"Guns," he said, waiting for each to reply.

"Two here ... Three, One ... Four," came their reply.

"Five ... Six, you there?" yelled Lee.

"Five ... Six," they responded.

"Height two four seven zero," Lee began; "deflection niner four zero!"

"Height two four seven zero, deflection niner four zero," the guns repeated.

"Shell H E, charge six, fuze impact," Lee commanded. Each gun again repeated the instructions for the "heavy explosive" charge.

"Report when ready," Lee said.

"Ready on One ... Two ready ... ready on Three..." All six guns replied.

"Battery ready?" He paused. "Fire!"

Six guns thundered in unison. Gianettino notified the infantry.

"Delta Redbird this is Killer Six Niner, over," he said. "Fire out."

"Fire out," came the reply, followed by a slight pause.

"Fire on target," came the FO's excited voice. "Give 'em hell, over."

"Delta Redbird, roger, fire on target, over," Gianettino replied, smiling.

46

In an hour and ten minutes we dropped 2,409 pounds of explosives on the Viet Cong location and fire from the enemy position ended. D Company then proceeded to search the area but not before we monitored this transmission.

"Delta Redbird, this is Killer Six, over."

"Killer Six, this is Delta Redbird, over," the infantry FO replied.

"Delta Redbird, from now on you will use correct procedures when transmitting over the radio. That is to include your call sign and all other standard operating procedures. Is that understood, over?" said the major sternly.

"Killer Six, that is a roger, over," the FO replied.

"Killer Six, out."

"Whoee," Gianettino said. "I sure wouldn't want to be in the shoes of anybody having to face the major. He can be a mean mother when he wants."

I wondered why the major made such a big deal of procedure. Shit, if the infantry was in big trouble, so what if they failed to use all the procedures and skipped what was unnecessary. We knew what was happening. I thought the major was just a prick!

Fifteen minutes later we received a report from D Company, this time with all the correct procedures.

"Killer Six Niner, this is Delta Redbird, over," it began.

"Delta Redbird, this is Killer Six Niner, over," Gianettino answered.

"Killer Six Niner, sit rep follows: We have one Uniform Sierra Kilo India Alpha at our location and six Whiskey India Alphas. After sweeping the area we have ten, that is one-zero Victor Charlie who are Kilo India Alphas. . . . I repeat, this is one zero positive IDs. We have evidence of three other possibles, over."

"Delta Redbird this is Killer Six Niner, one Uniform Sierra Kilo India Alpha, six Whiskey India Alphas and one zero Victor Charlie Kilo India Alphas with three possible, over."

"Killer Six Niner, that is affirmative, over."

"Delta Redbird, this is Killer Six Niner, do you have need of any more assistance at this time, over."

"Killer Six Niner, that is a negative, over. Thanks a lot."

"Delta Redbird, Killer Six Niner, we will leave two guns trained on your location. If you need further assistance, the battery can be made ready. Do you copy, over."

"Killer Six Niner, this is Delta Redbird, I copy, over."

"Delta Redbird, this is Killer Six Niner, out," finished Gianettino.

"Tell the guns to stand down," the lieutenant told Lee.

"Guns? . . . guns? . . ." Lee asked over the telephone.

"Gun one . . . two . . . gun three . . . . four . . . five . . . gun six," they replied.

"Stand down," Lee said. "Guns one and two, remain laid at this data. Keep one man posted on the phone, roger?"

"Roger!" they replied in unison.

"Hey, lieutenant?" one of the gun sergeants asked. "Does that mean we have to keep a full crew on shift, or can I let some of the guys sleep?"

The lieutenant reached over and grabbed the phone from Lee's hand.

"That means a full crew awake and ready sergeant!" he shot back.

"Yes, sir," came a weak and disappointed reply.

"Let the rest of the guns know they can keep on a half crew," the lieutenant told Lee, "but to keep someone within hearing distance of the phone."

Lee did as he was told and hung up the phone.

I wondered why the lieutenant was so uptight but quickly let it slide. After all, we could now lay low. Two base camps had been destroyed; that included numerous bunkers, ammunition, various assortments of VC clothing and gear, and valuable rice caches—their food supply. We had killed ten of theirs and lost only one of ours. We not only had been victorious, we had taken vengeance.

As the days went by, things settled down, and we began to develop a routine. We continued to fire a pattern of either destroying, neutralizing or suppressing enemy fire. And, as we continued to evaluate the FO's information, determine firing data, transmit fire commands to the guns and collect and disperse information, the routine became easier. The pace and stress less strenuous. It became easier to stay clean. The rains came occasionally, dropping without a moment's notice, drenching us and then fizzling out. Often as not, they stopped as suddenly as they began and within minutes, the sun would emerge, relentlessly baking the earth and its inhabitants. Although it remained muggy and humid, the earth dried out quickly. Sometimes, you couldn't tell it had rained at all except for the puddles which remained in the low area or wheel ruts.

It only took one night of trying to sleep on a floating air mattress to learn what had to be done to keep my bunker from flooding. Or, when it flooded, how to keep myself dry. Still, even when I got caught in the soaking rain, my fatigues dried quickly, as did my canvas boots and camouflaged blanket, being made of special material. But the damp clothes I had left in my duffel bag became moldy. Humidity and heat slowly wrinkled my writing tablets and they and nearly everything else in my bag got moldy too.

With each passing shift, I became more acquainted with the operation of the control center, picking up radio transmission lingo, which Gianettino explained to me. Almost all communication was cloaked in secrecy having a primary code which remained constant and a secondary code which changed each month. The new code was personally transported from headquarters to our location by air or convoy.

Each day the infantry went out searching the surrounding area while other elements conducted air mobile assaults into the Iron Triangle or between the Triangle and us, and we supplied direct fire support for both. But not us alone. We were always within firing distance of at least one other battery so we could also provide cover fire for their fire support base, and they for us.

The radios clattered every day with an uneven flow of traffic, and while our responsibility remained to cordon and search the area, the 7th ARVN Regiment was supposed to search and clear the village every day, executing control over its population under the pacification program. Occasionally, we intercepted their transmissions on our radio but we never understood what they were saying. We had no idea of what kind of resistance or fighting they encountered, if any.

Intelligence prior to our operation had indicated the presence of three battalions of Viet Cong regulars operating in our area with an estimated strength of 600 to 900 men. In addition, a Viet Cong platoon made up of local people was known to exist. With us being located on the western edge of the Philhol Rubber Plantation and both the plantation and the Triangle known to be influential in the activities of the village and surrounding areas, the infantry repeatedly found Viet Cong fortifications, installations, tunnels, booby traps and mines. And, throughout the operation, they consistently encountered small groups of armed VC.

Again and again, the 1st Battalion 5th Mechanized Armored Cavalry encountered small arms fire and enemy resistance as they fought to secure the river. Previous nights' ambushes had killed three Cong and destroyed two sampans as the VC tried to move their supplies on the river after dark. And though the surrounding terrain held great obstacles to ground movement, it didn't deter the grunts. They walked, crawled and sludged through streams, marsh grass and jungle, uncovering and uprooting enemy strongholds. However, our own losses began rising.

5

29 November 1967
Fire Support Base Janet
Phu Hoa

Developing my own routine, I made sure I washed my dirty fatigues and hung them out to dry during my off shifts, and took the time to make improvements on my living quarters. We had been at Janet for more than a week and I began to find time to write, visit the guns and the ammo bunker, and acquaint myself with some of the guys I was serving with.

One day while walking past Gun No. 1 I heard someone yell, "Hey, Olsen." I stopped, wondering who would be calling my name or, for that matter, who knew it. A young man with light sandy hair waved me over.

"Hey man, you're with the FDC aren't you?" he asked grinning.

"Yes."

"Well, I'm White," he said, extending his hand. "I heard there was another flower child in the battery. The word has it, it's you!"

"White?" I repeated. "Far out ... glad to meet you brother."

Leslie White, a Californian, was a thorough "head" whom I immediately took a liking to. It was exciting to meet someone who was coming from the same place I was philosophically, and as we sat and talked, getting acquainted, a bond of friendship quickly developed. Both of our experiences coming into the military were surprisingly similar. He had endured ridicule and harassment for his long hair as I had. Even here he felt alienated from most of the other GIs. All of the other men on his gun section were jocks and juicers, people who drank heavily and were caught up in the traditional male macho image that we were both beginning to question. Any talk of drugs, brotherhood, peace or love brought a verbal assault, and he, like I, had learned quickly not to be too open about his feelings or beliefs.

White, like myself, was new in country. He had been assigned to Gun No. 1 with another buddy from his hometown area. He called him over.

"Hey, Larry, I want you to meet Olsen," he said. "He's from the FDC."

"Hey, just call me Surfer Joe," Larry said, puffing up his chest and pointing both thumbs at his well muscled, tan body. He seemed friendly enough but it didn't take long for me to see that he was really hung up on himself, a real braggart.

"Hey, you didn't pick that tan up over here, did you?" I asked when I could squeeze a word in.

"Hell, no," he said lifting his chin, "I'm part Filipino, on my Mom's side."

We rapped for a couple of hours, with Larry hogging most of the conversation. He talked about how rich his folks were, about the new sports car he had to leave behind, and the girls that he said beat a path to his door. It didn't take long for me to become sick of his boasting, but I also felt kind of sorry for him. I sensed that all his bragging was just a front. He tried too hard to be friendly and flung his background around like it was his ticket to acceptance. I sensed he was just insecure. Still, I was glad when the gun sergeant finally called him over to do some work and White and I could talk.

Walking back to the FDC that afternoon, I thought about our conversation. I remembered how alone I had felt boarding the bus in Portland, waiting to be transported to Basic Training in Fort Lewis. That scene seemed as real to me now as it had that day, and my thoughts drifted back to it.

Much to my dismay, I had passed the induction physical that morning and after a brief swearing-in process, pledging my allegiance to God, the Army and the flag, I was herded outside with forty or fifty others to board the bus. Sitting quietly, feeling suddenly alone again, I tried to rid myself of the fear that clung like a leech on my mind. Where would I look for support now? I was being separated from the only support group I knew, the only real sense of family I had—my friends!

What was it going to be like in the Army? Looking around the crowded bus I could see that I was the only person with long hair, the only so-called hippie. I suddenly felt self-conscious about my appearance. My dress was radically different from those around me. I easily stood out in my bell-bottom cords and purple and orange polka-dotted shirt. Man, everyone else was straight. Jocks with very short haircuts, as if they had cut them in preparation for the Army, wearing slacks and madras shirts. Greasers in tight black slacks with black pointed shoes, the kind I used to wear a couple of years ago. Clean-cut college types and those who looked like they were on the down and out. But no freaks. How was the Army treating hippies anyway? Would I be treated like an outcast, subject to the same verbal abuse I got as a civilian?

What about physical violence? Man, I had heard some pretty weird stories about what people could get away with in the service. I had always thought they were just tales but what if the things they had said turned out to be true?

Looking back at the events of that morning, I wondered why my life had taken the turn it did. The closer Mike Finn and I had gotten to Portland, the surer I had become that going into the Army wasn't what I wanted to do. I wanted to back out of the commitment I had made two weeks prior, but I couldn't find a way. It just didn't seem fair. I had volunteered for the draft after the recruiter had promised me that I wouldn't have to be inducted until after the summer, and here it was, the beginning of May. Summer hadn't even started. Man, what a liar he had been.

It all happened too soon: the probability of my having to go to war was just too high and I still hadn't made up my mind about Vietnam, about the moral question of killing another human being.

It seemed odd to be grappling with that question again. I had been raised on violence. It was a part of my male heritage and I had been a fighter and a scrapper all my life. Why was I now questioning the sanctity of life? It seemed such a foreign idea, yet somehow, there was this compelling urge to identify with this new philosophy I was hearing – as if it fit better than the roles I had previously played. But, I wasn't sure. Being right in the middle of the growing controversy concerning Vietnam didn't help either. I felt I was being forced to take sides and I wasn't sure even what the issues were. Some of them seemed clear; I mean, how could I be against the war when to do so was synonymous with being for communism? Yet I barely knew anything about Vietnam other than the fact that we were fighting communists there. And then, I only knew what I had been told in high school. Christ! I had heard from friends that some people were even leaving the country, skipping to Canada to avoid the draft. I wasn't about to do that. Those people were considered criminals, and rightly so. I mean I knew I had a criminal past but I sure as hell wasn't a coward, and that's what people were saying about them.

Frustrated, I pushed those questions aside. It did little good to think about it now. Suddenly, I regretted my past, regretted all the times I had gotten into trouble and had been arrested. If it hadn't been for my police record, I could have gotten into the Navy or the Air Force. God knows I had tried. It was only after being turned down by both of them that I had turned to the Army, knowing for sure that I didn't want to be drafted into the Marines. I had purposely neglected to tell my local draft board where I had been for over a year, and the last few months the board had been sending out letters to my home address. My parents had forwarded them to Finn's, along with a note saying the board had been calling them, wanting to know where I was. It was a good thing my parents didn't know for sure. They had only heard rumors that I was living with the Finns. There had been the lingering fear that I could be sent to jail if I continued to evade the draft and I felt pressured to respond to what I had been taught was my patriotic duty. Slowly, I had just tired of the whole thing, and in fact, of life itself. I wasn't going anywhere with my life so after failing to enlist, I simply volunteered for the draft. Riding the bus to Portland that all seemed far away. Even if I wasn't going anywhere with my life, I didn't want that somewhere to be the Army.

Turning in my seat to look out the bus window, I leaned back and breathed a heavy sigh. I was trapped. I might as well accept it. I had tried everything possible to flunk my physical. I had gotten drunk just before going in. I tried to con the psychiatrist during my examination, trying to capitalize on what others considered my oddities. I exaggerated my use of marijuana, saying I used it daily even though I had only experimented with it a couple of times. I told him how much alcohol I was really drinking but he didn't believe it. I complained about my knees, about my back, about my feet, but nothing worked. They were drafting anything that walked, crawled or hobbled in that morning. They must have had a quota to fill.

I wondered if everyone on the bus wasn't as lost in thought as I. It may have been early morning when we left, but for most of us it was a late night in our lives. My fears were justified the hour the bus rolled into the basic training area. The abuse started even before we got off the bus when some jerk in uniform got aboard and began yelling obscenities at us, screaming for us to get out. We were herded and cussed from one place to the next. When the time came for haircuts it left little doubt in my mind as to where the military stood.

A tall, thin drill sergeant stood before us, hands on his hips, screaming in our ears. "There aren't gonna be no fuckin' individuals in this Army. Do you hear me! You're all gonna think alike, feel alike and look alike. Do you understand? You fuckin' shitheads are gonna learn that in the Army there is only one way. There is the right way, the wrong way and the Army way. Do you understand! There is only one way here, and that's the Army way. You dropped your own fuckin' thoughts on the other side of the fence when you entered this compound and that's just where the hell you're gonna leave 'em. You're gonna learn that when I say shit, you're gonna shit—and not before. By the time you leave here, you're gonna learn to respond immediately to any given command, without any hesitation, without any thought of right or wrong. Do you understand! You shitheads better be listening! There is no room for differences of opinion in this man's Army. You will do as you are told and that's that. By the time you leave here, you'll operate as one unit, like one man, or you won't be here at all. And if any of you shitheads are thinking of running home to mommy, there's only one way out and that's either in a pine box or over the fence, and if I catch as much as one of you chicken-shitted bastards going AWOL you can bet your ass you'll never do it again. Do you understand? When we are through here you won't be able to tell yourselves apart. We're gonna make you into one responsive fighting team and you'd better listen closely because your life might depend upon it."

When the sergeant was finished with his threats, he jerked the company into order and marched us down to the barbers.

Rows and rows of recruits stood outside the long thin barracks building that served as the barber shop and we marched up and took our place alongside hundreds of others who were waiting. Slowly, methodically, one line after another was called to order and made to march up the steps of the platform, which was about sixty feet long.

One line entered a door on the right side of the building and another came out the left, minus their hair. We stood in formation a full hour before our company began its trek through the doors and yet another forty-five minutes before I ascended the stairs. I could see the four drill sergeants who led our company huddled together at the top of the stairs, laughing and looking down in my direction.

Even when I realized that the focus of their attention and laughter was me, I had no suspicion that they would do anything more than just make me the subject of their taunts. Mutely, I followed the others, like sheep, but anger and defiance bristled in my heart. It was embarrassing enough to have my head shaven, but to be humbled, like a slave before these, my captors, that was too much!

When I reached the top of the stairs, all four sergeants followed me inside, drawing everyone's attention.

"Hey, we got one of them peace-niks here," one of them shouted. "Another hippie love child. Watch what we're gonna do to this fucker!"

Everyone laughed, even the recruits sitting in the chairs next to me.

I drew tense and gripped the arms of the chair. My immediate thoughts were those of self-defense. Should I make a run for it? Should I slug one of these bastards if he lays a hand on me? I knew I was hopelessly outnumbered but I was ready for whatever was going to happen, and whatever it was I wasn't going to take it lying down. Still, I thought, if I make it past them, just where the hell would I go. The drill sergeant's speech was fresh in my mind. Everything inside me was coiled to strike but an inner voice was saying forget it, you'll never win. Just let it happen!

I stared hard at the soldiers in front of me. God, how I hated their smirking faces. O.K., I thought, you bastards win today, but not forever. I forced a smile to hide the rage I felt inside and to let them know that they didn't scare me one bit. I said nothing. Slowly, I sat back down and relaxed my grip. No matter what these bastards do, I thought, I'm not gonna let it hurt me. I'm just gonna make like this is smoke in the wind. But, I won't forget, and I'll never forget their faces.

One of the sergeants walked over to my side, watching the barber as he clipped my hair. Long bunches of hair fell to my face and shoulders.

"Leave two long strands on both sides of his head in the back, like a China-man's pigtails," he said. "Then we'll see how pretty he looks!"

The barber did as he was told, laughing, adding his own insults. When he finished, to the accompaniment of laughter from everyone inside, I was ordered to my feet.

What now, I thought, are they gonna leave it this way?

"Out here, Olsen!" the drill sergeant ordered.

I obeyed, marching out through the front door and onto the platform before the waiting troops.

"Call these fuckheads to attention," one sergeant whispered to another.

"At-ten-tion!" the sergeant screamed.

Hundreds of heads snapped into position, all eyes to the front. I could see the officers who commanded the companies talking below and they too looked up to see what was going on. They smiled, immediately catching on.

"What do you think of your god-damned homosexual hippie now?" the sergeant shouted. "There had better not be anymore of you pansies with ponytails out here today. These fucking faggots don't belong to a man's Army. There had better not be any of you chicken-shits in this outfit like this one!"

Laughter echoed across the parade grounds.

I stood frozen at attention, my gaze fixed hard into the distance. I wanted to kill the bastard! I fought with every ounce of strength to keep back tears of frustration and humiliation. A crushing pain settled on top of my chest as I struggled to retain my composure. I felt my hurt and anger flash and then fizzle in defeat. A feeling of contempt mushroomed within me, contempt for both myself and them. I was disgusted by my own cowardice and their lack of compassion, but I would not let them see that they had hurt me. I would not make myself more vulnerable than I already was. Reining in my feelings, I smiled broadly and said nothing, then walked back into the barber shop at their command.

It seemed like only yesterday. Was that world real? Was this?

As I approached the FDC bunker I could see some of the crew outside. A poncho had been tied to the corners of the three-quarter and stretched out on two poles, forming a small haven of shade. A couple of the guys were under it. It must have been chow-time because they were assembling their mess plates and canteen cups. I picked up my gear, wandered over to the chow line and joined them. I could hear Vechione riding Vanous about something or other as I approached. Man, he was always riding someone! Always making some cheap shot. I wondered why he was so bitter, or why he chose to take it out on everyone around him. Lee seemed to be his only friend and even he was not immune to Vechione's criticism. I sat down next to Vanous and listened, keeping my distance from Vechione.

Vechione was talking about how "short" he was, an expression meaning he had little time left to serve in country. He had fewer than ninety days before his discharge and was rubbing it in, kidding Vanous about the fact that he was a "longtimer."

"Here's another one of them silly bastards," he said as I sat down. "365 days left to serve."

"Are you kidding," I said, winking at Vanous. "I'm short too. Only 339 days left!"

Vechione didn't like that. It really set him off.

"Shit, you don't know what short is, motherfucker!" he started. "You don't even say short over here until you have less than ninety days, and you don't start counting until you're under thirty!"

"That's right!" Lee joined in. He too for some reason had taken offense. "I'm not short yet, but I will be soon," he said. "You're lucky if you make it through your first ninety days here, and you don't even think to start counting until you're so close to leaving you could reach out and touch it with your pisser. You never know what day will be your last. I've heard of plenty of guys getting wasted with ti-ti time to serve and it's nothing to joke about."

I had touched a nerve and I knew enough to withdraw quietly before I offended anyone more. There was this fierce pride attached to being short but I didn't understand it. A lot of these guys were that way and this wasn't the first negative reaction I had observed when new recruits joked about it.

55

That afternoon went by normally. Infantry elements continued to experience light contact with the enemy. The 1st Battalion 5th Mech arrived with a platoon to secure the base while the 1st of the 27th and the 2nd of the 27th continued search and destroy operations. Company C had discovered a large tunnel complex 300 meters northeast of our perimeter and were in the process of searching it. They had already lost one man to a VC who was hiding in the tunnel. The Viet Cong had opened up on him with an AK-47, nearly cutting him in half. Two hours later they came upon the VC twenty meters further on down the tunnel and took revenge by blowing him to pieces with a hand grenade.

How lucky I was, I thought, being assigned to the artillery. At least I didn't have to go crawling through those tunnels staring death in the face.

By the time I left shift, the 1st and the 2nd had reported two more wounded with not much more to show for it than some captured rice, documents and a small assortment of weapons and ammunition.

Although Vanous and I had grown to be friends, there was a certain distance that the rest of the crew kept from us. It seemed difficult to get close to anyone who had been in country for a while. It was like they really didn't want to get involved with anyone. I wondered why.

Still, White and I had hit it off and I looked forward to the times when we could talk, and headed off to visit him.

When I arrived at the gun, he was busy humping ammo off a deuce-and-a-half, stacking it in a bunker for protection. I took my shirt off and walked over to help out.

"Hey, Hippie!" he said. "What's happening?"

White was straining under the load of a box of 105 shells but he flashed me a quick grin. He had started calling me Hippie as a private joke. I hustled over to help him lower the shells off his back and we slid the box under overhead cover.

"Fuck man, I'm sure glad to see you. Thanks for the help. This shit gets old in a hurry!"

I could tell by his voice that he was sincerely grateful.

"Hey, let's go!" the sergeant yelled from atop the truck. White and I hustled over.

"Hey, look," one of the gunnies sneered, "here's one of those brains from the F...D...C. I wonder what he's doing here."

"Maybe he's slumming," someone joked. The crew laughed.

"Yeah, hanging out with us common folk."

"Or maybe he just wants to see what it's like to sweat."

"Hey, knock it off!" Sgt. Lightfoot grunted. "Let's just get this shit unloaded so we can take a break. Put your energy where your mouth is."

I didn't know why all of a sudden I had become the brunt of their jokes but their hostility was evident. I was glad that Lightfoot had brought it to a halt. I had been watching White's face during the incident, looking to see if he knew what was going on, but all I got out of him was a sheepish grin. I couldn't tell if he felt the same or if he felt just like me, too new and insecure to offer an

56

opposing opinion. I kept my mouth shut and humped ammo with White until we were done.

After unloading, one of the gun crew came over and gave me a friendly slap on the back.

"Hey," he said jokingly, "I didn't know that anyone in the FDC even knew what the word 'work' meant. Y'all must be part of a new breed."

I didn't say anything. I was embarrassed by the attention I was beginning to receive as the rest of the crew gathered around. Besides, I felt we worked our asses off building bunkers that were twice the size of theirs and always took longer to build.

"You'd better send a few more o' those boys down 'ere so's we can teach 'em what work means," added another.

The rest of the crew laughed, and so did I.

"Tell 'em we could use a few more like you," Sergeant Lightfoot said.

"Hey c'mon guys, lighten up!" White said. "You're gonna scare him away an' then we won't get him to help anymore."

"Well, thanks anyway," a crew member said, his massive hand shaking mine.

I could sense that I had gained their respect and though I was surprised by their response, I was pleased.

"Hey, Olsen, come over here, man," White said, slipping away from the rest of the crew.

We walked over to the edge of the bunker where he picked up his grimy fatigue shirt, and after looking around to make sure no one was watching, carefully extracted two joints from a pocket.

"Far out," I whispered. "Where did you get that?"

White smiled. "I got them in the mail today from a friend back in the states. Man, I can't wait to try it but it won't be safe until I'm off shift. I'll come up to the FDC as soon as I get off tonight and we'll get stoned together."

It was nearly 2300 hours when White finally returned to the guns, leaving Vanous and me sitting on top of the hood of the three-quarter. Still high, we were just lying back enjoying the still, quiet tranquility. As I retreated deep into my thoughts, darkness hid the surrounding jungle, shrouding reality. It was mystifying. I couldn't remember being in any other place where I felt so completely insulated from harm. The darkness was like a curtain separating us from the hectic activity of the day.

"Hey, how you feeling?" I whispered to Vanous.

This was the first time he had ever gotten stoned, and I didn't want him freaking out.

"Fine," he whispered. "I feel happy . . . relaxed . . . kind of funny."

"Far out," I said, and left it at that.

We had been lying there, looking at the stars for twenty or thirty minutes when we heard an explosion. A bright light flashed on the edge of the perimeter and was quickly followed by two more.

57

"Far out!" I exclaimed, sitting up. "Look at those lights man." The area had been lit up like a flashbulb.

"Wow, what's happening?" Vanous asked dreamily.

Two or three more explosions shook the earth, each in rapid succession. An instant later a red trail of tracer rounds burst from a fifty-caliber machine-gun emplacement, penetrating the black sky. It was soon followed by a chorus of M-16s. Suddenly it dawned.

"We're being hit . . . mortars!" I yelled. "Those are mortars!"

We both leapt simultaneously from the top of the hood and scrambled underneath the bed of the three-quarter, our M-16s in tow.

"Wow . . . far out," I said. "Look at that shit!"

"Fuck!" said Vanous, his chest heaving, "I didn't know what the fuck was happening!" He was almost apologetic as he clung to his helmet, pressing it firmly on his head. Six or seven more mortars exploded as we huddled together under the truck, then, just as suddenly as it had started, it stopped.

"Shit," I said, "I'd better get inside. I'm supposed to be on duty now." Still, I didn't go. I hadn't heard anyone call for me and I was still hesitant to leave the protection of the three-quarter. We both stayed at least ten minutes more before cautiously crawling out. I headed for the bunker.

"Wow, what a trip that was, huh!" I said to Vanous while leaving. "Just like the Fourth of July!"

Vanous laughed. We were both still high and everything had happened so quickly that I had failed to realize the seriousness of it. Both of us had failed to recognize the sound of mortars, of incoming rounds. One thing was sure though. Neither of us would forget after tonight.

The following day seemed routine. Nothing unusual happened. We picked up support for a platoon of the 1st of the 5th Mech and found our fire missions increasing. That helped to improve my operation of the charts. I was beginning to understand radio transmissions better and was asked to help in the daily decoding of information from headquarters. Every night, starting around 2300 hours, we would fire our H & I's, harassment and interdiction targets, periodically and keep it up throughout the night. Intelligence would speculate which trails the Viet Cong would be using to transport supplies and would pick some spot on the trail on which to drop a few rounds. The intent was to confuse and delay enemy movement. Even if we didn't have a listening post or ambush patrol set up in the area, the Viet Cong might think so if we happened to drop a round close to them. Then hopefully they would disperse, thinking they had been spotted. We rotated the responsibility of firing these targets to the guns so that all would not have to keep a full crew up. After last night's mortar attack Division HQ had added a group of counter-mortar targets to our list of H & I fire, plotting them around other fire support bases in our area in hopes of keeping down enemy harassment. It seemed we were both playing the same game.

The infantry continued to report their daily findings and I was amazed at the extent of underground operations the enemy had managed to build in the area. The 1st of the 5th found 8000 pounds of rice about two klicks from our location and had detonated an APC mine near it. The 1st and 2nd of the 27th reported items that read like a department store shopping list: bunkers, base camps, bicycles, tunnels, notebooks, ponchos, rations, hammocks and antipersonnel mines. No one location held a lot of supplies; they were scattered all over the area—a tunnel here, a bunker there, or in a base camp at yet another location. One location would have mortar rounds, another location a hundred meters from it, mortar tubes, and yet another would have the base plate from which they were fired. If the VC lost one item they were sure to have a replacement not far away and they made sure that if one location was discovered they never lost all they had. Even if they were the enemy, I certainly had to respect their wit.

Although VC had been spotted moving in small groups all around our location, we had not been attacked. We knew that we were somewhat secure from direct attack during daylight because it would take a major unified effort from the VC to overrun a base camp with the capability of direct artillery fire. A direct offensive daylight assault was sure suicide. Our primary concern was night assaults. Therefore, we were caught off guard when on the morning of November 26 the enemy opened up from the woodline, firing RPGs into the bunker line on our perimeter. Simultaneously, the listening post outside our area, just due to come in, began receiving small arms fire as they ran smack into the retreating Viet Cong. It only took minutes for the Viet Cong to hit, run and disappear, but they left behind two dead GIs.

The attack took place barely an hour after I had gotten off shift, rousing me from sleep. Fearful and unsure of the enemy's next move, I decided not to get caught napping and decided to stay up the remainder of the morning.

That afternoon the resupply chopper brought the top sergeant out from base camp, and with him, a new shift in our defensive posture. The 2nd Battalion 22nd Infantry operating to our north had made contact with a large enemy force near the mushroom bend on the Saigon River and reported a body count of 20 VC with 22 possibles. The enemy appeared to be changing his tactics and becoming far more aggressive and HQ responded with new directives.

After conferring with the captain, the top called the section leaders together to disperse changes to their respective crews. "Stand to" was initiated, meaning that every morning at five o'clock the entire battery had to be awake and on its feet, clothed in helmets, flak jackets and M-16s in case of a possible attack. The grumbling that rose from the battery was almost audible. Available periods of sleep during off shifts were already frequently disrupted by the enemy and having to get up an hour earlier every morning just to stand around and wait for a possible attack seemed ridiculous.

Discontent was more than evident every morning when I had to get the crew up. Most of the time they simply wouldn't respond and the top had to make rounds every morning to make sure everyone complied. If he found someone sleeping, he gave them a swift kick in the ass which soon had them on their feet. But, he soon tired of that and called a meeting of the section leaders and threatened each one with an Article 15 if their crews didn't comply with orders. That changed things, not because anyone was necessarily afraid of the Article 15, but because there was a close tie between most crews and their leaders; no one wanted to see their leaders suffer because of their own behavior. Even so, the top still made rounds, making sure that no one was smoking and that everyone was wearing all their gear. We simply posted a guard who kept a lookout for him and whenever he approached, we quickly doused our cigarettes and put on our helmets and flak jackets. If anyone was having a problem getting up, one or two others would drag him out of his bunker and see that a vest and helmet were put on him and that he remained in a standing position. As soon as the sun came up, we were allowed to stand down, and never welcomed anything more.

At the same time, the 1st of the 5th Mech received orders to retire most of its company to Cu Chi for maintenance and training and when they pulled out they were replaced with a platoon from the 2nd of the 27th Infantry. With most of the Mech gone, the 4th Battalion 23rd Armored Division pulled in to take its place and began OPCON (continued operations) in its place.

Having nothing better to do with my free time, I began exploring the bunker line of our perimeter, looking for a familiar face or the opportunity to talk with some of the grunts about what was happening in the field. Climbing over the dikes that crisscrossed the outer edge of our perimeter, I walked along the bunker lines shouldering my M-16. It was interesting to note the contrast between the infantry and ourselves. The grunts' uniforms always seemed to look as if they had been playing football in a muddy field. Most of them were unshaven and a few even sported mustaches. I wondered how they got away with it. Army regulations required a strict regimen of shaving every day, something strictly enforced for us. Even in our short stay here, command had managed to fly a gook barber to the field to make sure that everyone kept their hair clipped to regulation length. In spite of the inconvenience and hardship, our unit still managed to enforce regulations so that no one went without a shave for more than a day.

I could see the exhaustion deeply etched in the faces of the grunts I passed and I wondered what it was like for them. I knew the grunts were accustomed to working in almost any type of terrain, from dusty fields to broad rivers and swamps. Stalking through the rubber plantations that massed to our east was no easy job either and required a sharp watch for VC bunker complexes hidden between the endless stands of rubber trees and bamboo thickets. That didn't even take into account the trip wires and booby traps scattered in those areas. The tension that existed on patrol must have been enormous. Crossing open rice paddies which were the frequent site of ambushes; caught in crossfires from dense woodlines; searching the intricate bunker and tunnel systems in thickets so thick you could barely peer through them; it seemed unimaginable. There were even teams whose responsibility it was to wade into the river beds to look under the hidden canopy of vegetation that covered the banks. They often uncovered caves with small entrances that had to be searched for enemy contraband. Some went in and never came out.

It was on one of those forays around the southern end of our perimeter that I met Roach. Seeing him made me stop and laugh. He was perched on top of a layer of sandbags grooming one of the largest red mustaches I had ever seen. He reminded me of the Bugs Bunny cartoon character Yosemite Sam. He was hunched over a can of C's, sitting on his haunches like a gook. His unshaven face bristled and his hair hung over his ears like a mop. I couldn't believe it! He must have seen me staring at him because he looked up and after a moment of looking me over, said "What's happening?"

"Sorry," I added quickly. "I was just a little surprised to see anyone out here looking like you."

He grinned and invited me to sit down.

"My name's Roach," he said. "What's yours?"

"Olsen," I replied.

"You with the arty here?" he inquired.

"Yah," I said.

"New in country?" he asked.

"Yah," I said. "How'd you know?"

"Just a guess," he replied.

In the course of our conversation I discovered that he was from San Francisco, and that he was familiar with the Haight-Ashbury district where I had stayed during leave. The band around his camouflage helmet liner had been deeply penned with "make love not war." I asked him about it. As he talked about the need for people to show one another a greater sense of trust and compassion instead of killing one another, I listened closely. I realized that even though it was compelling to believe in what he said, and I wanted those things in my own life, I had shown little trust in others and even less compassion. Instead, as I grew up I had gotten progressively harder. For me, showing trust and love had only resulted in disappointment and rejection. By the time I finished high school I had formed a protective and nearly impenetrable wall around my emotions. Yet I knew in the last two years I had begun questioning my beliefs and examining the kind of person I was. When a friend who had been staying in San Francisco hitch-hiked up to Oregon and told me about the Hippie movement that was going on there, I found myself curiously identifying with its philosophy, but not so much that I made my feelings public.

I had grown disillusioned with the lifestyle my parents were living early in my childhood and it didn't take long for me to abandon the principles they had lived by. Those of society in general reflected the traditional views my parents held, so I abandoned them also. Of course turning my back on all the values my parents held sacred left a void in my life that I had been trying to fill. I had promised myself, like Bob Dylan, that I wasn't going to work on Maggie's farm no more; I wasn't going to give my life to an oppressive economic system—but now here was this. If ever I had jumped from the frying pan into the fire, it was here. The Army was as oppressive as any system I had been under. I found myself curiously attracted to this philosophy of brotherhood and love with its emphasis on creativity, personal liberty and freedom. Now Roach was talking about those same things and I found myself drawn even further to those ideals. Yet my life was certainly inconsistent with them. Still, I felt in my heart that these concepts were right. Right for me and for the world.

Roach soon tired of philosophizing. After all, he said, those ideals were fine for the "real world," but this wasn't the real world, this was war, and in a faraway never-never land. With cynicism, he began talking about what was happening now.

"Did you know that we came upon this grave yesterday? We were working with the Fourth of the Twenty-third Armor on this sweep, and we uncovered a grave with sixteen bodies in it. Man it was nasty, they must have been dead three or four days. There were a number of them that had shrapnel wounds. Listen, I want you to know that we really appreciate the job you guys are doing. Man, if it wasn't for you guys, we would have lost our shit a number of times! But you guys came through and man, we don't forget it."

I must have talked with him and his buddies close to three hours before leaving. It felt good knowing that we were helping to protect these guys. It made the war seem less impersonal.

It was early afternoon, November 28, when I first noticed them entering the perimeter. There were three or four Vietnamese – ARVN Rangers I thought – and two Americans. They were prodding two blindfolded peasants ahead of them whose black silk shirts and short pants barely covered their long, thin, brown legs. Viet Cong, I thought to myself. Why else would they be bound and blindfolded?

My curiosity was piqued as I watched them pass in front of our bunker heading for the Infantry CP less than sixty feet away. I heard the Vietnamese ARVNs bark some kind of order and the two gooks quickly dropped to their haunches. The two Americans went inside the command post, emerging with the infantry captain a few minutes later. I could tell that they were discussing the prisoners, but I couldn't hear what they were saying. Soon the ARVNs entered the conversation. Suddenly, one of the ARVNs grabbed one of the peasants by his hair and pulled his head back, yelling at him in Vietnamese.

"What the hell's going on over there?" I asked Lee.

Lee had been coming out of the FDC bunker when the prisoners first appeared but had ducked back in as soon as they passed. He had now re-emerged and was staring as intently as I was at the situation. I wondered how many others were doing the same.

"It's a CRIP Team," Lee said. "Special forces who operate with the ARVNs. Only these gooks are supposedly *hoi chanh*. They're like the long range reconnaissance patrols that operate in the jungle, except they're even more secretive. It's called a combined reconnaissance intelligence platoon. What they've got is a couple of suspected VC. You see that weapon the American is carrying, the one that looks like a mini M-16? Well, that thing fires more rounds per second than five M-16s, and it's twice as light and more compact. There's a rumor that only the CIA have them."

CIA? What the hell would the CIA be doing over here? If those weapons were so good, how come they weren't standard issue?

We watched as the ARVN pushed the peasant's face into the dirt, stomping his foot repeatedly on top of his head. He kept shouting something in Vietnamese. He must have been trying to extract information, or a confession, I didn't know which. I wondered if it was right to treat him that way if they didn't know for sure they were Viet Cong. One thing for sure was that if he wasn't Cong now, he sure would be after the interrogation was over.

Another ARVN kicked the peasant hard in the side. I could see the pain spread across his face, but he didn't say anything. The other peasant kept his head down, not looking up as the beating and questioning continued. One of the Americans started looking around the base camp, suddenly aware of all the eyes that were watching. He turned quickly to the ARVN and barked a sharp command. The ARVN stopped, looking up, and the American motioned towards a tent erected next to the CP. Two of the ARVNs grabbed the peasant by his arms and jerking him to his knees, dragged him into the tent. The remaining ARVNs stepped up behind the other peasant while the two Americans and the infantry captain went into the tent.

"Do those guys know that these are Viet Cong?" I asked Lee.

"It doesn't matter," he replied. "They're gonna find out one way or another. No doubt they'll work him over until he confesses. I've heard that one of their favorite tricks is to shove bamboo slivers under their fingernails or to take a field telephone and hook up the wires to his balls and crank away until they get a response. It don't mean shit," he added. "Just forget about it!"

Forget about it, I thought. What if the guy's just a civilian? I thought it strange that none of the Americans had laid a hand on the prisoners. It was just the ARVNs who inflicted punishment. It was just like them, I thought, to give the orders but keep their hands clean in case something went wrong. That was the Army way.

Just then the lieutenant stuck his head out the bunker and yelled, "Fire mission!" I ran in. When it was all over, I looked for the Vietnamese prisoners that had been brought in, but they were gone. It was the last I ever heard of them.

Later that afternoon C Company found a Viet Cong base camp which had five interconnected tunnels. One of the tunnels was fairly large and, surprisingly, contained a printing press. While searching the area they uncovered six booby-trapped grenades, one stick mine and two butterfly bombs. That was, of course, in addition to the three dead fish.

Even as we added to the growing list that day, one of the crew who was digging a new latrine in a rice paddy dike uncovered two Viet Cong gas masks.

Sometimes the findings that the infantry reported were hilarious, but as the body count of American soldiers grew, not a day passed in which our reports didn't leave sobering thoughts or a dull ache in my stomach.

That afternoon, one of the tanks on patrol was hit by an RPG. One man inside caught fire and when he jumped out, he landed in front of the moving tank and was crushed to death. Two more were severely wounded. By the end of their sweep they had uncovered 45,000 pounds of rice but it seemed an unfair trade for the lives of three people.

One November 30 I sat back in the security of the FDC bunker and listened to Gianettino relay the intelligence summary for the month to headquarters. I couldn't help but feel a sense of pride in our accomplishments.

". . .B/2/27 found at grid 699336, one eight inch butterfly bomb, tools, one well of good water, clothing, Victor Charlie canteen, one bunker, one and one-half pounds of documents, one pistol holder, one Mike sixteen magazine, 100 rounds of ammo, and two kegs of rice, over.

". . .At grid 700238 found one Victor Charlie hootch, one bicycle, one tunnel, one straight razor, five yards of fabric, two entrenching tools, one canteen, one file, one pot, and thirty inches of claymore wire, over.

". . .At grid 701239 found two bunkers, two tunnels, candles, 1500 pounds of rice, over.

". . .At grid 691234 found thirty-one Victor Charlie fishing poles, one tunnel, seventy-five pounds of rice, one butterfly bomb, two tunnels, two booby-trapped grenades, two butterfly grenades, seventy-five pounds of salt, over."

As he continued I thought about how good it felt destroying the enemy's source of cover and supply. Especially when we rarely saw them and never really knew the total harm we were inflicting in terms of casualties. If we couldn't destroy them, at least we could destroy their food supplies, safe places, and weaponry. Enough of that, and the war would eventually grind to a halt. There was no way the enemy could continue to fight if we remained this effective. Eventually they would give up and we would win, and it wouldn't take long.

Suddenly, I was alerted by a transmission on our secondary push. "Muddy Waters, this is Alpha Three, over," a voice whispered over the radio. "We have spotted three Victor Charlie running across our Alpha Peter. We have engaged with small arms and automatic weapons. Negative results, over."

A night ambush patrol in our area was reporting contact to the infantry command post. Charlie was on the move and that meant he might be heading in our direction. My mind and body immediately switched gears, propelled by possible danger. I felt the adrenalin surge through my body. I remained in a hyperalert state for nearly an hour. It took that long to convince myself that it was just an isolated incident and that I needn't worry.

Shortly before going off shift, battalion headquarters relayed to us that forty Viet Cong had been spotted near Duc Hoa in our vicinity, and that we were to stay alert for a possible attack. It didn't help me to sleep!

III OPERATIONS CAMDEN AND SARATOGA

6

2 December 1967
Fire Base Hale
An Thuam

It was around 0600 that we received word to be ready to march. Brigade was thinking of moving its operation further north where a large battalion of local Viet Cong were active. If the infantry moved, we would move with them. Lee woke Lieutenant Voss to give him the news. The lieutenant said we should notify the captain.

I'm glad I've just come on duty, I thought. At least we won't be moving when I'm off shift and losing more sleep.

During the night the crew had fired fifteen missions. At first the outgoing fire had awakened me. Tense, I had listened for the explosions trying to figure out whether they were outgoing or incoming. As soon as I knew they were outgoing I fell back asleep. That had happened several times, but later, overcome by exhaustion, I slept through it.

I was still half asleep as Gianettino called our situation report in.

"Killer One Three, this is Killer Six Niner. Over." The handset pressed his lips.

"Killer Six Niner, this is Killer One Three. Over."

"Killer One Three, sit rep follows. Charlie fired one-five missions last night. Three zero rounds expended. Over," Gianettino continued.

"Killer Six Niner, I read you as follows: One-five missions, three zero rounds. Is that correct? Over."

"Killer One Three, that is affirmative. Over."

Another voice began transmitting and I recognized it right away.

"Killer Six Niner, this is Killer Three. Tell your Charlie Oscar to meet me on Code Three push. Over," he commanded.

"Killer Three, I roger your command. Over."

"Killer Six Niner, Killer Three, out," said the colonel.

Ten minutes later our new captain pushed aside the poncho covering the door and gave the order to march. The lieutenant immediately telephoned the guns and the procedure began. This was my first move in the field and I didn't know where to begin, so I listened intently. Lee told me to go wake the rest of the crew and tell them to march order; I did and quickly returned. I heard the captain explaining to the lieutenant that we would keep one radio on our present push and one tuned to the station that Killer Three was on. We were to tear down the bunker but keep everything else operable until the final order came to move out. A convoy would be arriving in a couple of hours to transport us to our next location, and the Mech was sending a couple of APCs to provide security.

Myers appeared in the door of the bunker, pulling his fatigue shirt on and grumbling. His eyes were swollen from a lack of sleep.

"O.K. guys, let's get the tent off the top of the bunker first," he said. "Set it aside with the poles. If it rains we might need it. Just lay it out so it can be set up or rolled up with just a few seconds notice." He turned and lifted the tent flap and yelled to Vanous, "Check everything on the three-quarter and make sure it's ready to roll. Vechione! Fill up those water cans and start stripping the sandbags off the bunker, personnel bunkers first." Turning back inside, he continued, "Olsen, get your personal gear together and help Vechione on the bunkers. Empty the dirt out but keep the bags, and as many ammo boxes as we can take along."

I quickly complied. Within the hour, the three of us had stripped every bunker including the roof of the Fire Direction Center. A half hour later the walls had been stripped to ground level and the perforated steel planking stacked near a pile of sandbags. All that remained was for the convoy to arrive. We waited. An hour and a half later it rolled into camp.

Hurry up and wait, I thought, hurry up and wait. The Army's no more efficient here than it was in training. You'd think they would coordinate their efforts a little better over here.

Fifteen minutes after the convoy arrived the entire battery was ready to move. Two artillery pieces were left unhooked in case of attack, for immediate defense. In addition, our radio charts, transmission equipment and generators were still up. We reported our status to headquarters and waited. At 1000 hours the order came. The two guns and we rushed through final teardown and loaded everything up. At the same time the armored tanks and the APCs moved into position at the front and rear of the convoy. The lead truck pulled out before we had finished and we rushed to take up our middle position in the convoy before we got chewed out for holding it up. Finally, our three-quarter roared up from the back of the convoy and slid into place.

The last to go down, the first to be up.

As soon as we were on our way, I asked Vechione where we were headed.

"Ben Cat," he leered. "Boy, the last time we were up there we really got into some heavy shit!"

I couldn't tell if he was kidding or not. He was always trying to scare us, to get us to expect the worst. He delighted in it.

"Hey Lee, is that right?" I asked.

"Fuckin' A!" he replied.

For three hours the convoy trucked over the narrow country roads, stopping frequently to remove bombs and mines that had been planted. When we finally arrived we had traveled only three klicks.

Pulling off a narrow road the convoy began to fan out in the middle of a rice paddy. The tanks that had provided security for the convoy did the same. They rolled over the dikes that separated each rice paddy into neat squares, and, backing over them, quickly crushed a flat path for the gun trucks. Two hours earlier an infantry company had been flown in to secure spots around the perimeter. Some were keeping guard, others were digging in. As the convoy dispersed, a bubble copter entered our air space and landed in the middle of the area.

The captain and his driver raced their jeep over to the settling helicopter and both the captain and top sergeant scrambled out to meet it. An officer ran out from under the swirling chopper blades and both the captain and top stiffened and saluted. They were too far away for me to recognize the rank, but whoever he was, he outranked the captain. They pulled out a map and began pointing in various directions, making repeated reference to the map. Soon, top broke away from the group at a crisp walk and began shouting orders to the gun crews. The lieutenant was just approaching the group as top left. With a quick salute the lieutenant joined their conversation. After jotting something in his notebook and pointing toward a position on our left, he turned on his heels and left, waving us over while shouting orders. Trucks, guns, APCs, tanks and jeeps all moved in unison, demolishing the rice paddy under treads and wheels. A cloud of dust rose from the area as our perimeter began to take shape. Again, half of the crew set up the tent while the other half set up the equipment necessary to lay the battery.

The ammo crew was responsible for setting up communications within the battery and I could see one of the blacks running from their deuce-and-a-half with a bale of wire in his hands. Within minutes he had connected Gun One's telephone to ours and was on his way to Gun Two's position. Since I was officially off duty, I wasn't involved in the set up, but I observed as much as I could while struggling to help put up the tent. With the tent firmly roped into place and the sides up, the on-duty crew moved their equipment inside. The sun was at its zenith and sweat ran down my legs.

Once our exact position had been determined and mapped on the charts the lieutenant and captain placed the guns, designating different areas of fire to each.

"Get that telephone line in!" the captain yelled to the guy tailing the wire.

"One more gun, sir," he replied, running in pursuit of Gun Six.

Unhooking each gun, the crews pulled and pushed them into position, setting the muzzles toward the perimeter. As we set up, the guns took their cue from us and jockeyed into surrounding positions, making us the center of the fire base. When the last telephone was hooked up the lieutenant took over and began laying each gun separately, giving each a direction of fire so that overlapping fire zones were established without the guns having to be drastically traversed.

Stripping off our flak jackets, helmets and shirts, we unloaded the rest of the three-quarter and then the PSP, sandbags, boxes and personal equipment. Tossing everything into a pile, we unloaded as quickly as possible so the trucks could move back into formation and return to Cu Chi before dark. As soon as we finished the lieutenant told us to start digging and we began the dreary, long process of building another bunker.

Twenty minutes later Myers walked over. "The captain wants each crew to send one person to the Ammo Bunker to help unload and disperse ammunition to the guns," he said.

"Shit!" spat Lee. "We'll never get this bunker built with only two people working. Why the fuck don't the guns take care of their own duties. You don't hear him asking the guns to come up here and help us build our bunker, do you?"

"Olsen, you're low man on the totem pole. Grab your helmet and get over to Gun One," Myers barked. "I think they're already unloading there."

I could hear Lee still grumbling as I picked up my helmet and M-16 and trudged over toward the gun.

"Fuck, the next thing you know that pansy-assed captain will be ordering one of us to come over and help build his bunker too," he was saying.

Within the hour the ammo was unloaded and the convoy assembled to leave. I made my way slowly back to the FDC. Exhausted, I was dreading the backbreaking work that still lay ahead.

As I approached the bunker I could see that Lee and Gianettino had made little progress. A hole about nine feet wide and ten feet long had been started. About thirty sandbags were filled and strewn around the outside.

I started dragging over the few boxes we had managed to salvage from our last position and began filling them with dirt. Five hours later we had dug the hole down two feet and erected walls another two feet higher. The infantry had already made light contact with enemy forces and occasionally one or two of the guns had to fire to support them. Whenever he could, Vanous helped us with the digging. By dusk we had the wall up another foot, PSP on the roof, and one layer of covering. The on-duty crew moved all the equipment into the bunker even though you had to stoop to move around. We strung a light for night operations and started up the generator to charge up the batteries so the generator wouldn't have to run at night. We didn't want the enemy to zero in on the sound and lob a few RPGs in our direction.

The lieutenant told us to pull the tent over the top of the bunker to block out light and to pile sandbags directly on top of it.

Two more layers on top meant we could stop working and get some rest—if we were lucky enough to be off shift. I would be back on duty by then I figured.

Somewhere around 0400 the next morning, we finished the last two layers. I didn't have to go on duty for two whole hours. Lying down on top of the bunker, I fell instantly asleep. At 0600 I was shaken awake. I was still exhausted.

Now it was time to start on the personnel bunker. With all of us anxious to get some rest, we decided we would do what was easiest. We dug down a foot and put the end wall up two or three layers high. That would make the height around two feet. It would enable us to crawl in and sleep and that was all. Attaching one side to the FDC bunker saved us building one wall and created head space on one end and a slope to drain off water if it rained. Since it was the beginning of the dry season we wouldn't have to worry much about run-off. With one layer on the roof we could get back to swing shifts and then the on-duty crew could complete the rest.

Around 0800 we got a fire mission. Battalion had planned an airmobile assault at 0830 hours for Charlie and Bravo companies of the 2nd/27th Wolf-hounds, and we had to prep the area before they went in. Headquarters sent us the coordinates for the landing zones over the radio. I still had not caught on entirely to the various codes used, but I was beginning to understand some of the references.

Lee called me in as soon as Battalion HQ radioed. I was grateful for the opportunity to get into the shade and sit down. The temperature was already in the nineties and slowly climbing. I made my way down the clay steps that had been dug out and entered the bunker. A cool breeze was blowing through the gaps in the sandbags that were left as windows. It was refreshing but I knew that when evening came and the tent flaps came down, the inside would be like an oven and stink of sweat.

Lee handed me the code book for December which had been brought out on the convoy.

"Here," he said, "I want you to follow along as Ginchi and I decode these coordinates."

He explained the procedure to me, and as Gianettino read off the letters, he showed me how to decode them.

"X-ray, Tango, Alpha, Peter, Lima, Foxtrot, Delta, Tango, Lima, Foxtrot," read Gianettino.

"Hold it," said Lee. "Do them slower and start from the beginning again."

"X-ray Tango," Lee advised, "stands for the letters X and T. The first two letters dictate code for the coordinates. With the remaining letters, you take them in pairs. Each pair denotes one number. We turn to the code page which has today's date and read across and down from where the letters are located and where they come together, we use that number. Now you decode a number and I'll tell you if it's correct."

Gianettino read the numbers and I deciphered. The code was easy to break if you had a book. Once they finished, I transferred the coordinates to the charts and Lee began figuring out the range and direction of fire. He then took out a slide rule and a book of graphs and calculated the height and traverse. After that he figured what type of shell, explosive charge and type of fuse to use. After the lieutenant checked his data, Lee brought the guns up on the phone.

"Battery!" he commanded. Each gun responded.

"Six," he asked, "Six, you there? Somebody yell over at Gun Six and tell them to pick up their phone!"

In a few seconds someone picked up the phone and yelled, "Six here!"

"Fire mission," Lee responded.

"Shell HE," he began, waiting for the designated gun sergeant to repeat back the instructions. "Charge six . . . fuse time . . . time, one point zero six . . . azimuth one six hundred . . . height three two four zero . . . deflection six two four . . . do not load, report when ready."

While they set the guns, Lee explained the mission. Within minutes each gun reported ready and Lee told them to hang loose but to keep one man on the phone.

"Olsen," he said, "you can drop back out and help those guys sandbag till we need you."

I crawled up the stairs and walked over to the bunker where Vanous, Vechione and Myers were working. It was unusual for Myers to be out filling sandbags. He always stayed at the helm of operations until both bunkers were built and all the work had been done. We all knew it was his responsibility to be in charge during the moves but most everyone resented his not helping. He didn't get any more sleep than anyone else, but he never had to do what the other guys figured was his share of the work either. He simply bumped the crew chief on duty and had the crew chief bump the RTO. That's the way it was supposed to work, the advantages of the so-called chain of command. I knew he hadn't always been the crew chief; he must have done his share of work some time.

"Hey, Olsen," Vechione said after I sat down, "do you want to see something unbelievable? A real fuckin' miracle? Look over there! Do you see what I see? That's the first time we've ever had a fucking captain that's dug his own bunker. Look at that shit! He's actually got his shirt off and getting his fuckin' hands dirty."

I looked over his shoulder to a position twenty yards from us. There, stripped to his tee-shirt, the captain was digging with a shovel while his driver held sandbags. They had two or three layers of sandbags stacked around a narrow hole and it looked like they were constructing a bunker just big enough to accommodate two people.

"Jesus!" said Vechione. "It actually looks like he's going to room with an enlisted man too! Every other fucking captain we've had always had one person from each gun and sometimes two from the FDC build his bunker. And, they generally didn't settle for small ones either; they've always kept one man on to help their aide build one for himself, and ya know where that one came from!"

The way the sarcasm dripped from his words, I could tell he meant they came from FDC. I could identify with the contempt he felt, but sometimes Vechione frightened me. He had become so deeply embittered that I rarely heard him speak a civilized word. Lee too was sometimes harsh and cynical, but at least he was still able to carry on a civil conversation.

My thoughts were interrupted by Vechione and I picked up the end of his conversation.

"First thing these bastards do is cover their own asses," he spat. "Let everyone else take care of their own shit later."

72

Lee's head emerged above the stairway and I caught the movement out of the corner of my eye.

"Hey Lee, what's happening with the prep?" I asked, hoping I would be called in.

"Nothing," he replied. "Headquarters is having A and B batteries fire it. They want us to come up on another push and cover A Company with the 1st of the 27th. I just told the guns to stand down."

"Hey," he continued, walking over, "the new captain is calling a battery formation at 0900. The lieutenant says we're supposed to show up with shirts on, helmets and weapons. Make sure they're cleaned by then just in case he's holding a surprise inspection."

He turned and went back inside.

"Jesus Christ!" exclaimed Myers. "I wonder what this is all about. I hope it's not another fucking pep talk!"

Myers' language caught me by surprise, he rarely swore. It always sounded like he was forcing it when he did; like it was uncomfortable for him. I felt he swore to be one of the guys.

"Well, let's get it done," he whined. "You guys make sure you get your sixteen's cleaned."

I dropped my shovel and walked over to the three-quarter and pulled my duffel bag out. Loosening the strap and clip, I began to rummage through my gear trying to find my cleaning kit. Shit, I thought, there's got to be a better way to store my crap than this. What the fuck do I need all this shit for anyway! I needed to discard some excess baggage.

Vechione and Myers pulled square, grey ammo boxes out of the back of the three-quarter and set them by the side of the bunker. Flipping their metal lids open, they pulled out their kits.

"Hey Vechione," I yelled. "Where can I get another ammo box like that?"

"Come over here and I'll tell ya," he replied.

I grabbed my M-16 and pulled my duffel bag over to their position.

"We got these from the infantry," he began. "They're fifty caliber ammo boxes. Every once and awhile the ammo bunker uses one up but they're snatched up pretty quickly. You almost have to go out to the perimeter to where one of the fifties is set up and ask 'em for one."

Gianettino dragged his ammo box over and sat down. "Hey," he said, "you should get ahold of one of these boxes. If you leave your clothes in your duffel bag they'll mold, then rot."

"We were just saying that, stupid," spat Vechione.

"Hey, fuck you!" Gianettino shot back, taking us both by surprise. Gianettino was really a mild-mannered sort of person, a real Clark Kent. He rarely got angry.

"Hey, watch your mouth or I'll have your ass!" Vechione threatened, rising from his seat. Gianettino dropped his eyes and mumbled something, avoiding any confrontation. Since Gianettino was just a PFC and Vechione was a corporal, I knew he could do as he threatened. Rank did have its privileges.

"Listen," Gianettino offered a little later. "The next time we get into base you can drop off some of that shit and keep it there. You can always have something brought out if you really need it, just don't carry anything you don't absolutely need. It just makes it harder for all of us everytime we move."

"Besides," added Myers, "if you don't use it up right away, everything spoils over here really quick, including your fatigues. If you get an ammo box your stuff will stay drier and we can pack all our boxes in less space. You'd better keep your duffel though, for your dirty clothes."

I began tearing my M-16 down, wiping away the dust that encased every working piece. Every time we convoyed my M-16 ended up looking like shit. All the dust raised building the base camp only made it worse.

"You'd better learn to wrap a towel around the handle and magazine when we travel," said Vechione, "or you're gonna end up with a gun that doesn't work!"

That evening I sat in the quiet of the FDC bunker, deep in thought. By mid-afternoon we had finished the required layer of sandbags on our personnel bunker but battalion HQ sent out new field orders requiring a second layer of sandbags to be added to all existing bunkers, including the walls. I was still angry about it. I had slept only two hours in the last 36 and being on duty, it would be another six before I could get any more.

Damn, I thought, this fuckin' Army's crazy!

I was thinking about the things Captain Nyberg had said at this morning's assembly. He had said he was going to expect the most he could from us and would push us to excellence, but that he wouldn't ask us to do anything he wouldn't do himself. For some, he had already gained their respect by building his own bunker and sharing it with an enlisted man, but I wondered if now he wasn't sleeping while we were awake. If he expected my loyalty he would have to do more than just talk about it.

Shift had changed an hour ago, and the rest of the crew had immediately zonked out. I envied them. This on-again, off-again, every six hours was a drag. I wondered if there wasn't a more equitable way to work shifts.

I was fighting to stay awake, my head nodding, when simultaneous voices burst over the gun lines and the radio. Tripflares! Tripflares had been detonated on the perimeter! A gun crew and the infantry bunker had spotted them at the same time.

There were three VC! The infantry scrambled to get a squad together to go in pursuit. We couldn't fire at them because they were between us and the night listening post outside the perimeter. We would endanger our own site if we did. By the time the infantry set out the Viet Cong has disappeared.

I had no problem staying awake the rest of my shift.

I pushed my chair back, got up and stretched. A cool breeze blew through the bunker, cleansing it of the night's heat and stench. I could smell the upturned soil and the sweet scent of grass and plants that surrounded our location. Taking a deep breath, I detected another familiar odor and leapt to the window to see where it was coming from. The window was at ground height, a little over chin high for me, and all I could see were boots and legs.

I had smelled marijuana but I couldn't see anyone smoking it. I hustled over to the bunker door and climbed up the dirt steps. Looking over the top of the bunker I surveyed the area. I couldn't smell it anymore but I knew that it had been more than just my imagination.

As I walked back down my legs trembled slightly. I still felt physically weak, but after 42 hours I had finally gotten some sleep and those few hours had done wonders for my mind and body.

I looked up as Lieutenant Voss entered the bunker. He had been in conference with both the infantry captain and ours and seemed excited. He spoke with a thick German accent and I had to concentrate to understand what he was saying.

"A couple of grunts have discovered a tunnel entrance in the bamboo thickets growing in the corner of the rice paddy. It runs through the berm directly behind our bunker. The damn tunnel apparently runs right under our base," he said. "You get your helmets and keep your M-16s close by in case anything breaks out as we search the tunnel. We've decided to pull one man off each gun to search the area with the infantry. We aren't required to send anyone because we're short-handed."

How nice, I thought! I sat down at the folding table near the radios and pulled out the battery log. I wanted to see if anything had been reported while I had slept. I was especially curious to see if those three VC had been accounted for. Glancing over the reports I read:

...December 2nd: arrived FSB Hale at 1300 hours. XT 7254 2325, 1-27 INF, negative enemy contact.

...Dec. 3: 0600 Ammo report: 1509 HE 124WP 160ILL 53SMIC 60BH.

0830-Air strikes in grid 4209 at 0930 hrs., grid 4110 at 1550 hrs.

0908-2-27 INF reports gunships engaged 1 sampan XT 423098 resulting in 2 VC captured.

0930: C/1/27 had 2VC KIA at grid 423098 and 1 weapon.

0941: B/2/27 had 4 female detainees at grid 412082.

C/2/27 found 1 VC dead about 2 days from 2 headwounds.

1350: 2/27, gunships engaged VC, 2VC KIA (BC).

1425: A/1/27 found 3 tunnels, 1 homemade gas mask, 6 bottles medicine, 1 lantern, 1 pair glasses, 1 multi-level tunnel at grid 728262.

That's only 200 meters from our location, I thought, I wonder if it's hooked into the one that we're on top of?

1900: C/1/8 had trip flare on perimeter detonated, 3 VC spotted.

2400: journal closed.

Nothing had been entered about the VC so I closed the journal, but after a second thought said, "Hey, Lieutenant, do you want me to add the tunnel to the log?"

Vanous and I had just returned from the mess tent and were sitting on top of our bunker eating when we heard an explosion not fifty feet from us. Startled, we jumped off the bunker. I dived onto the dirt, spilling my food onto the side of the bunker.

"What the hell was that?" I asked as I crawled up close and pulled my M-16 up tight.

"I don't know," whispered Vanous. "Sounded like a mortar to me!"

"That's no mortar!" yelled Lee, who was crouched down alongside the bunker entrance. "It sounded like a grenade!"

Grenade? Shit, is Charlie that close? I could see people all around me scattering for cover as a cloud of dust rose from the infantry location. People who were in the open, carrying their mess trays and M-16s, had simply squatted down, holding one hand on their helmets and balancing their trays with the other. They were frantically looking around, trying to figure out where the explosion came from and looking for someplace to hide.

"Fire in the hole," someone yelled from the area of explosion. The word quickly spread.

Fire in the hole? I thought. That was something you were supposed to yell before you set off an explosion, not afterwards. Who the fuck was the monkey who did this? Nice warning! I could feel a knot in the pit of my stomach so I tried to relax, but couldn't shake off my anger.

About five minutes later Myers came out of the bunker and explained what had happened.

"Some guy blew himself away over in the infantry section," he said. "Apparently two grunts were playing catch with a live grenade and it went off. They're calling in a Medevac for him now."

I couldn't believe it!

"How the fuck could that happen?" I asked. I knew grenades didn't explode unless somebody pulled the safety pin, but they wouldn't have done anything as foolish as that. That was sheer suicide!

"Well, apparently they pulled the pin and then played catch," he said.

"Hey, bullshit!" I said, shaking my head. "Nobody does shit like that. Why, you'd have to be crazy!"

Three days following the grenade incident, we were tearing the fire base down and moving again. Word had come down around 0540, to march. By 0745 we were headed for Cu Chi. This time, we were being airlifted. Elements of the 27th Infantry division east and south of Cu Chi were encountering sizable VC forces which were threatening the security of the base camp, so we were off to support them. But, because we had encountered daily resistance here, battalion headquarters had decided to split the battery and to leave two guns in position while moving the other four.

Myers changed crews again! He and Gianettino were to remain at FSB Hale while the rest of us left. I was anxious to leave even though it meant going through the god-awful process of rebuilding our bunkers. We had been mortared twice in the last five days and had lost seven men. More than 12 were wounded.

This was the first time I had participated in an airmobile operation, and I looked forward to the arrival of the giant Chinooks. This would be my first opportunity to fly in one.

This time the FDC would be the first to leave. I could see Captain Nyberg standing by his jeep on the edge of our perimeter coordinating the airlift. He was speaking into the mike on the jeep radio, talking with the chopper pilots as they approached. He began to yell in our direction, waving us over to a spot where he had thrown a smoke canister. Minutes after reaching the marker we heard the steady thup-thup-thup of the approaching helicopter. The Chinook grew larger as it began its slow descent, its whirling blades creating a dust storm. Purple smoke filled the air and everything that wasn't tied down was tossed high into the air. Dust stung our nostrils. With clenched teeth we hung onto our helmets, in fear of losing them. We bent over bracing ourselves against the fierce draft. Tucking our heads into our shirts we scrambled toward the chopper, against the stinging sand. As the back door of the Chinook dropped, the lieutenant shouted, "Go, go, go!" Vanous, who was driving the truck, pulled his helmet down and pushed the accelerator to the floor. Off we lurched. Behind us, a squad of grunts, their towels waving in the air, began their dash. They tried to follow close behind us to block the gale. Seconds later we were all inside the cavernous belly.

Rocking back and forth, the Chinook lifted off. The crew rushed to hook straps to the back and front of the three-quarter to keep it from rolling. I crawled over the back tailgate, and moving cautiously toward the side of the chopper, I struggled to keep my balance as the helicopter lurched. I made my way over to one of the windows near the door gunner's position and sat down. The camp below became increasingly smaller as we rose in the air and began our journey southward.

God, I thought, this is great! Traveling by helicopter is really a trip. Not half as dirty as trucks, either!

I was excited but a little apprehensive. I wondered if we would take any ground fire. Yesterday a Chinook had taken automatic weapons fire from a small village near our location, in the same direction we were going. I hadn't heard if anyone was injured but the infantry and the gunships who swept the village later demolished it, destroying with flame throwers what had been left standing.

I tapped the door gunner on the shoulder. "Have you been seeing much action on this route?" I yelled, trying to be heard over the whine of the engine and the helmet he wore.

"What?" he yelled back, leaning his head closer.

"Have you seen much action on this route?"

"Some," he yelled.

"Are we in range of rifle fire?" I continued.

"Yeah, they can reach us, but we're flying higher than usual and accuracy and impact is a little harder up here."

"How long will it take us to get to Cu Chi?"

"About fifteen minutes, give or take a few!"

I settled back against the hull of the helicopter and watched the patchwork fields and grass-thatched roofs of the villages pass below. Occasionally I saw a few peasants in the fields, but none of them carried weapons.

We left Cu Chi on convoy to Xom Bao Cong, a small hamlet about 45 minutes to the south. It was probably going to take us five times longer than the 18 minutes it took us to be airlifted from FSB Hale, even though our destination was only half the distance away.

Riding in the back of a truck, I wondered what it would be like in Xom Bao. As we made our way through the open countryside, I slouched further down in the truck, trying to avoid the dust. There was no way of escaping it but I did my best to try. Taking Vechione's advice, I had wrapped a towel around the bolt assembly of my M-16 and stuck a wad of cloth down the barrel, making sure it was large enough to be easily visible. I didn't want to forget it was there and fire it, and kill myself.

Our morning's intelligence briefing had warned us that the 190th Assault Helicopter Company had two choppers shot down approaching an LZ yesterday near where we were headed. Last night the 549th ARVN had come into contact with what was estimated as a VC company in the same area. A chopper from the 190th had been shot down while assisting them. Even the dust-off ship was shot down when it tried to evacuate the wounded. Three other aircraft had received direct hits but had managed to remain in the air. I couldn't figure out what the heck the ARVNs had been doing in the woods so late at night. The whole fuckin' country seemed to belong to Charlie at night. The only safe place to be was inside your own perimeter, and even then there were no guarantees.

I tried to remember everything that had been said at yesterday's briefing. Battalion command had given the lieutenant a list of updated observations and changes, and he had passed them on to us.

The first item had dealt with the construction of bunkers. Commanders were to insure that all bunkers were mutually supporting by having firing ports to the front and both flanks. All bunkers were to be constructed with a side entrance, with sufficient cover to the rear of the bunker to prevent casualties from artillery fired directly onto their position.

Secondly, because night LPs were frequently ineffective due to their incorrect or uncertain position, the infantry was supposed to have at least one man move to the site of the planned route during daylight to insure familiarity with the area to be occupied. For sure, I had thought, lots of luck. I knew the brass stood as much chance of enforcing that as to make us build additional entrances into our bunkers. The infantry were as short of men as we were and could hardly spare two men to check one area while they were sweeping another. I just couldn't imagine one man wanting to patrol on his own in enemy territory. You could tell that these were orders from men who just made up rules for others to follow

78

without having to do it themselves. Shit, if they had to do it, it wouldn't be a rule.

Another item was the use of illumination shells. The artillery had discovered that illumination shells could be fired at a low height of burst, at a range much closer than previously thought possible. The shells would then burn on the ground, illuminating and silhouetting targets between the point of impact and the perimeter. This had proved extremely effective when a large force of Viet Cong had initiated a well-coordinated attack at Dah Song three days ago. The enemy, using a familiar m.o., had laid down a heavy barrage of mortar fire and then conducted a ground assault. Since the fire support base couldn't get an airship in right away to drop flares, the 23rd Arty had fired their own. Usually, illumination was simply fired at the highest elevation of the guns but that had been impeded when gunships had arrived.

It was nice to know that command was passing that kind of information on to us.

We were beginning the first phase of another Brigade operation, code-named Saratoga. It was going to be run in conjunction with Operation Yellowstone. We would be working jointly with ARVN forces and province officials in the TAOI portions of Long An, Binh Duong and Hau Nghia. Our job was to pacify those areas, secure allied bases and prevent VC rice taxation in the two remaining months of harvest. We were also supposed to prevent harvesting or transportation of rice by the Viet Cong and destroy any VC or NVA forces operating in the area. Headquarters had said we could look forward to working with the 3rd Squadron 4th Cavalry for a change. Those mechanized divisions had a reputation for being mean mothers. I wouldn't mind having them around at night.

I peered over the side of the truck to check out the scenery. Everything in the area looked much the same. There were dry, hard rice paddies as far as I could see. Occasionally there were lush bamboo thickets or a foreboding wood line.

"Hey, Lee," I said, "what do you suppose it'll be like here?"

"I don't know," he replied. "But it shouldn't be too bad. There have been occasional sorties of VC and NVA units through the area from up north but we haven't had any extensive contact lately in this area. Last year most of Duc Hoa, Duc Hue and portions of Cu Chi and Trang Bang were openly under Viet Cong control—they say as much as sixty percent of the population. Ol' Charlie had his foot so firmly entrenched in the door even our heaviest weapons couldn't dislodge him. Man, there are so many tunnels in this area Charlie can literally maneuver his forces below the ground."

I could tell that Lee was trying to be optimistic, but he didn't sound very positive to me. Still, the fact was, this operation was using the combined forces of ten infantry battalions and I was sure we could take care of any enemy we ran into.

We finally pulled off the road around 1300 hours, near a small village directly off Highway 8, and the building process began again.

Because we encountered intense resistance, it didn't take long for us to realize that something was in the air. We began to expect the unexpected. The first day out, the 1st of the 27th apprehended 36 detainees and had them evacuated for interrogation. Running across that many people without identification, or whose activity warranted further questioning, was unusual.

The same day, the 4/23rd Infantry discovered a grave containing one VC dead from gunshot wounds and also three weapons caches and numerous ammunition caches. A Division C & C ship spotted a VC platoon in the open and engaged them, taking fire. It was unusual for the VC not to run. A company of the 3rd of the 4th Cavalry found antitank mines in the road near their location and came under heavy automatic weapons fire about the same time the C & C ship spotted the enemy. Forty meters from Alpha's location, Bravo Company of the 3rd Battalion 17th Cavalry walked into an ambush during the same period the infantry with the 2nd Battalion 14th Infantry received sniper fire.

C Company of the 3/4 Cavalry discovered two bunkers on their sweep, one containing fresh blood-soaked bandages. All this was taking place in a relatively small area around our location.

That first evening the area around us exploded with activity. The 7th Battalion 11th Artillery's location received 12 to 15 rounds of 82 millimeter mortar fire and CID-6, not far from us, received over 200 RPGs, and small arms fire. The ARVN outpost, not 2000 meters from our location, was assaulted by an unknown number of Viet Cong and lost 16 men.

With all the action that was going on and because we were short of help, the construction of our bunkers went slowly. And what made us even angrier was the fact that Battalion HQ sent down orders that every bunker, including personnel bunkers, had to have three layers of sandbags on them before anyone could sleep.

We fired preps daily on the LZs where the combat assaults were taking place; even then they turned out to be hot. Twelve guys were wounded by booby traps alone in the first two days. On one sweep the grunts found a black pair of pajamas, a Viet Cong uniform, hidden in a haystack. Shortly afterwards, they saw a male enter a thatched hut near their find and went after him, securing the hut against escape. But after surrounding it, they assaulted it only to find it empty. Undoubtedly a tunnel entrance existed somewhere inside, but they could never find it so they just planted C-4 explosives in it and blew it in place; then set fire to its remains—and to all the haystacks in the area. I had no idea of how long it might have taken that man's family to build the hut, or how long it took them to grow a half-year's provision for their livestock, but I didn't care either. If they were the enemy, we had to destroy everything they had so they could not continue their aggression.

The third day at FSB Meade, communications came down from headquarters that eight VC companies had been dispersed in the area near Go Dau Hau, just to our north, and that we were to be on the alert for possible infiltration into our area within the next day or two.

80

"Next day or two," I had thought; that was probably them coming through last night. Army intelligence always seemed to be a day or two late.

Brigade headquarters sent us a communication saying that some local Vietnamese, 900 meters from our position, had been detained by Viet Cong for four hours and made to gather wood for them. HQ also added that a VC company with an estimated strength of 100 men had been spotted about two and a half klicks from our location on the first of December and that they too were thought to be headed in our direction, toward Trai My. They were unsure if they were in our sector anymore but we were supposed to keep it in mind. How could we forget?

Later, HQ called again and said that during the month of November, at Thanh An, a VC meeting was held whose purpose was to make plans for attacking Tri Tam, and that they might be using our area as a holding zone for VC and NVA infiltrators. A government source had just observed a large number of VC between Thanh An and our location. They were alongside a road and moving north. He was unable to distinguish the type of weapons they were carrying, and their type of uniform was unknown to him.

Two and a half hours after their report, about 200 meters from the position the VC had been spotted, Delta Company made contact with approximately 400 men who were sporting 60mm mortars, .30 caliber machine guns, and small arms. Gunships and C & C ships swarmed to the area to fire support. The forward observer's helicopter was taking small arms fire and we listened to his excited transmissions as bullets tore through his bubble. When it was over, the infantry had captured 16 RPGs, eight 81 and 60mm mortars, and four heavy machine guns. They also managed to take one prisoner who through interrogation had revealed that their mission was to attack the 34th ARVN Ranger Battalion. During the battle the infantry had sustained only two casualties. Later, while being extracted by helicopter, they received sniper fire and lost another man.

After their extraction, Brigade forces hammered the area with repeated air strikes. We had seen the smoke from the explosions mushrooming in the distance. I wondered how Charlie, even in his tunnels, could survive a pounding like that.

We were still working on the construction of our personnel bunker well into the later part of the third day of occupation. The loss of sleep, exhausting physical labor, and insufferable heat took their toll.

We had been able to send one person into the PX for supplies for all of us during our stopover in Cu Chi and on the top of my shopping list had been sun tan lotion. It wasn't a purchase of leisure, it was a necessity. It was a weapon of defense against a merciless sun which beat down on our neck and shoulders from early morning until late into the evening. Even with sun-screen, my face, arms and back burned. The tops of my ears blistered repeatedly and I had taken to wearing my jungle fatigue hat almost all the time. The intense heat pushed the temperature up into the hundreds every day and that was in the shade. Every ounce of sweat that poured from my body seemed to rob me of strength. When the heat became unbearable we stopped to take short breaks in the shadow of the three-quarter, and gulp down salt tablets. We knew that if we didn't we might end up with convulsions in the dirt and possibly dying.

We were on the move again. The 1/27th had swept an area west of Trung Lap, nine klicks north, and their base had come under attack. An NVA battalion had tried to overrun it. This was the first engagement with a North Vietnamese Army unit in the Hau Nghia District, or for that matter, in the whole 2nd Brigade TAOI. The 1st of the 27th lost 10 men, but the NVA lost 39. It was even possible that more were killed but because of the enemy's habit of never leaving their wounded or dead, we didn't know. Following the attack the NVA had moved into the Ho Bo Woods. It was rumored that we were heading there. I had seen enough action the way it was, I had no desire for more.

By the time we left FSB Meade we had fired over 6,700 rounds in support of infantry operations. The score was U.S. 87 KIA, VC 16 KIA: but it didn't include the 51 wounded on our side or the 139 detainees on theirs. Nor did it include the extensive list of supplies or enemy emplacements we had destroyed. I was beginning to get an inkling of the cost of war . . . to both sides.

Again, we airlifted to Cu Chi to pick up further orders. The next day we were on the road again, headed back in the same direction we had come. This time we were going to Bao Trai, a small hamlet northwest of Duc Hoa, on Highway 10. The 1st Battalion 27th Infantry was conducting a multibattalion assault with the 2nd of the 23rd Armor and they had encountered an unknown size VC force and we were returning to assist them.

On the convoy, it became my turn to drive the three-quarter. The lieutenant was riding shotgun. Because Lieutenant Voss thought it necessary to follow battalion orders, he wore his helmet and flak jacket and insisted that I did also. It was too damn hot to wear it but to satisfy him, I did. I stripped off my fatigue shirt first though.

Since we were riding together, I tried to get as much information from him as I could about what was going on, and bored with the long drive and maybe even hungry for some kind of companionship, he talked freely.

He let me know that brigade flights over Bao Trai, which were being conducted on a daily basis, had spotted a number of Viet Cong battalions in our area. In addition, S-2, command intelligence, had said that agents reported sighting two VC battalions northeast of us, one VC company east of us, and two VC companies northwest of our previous firebase. S-2 also reported that civilians reportedly had been ordered to Giong Giong, Tun Pho, Thu-Rung and Xuan Than to dig trenches for the Viet Cong.

Definite concern was evident in his face as he talked. He didn't like having to conduct offensive operations against a thoroughly dug in Viet Cong and made no effort to hide it.

"This is highly unnatural," he said in his thick German accent. "Those Viet Cong are rarely willing to stand and fight. It's not like them. They know what awesome destruction we are capable of with the firepower we have available. They know they can't survive against American firepower!" His voice quivered as he talked. He appeared a little more hyper than usual. He generally wasn't this talkative, and the more he talked, the angrier he became.

"Ah, this fuckin' heat!" he spat, grabbing his helmet. He pulled a handkerchief out of his pocket and wiped his brow. His forehead, enlarged by a receding hairline, was covered in sweat. His face was unusually flush, a bright pink instead of his usual pale skin. I couldn't figure out why he was so agitated. I hoped it didn't have to do with the area we were headed into.

"You O.K., lieutenant?" I asked.

"Ya, ya, I'm fine," he replied. "It's the god-damned heat! And this god-damned dust!" He leaned his head out the window. Picking up his helmet, he tossed it to the floor of the cab. "God-damned dust," he yelled. "You can't even get your face cooled off without getting covered with dirt."

We could see two villagers out in a rice field as we passed; their black pajamas and wide brimmed straw hats made them easily identifiable.

"Those fuckin' gooks!" the lieutenant continued. "Those bastards are probably VC. We should stop and kill them right now. You can't tell the difference, ya know. They all wear black pajamas. Better we kill them now than they kill us tonight!" He stuck his fist in the air and cursed them at the top of his voice.

By now he was even attracting the attention of the guys in the back of the three-quarter. I was secretly amused by the lieutenant's antics, but the more he continued, the less funny it got, and the more concerned I became about his leadership ability. I wasn't trusting my life to just any man, regardless of his rank, and this wasn't the first time the lieutenant had seemed unstable. I had been on duty during previous tirades, when Myers had been the subject of one such outburst. I had been glad then I wasn't in his shoes. I had seen the lieutenant lose his cool under fire too, and that bothered me. He just didn't seem to have his shit together! But, I was learning that wasn't too unusual for officers, in spite of the fact that all of them were older. Most of the lieutenants were in their twenties but Voss must have been in his early thirties. The thing that bothered me the most was that he wasn't respected by the rest of the crew, especially the longtimers.

When we arrived at Bao Trai we worked all night and the next day building a firebase, but the third day we were ordered back to Cu Chi and had to tear it all back down. Man, I figured either the brass didn't know what was going on or they didn't give a shit.

We spent the next four days in base camp. It was like being on vacation. We pulled shift whenever we were on duty but the remainder of the time we were free! We didn't have to break our backs digging bunkers or filling sandbags. I hardly knew what to do. The first thing I did was take a shower, with actual hot running water. It was even indoors! I visited the PX with a couple of guys from the ammo bunker and even shopped at some new Vietnamese stalls near it. Here was actually someplace I could spend the money I was making. I put on clean fatigues and washed my old ones, which were beginning to rot. I took the time to begin some letters to friends back in the world.

Command had moved our battery to a new location on the perimeter so I spent some time looking through the stacks of footlockers in the barracks hootches, trying to locate mine. The only thing I missed was the opportunity to visit the E.M. club, hindered because my work shift ran concurrent with its hours.

Having few extra duties and being lucky enough not to be assigned the despicable job of burning shit, I seized the opportunity to socialize. I became better acquainted with the crew at the ammo bunker. I met Sergeant Ramos, a Puerto Rican who headed the section; Santiago, another Puerto Rican whose friendly behavior and boastful kidding nature made him an immediate favorite; T.J., a skinny black kid from the ghetto who was always coming on as "bad"; Winston, the black "commo man," who put together the telephone lines; and LeRoy Pearson, a black, smiling, round-faced boy whose exuberance and humor drew me to him.

I quickly became attached to the ammo crew, and especially to LeRoy. I didn't know what it was about the "brothers" that attracted me but I was drawn to black people, and had been ever since LPC School. There was something about blacks that made me feel like I belonged. There were a lot of things I felt in common with them; their music, their sense of being a persecuted minority and their sense of loyalty and commitment. They had a looseness about them, a certain sense of freedom of the soul. They were capable of feeling and expressing deep emotions, the kind of emotions I often felt but rarely expressed. They had a sense of family, of brotherhood that most whites lacked. It reminded me of belonging to the gang I had grown up with, the Keemos. The Keemos had become my family as I had increasingly become alienated from my parents. Most of the blacks were heads too, and that provided a real link in the chain that bound me to them.

Everyone's hope was that we would get to spend Christmas, now only six days away, in base camp. Shit, I didn't care if it was Christmas or not, but I sure wanted to stay in from the field. As long as possible!

I could feel myself slipping into depression, the kind that seemed to accompany every Christmas and I tried not to think about it. But it grew more evident as I reread the letters I had started writing in the field. I really was hoping to hear from someone before Christmas but I just didn't want to get my hopes up. Christmas was always like that. Some kind of major disappointment always accompanied it.

I began asking myself questions like, If my life ended tomorrow—and it could—would there have been any value to it? What had I done with it? Did it mean anything to me . . . or to others? Had I done anything worthwhile at all? Would anyone really care if I died? Just what was it I was living for anyway?

There wasn't a day that passed where someone wasn't asking me whether we would be staying in camp. They knew the FDC would know first. All I could ever tell them was what headquarters was telling us, and they gave us every assurance that it looked good for us to stay for Christmas. But telling them never seemed to assure them. I never felt assured myself. One thing I was learning about the Army was that those in authority did their best to keep everybody below their rank in the dark. There was a purposeful gulf between officers and enlisted men and I was a long way down the totem pole. Luckily for me, the FDC generally had access to almost all the information that was shared on a captain's level, but even then there were times that command sent him coded messages that were for his eyes only. And there were no personal conversations with the big brass, because the big brass never came out to the field.

It came as no surprise on the 24th when we received orders to prepare to march. As we passed down the word to the guns, I remembered one of the sergeants saying, "Damn it, Olsen, I thought you said we were going to stay over till Christmas."

"Don't blame me," I had answered. "I just passed on what the brass told us, and I told you so at the time." I didn't like having to represent authority and then be wrong.

I should have known better. I had seen the scenario slowly developing. There had been a rapid increase in the contacts we had monitored on the radio. We had even been called to fire a number of missions from base camp which was unusual because of the limited range of our 105s. Then, we heard rumors that the 4th Battalion 9th Infantry had run into an NVA regiment, experiencing major casualties. It was really unusual for an enemy force of regiment size to be in our vicinity, especially grouped together. Then, the Wolfhounds got into a major skirmish and ended up with a larger than usual VC body count. Another major battle had taken place on the 22nd, just six miles northwest of us, so, on the 23rd, when the captain was called to a major briefing, I knew something was about to happen. Still, headquarters insisted that we would be staying in camp over Christmas. What a bunch of bullshit! It made me angry. They must have known what they were planning, why didn't they just play it straight with us. You couldn't trust anyone in authority.

We were heading for the notorious Iron Triangle, a favorite sanctuary for Charlie.

The Iron Triangle was a nickname given to a large area of transition jungle which contained the Boi Loi Woods, the Ho Bo Woods and the Filhol Rubber Plantation. Each of these areas bordered the three corners of the heavily wooded, triangular shaped forest. Because of its shape and reputation, it had earned its nickname. The Triangle was believed to contain one of the heaviest concentrations of Viet Cong in the 2nd Brigade area. They used a different battle style. In the flat open country, which contained mostly rice paddies, there was little natural shelter and the Viet Cong were content merely to harass us on a small scale and then fall back in to the foliage and disappear. In the Triangle you could almost disappear anyplace. You could pass within a foot of Charlie or even walk directly over his head and not know it. The Viet Cong had been busy building large tunnels in the rice country but they were merely enlarging their control from

85

the wooded areas that were already like large underground cities. The rubber plantations were like that also; they were favorite sanctuaries for the Viet Cong.

The Triangle also contained two large rivers which branched out from the Saigon River directly north and east of the forest. The Saigon River was considered a main supply route. These three rivers ran the length and width of the whole area. The Truong Chua River ran west through the Boi Loi Woods. The Suoio Ba Ca ran through the middle of the Triangle and directly south to the Ho Bo. The Saigon ran directly east and bordered both the Filhol and Ho Bo Woods. For years the Vietnamese from the north had been sending supplies and ammunition to the south and these had been stockpiled in the Triangle. There, they were slowly dispersed throughout the country—overland by night and underground by day.

In the Iron Triangle the enemy was not satisfied just to hit and run. After all, the enemy generally retreated toward the Triangle after hit-and-run tactics, it being their base. Since December 8 we had been monitoring elements of the 4/23rd who were involved in securing Rome Plow clearing operations there. They had been conducting S & D missions concurrent with the 65th Engineers' land clearing operation. We were not giving direct support to them, but were monitoring their activity in case they needed additional artillery support. The majority of their contact consisted of mechanized infantry attacks on heavily fortified enemy emplacements, which the enemy fiercely defended. During their sweeps they had reported several large underground rice and equipment caches, multiple freshly dug graves and several bunker and tunnel complexes. One tunnel complex was so large it took the Kit Carson Scout platoons three days to search it. Myers had said that a body count of 1,467 had been reported during their 35 day operation. Those gains had not taken place without losses. Even though the engineers had destroyed approximately 10,000 meters of interconnecting tunnels, they had suffered a huge loss of machines, equipment and men.

One thing the Army had begun doing to cut down on the number of American casualties was the formation of Kit Carson platoons. These platoons, made up of Americans, Hoi Chanhs and ARVNs, were being used to search the tunnels. They figured one way the Hoi Chanhs could prove their loyalty was to volunteer in searching the tunnels. That was the most risky position. We were finding that many of the tunnels and bunker locations reported by Hoi Chanhs and civilian do-gooders turned out to be highly booby-trapped, with little there of any worth. Often as not, we were simply being set up.

We were to be part of a clean-up operation in the area called Operation Camden. Considering that during operations Kole Kole and Barking Sands, Rome Plows had cleared a total of 19,995 acres in the Triangle, and on Operation Atlanta had downed 5,250 more, I wondered if there was still jungle standing.

No one was looking forward to this mission. Lee mentioned that he was sure glad he was getting short. If what we had been hearing was any hint of the defensive tenacity we could expect from the enemy in future operations, he was glad he was getting out soon.

The operation added weight to the rumors that indicated a large buildup of

NVA units was occurring and that additional NVA soldiers were being added to already existing Viet Cong units in our area. Up to now, enemy elements within our TAOI were primarily local force units, operating with little deviation from established m.o.'s, but we sensed we might be in for a change.

Word came down that we would be hooking up with the other two guns in our battery while on convoy. It was good to know there would be two more people to help construct the next bunker. As we rushed to break down the equipment in the FDC bunker and load it into the three-quarter, Sergeant Clinton, one of the gun chiefs, approached our bunker carrying a telephone in his arms.

"This baby's sick," he said when he arrived. "Maybe you could urge the lieutenant to have headquarters send us out a new one. I need to pick up some batteries for it but it needs more than that!"

He thrust the phone in my hands and continued talking. "Hey, did you ever find out what that explosion was in front of our bunker last night?"

"Yeah," I replied. "It was a short round. The 1st of the 321st Artillery was firing over our location using MT fuses set on safe. Apparently the fuse was defective and it exploded before it was supposed to. Headquarters said they suspended the complete lot. I told one of the men from each gun that they were to check all our fuses for lot number UST1-89 and to turn in any that they found for replacement. Didn't you get the word?"

"Oh," he said. "That's what that was all about. All right!" He turned and headed toward the ammo bunker.

When the convoy finally left, we pulled onto Highway 8. The long trail of tanks, trucks and APCs kicked up dust as we moved northeast up Highway 237 toward Trung Lap. Before long, my sweat-saturated shirt began sticking to the blisters on my back and my fatigues started collecting dust. I knew that before we reached our destination I would be covered in a filthy grime. I took off my helmet, and taking a pen from my shirt pocket I began inking the words "Fuck it" on the cloth band that circled my camouflage cover. It was against Army regulations to write on part of your uniform. It was government property. Damaging it was considered a felony. But, I just figured, fuck it. I was just gonna go with the flow.

Shortly after passing Gia Be we swung north on Highway 7 and joined up with the other two howitzers at an intersection there. Near Trung Lap we swung off the main dirt road onto a road that seemed more a trail and began our ascent into the Triangle. The vegetation and foliage began to change gradually as we traveled north. Then, as we neared the forest area, it began to differ rapidly. Tall trees and thick foliage dominated the area, thickly spanning both sides of the road. There was a twenty yard buffer on each side of the road that had been completely stripped of jungle. In some areas, only the stumps of trees remained, dotting the sides like straw stubble. As we drove deeper into the sanctuary we made ready. Our eyes strained to catch any enemy movement in the woodline.

The 2/27th had conducted an air mobile assault into the area to secure a bridge site for the convoy and Company A of the 2nd Battalion 34th Armor were to provide security for our base. We began to see some of their tanks patrolling the road and knew we must be close to our destination. Further up we passed more, guarding an engineering unit that was clearing a path even further into the jungle.

The convoy stopped about thirty yards beyond the tanks and was quickly approached by an infantry captain, who was directed to Captain Nyberg. After some quick conversing, Captain Nyberg waved the convoy on and we pulled off the road to wait directions. I jumped down from the deuce-and-a-half, clutching my M-16, and headed toward the three-quarter. The lieutenant pointed to an open area about thirty yards from the woodline and the three-quarter spun off toward it. We hustled to establish communications and set up the charts. This time Vanous and I were doing it. While the lieutenant removed a cap from a long round cardboard container and slipped out the enlarged maps of the area, we quickly removed the old ones from the top of the charts and put them in like containers. Cutting and pressing transparency paper over the new maps, we began to lay out the area, which was plotted in 1000 meter squares. Following the lieutenant's directions, we pin-pointed the battery center and laid out azimuths of fire around it. Once we did that, and communications were established, we helped to unload the rest of the equipment. In the midst of our labor, the lieutenant slipped over to the engineer battalion and fifteen minutes later returned with a bulldozer trailing behind him.

"Hey, look vat I vas able to dig up!" he shouted. "Zis time we von't haff to dig a bunker."

The bulldozer rapidly scraped out a huge pit in the earth, large enough for both the FDC bunker and a personnel bunker. What a relief! Since the PSP would not stretch across the top, the lieutenant managed to secure three long timbers that would. Each one was 18 inches square and it took three of us on each end to shove and pull them into position. Laying the PSP on top of them, we immediately began covering them with sandbags, all the while cheering this unique stroke of luck. Man, it was a pleasure working with the engineers. They had all kinds of stuff available, including C-4 which the infantry was using to blow holes for their bunkers. Before evening we had two layers of sandbags on the roof and were just starting on the third when Myers stuck his head out the bunker and yelled for Lee. Lee left, but soon returned, dragging his M-16 and helmet.

"Hey guys," he drawled. "You're all supposed to find your guns, helmets, flak jackets and magazines. Around dusk we're going to have a show of fire power around the edge of the perimeter."

"Show of fire power?" I asked. "What's that?"

"Well...," Lee drawled, "all the infantry, the tanks, and the artillery are going to gather at the edge of the perimeter tonight with all nonfunctioning personnel. Then we're going to have a mad minute where everyone fires their weapons at once. It's supposed to let Charlie know what he's in for tonight if he tries to attack. The captain feels that a show of force now will help to deter an attack later. Who knows, maybe it'll scare 'em off."

"Wow," I said. "Far out. That ought to create some fireworks, especially since it's going to be just dark enough to see all those tracer rounds going off."

"Fuck you, 'far out,'" spat Vechione. "What the fuck kind of bimbo are you anyway? Why don't you stop with the fuckin' hippie talk. Shit, that flowerchild shit makes me sick!"

"Hey, fuck you man!" I shot back. I was tired of his bullshit.

"Yeah, well, why don't you try it?" he said.

"Just keep it up man, and I will," I replied.

"Hey, we got enough to worry about without fighting among ourselves," Lee interjected. "Just keep your head down. I wouldn't get too excited about it if I was you."

As dusk settled, every available man could be seen trucking his rifle down to the perimeter. I headed over to Gun Three to see if White was off duty. He was. We both headed off to the ammo bunker which was directly on the edge of the perimeter. When we arrived, Sergeant Ramos was sitting behind the .50 caliber machine gun atop their bunker. I waved at him and then to LeRoy, who was lying behind a small ridge. He waved us over.

"Wow, this is gonna be some show," I said, lying down beside him. "It's too bad we don't have something to toke up on."

"Wow, I can dig it," added White.

LeRoy laughed and rolled over on his back, tipping his helmet back. His wet, black skin shone in the diminished sunlight. His fatigues, like ours, were soaked and caked with dirt.

"Ho boy," he said, "I hear that some of them guns is gonna fire up some of those new beehive rounds tonight. I'm sure lookin' forward to see what they's gonna do."

I was too! I had never seen a beehive round fired. They were a recent addition to our arsenal and had been developed specifically for use by the artillery for point blank fire in the event of a ground attack. The rounds were like giant shotgun shells and were filled with thousands of small steel darts. The shell exploded within the chamber of the 105 and the darts began to fan out almost immediately out of the barrel. It was said that the darts utterly ripped apart anything in their path from 100 meters out. Only two of the guns were firing beehive and Captain Nyberg was manning one of them. The infantry captain and the lieutenant were also on hand to see what they would do. The rest of the guns were firing Killer Junior, a technique of utilizing close-in, low air bursts of heavy explosives with timed fuses.

"OK, you guys, get ready!" Ray yelled from the ammo bunker, the telephone cupped next to his ear. "They're gonna shoot any minute now."

Two minutes later the perimeter erupted. The noise was terrifying. For nearly one full minute every kind of weapon we had poured continuous fire into the wood line. Shee-iittt! I thought. If Charlie was hiding out there now he was undoubtedly filling his pants. When the all-clear command came and the smoke finally settled, you could see a path in front of Gun Six that looked like it had been cleared by a lawnmower.

"By the way," I said, getting to my knees to leave, "Merry Christmas!"

Soon I began to discover just what a Rome Plow operation was. While we were digging and building, the engineers and tanks were blowing up and pushing down everything in sight. The woods were slowly being transformed into flat, empty sand lots. Any tunnels, bunkers, or graves uncovered were thoroughly searched, emptied and destroyed. And there were plenty of them. Toward the outer woodline, where defoliating chemicals had earlier stripped the trees of all their leaves, helicopters were spraying, finishing off the secondary growth with a chemical spray called Agent Orange. The area surrounding our position was extensively booby-trapped and honeycombed with trenches and tunnels. I could hear explosions being set off every few minutes as "fire-in-the-hole" sounded across the base area. The infantry was blowing in place all the booby-traps they found, trying not to risk lives by dismantling them. Toward the middle of the afternoon I heard one of the grunts excitedly report a major rice cache about ten yards outside our perimeter. I walked out with my M-16 to watch as they dug the rice out of the tunnel. I kept my eyes open for any souvenirs. I was kicking around the tunnel opening when shots rang out.

"Sniper! Sniper!" someone yelled. "Get down! Get down!"

Panic, like electricity, surged through my chest. I dove to the ground. Sliding up next to the nearest berm, I inched my head up to try and see where it was coming from. I heard some sporadic gun fire coming from about twenty meters to my left and dropped my head back down. Three or four guys were now laying sprawled beside me. I could hear people yelling. "What's going on . . . where's the fire coming from?"

Another five minutes passed before I saw guys beginning to sit up and look around. By then, Charlie had already dropped down inside a spider hole and di-di mau'd. The enemy remained invisible. I sat up on my haunches, still keeping the berm as a wall in front of me, and watched as one of the APCs barreled across the edge of the clearing, kicking up dust. Five GIs rode across the top, their bare skin covered with flak jackets. Each one was poised for action, scouting the perimeter.

Well, I thought, with those guys parading around the perimeter it ought to be safe for awhile. I got up and jogged back to the FDC, forgetting about souvenirs.

That evening, around 2320 hours, the commo bunker spotted five VC through their starlight scope, an infrared device which enabled them to see in the dark. They were 80 meters outside our perimeter. We quickly notified the listening post to be on the alert for a possible attack. One of the ambush patrols that was nearest the Viet Cong's position began to move silently, trying to get into a position to make contact. When I went off shift forty minutes later, the night AP had still not found them.

Crawling onto my air mattress in the back of the bunker, which was separated from the front by two hanging Army blankets, I lay down but sleep never came. I propped my M-16 against the wall next to my air mattress and positioned my helmet right next to my head, just in case. I didn't have to wait long. In about an hour mortar rounds began falling like rain. Sixty and 81 millimeter rounds exploded everywhere. Myers immediately got the guns up for a fire mission. At the same time, the lieutenant dispatched a call to headquarters telling them we were under attack. I grabbed my gun and helmet and bolted for the rear entrance, waiting, crouched by the opening, for the mortars to stop. I knew my job was to be outside taking up a defensive position in case of ground attack, but I didn't want to leave the safety of the bunker while mortars were still falling.

"Shit, what do you suppose we should do?" Vanous crawled up next to me and slid down against the wall.

"Fuck, man," I said, "I don't know . . . but I sure as hell don't want to go out now!"

"Come on!" Lee yelled as he slid up next to us and darted out the entrance. "Let's get at it!" Vanous and I reluctantly followed.

Around 0600 the next morning we fired a prep for an air assault which was to take place at 0630. Our prep followed earlier air strikes which were being used to soften enemy resistance, and to destroy any fortifications in the landing zone.

The infantry had engaged 50 Viet Cong in the area yesterday, and today they were going back in to it. Around 0900 the sweep became bogged down when an extensive bunker and tunnel complex was uncovered. Efforts to investigate were greeted by enemy machine gun fire. The Mech, which was accompanying the foot soldiers, attacked the complex in their tanks and APCs; first head on and then from the flank as enemy rifle fire and rocket propelled grenades exploded around them. They pounded the bunkers and spider holes lining the road but soon had to withdraw because of heavy casualties. They retreated only far enough to allow artillery strikes and then radioed for help. As soon as we targeted their position we began to fire for effect and saturated the enemy bunker line with heavy explosives.

And that's the way the battle progressed. The infantry would strike, pull back when heavy resistance was offered, and send in artillery. Inch by inch, little by little, the enemy relinquished ground, but not without substantial losses on our part.

That evening we had another mad minute, hoping to deter another enemy attack. Our bunker had taken two direct hits from mortars last night and one of them had blown a hole down to the PSP. I didn't want to have to face another evening like the last. Still, shortly before midnight, our night LP spotted flashlights 300 meters in front of their position and we fired three Killer Junior bursts in the area, extinguishing the lights. We hoped that along with the lights, the VC had been snuffed.

It soon became obvious that the cleverness of the enemy in constructing and concealing tunnels was proving to be a step or so beyond the ability of the engineers. Some tunnels had been demolished by cratering charges placed every forty meters but when this method, though effective, proved burdensome, it was decided to try flooding the tunnels in hopes they would collapse. First, jungle and foliage had to be cleared from the river to the mouth of the tunnel. When a shortage of pipe developed, the enginners simply ditched the water source to the tunnel and then floated explosive charges into them. Still, they could not destroy them all.

Every day we experienced significant enemy contact and every evening we or one of our night ambush sites received incoming mortar or RPG rounds. They were rarely followed by any ground force action but occasionally we received small arms fire or machine gun fire as the enemy probed for weaknesses in our perimeter. By now I had learned to detect the cold klack-klack-klack of an AK-47; it always sent shivers up my spine. Hearing that AK only meant one thing— Charlie was dangerously close and my life was in immediate danger.

Each day the infantry swept the area, making contact, then withdrawing, contact, then withdrawing. Air strikes followed or preceded our preps and although the elusive enemy always seemed to remain hidden, daily sweeps uncovered fresh graves, and the VC body count mounted. Whenever bodies were discovered there was always disagreement about who was responsible for the kill. We all wanted our share of the credit. It was obvious that bodies found mangled or in pieces had been killed by heavy explosives but sometimes they were credited to air strikes rather than to artillery fire. There was stiff competition involved in who got credit. It wasn't only related to our sense of accomplishment; since we rarely saw the enemy, it began to be the gauge which determined whether we were winning the war.

Whenever it was possible I drifted out to the perimeter and talked with the infantry. It was a good way for me to find out more about what was actually happening. The more I knew and understood, the more in control of the situation I felt, and a little safer. Little by little I began to notice some discrepancies between what the brass was saying and what the grunts in the field knew.

I soon learned the various nicknames the infantry units had adopted. They sounded just like street gangs to me. There were the Tomahawks, the Regulars, Wolfhounds, Mech, Golden Dragons and others, each name somehow fitting their militant character. As I talked to the convoy guards or to crew members from sister batteries, I slowly began to get a large picture of what was going on. A more complete picture. Not all the information that was being fed to us by command was in line with what those who were actually involved in battles said. That began to weigh on my mind.

At the end of nearly a week's stay we received a long awaited resupply chopper. I had been hoping we would receive mail before Christmas, but it never came. I heard the giant Chinook's twin wings beating the air as it approached and my heart lifted. Three days earlier a resupply chopper had taken small arms fire and had to return, but with the amount of jungle that had been destroyed in the last few days, the helicopter now had a safer approach. The Aviation's policy was to try to deliver personnel and mail to forward positions every day but it wasn't always possible. When they did come, the Chinooks always created excitement.

Invariably, the choppers not only brought mail and recruits, but ice, soda, beer and sometimes hot meals. At the same time they allowed for prompt evacuation of the wounded or sick and really raised the odds that the wounded would survive. I never knew when I might be next so I appreciated it. Sometimes I felt as if we were all participating in an all encompassing game of Russian roulette. Each day the chamber of the revolver swung into place, each night the trigger was squeezed. And every day I listened for the hammer to fall.

"Vanous . . . Olsen!" Myers shouted, sliding his head outside the bunker. "Pick up our share of the resupply. It's sitting down on the south end of the perimeter!"

"Roger," I yelled, picking up my M-16. "C'mon Vanous, let's do it."

The Chinook was dropping its supply net as we approached and we waited until it had set down a short distance away. We could see people from each of the crews heading toward the net and hustled over.

"First of the Eighth!" a grunt sergeant shouted, separating our mailbag from the others and tossing it to Sergeant Clinton.

"Yo!" the sergeant replied, catching the bag.

Mail call was something almost everyone personally attended, so a small crowd quickly gathered around him, everyone pushing to be closest. I hung back. I wasn't expecting to hear from anyone anyway and didn't want to be one of the guys to walk away disappointed.

"Gianettino!" Clinton started.

"Here!" cried Vanous, pushing forward to get the letter for his friend. It was quickly passed overhead to him.

"Johnson!" Clinton shouted, pulling a large box out.

"Here Sarge!" he responded, squeezing his way through the crowd. Oh's and ah's broke out as he lifted the box for everyone to see. He did nothing to hide his excitement.

"Lee, Jarovich, Douglas!" the sergeant continued. Vanous picked up Lee's letter.

"Santiago, Lee, Manning!" I could see faces turning as Vanous reached in to pick up another letter for Lee.

"Lee!" the sergeant repeated, this time more slowly. This time the crowd parted as Vanous walked up to get it. I had this happen before although not often. One guy getting lots of letters in one day. There was a kind of mystique about it and for a moment everyone held that person in awe. I felt good for Lee but couldn't help but feel my own disappointment as the bag was slowly emptied. A lot of the guys were walking away beaming, clutching their mail, but all I could feel was emptiness. Fuck it, I thought, it don't mean a thing. I didn't need the aggravation.

As soon as we picked up the mail for the FDC, and a special dispatch from headquarters, we made our way over to the net where the others had gathered. I could see Wheatstraw, the black cook, bending over three long chunks of ice that were in the net, chopping away, distributing the pieces evenly among the gun crews.

93

"Hey, what's happening Wheatstraw?" I asked.

"Oh, not too much," he replied, grinning. He was always like that, shuckin' and jivin'! Telling me to "be cool" whenever I got uptight at the Army or with his cooking.

"Hey, you guys," Wheatstraw continued, "I'm sorry there ain't too much to go around this time, but the cooler in the mess tent is gettin' low and that's where most of it's gotta go." The men started grumbling but it didn't bother Wheatstraw; he kept right on talking. "Man, now, be cool," he said. "You know that we have first priority over the ice. If we don't keep the food cold it spoils overnight and you know that this ice just don't last too long. Right man? Now, if you want fresh food, you're just gonna have to put up with it, right?"

"What do you mean, food?" someone kidded. "You call that slop you feed us food?" The smile on Wheatstraw's face faded.

I was just getting to know Wheatstraw, having been introduced to him at the ammo bunker. Every black in the outfit knew one another and frequently hung out together. I began meeting all the other blacks. It didn't take long for me to see why the ammo bunker always seemed to have ice in their cooler, or cold water to drink. As my relationship with Wheatstraw deepened the cooler in the FDC grew colder.

It was funny, but ice was beginning to take on a value greatly exceeding money. Sometimes the men would conduct raids on the mess tent at night, searching for it. Occasionally they would make off with small chunks from the mess cooler, but at other times Wheatstraw or Tiny would be sitting on top of the cooler, guarding it with a shotgun. We all knew Wheatstraw would never shoot anyone but it was a good deterrent anyway.

After delivering the dispatches to the captain's bunker, I returned to sit out my duty in the cool shade of the FDC. Gianettino asked me if I would monitor the radios for him while he went off to read his mail and I said sure.

I picked up the notebook that he had been using to monitor calls and dispatch information to headquarters.

. . .0684 C/1/8 56 missions 112 rounds expended.

. . .0845 C/1/27 destroyed 2 bunkers at XT 515288.

. . .0930 1/27/ at XT 514292 found 1 hootch with false bottom, underneath was undetermined amount of loose rice.

. . .0940 1/27 at grid XT 549317 found 10-101 lb. bags of rice.

. . .1130 Gunships engaged VC at XT 520265. 1 VC WIA, 1 woman and 1 child killed. Dust-off called in.

One woman and one child, I thought . . . VC?

"Boy," I said to Myers, "they sure are finding a lot of rice in this area. What the heck are they doing with it all?"

"Well, if they can't evacuate it," he began, "they soak it in diesel fuel and then insert bangalore torpedos into the rice and blow it. If the cache is too large to blow, sometimes they drop fifty-five gallon drums of CS gas with a detonation device from a helicopter. That generally makes it unfit for consumption."

"What do they do with the evacuated rice?" I asked.

"Generally, they distribute it to the villages through Civic Action Programs," he answered, "but they found that people were getting sick eating it. Sometimes the rice is contaminated with an insecticide called parathion. Apparently the insecticide contained toxins which produced poisoning. We had an item from headquarters saying that all rice caches had to be dispatched through S-2 channels for analysis from now on before distributing any of it to the people. Apparently you can get contaminated through the skin, your eyes or your intestinal tract, and it does strange things to your eyes, intestines, muscles, lungs and your nervous system. They said it's akin to nerve gas. I don't know how it got contaminated," he added, "they didn't say, but as far as I'm concerned, it could have been done deliberately by the Viet Cong. The people we were giving the rice to thought we were trying to poison them. It didn't do too much toward winning them to our side."

I watched Myers as he talked. How did he ever get messed up in this? He was just not cut out for war. He was too much of a namby-pamby, a mama's boy. He had no stomach for what had to be done. I detested the softness I saw in him. I hated the whiney way he tried to get people to follow his orders. He didn't have the respect of either Lee or Vechione and I could see why. Still, I felt sorry for him. I doubted that he was here by his own choice.

Still, I knew that by the "RA" prefix to his military serial number he had enlisted and I felt a growing contempt for those who had. At least my prefix was "US," which meant I had been drafted. Surely anyone who was dumb enough to enlist for four years deserved what he got. But the other side of it was that Myers was certainly no dummy. It obviously took a lot more brains than I had to run the FDC. It took a pretty straight head for that. At least I could respect him for that.

"I wonder if we'll be here in January, or if we'll leave soon?" Myers said. "Intelligence says that the Viet Cong–controlled province of Binh Duong has established a recruit training school for VC in the Hoc Tran area, just north of us. They're supposedly using the woods as a training area for locals. Intelligence says they've designated January first as their opening day. The VC supposedly have a complete set of school facilities established and a network of tunnels where they are assembling supplies. Approximately 200 men, 16 to 19 years old, are supposed to be training there. Hey, at least that's a little less than we got! The Viet Cong are supposed to have a VC company in the area to protect the school while it's operating. That's nice to know, huh?"

Maybe it was just a premonition that Myers had, but by 1100 hours the next day we had completely dissassembled our bunker and were on the move again. I was thankful. Anywhere else had to be safer than here.

95

7

The convoy to Cu Chi was a welcome break from the frenzied activity that followed each move. With my weapon locked and loaded, I could relax as we headed home. Some villages and landmarks were now becoming familiar. The pagodas, Buddhist temples, were especially easy to recognize, there were so few of them. With the rice harvest almost over there were few peasants in the field. Occasionally as we passed they would straighten up and look our way, but otherwise they paid us little mind. There were no friendly waves. No assurance that they weren't the enemy. No sign that they even appreciated our being there. They were mostly mama-sans, papa-sans, or young children, rarely any young men. I wondered where they all were. They either looked nine or ninety, no ages in between.

I wondered why the peasants all dressed the same way, and why black of all colors? Vietnam seemed a nation in uniform. You'd think as hot as it was black would be the last color anyone would wear. These people . . . all the same. Always quiet and withdrawn. All but the whores and the children. They seemed friendly enough but I knew very little about them. Why was there such a great gulf between us and why such mistrust?

As we rode through the villages I observed the differences in the people's responses to us. Baby-sans and children continued to flock to the side of the road, waving and yelling, but by now I realized that most of them were only selling or begging. Did any of them really care about us or about what we were doing . . . or was the only attraction our money and the free food. Regardless, I greatly admired their beauty. In the larger villages the people often wore white tunics over black pajamas, a noticeable change from the all-black pajamas of the peasants. Sometimes the young girls wore long colorful tunics that covered their pajama-like trousers but only in the villages that were large enough to have a small business section. Occasionally young women wore long slinky, tight dresses that were a variation of the tunic, but they were mostly the bar girls in Saigon.

As we neared Cu Chi I felt a growing anticipation. At last I could get some

96

clean clothes, a shower, hot food—even the chance to go shopping at the PX. Maybe I'd even get to the E.M. club.

The second day in base LeRoy, Wheatstraw and I hiked to the PX. After browsing through the Vietnamese gift shop we headed inside. The PX straddled a huge Officers' Bar and a Post Office and the compound area had kind of a carnival atmosphere with lights and brightly colored decorations. We excitedly searched every shelf in the place. It was like being in Toyland. We found magazines, books, shaving equipment, packaged cookies, toothpaste, canned meat, chips and candy bars. We went on a buying binge—and why not? This could be the last time we were in base camp for weeks, even months! We talked and laughed like excited children. Wheatstraw's quick sense of humor and sense of irony kept us in stitches and I laughed like I hadn't in months.

"Hey look!" I said, pulling out a paper as we left the PX, "I picked this up inside. It's called *Stars and Stripes*. It looks like it's reporting on the action over here. Let's find a place to sit down and grab a smoke, I'd like to look at it."

We found a bench and I opened the paper. I skirted the headlines, looking for anything on the 9th Infantry where Glover was stationed.

"Hey man, look!" I said. "Here's an article about the Twenty-fifth. It's about one of the last operations we were on."

I began to read it out loud.

"'25th Infantry Division Finishes Operation. A pacification and jungle clearing operation was recently cleaned up by the First Brigade, 25th Infantry Division in the Cu Chi and Trang Bang Districts of the Hau Nghia Province and the Phu Hoa District of Binh Duong Province.'"

"Trang bang hah nie fu wa ding dong!" interrupted Wheatstraw. "Is that how you say that shit!" he kidded. "You sure you know what the hell you is saying?"

"Fuck man, I don't know," I replied. "Some of it sounds familiar! I'm just saying it as I see it. Let me continue, will ya? 'Numerous small unit actions which included Bushmaster patrols, cordon and search operations of suspected Viet Cong hamlets, Roadrunners and Checkmates enabled the Brigade to reduce Viet Cong capability to move freely. In addition, Search and Destroy missions employing airmobile combat assaults into the Iron Triangle were conducted. These assaults were the result of intelligence reports locating Viet Cong units in those areas and led to a profitable return on the Division's part.

"'Artillery support for Operation Barking Sands envisioned many new concepts which proved to be highly successful in a jungle war against guerilla forces. Barking Sands, as never before, utilized the concept of airlift of light artillery batteries to exploit important intelligence data. Further, it was in Operation Barking Sands that the concept of a minimum of one artillery battalion equivalent would be used to support any maneuver force larger than a platoon. The results of these new ideas were a greater kill ratio per artillery round fired and most certainly added a confusion factor to the enemy as to the size force opposing him.'"

"Confusion factor!" I said. "I sure hope so; we need all the confusion we can create!"

97

"'During November and December the Viet Cong's efforts consisted primarily of efforts to delay allied clearing operations, counter-sweep operations and harassing activities along the main supply route of Highway 1. Some harassing activities also plagued base camp and field locations....'"

"Shee-it," drawled Wheatstraw, "is that what they're calling them ... harassing activities! Let me see that paper!" He muttered as he looked over the article. "Look here. 'During November the Golden Dragons of the 2nd Battalion, 14th Infantry, were busy in Hau Nghia and Binh Duong Provinces keeping enemy movement to a minimum.'"

He paused. "It sure wasn't that way in December, was it? Man, there sure seemed to be more activity last month than they's talkin' about here."

"'The Dragons,'" he continued, "'primarily using ambushes and combined patrols with ARVN forces, engaged the enemy frequently during the two months of action. Dragon recon teams and ambush patrols kept the enemy off balance and at the same time discovered many supply caches.

"'In early November, on a routine reconnaissance, the Dragons engaged an unknown size enemy force. With help from the 116th Assault Helicopter Company, Bravo Company defeated the enemy and captured 4,000 rounds of small arms ammunition and 300 pounds of rice and destroyed three tunnels. Throughout the month, the Dragons penetrated deep into the Ho Bo and Boi Loi Woods, constantly harassing the already beaten enemy. Rice, an important item, was being captured from tunnel complexes throughout the area. The Dragons controlled both the Ho Bo and Boi Loi Woods, and the enemy was finding it increasingly difficult to move around without fear of detection. This was just a hint of what was throughout the Division's area of operation.'"

"Hey, Olsen, weren't we just up in the Ho Bo Woods?" he asked.

"Yeah," I said, "but we were on operations with the 2nd Battalion, 27th Infantry, not the 2nd of the 14th. I don't know who they're with."

Wheatstraw handed the paper to LeRoy.

"Hey, Olsen," LeRoy asked, "was we on any operation called Kole Kole?"

"Yeah, that sounds familiar." I said. "It was supposed to have ended sometime last month I think. What about it?"

"Well, it says here that we was working in the pineapple area south of Duc Hoa. I never seen any pineapples where we was at!"

Grabbing the paper from his hands I began reading. "'Soon after Manhattan came the longest operation of the year, Operation Kole Kole. The operation lasted almost seven months. From May 13, 1967 until December 7, the 1st Battalion, 8th Artillery, provided direct support for the 2nd Brigade which was working in the pineapple area south of Duc Hoa. B Battery of the "Automatic Eight" did an outstanding job on this operation getting over half of the VC body count for the Battalion. A and C Batteries did their usual fine jobs also, as the final results on enemy losses show. This operation marked the introduction of the electronic computer FADAC in the program of the 1st Bn 8th Arty. This extremely effective device was put to the test at once by the Eighth, and it came through in the

98

highest tradition of the artillery. The 1st Battalion 8th Artillery, with its lethal firepower, had 38 VC KIA (bodycount), 273 VC KIA (possible), destroyed 18 buildings, one bridge, 30 sampans, damaged or destroyed 19 bunkers and had 15 secondary explosions. These offensive operations against Viet Cong units provided security for engineer activities and denied the Viet Cong the use of lines of communication in the TAOI, reinforcing Vietnamese operations and bringing enemy movement to a literal standstill.'"

"Who wrote this hype!" I spat. "They make it all sound like guts and glory. Fuck, who they trying to kid? Who do they think is reading this shit anyway?"

I put the paper down. I had heard about the computer mentioned in the article but we hadn't been given one yet. As far as I knew, A Battery was the only battery having one, testing its function and accuracy before others would be distributed to the rest of the battalion. Apparently they were working it out thoroughly.

Eventually we gathered our booty together and headed back to the battery area. The walk back was over two miles so I occasionally stuck out my thumb, trying to catch a ride. Every time a truck passed it funneled clouds of dust into our eyes and lungs. The pungent smell of diesel fuel, which was sprayed on the roads to keep down the dust, filled our nostrils. I caught the familiar stench of shit being burned in diesel fuel as we walked and thought back to my first days in country. It seemed a long way off now. Eventually a three-quarter stopped and picked us up. None too soon for me.

When I got back to the FDC I found two surprises waiting. One was the new FADAC computer, and the other was two new recruits: PFC Campbell, who had been transferred in from another unit, and Larry Dangerfield, a greenhorn. With additional men, Myers scrambled crews again. My shift changed. I was free until 2400 hours.

Now, I thought, I'll get a chance to get to the E.M. club.

The walk over to the enlisted men's bar took ten or fifteen minutes during daylight, but at night it took much longer. The path took us through a series of unit areas and back roads that ran like a maze and it was difficult to navigate in the dark. LeRoy, Wheatstraw, White and I struck out while the sun was setting, guided by one of the rear personnel who was familiar with the area. As we approached the club I was surprised to see it looked like all the Quonsets that surrounded it. I suppose that was for precautionary reasons. It was about 24 feet wide and 40 feet long, with large wooden shutters that were propped up on boards at the roof line. The shutters encompassed the building, giving it the appearance of a hat with an elongated brim. Screens covered the upper half of the building, filtering out the hordes of mosquitos that filled the air.

Two GIs walked out of the club and began lowering the shutters as we approached. The shutters had not been closed tight, but simply hung lower than the window openings, preventing light leakage. There was a space about ten inches wide which let air pass through. Lights were going off everywhere as the base prepared for night discipline. We pushed open the screen door and walked in. I looked for a table that would seat four. The air was already thick with smoke. The place reeked of beer. We could see the club was filling fast so we headed for an open table. I grabbed a free chair and passed it overhead to White.

"Hey, what do you want to drink?" asked LeRoy.

"I'll have a whiskey sour," I said. "Fuckin' A, man, this is gonna be great!"

"Shee-it," said Wheatstraw, "you can't get no hard liquor in here. You got to be an officer to get that kind of shit."

"Whad daya mean, man," I said, "you must be shittin' me!"

"No shit?" said White.

"Ain't no enlisted men can buy anything but beer here, man," said Wheatstraw. "You didn't know that?"

"They's just new boys in town," LeRoy said. "They don't know no better. They's got hard liquor at the Officers' Club, but they ain't allowed to sell it to no enlisted men. We's too low on the ladder."

"Hey man, I don't believe this shit!" I said. "You telling me that I'm out in the boonies fighting my ass off while the fuckin' brass are sitting back in base and they get hard liquor, and we don't. Wow, this fuckin' Army ... it never ceases to amaze me. What a stinkin' class system."

"Right on!" replied White.

"Hey, let's just get some beer," said LeRoy, "and take it easy."

"Bring me a Schlitz," said Wheatstraw, making it clear that he wasn't going to be the one picking it up. "An' make it cold."

"I'll take a Pabst."

"Me too."

LeRoy headed for the bar, squeezing his way through the crowd.

Still angry about the lack of liquor, I continued to bitch. "What gets me man, is how they can get away with it. We're fighting the same war ain't we?"

"Right on!" said White. "Look at the Officers' Club we saw today. Man, it must sit on two city blocks."

LeRoy sat down, and we grabbed our beers.

"Man, this'll do right well for me," Wheatstraw said, chugging his beer. "There's nothing like an ice cold beer an I don' give a fuck if it comes in a tin can!

"You just gettin' your dander up," he said to me, "'cause you finally starting to see what it's like to be treated like a nigger. I been used to that most of my life. That's one of the reasons I joined the Army in the first place. I don' know what it was like for you, but for where I was at, there was no place to go but up. The more rank I get the more respect I'm gonna get, and Nam is the fastest way to get it. Man, that's why I'm in it for the duration."

LeRoy said, "You know that you gotta put in a lot more time than the white man to make the same grade. What's to assure you won't get your shit blown away in the process. Man, I'm getting my ass out of here just as soon as my time's up."

"Shee-it, once I get my stripes, I'se seen the last of the jungle," Wheatstraw replied. "And once I'm back in the States they ain't no one gonna give me no more crap just 'cause I'm black. Without rank you ain't shit in this man's Army and once you get it, no one can fuck with you."

100

"Fuck you, man," LeRoy said. "You just stupid, man. You're gonna be just as black back in the world as you are here, maybe blacker. Just look who's pulling all the shit details. It's blacks and Puerto Ricans, man. You don't see any white skin on the ammo detail do you? If you want to get at the front of the line maybe you'd better change your MOS and join the infantry. You can walk in the front then, right at the point."

"Yeah, shit," Wheatstraw said. "The front of the line in Vietnam and the back of the line in the world."

It grew silent for a minute. I couldn't pretend to know what it was like to be black so I had just listened. Still, I empathized. I knew what it was like to be treated like an outcast. I, like them, had grown up on the "wrong side of the tracks," so to speak, and knew what social ostracism was. There had been plenty of mothers and fathers who wouldn't let their precious children hang around with me, or their daughters go out with me. I knew what it meant to be singled out—to have people look down their nose at you. And I knew what it meant to be threatened with physical violence and spit on. Somehow I felt their hurt wasn't much different from mine. Maybe that was what bound us together. After all, even before I was drafted I had heard the phrase "the hippies are the new niggers of the north!"

"Fuck, man, the system's the same all over," I finally said. "It just depends on who's got the power. Fuckin' officers, school principals, policemen or bosses. The Army treats us all like slaves and so did the people I worked for back in the States. They all try to indoctrinate us full of their bullshit."

"Yeah, we might all wear the same uniform, it's just that some of these bastards wear it differently," White said.

"Man, it's the fuckin' shits!" spat LeRoy.

"At least back in the world if someone in authority was fuckin' with me I could walk off the job. No such luck over here. Anyway, where the hell would I go?"

Wheatstraw added, "And I ain't ready to spend my time in LBJ."

We talked late into the night, each taking a turn at buying and delivering the beer until our conversation slurred and our bladders gave out. As we shared personal experiences I could feel a bond deepening between us. I was finally finding someone who really knew what it was like to have gone through the same rejection I had. Someone who in turn felt as deeply bitter about prejudice and injustice.

By the time we left, we were all flat-out stinking drunk. In the pitch black outside we didn't know where the hell we were or how to get back, but for once I didn't feel threatened. I was in the company of friends.

That evening, the rumored truce that was supposed to be taking place for New Year's was initiated in the form of a 36-hour cease-fire. The enemy had agreed not to initiate any personal attacks nor to move any supplies or equipment during our celebration of New Year. A break in combat was great, but how absurd! If the Viet Cong were truly our enemies how could we possibly believe them! If someone picked a fight with you, you fought back, and you fought back to win.

That's what survival in the streets was all about. Why would war be any different? What a game. Rules! The "right" way to kill someone. I didn't want to be playing no fuckin' games.

When the morning shift ended I passed up breakfast at the Chow Hall and headed straight for a cot. I pulled off my sweat-soaked fatigues and lay down in my shorts, spreading my poncho liner beneath me. The liner was cool to the touch as I stretched out and pulled my mosquito netting down. A slight, lingering breeze blew through. I stuck my hands behind my head and closed my eyes. How good it felt just to lie there and rest.

I wondered how Glover was doing. He frequently crossed my mind. I hoped he was safe. If there was a God, I sure hoped he was watching over him.

Maybe the affinity I felt for blacks wasn't so strange after all. Maybe it was no fluke. I had gotten closer to Glover than anyone else I had known since high school, and he had been the first black I had known personally. Blacks and hippies! They both seemed to be my type. I had never known any blacks growing up, rarely even seen any until I moved to Minneapolis. At least other than on T.V.—Selma, Alabama, and all that stuff! There had been blacks in some of the units we had trained with in Fort Lewis, but even then, I hadn't really known them. In Minneapolis, black gangs liked to beat up whites and I stayed clear of the areas where gangs roamed. Just the same, there were also areas I stayed clear of because they were inhabited by white gangs, and they beat up whites too.

In Basic all the other squad leaders in my company had been from the south and despised blacks. I never heard anything but derogatory comments about them. "Niggers" and "Coons!" Those guys thought blacks were inferior and frequently told me so. I had yet to see any truth to it. The negative traits they applied to blacks could just have easily been applied to any number of white people I knew. What was going on in the South, the way whites treated blacks, that whole issue never did set right with me. Segregation was a curse.

It hadn't been my desire to go to Leadership Preparation School after Basic, but since I declined the Army's request to go to Officer's Candidate School, they said I would "have to" go to LPC Academy. There, I would be trained to be a non-commissioned officer. The Army must have thought I was capable of a whole lot more than I did! I wasn't looking for any more authority or responsibility. I could do without the hassles. My experience as a squad leader in Basic had taught me that. I didn't care for the pressure of someone else's expectations and I hated to be mistreated by people who hid behind their rank. I didn't like anyone telling me what to do, and I didn't want to be in that position over anyone else! Having authority gave you certain privileges, but the price you paid outweighed them! The more rank, the fewer people you had to answer to, but, at the same time there became a greater number of people you had to harangue and threaten to keep in line. I was no John Wayne. I didn't want to be anyone's leader and I wasn't anyone's hero. The true cost of heroism wasn't shown in the movies, it couldn't be. Ole John had been a childhood hero, but this was real life. The good guy didn't always win!

I was sent to LPC School despite my wishes. The Army controlled my life and I danced to their tune. I didn't want to go to the stockade and I couldn't just chicken out and go AWOL.

Half of the company at LPC School had been black, and blacks and whites were divided into four squads on an even basis. It was impossible not to get acquainted. We ate, drank, slept, and shit next to one another. But there was always this tension that hung in the air, and when sleeping quarters were chosen, the whites and blacks split right down the middle of the barracks; whites on one side, blacks on the other.

Our first week of training was intensely competitive and when it ended, the training officers chose the company's four squad leaders based on performance, record, test scores and evaluations. They chose two blacks and two whites and I was one of them. Glover and a guy named Marshall were the two blacks, and a Southern boy whose name I had already forgotten was the other white. To most of the blacks we two were simply "white boys!" Away from the eyes of the training cadre there was little effort made to hide the animosity between whites and blacks. The training officers had instructed us that by the last week of training they would determine which one of the squad leaders would be trainee commanding officer of the company. Until that time we would all be acting drill sergeants. Each one of us would lead a squad-sized "platoon." The person showing the highest merit would be given the commander's position and command the company for the last week. That person would also be the first to receive his PFC stripes upon transfer to A.I.T. and would be guaranteed a platoon leader's position. The chances of receiving his corporal stripes after finishing A.I.T. would be almost certain. Having corporal's stripes would put him one full rank above all the others in his company, and of course, he would receive higher pay.

That day, in front of a platoon-sized company, the four of us stepped forward to receive our black armbands and acting sergeant's stripes. The black armbands were most significant.

As classes and training progressed it was announced that according to test scores and performance, the highest leadership ability was being shown by Marshall and me and that the commander's position would go to one of us. I was determined to do my best in whatever was asked, but I had no desire to win that position. I didn't want the authority I had, and certainly had no desire for more. Marshall, on the other hand, was determined to win. He openly challenged me in front of the company and told me there was no way he was gonna lose, especially to some white boy. I didn't care about winning but I resented the hell out of his insults and arrogance. I especially didn't like the way he made the challenge in front of the whole company.

Marshall towered six inches above me and his polished, muscular body mirrored strength and athletic achievement. Marshall had grown up in the ghetto and had little love for whites. He talked openly about whites the way white Southerners talked about niggers. The Southern white boys in the company hated it! In addition, he was constantly boasting of his athletic ability and considered himself another Cassius Clay.

It didn't help that all the Southern white boys began looking to me to win the competition, "so that black nigger bastard can be put in his place!" I never backed down from a fight in my life, and this certainly looked like one to me, but I wasn't looking forward to it.

As training progressed Marshall never missed an opportunity to put me down or to show me up in front of the company, especially when the training officers were around. He used every opportunity to humiliate me—and sometimes succeeded. Resentment smoldered underneath the calm exterior I strove to portray. Physical threats I could handle, but this guy was threatening my self-esteem. When he goaded me publicly, only common sense controlled my rage. I knew if we got caught fighting, I could be thrown in the stockade, especially if I threw the first punch. Still, I was tempted. I hated backing down to his constant challenges. There was a small group of Southern boys who took it even harder than I; I overheard them one night planning to jump him and "clean his clock." Marshall became so obnoxious with his constant boasting that even the other blacks got annoyed.

One night I simply blew up and charged him, unable to control my rage, but an officer quickly broke up the fight. Afterwards, Glover and another black dude named Carr came over and told me just to shake it off. Not to let him get to me. It really surprised me. It was unusual for blacks to take sides against each other. But the fact was, sides were being formed and allegiances were thrown behind either Marshall or myself. Racial slurs became more common. The fact that Glover and Carr continued to encourage me, blew my mind! I told them I wasn't afraid of Marshall and that I wasn't going to let him push me around no matter how big he was, but with their encouragement it became easier to tolerate his goading.

Things deteriorated rapidly the last two weeks when each of us had to assume a week as acting commander, taking the training officer's place. Command's evaluation of our performance that week would determine who was the best qualified leader. Marshall was given leadership the first week. I caught the gleam in his eyes as he strutted out to the front of the company to take charge. He looked over at me. With his eyes glued to mine, he barked his first orders. With every opportunity he drilled me under the watchful eyes of the training officers, trying as hard as he could to make me slip up. He pushed me to my fullest, probing my memory for mistakes on the material we were being forced to digest; checking my understanding of military rules and procedures; and singling out my platoon for drill and endurance.

The last night of his command was the worst. There was to be a general inspection by the real company commander and Marshall was to be held responsible for the condition of the barracks and each of the men. That night, at lights out, he decided that things weren't quite ship-shape and that the floors needed to be rewaxed and repolished. In addition, he was going to personally inspect everyone's shoes and brass to see that they passed his standards. When the floors were finally redone to his satisfaction, it was late into the night. Everyone was exhausted from an already draining afternoon and tempers flared easily. As we shined our brass and polished our shoes, he sat on his bunk and waited for everyone to bring him their items for inspection. When I brought mine, they weren't good enough. When I brought them a second time and they still didn't meet his approval, I knew they never would. That was the final straw!

"Eat shit!" I said coldly, when he told me they would have to be done over. "I'm not doing them again." I turned and started walking away. That was all he was waiting for.

"What did you say?" he yelled, leaping to his feet.

"You heard me."

"Your gonna do just what the fuck I said! Or your ass is grass and I'm gonna be the lawnmower."

"I ain't doing it, Marshall," I said flatly. "So you'd better think twice about what you're saying."

I knew I was no physical match for him and that if he came at me I was in deep shit, but I wasn't backing down. The barracks grew quiet.

"Whooee!" Marshall laughed in feigned horror. A grimace came over his face. "I'm gonna kick your shit, boy."

He came at me, hell bent on destruction. I braced myself. Suddenly I heard a scuffling behind me and an audible murmur. A group of whites were gathering, mostly Southern boys. Marshall stopped! Instinctively, a group of blacks grouped behind him.

"So these white boys want a fight do they," said Marshall. "Well let's show them who's best."

It wasn't until Marshall took his first step forward that Glover walked out in front of him and squared off.

"Knock it off," he warned in his deep foghorn voice. "This ain't no racial fight an' you know it! You've been puttin' all kinds of shit on Olsen here. I'm not gonna let your personal battles get everyone else here in hot water. You dig? We'd all lose our asses if this thing got started and I ain't gonna lose mine, boy. You're gonna have to take me on first an' I'm gonna . . . jump . . . in . . . your . . . shit!" He poked his finger at Marshall's chest and continued, "You're talking to someone your own size now, you dig!"

Marshall was taller than Glover by at least three inches but Glover was broad, like a barrel. It was like a bear and a panther facing off. No one said a word as they both glared at each other in defiance. Then it happened: Marshall turned on his heels and stormed back to his bunk, shouting as he went. "Get your asses back to work! There's still plenty that has to be done yet tonight."

When it came my turn to command the company I was tempted to treat Marshall the way he treated me, but I just couldn't find it in my heart. It seemed such a petty thing to do. Besides, I hadn't lost face and had proven myself in a way that seemed to gain the respect of the other guys in the company, including many of the blacks. So I let it rest. Inwardly, I knew I was having enough troubles with the system, I didn't need any more enemies. I didn't want to be like Marshall anyway. There were times when I felt incompetent to command and insecure about my performance—but, I tried my best. Surprisingly, at the end of the training period I was awarded the Commander's position.

I stared at the ceiling and the surrounding mosquito net. Shit, I thought, this fucking army. Why hadn't they let Glover and me go to the same unit? What happened to the good ole buddy system the recruiter told me about? I took a deep breath and let it out slowly. Suddenly I felt overwhelmed. A tear ran from the corner of my eye. I just felt empty.

The air was still, not a breeze, not a whisper. I got tired of staring at the bunkers in front of me and closed my eyes. My ass was getting sore from sitting but I felt too relaxed to move. Dropping my head I stared at the paper in my lap. What more did I have to write? I was tired of pissing and moaning about the weather. What could they do about it anyway. Should I tell them about the fighting? I just didn't think they would understand. I didn't understand myself. It just seemed necessary in order to survive.

I wanted to tell Debbie how lonely I felt but I didn't want her or anybody thinking I was weak—that I *needed* anybody. But I did. I started writing again.

There it was again. I always seemed to come back to it. This feeling of loneliness! This constant companion. I wondered if the life of solitude I had slowly developed was really for the best.... I wasn't sure if I had pulled away from others because I felt so alone, or if I felt so alone because I had pulled away. Where was I at anyway? Where was the real me? I certainly wasn't being up front with Debbie, hiding the things I wanted to say openly. Never really taking a risk. Never leaving myself truly vulnerable. What if I were killed tomorrow? Was there anybody who would have known the real me? Would most of my life have been just a sham?

Man, I thought, this is really "desolation row."

Dylan's song went through my mind. If there was truly anyone I believed in, it was him. He had been there before and I knew he understood. His music and words continually struck a responsive chord in my life! The longer I lived the more I saw just how deep his understanding of human nature and life was. Man, it was like the man was prophetic!

I didn't expect the R and R we were experiencing in base to last too long. Rumors were that we would be heading out soon, possibly toward the Cambodian border. The Viet Cong depended heavily on the flow of equipment and supplies coming down from up North and much of it was coming through Cambodia. A series of border battles had recently taken place in what was believed to be a communist attempt to embarrass the South Vietnamese government on the eve of the elections, but continuing enemy movement along the border possibly signaled something else. Intelligence reports indicated that major contact with North Vietnamese forces was taking place up near the DMZ, the demilitarized zone. That was to be expected, but North Vietnamese Regulars had been spotted further south in Binh Long Province where the 3rd Brigade was operating, and that was just north of us. The Battalion grapevine said that they were expecting more action in the DMZ but weren't expecting anything here. Command said that the enemy had sustained heavy losses in our TAOI—that our kill ratio was about ten to one so we didn't have to worry about any major offenses. Still, I was uneasy.

Two days ago a 3rd Brigade fire support base named Burt had been attacked by a major Viet Cong regiment. I had heard some people talking about it in the E.M. club. They had said that the enemy had launched human-wave attacks on the base much like the Chinese had done in Korea. They said that the VC must have been doped up or crazy or something, because they just kept coming and coming. The Viet Cong didn't even stop when they were shot. You had to blow their heads or legs off to stop them. The base had gone through repeated assaults for five hours. Over 152 GIs had been wounded. The VC body count had been 355.

It appeared to me that the size of the enemy forces was growing and so was the traffic on the Saigon River. We were getting sitings from there on the radio all the time.

On January 4 I watched a convoy of 28 Rome Plows leave Cu Chi. We followed right behind, off again on a major operation which was drawing the whole battalion together. Headquarters Battery, A Battery, B Battery, and we would be assembling at the same night location near Trung An, on the western banks of the Saigon River. We were going to support both the 1/27th and the 2/27th Infantry as they conducted a major reconnaissance there.

As we approached the main gates, I could see one battery was already in position. We fell in behind them. As we waited, three deuce-and-a-halfs pulled up alongside us and stopped.

"Hey man," I called to one of the grunts, "who ya with?"

"First of the Twenty-seventh," he replied.

"You guys going with us?" I asked.

"Looks like it," he answered. "I hear there's supposed to be some mean shit where we're going. You guys know anything about it?"

"Well, only that it's supposed to be mostly river patrol," I said. "Apparently elements of the Second Local Force VC Battalion are headquartered there. I hear we'll be getting a chance to see the ARVNs in action too. We're supposed to provide cover fire for a regional force platoon in that area."

"Shit man," he replied, "I hope we don't have to work with those motherfuckers. They don't do shit. Most of those bastards hang back when we get into any contact and they don't do diddly on their own. They're afraid the VC will kill them off as soon as we're not around to protect them so they try not to do anything to offend them. Can you believe that shit? I wouldn't doubt they were the fuckin' gooks themselves."

I agreed: "Sometimes we'll be set up only a couple hundred meters from an

ARVN compound, and we'll get our shit mortared, and they don't get nothing," I replied.

B Battery began pulling into position behind us. It was still dark out but dawn was beginning. Cool air would be nothing more than a memory soon.

What should have been a thirty or forty minute convoy turned into an hour and a half ride. The road had been heavily mined near Vinh Cu and had to be cleared more than once. Once the convoy had come to an abrupt halt when a shuddering blast blew up an APC. The whole convoy had been immobilized until the lead tank could work its way around the flaming wreck and pull it out of the center of the road. At the same time, demolition experts had to fan the road in front, to check for other mines. I knew for sure the driver of the "track" had been killed and possibly the copilot also. The explosion had blown the rest of the crew off the top. It was a good thing the deck had been covered with sandbags. I could see why the grunts chose to ride on the top instead of inside. The APC was still burning as we passed.

We set up our new base, FSB Crockett, near a small hamlet called Tan Hoa. We got into heavy shit the moment we arrived. After two days of continuous contact, we had killed 89 Viet Cong. The body count was soaring. We suffered our own casualties too, but nowhere near enemy losses. Besides, mishaps accounted for some of our losses. Nineteen men from the infantry had been wounded by napalm mistakenly dropped too close during a prep, and five men on the west side of our perimeter had to be "dusted off" after receiving small arms fire from our own troops.

As one crew plotted, recorded, and coordinated troop movement, the other worked to fill sandbags. Day and night we worked and fired, constantly awaiting the unexpected. We nearly covered the 11,500 meter range of fire of our 105s, firing even for the 4th Battalion 23rd Infantry who were working alongside the Rome Plows I had seen leaving Cu Chi. We fired our first "woodchopper" prep, utilizing a new technique the artillery had developed for clearing heavily wooded areas. Instead of trying to blow the trees up with heavy explosives, rounds which ignited on impact, we started using HE rounds with a timed fuse, causing the rounds to explode at the top of the tree line. That sent thousands of metal particles flying through the air, ripping off branches and leaves, first destroying the upper layer of jungle canopy that covered the area, and then the second and third. With the woodline better exposed the Plows and grunts could advance with less risk from snipers. Even if explosives were not as effective as chemical herbicides, they worked quicker. Besides, the Air Force usually sent in helicopters afterwards to spray any remaining growth.

On day three, a lone VC ran up to the listening post on our perimeter and threw a hand grenade in it. No one was killed, not even the Viet Cong, but it was a start of similar explosive events.

Fire Base Burt, a victim of "human wave" assaults earlier, came under siege again and so did FSB Bouregard. We fired to assist them and were credited with five body count. Later, both the 1st and 2nd battalions uncovered mass graves in our area, probably from those attacks. They dug up 24 bodies, all estimated to be 16 or 17 years old. The Viet Cong were getting younger! Ammunition caches and weapons were turning up everywhere. One location alone yielded 275 rockets. It was highly unusual for so much of one item to be buried in one location.

The 1/27th and the 2/27th ended up having a fire fight with each other. The area the 2/27th was searching had been cleared by the LNO of the 1/27th as having no friendly troops, so when the 2/27th heard movement they opened fire, expecting it to be Charlie. Luckily only one man was wounded.

But it had become like that. We had designated areas as Free Fire Zones, which were basically free *kill* zones. If we didn't have known friendly units in those areas, everything that moved was considered fair game. We fired first and asked questions later. The ARVNs had the responsibility of notifying us if they had any troops in those areas, or if civilians went in. All inhabited villages in those areas were considered Viet Cong–controlled, so if people stayed in them they were considered VC.

It didn't make any difference whether it had been their home all their life or not. Anyone in those areas had to have identification, and it had better be in order or they were in for a rough time of questioning. Sometimes anyone who stayed in those areas was considered Viet Cong, identification or not, and was shot on sight.

As the day progressed the infantry sweeping our perimeter began taking automatic weapons fire from our direction. We soon pin-pointed it to A Battery's position next to us but it turned out that it wasn't them firing. Some gooks had emerged from an underground tunnel between A Battery and the infantry. The VC had been there overnight and were trying to get out. They fired at the infantry knowing that the infantry wouldn't fire back because of the risk of hitting our own troops. In all the confusion, they made good their escape.

That night we were mortared twice, at 2225 hours and again a half-hour later. By early morning we had dusted off five men suffering severe head lacerations and multiple body wounds. The order came down to march again as I watched the dust-offs trail away. Shit, I was ready. We had only finished building our bunker a few hours ago, but I didn't care. I wouldn't have felt safe here no matter how many layers of sandbags we had.

Three days later I had forgotten all about the fear I had felt at Crockett. I was dirt shit tired. We had traveled only two hours before stopping to set up, but had remained in that position only five hours before dismantling and moving again. All that time we had been filling sandbags. As night fell, we pulled into Go Dau Ha, 19 miles northwest of Go Mon and only a short distance from the Cambodian border. We had only four howitzers. Two had been airlifted to Cu Chi for repairs suffered during the mortar attack. Right after we arrived the Viet Cong blew the bridge at Trang Bang, cutting us off from any resupply by convoy. While we provided cover fire for the infantry, we struggled to finish our bunkers so we could get some sleep.

I thought about the grunts while my back ached from filling sandbags. At least walking through the jungle they didn't have to do any of this shit. I wondered which of us was really better off. Theirs was no easy row to hoe, but neither was ours. Daylight reconnaissance was daily tedium and terror but at night every fire base was a prime target, constantly mortared and often assaulted. It looked like a pretty even trade-off.

Fifty-four hours after leaving FSB Crockett we finished both bunkers and the rice paddy we invaded had been reduced to a bowl of dust called Fire Support Base York. Since I was off shift I decided to crawl under the back of the three-quarter and sleep. I knew the bunker would already be hot and stuffy. A cool breeze was blowing outside and I knew how good it would feel. Vanous thought it a good idea too and crawled in beside me. Campbell followed him in. Not bothering with an air mattress, I stretched out my poncho liner and slept.

I hadn't closed my eyes fifteen minutes when I heard Dangerfield yelling. I rolled over, blinking my eyes. As I stared in the direction of the FDC bunker, vapor shimmied in the bright sunlight, distorting my vision. I shook my head; was I really awake? What is it that he was saying?

"March order . . . march order!" Dangerfield yelled, running. His long gangly arms swung back and forth and his gait reminded me of the Scarecrow in the Wizard of Oz.

"Sorry, boys," he said, grinning. "We gotta go. The brass just gave us orders to move and we gotta go now!"

"Hey fuck!" moaned Vanous. "I don't believe it. What kind of shit is this anyway? What the fuck is happening?"

"Those motha-fuckin' shit heads," I grumbled. "They couldn't give a shit about us. I'd strangle 'em if I could get my hands on 'em. But no, you'll never see those pricks in the field."

"Well, quit your bitchin', boys," said Dangerfield. "There ain't nothing we can do about it."

"Hey, you should talk motha-fucker," growled Vanous. "You've been on shift the last six hours and haven't done a thing but watch that fuckin' radio. You probably even got a chance to sleep last night."

"Hey, watch it, boy," shot out Dangerfield in his heavy Southern accent. "Those are fightin' words."

"Hey, shit! C'mon you guys," I said. "We're not the enemy."

We dismantled the camp in two hours, making sure no loose ammunition or anything else usable was left behind. Of course, our idea of what was usable and what wasn't was different from the Vietnamese; that was evident every time we tore down a position and left. Even before the trucks arrived the Vietnamese children began gathering at the edge of our perimeter. Sometimes they began gathering even before we started tearing down. It was uncanny. I wondered how they knew.

Scavengers, they would swoop down over the area as soon as we left, looking for anything usable or edible. Many of the bullet booby traps that the infantry discovered were made from M-16 ammo, so command had issued a stern warning at our last location, directing all units to do a thorough search for loose ammunition. They felt the rounds were coming from discarded ammo at base camps. We had been ordered to destroy all sandbags left behind as they, too, were being used to fortify enemy positions. Still, it was impossible to destroy everything. We always wondered how much of what we left behind was going to haunt us. The Vietnamese were like the American Indian; they didn't waste a thing. How different we were, how wasteful. I wondered if perhaps we hadn't lost our perspective. By American standards my parents had been far from rich but I had no idea of what it was really like to be poor until here.

Captain Nyberg came over as we waited the final tear-down. He was using our radio to keep in touch with the convoy. He wanted a "sit rep" from command headquarters again.

"Hey, captain, where we headed, sir?" I asked. I always felt at ease in Nyberg's presence. He didn't demand any kind of formality, but neither did he allow any disrespect. I had learned to trust and respect him. He always seemed to have a word of encouragement no matter how dismal the circumstances. The fact was, he was one of the few officers I had ever respected.

"It looks like we're headed for the Bao Trai area again," he said. "I don't relish going back there, but apparently they've hit some pretty rough stuff and we should be there to help 'em out."

"I don't understand, sir," I said. "We just left there a couple of weeks ago. How come they got us running back and forth hopping from one position to another?"

"Look, I'm not sure that I agree with the way they're handling this operation, but command figures that an aggressive and systematic patrol of the Cambodian border requires a constantly moving base. We don't have enough personnel to carry on an effective patrol of the border without moving from one place to another, so command figures we'll just have to do the best we can with what we have."

"Well why don't they send us more troops then?" I asked in frustration. "What I see happening is that as soon as we leave a position another battery often pulls in and takes our place, sometimes within one or two days. I just don't understand why they couldn't have left us there!"

"Look," Captain Nyberg replied with an air of finality, "I don't know all the answers but I do know that ours is not to question why, but to do, or die."

Shit, I said to myself, dropping my eyes. It pissed me off! How could the captain drop that kind of career rhetoric on me. Maybe that was a creed he had to follow as an officer, but it wasn't mine. It just wasn't like him to use a cliche like that to bring an end to a conversation. He generally tried to help us understand things.

Maybe he's just as frustrated as I am. Maybe he's told me all he knows. I walked away to think about it. I knew it would possibly take us a couple of hours to get to Bao Trai so I walked down the convoy to White's gun and hopped in the back of their deuce-and-a-half, determined to get some sleep. I crawled on top of the duffel bags that lay piled at the front of the truck.

"You'd better not sleep on this convoy," White warned. "We're liable to see some real shit and you'll get caught with your pants down."

I didn't listen. I didn't care.

At one point the truck bounced over a large crater in the road and threw me off the bags. I tried to go back to sleep, but the truck kept bouncing from side to side, throwing me off the duffel bags. I was soaked. God I stank! It had been days since I had been able to change and my fatigues were crusty. I pulled out a bandanna and tied it around my mouth to keep from breathing the dust from the road.

The road we followed wound along parallel to the Co Dong River. The Co Dong stretched from the northern end of the Third Corp area to the MeKong Delta, where Glover was stationed. It provided direct access from the Ho Chi Minh Trail to the south and was a heavily traveled river, especially at night. As we traveled, we passed several hamlets on either side of the river. They weren't much more than a collection of thatched huts perched on long bamboo poles. Many of them were built on the bank, suspended over the river. Almost every hut had its front to the river. As thick, green, bamboo groves flanked each end of the hamlets we were careful to watch them closely for snipers.

We finally pulled off the road near Hiep Hoa about 500 meters west of Bao Trai and began lining out our perimeter. This was to be FSB Houston. Borrowing C-4 explosives from the infantry, the lieutenant and captain lowered them into a hole I had dug and lit the fuse. Everyone took cover as the lieutenant yelled, "Fire in the hole!" A huge explosion shook the earth and dust and debris filled the air. In a matter of seconds the explosives had reduced the brick-hard clay into dust and brick-sized pieces. We began enlarging the crater, filling sandbags and stacking them around the edge. At 1800 I went on duty, embracing the change and the opportunity to rest. This time Lee, Vechione, Vanous and I were teamed together, all standing by on a fire mission.

It had been two hours since I had lifted a shovel, but I was so exhausted I couldn't stand. I knew that if we didn't receive clearance on our fire mission soon, Vanous and I would be sent outside, and for us, the digging would resume. The inside of the bunker slowly grew darker as our lone light bulb began to dim, a sure sign that the batteries were weakening. The generators needed to be turned on but I was too tired to get up and do anything about it. Too tired to even care. I secretly hoped that when Myers told someone to go see to it, it wouldn't be me.

"Vanous!" Myers barked. "Go turn on the generator. Damn it, I told you to make sure the batteries were charged before dark. You know the VC can zero in on the sound of it!"

Vanous quickly left and a minute later I heard the generator start.

I watched Myers. His face was red. I wasn't sure if it was anger or the heat. The inside of the bunker was sweltering, like a sauna. I wrestled my wet fatigue shirt off and laid it across the back of my chair. Myers was off shift but still inside.

112

I wondered what the rest of his crew was saying behind his back. He was explaining the operation of the FADAC to Lee but I knew it was just an excuse not to be outside digging.

The lieutenant, bent over charts showing the location of the infantry elements, asked Vechione to get a situation report from the infantry unit we were waiting on. Vechione picked up the mike.

"Mohawk Three Six, this is Killer Six Niner. Over," he whispered. He paused and repeated it.

"Killer Six Niner, this is Mohawk. Over," a voice finally whispered.

"Mohawk Three Six, sit rep. Over."

"Killer Six Niner, sit rep negative at this time. Over."

"Mohawk Three Six, sit rep negative. Out," Vechione ended.

"What's happening, lieutenant?" I asked.

"Apparently the LP is still waiting to verify the movement they spotted outside our perimeter. He wants to make sure it's the enemy before he calls in any fire."

"Shit," said Vanous who had re-entered, "that's all we need!"

"Just who the fuck else would be out there in the dark," I said casually, not really addressing anybody.

"I don't want any of that kind of language in here!" snapped the lieutenant.

Wow, what the fuck kind of soap box is he on tonight? I've heard him use stronger language. This lieutenant is really a squirrel. He must be tired and on edge like the rest of us.

I pulled a folding chair over to the chart table and slumped down on it, laying my head on the chart. No air circulated. The tent flap covering the entrance moved and the captain quietly entered.

"What's happening with this fire mission? The guns have been standing to for nearly two hours! What the hell is going on?"

"Still nothing, sir," Vechione replied. "I got a situation report just minutes ago and he hasn't confirmed spotting anything yet."

"Well, shit!" said the captain. "We're not gonna stand ready all night for this bastard! He should know by now whether there's anybody out there or if it was just an over-active imagination. Get him up on the line and let me talk to him."

"Yes, sir! Mohawk Three Six, this is Killer Six Niner. Over."

"Killer Six Niner, Mohawk Three Six. Over," the whisper answered.

"Mohawk Three Six, our Charlie Oscar would like to talk to you. Over."

"Killer Six Niner, roger. Over."

"Mohawk Three Six, this is Killer Six Zero. Do you have affirmative identification of Victor Charlie at this time? Over," the captain asked.

"Killer Six Zero, that is negative. Over," Mohawk replied.

"Mohawk Three Six, be advised that we are standing down until further notice. We will be available at moments' notice for positive sightings and will keep two guns trained on your Lima Poppa. Do you roger? Over."

"Killer Six Zero, I roger. Over," answered a slightly shaky voice.

The captain handed back the mike to Vechione.

"Mohawk Three Six, this is Killer Six Niner. Out," Vechione said.

"It sounds to me like maybe it's this lieutenant's first night at an ambush site and he's just jumpy and scared," said the captain. "Anyway, we don't need all of you down here when you've got to get another layer of sandbags on this bunker and build one of your own. Keep half this crew on duty," he said to the lieutenant, "and send the rest back out."

Any levity created by the captain's earlier remarks faded. None of us wanted to go back filling sandbags but I knew that it would be the lowest on the totem pole that had to, and that included me. Still, it didn't seem fair. We were all in this together—what difference should rank make?

"I know it ain't gonna be me," Vechione said, smirking. "Spec fours don't pull duty as long as there are privates around."

I was repulsed by him, his sullen, blood-shot eyes that held neither pity nor sympathy. I hated his arrogance, his sarcasm, the carpet of stubble that covered his face.

"So you two get off your asses and get with it!' Vechione snarled.

"Hey, I don't have to take no shit from you, Vechini," I spat back, deliberately mispronouncing his name. "I don't care whether you're a Spec Four or not."

"I don't take lip from no greenhorn," said Vechione. He pushed his chair out and headed for me. I rose to meet him.

Suddenly the captain's voice rang out: "Knock it off! I'm not gonna have any internal fighting in my command!"

Stepping between Vechione and me, he gave each of us a warning look. Dropping my eyes, I clenched my teeth. I sat back down. Tension filled the silence.

"I know you guys are dead tired," the captain finally said. "But I haven't gotten to sleep since we moved either. If I can take it, you can too. The only thing that keeps this battery functioning together in this kind of condition is its spirit. Fighting with each other tears and rips it apart. I won't have it! Do you understand?"

"Yes sir," said Vechione, scowling.

"Yes sir," I answered, embarrassed. "But it's just not fair, sir. I don't see you using your rank to gain advantage over anyone, so why should he? The least we could do is draw straws. All of us have worked our butts off, and none of us have slept in over seventy-two hours."

Vechione scowled at me but I wasn't going to be intimidated. The captain listened as we angrily exchanged words again. In the midst of our argument, I just gave up. I was just too fucking tired. Nothing was worth fighting for.

"Look, I'm sorry, Vechione," I said. "I didn't mean to lose my temper. I know that we're both tired." Vechione seemed to accept that, and suddenly it was all over.

"Look," said the captain, "I don't know what's happening tomorrow, men, but I know there won't be any surprise inspections tonight. Why don't you tell the crew outside that they can stand down for the evening. Just make sure they sleep under some kind of cover. We can finish the bunker tomorrow. Lee, you may as well notify the guns, too. Tell them to keep half a section on and to let the rest sleep!"

Shit, man, Nyberg I love you! I slipped out carefully through the outer tent flap so as not to expose any light.

"We're free, we're free!" I whispered to the others gleefully. I shook my fists in the air triumphantly. "Nyberg says you can hit the sack. Just be sure it's under cover somewhere. OK?"

"God-damn! All right!" they replied.

When I returned to the bunker, Lee said both Vanous and I could take off. It was almost 2400 anyway and he and Vechione would finish the shift.

As I stepped out of the bunker I leapt for joy. A cool evening breeze swept over my face.

I had been fighting sleep like a boxer, slamming and pushing it away. Yet now, I was experiencing a tremendous burst of energy. My adrenalin was pumping and sleep was the last thing on my mind. I decided to head out to the ammo bunker, inching my way in the moonless black. They saw me before I saw them.

"Shee-it, Olsen, what are you doing here?" Wheatstraw asked.

"I should ask you the same thing." I made my way through an opening in the sand bags they had tossed in piles around them. I had heard Wheatstraw, but I couldn't see him. In fact, I couldn't make out anybody, so I listened for their voices. My eyes strained to make them out in the dark.

"I decided to pack it in here tonight, man," Wheatstraw answered, lifting a shovel full of dirt, "instead of building my own bunker. That way I can get under one of these roofs a lot quicker."

"It sure as hell beats having to build the mansion you guys are building," giggled LeRoy. He opened the top of the sandbag he was holding so Wheatstraw could drop more dirt in. I began to make out two or three other people sitting a couple of feet away. One was a new guy. The others were Santiago and Ramos. Both Santiago and Ramos were sitting on top of upright sandbags. They held sandbags while Johnson shoveled.

"Listen man, I got some good news," I said. "Captain Nyberg says we can split shifts and go to sleep!"

"No shit!" said Santiago, his rich Spanish accent punctuating the air. "Hot damn!"

"Whew!" said LeRoy. "If he wasn't an officer he might be a soul brother."

"Olsen, you want a bottle of beer?" asked Wheatstraw, setting down his shovel. He stuck his arm into an Igloo, his white teeth flashing a grin. Pulling a couple of bottles out of the water he set one in front of me and handed the other to LeRoy.

"Beer!" I said skeptically, "Where did you get beer?"

"We picked it up from some gooks," laughed Wheatstraw, "just before we left on convoy. It's Number Thirty-Three."

"Vietnamese beer?" I asked incredulously. "You're not taking a chance drinking that stuff are you? Headquarters sent word down that no one was supposed to be drinking that shit. The Viet Cong have been putting battery acid in the stuff and selling it to G.I.'s."

"Hey, it's O.K.," laughed LeRoy. "We already checked it out—right Straw?"

"Why not?" I said, lifting the bottle. It tasted bitter but it was cold.

"Hey man, you'll never guess what else," giggled LeRoy. "Ole Johnson here came into the battery already equipped, and we's gonna smoke some of his stuff."

"Jesus," I said, "this can't be happening. This is too good to be true!"

Johnson dug out two joints and lit them up and passed them around. We cupped them carefully in our hands so as not to let any light show. When I finally got back to my bunker that night, three guys were already sacked out under the three-quarter trailer, and there was no more room. Fuck it, I thought. I dragged myself over to the bunker and crawled on top. As dark as it was outside I was sure nobody would see me up there anyway.

8

10 January 1968
FSB Patton
Trung Lap

It was close to 2100 hours when I left the battery area. I would be on duty in three hours. I grabbed a couple of cold beers from the cooler and headed for the perimeter. The last few days' activity weighed heavy on my mind.

Three days ago we had fired in support of A Battery when their night location was overrun. In addition to receiving heavy RPG fire and mortar rounds, their position had been assaulted by a battalion-sized force. The intense fighting left 113 Viet Cong dead.

Intelligence, questioning the VC prisoners that had been taken, learned that 50 percent of their unit, as well as others, now consisted of NVA soldiers. Some of the documents stripped from the bodies of the Vietnamese dead claimed that North Vietnamese artillery was moving down the Ho Chi Minh Trail, which was already experiencing a 200 percent increase in truck traffic. The inclusion of NVA soldiers with Viet Cong units had markedly increased the units' combat effectiveness.

Last night, an ambush patrol from the 2/27th made contact. They had first received three or four rounds of probing sniper fire. They should have realized what was going on then and moved, but they didn't. Later, around 0200 they started receiving in-coming small-arms fire and RPGs. They were only 80 meters outside our perimeter, so we saw the firefight. With the help of gunships, we surrounded their position with a ring of fire but we still lost one casualty. We reported one possible kill, but it was nothing we could confirm. But, it was becoming like that. Guesswork was replacing statistics; sacrificed for the almighty body count.

The company Roach was with had come in earlier to pull security, and since we had finished our bunkers I was going out to visit. I asked the first grunt I came to if his was C Company and he replied, "Affirmative." Knowing that they had been out in the field a couple of weeks, I figured that Roach would appreciate a cold beer.

117

It didn't take long to find his squad. As I approached their bunker I saw him standing outside. A towel was draped around his body. His hair was even longer than I remembered it; busy, unkempt. He looked like some old wino. He was staring into a small mirror propped up on sandbags, scraping the remnants of a three weeks' beard.

"Hey, Olsen!" he shouted, seeing me approach. "What's that you got?" He yelled to someone in a bunker. "Hey, Jim, look what's coming up the path. You're never gonna believe it!"

Some big hulk stuck his bullish frame through the entrance and crawled out.

"Well whaddya know?" he said, smiling. "A wise man bringing gifts."

"Hey, I figured you might like something like this," I said.

"Sit your ass down here till I finish shaving," said Roach. "Olsen, this is Big Jim. We've been together now about six weeks and he's saved my ass plenty of times already!"

Jim reached over and grasped my hand, entwining thumbs in a power shake that was becoming popular among blacks and stoners.

"Far out," I said.

"Hey, don't let Roach put anything on ya, man," Jim said. "He's done as much for me several times over."

It was evident that a real bond had developed between Jim and Roach. The more we talked, the easier it was to see why.

"Hey, what's it like working with the ARVNs?" I asked. "You guys are conducting sweeps with them, aren't you?"

"Shit," said Jim, "the only time we see their asses is when everything is cool or the C rations are being passed out. There's something about these gooks that gives me the creeps. If you ask me, they're as queer as three-dollar bills."

"Right on!" added Roach. "I'd like to be able to trust 'em but it ain't always easy. Sometimes I've seen 'em pull their own weight, at least when we worked with the Rangers. But you gotta watch 'em all the time. They're great to have along when the armored cavalry is sweeping, because they add additional ground strength. And it sure helps to have someone who speaks the language when you're interrogating the gooks but man, you gotta work with 'em on a one-to-one basis to control their movement or to get any kind of mission done."

"I don't like it!" Jim said. "A couple of days ago I heard that a night ambush site with the Twenty-seventh watched three Vietnamese change into Army fatigues. The only people I know wearing our uniforms are the ARVNs. Now either those bastards were out having group sex or they were changing back out of their black pajamas. I don't trust 'em. They might act friendly during the day, but once night falls they're Viet Cong!"

We rapped for nearly an hour as darkness fell over the base. Just before dusk, three other squad members straggled in from the perimeter trailing wire behind them from the claymore mines they had been stringing.

"How many claymores you got out there?" I asked.

"Not enough," Roach retorted.

"I sure wouldn't want to get caught in front of one of those!" I said. "I've seen them clear a swath of ground cleaner than a swarm of locusts."

Jim crawled out of the bunker and yelled at one of the men who was just climbing in over the front of the bunker. "Did you get all of those trip flares set?"

"All of 'em."

"Good. I don't want no VC climbing in on this side of the perimeter tonight without me having plenty of warning."

Shortly before midnight, as I was about to leave, a flare lit up the perimeter about twenty meters outside the concertina wire, directly in front of our position.

"Shit man, a trip flare just went off!" somebody whispered.

For a split second it was like time was frozen. Nobody moved. Then a tremendous urge to run hit the pit of my stomach as I realized the possible danger. I had come out here without my M-16 and a sense of panic gripped me.

"Jesus," I spat. "I forgot my fuckin' weapon!"

In that moment, a sudden flurry of activity began and I could only watch as the others began grabbing simultaneously for helmets and weapons.

"Jesus, Jesus," Roach kept repeating as if it was a chant to ward off evil. He and Jim began to yank people in line, shoving them left and right against the bunker and its surrounding walls.

SSSSSSSSZZZZZTT, thud! Wham! Wham! Wham!

RPGs and mortars began falling like rain. Their deafening explosions rocked the base.

"They're coming in over the wire!" someone shouted.

"Like shit they are!" shouted Roach, standing up. Laying his M-16 on top of the bunker, he began to hammer away at the approaching enemy.

Big Jim, who had already risen to a half-crouch, was pushing rounds into his M-79 and firing over the top of the bunker. He didn't even stop to look for a target. He just kept breaking the breech of the 79 open, stuffing in rounds, pointing it up and out and firing for effect.

The 60 millimeter mortar crew that was stationed next to Roach's bunker went into action. I could hear rounds sliding down the tube and the familiar thop! as it fired.

"Hand me those magazines!" Roach yelled, pointing to a stack of ammunition next to my position.

I reached down and began pumping them into his hands as fast as he could empty them from his rifle.

"Pass me those 79 rounds!" yelled Jim.

I leaned over to my right and began lobbing them one by one to him as he plugged them into the grenade launcher and fired. With my right hand I lobbed grenades to Jim and with my left I handed magazines to Roach.

Roach's face began to contort as his neck bulged and his lips pinched together tighter. I could see the veins puffing out on his neck as his face turned red. All of a sudden all of the grunts started screaming and yelling, as though a jolt of electricity had struck them simultaneously.

"Sons-a-bitches!" they screamed. "Bastards, dirty rotten bastards!"

"Killllll . . . killllll . . . killllll!" Roach screamed.

"Mother-fuckers! Bastards! Fuckers! Sons-a-bitchesssss!" Jim yelled at the top of his voice. "We'll kill you fuckers!"

Crazy screams and curses filled the air in a frenzy of motion and frustration.

Throw a grenade. Drop a mortar. Explode those claymores. Fire your rifle. The energy was electrifying. There was no thought given to anything but kill or be killed. The fear of death burned its way into us. We fought frantically to survive.

Artillery fire finally began coming from the gun placements and exploding artillery rounds saturated the perimeter. The guns are up, I thought excitedly. Good. Good. Good. The guns are up!

Lost in the bubbling cauldron of battle, I felt my muscles strain and my heart pound. The air, now thick with smoke, stung my eyes. My mouth was so dry my tongue stuck to my lips as I sucked in air.

As another barrage of artillery rounds shook the perimeter in front of our position, I heard the whizz of shrapnel as it flew over our heads. Someone who had a radio to his ear was yelling at everyone to put on their flak jackets and take cover. The artillery was going to be firing in close, so we could expect to get back-splash.

Another barrage of explosions shook the perimeter and I heard someone yelling, "Cease fire, cease fire." As abruptly as it had begun, it was over. Charlie was retreating! I could hear the familiar whup-whup-whup of helicopter blades breaking the air. Gunship! They've called in gunships and supporting artillery. That's why the cease-fire.

Jim and Roach stood, staring over the rim of the bunker into the clouds of dust and smoke that covered the perimeter. The smell of sulfur stung my nostrils.

"Shit, I'd better get back to the FDC in case they need me," I said, and took off in a crouching run. Overhead I could hear one of the Huey Slicks diving toward the perimeter, its miniguns pouring out lethal lead. I wondered how many days I had left in country.

I stretched out on my back, letting my mind wander. All I wanted to think about was what life had been like back in the world. What had it been like to sleep on a soft bed with clean, fresh smelling sheets, to open a refrigerator door and have a cold drink, to slip inside a real bathtub and soak in hot water. I stared overhead. The immense stretch of flickering stars reminded me of the Montana skies that filled the lonely nights I had hitch-hiked across the country. They twinkled like jewels. I lay in a daze, my mind thousands of miles away. I grappled with my feelings, trying to make sense of my life.

Things were happening around us so much quicker now. A lot of mistakes were being made and too many lives were being lost. Many of those mistakes had occurred too damn close for comfort. An ARVN artillery compound had recently fired rounds into the 4th Battalion 23rd Mechanized's position, killing some American soldiers. When questioned about it, the ARVNs claimed they had obtained clearance from Phu Hoa, where the Vietnamese command post was stationed. Apparently they had neglected to get U.S. ground clearance, or simply felt it unnecessary. I wondered which! Two positions within a thousand meters of us had been mortared and assaulted twice in the last two days. I was perplexed by the Viet Cong's unusual aggressiveness. Sampans were spotted daily on the Co Dung River, and even though we were sinking them like crazy, the flow hadn't stopped. I didn't like the sound of that. Five Hueys had gone down in the last three days in assault operations, one of which was shot down within sight of our base. That worried me. The enemy was tenacious. The infantry was spotting groups of 50 or more Viet Cong openly traveling in the daylight. More and more spottings occurred each day. That, too, was really out of the ordinary.

To top it off, this evening one of our own artillery units had dropped two 105mm rounds into the 1st of the 23rd's location. One WIA had to be dusted off. The 321st Artillery said they had fired the rounds believing it to be a suspected mortar position. Their radar had picked up movement there. An erroneous AO on their clearance map had said there were no U.S. gound troops in the vicinity.

I wondered where all the confusion was coming from. Something was sure in the wind. I was glad I wasn't in leadership. I could just imagine the kind of ass-chewing some FDC leader was getting for those rounds. Besides, I sure wouldn't want the deaths of Americans on my conscience; it was already beginning to give me problems.

I tried not to think about the war and drew back into a world I could create in my own mind; a world of memories which glittered with tender words and enticing smiles. A world of close friends and rugged Oregon beaches.

January 17 found us on the move again. The fifth time in nine days. This time we were headed back to the northern part of Hau Nghia Province, back to the infamous Boi Loi Woods. Although our orders were to continue giving the 27th Infantry direct support we would also be working alongside a unit of mechanized APCs called the Bobcats. Wolfhounds and Bobcats: it sounded like I was in a den of Cub Scouts.

The mech had just discovered a tunnel complex in the area so large that it included hospital wards complete with surgery facilities, mess halls, communication rooms and bunk-lined sleeping quarters. All underground! What the Viet Cong could do never ceased to amaze me.

For more than 48 hours we worked at FSB Pope to build another bunker, cursing the kind of decision-making policy that was forcing us through this relentless chain of stupid maneuvers. Without fail, as soon as we moved out of an area, another artillery battery with the same firing capability or size moved in behind us. I failed to understand the thinking or motivation behind these tactics. As far as I could tell, no one else understood them either. I had asked both Myers and the lieutenant about it and neither of them had an answer. When I wanted to question the captain about it again, the lieutenant gave me a definite no! In his eyes, you simply didn't question authority. You did what you were told, or else! And, of course, I knew what that "or else" could be. In Basic I had been threatened with an Article 15, and in A.I.T. it had been nip-and-tuck before court-martial proceedings against me had been dropped. I knew that here, in a war-time situation, you could easily end up in Long Binh Jail for direct disobedience.

After three days the bunkers were finally done. When the normal rotation of shifts began I was able to find the time to relax, and decided to read a letter I had gotten from Debbie Winger nearly two days earlier. I had not opened it because I had wanted to read her letter slowly, in order to savor every word. In the security of my bunker, I pulled pen and paper out of the plastic sack I kept it in, in my ammo box. I wanted to be ready to answer any questions she might have, and I was thinking about the hundreds in my own mind.

I was filled with longing as I read her letter. I closed my eyes and pictured the faces of the friends I had discovered in Oregon. God, how I missed them. More than anything else!

"Dear Debbie," I began to write, "you can't imagine what it means to me to hear from you. Everytime I hear Dusty Springfield sing "the look of love," I think of you. I've never met anyone so beautiful. I can see your long blonde hair shining and a smile warming your face. . . . We've been moving so much that I've hardly had time to read your letter, nearly every three days. . . . It's really crazy over here Deb, you wouldn't believe it if . . ."

I was in the middle of a sentence when I heard my name being called and recognized White's voice. "Hey man," I called out of the bunker. "I'm in here!"

A few seconds later White appeared in the entrance and, dropping down to his knees, crawled in. "Hey, how ya doing?" he asked, sliding up alongside the wall and making himself comfortable. "Look what I got in the mail!" He unfolded a newspaper and laid it in my lap. "The paper's a few days old but you should hear what they're saying about the war. It says here that Westmoreland says that we've reached an important point in the war when the end begins to come into view. Can you believe that? Hey, those people in the world must believe that we're just mopping up the enemy left and right."

"Shit, maybe it's true," I said hopefully. "We've been picking up a lot of weapons and supplies that Charlie's got hidden, and, man, they've hauled away tons and tons of rice. Their body count is also rising. Charlie must be on the run or why would we be chasing him all over like we're doing?" As much as I tried to sound convincing, it was hard for even me to believe.

I finally said, "Hey man, who am I trying to kid. I'd like to believe that the end of this war is really close but I don't know if what Westmoreland says is true or not. But he's the one who should know, right?"

"Right on!" exclaimed White.

"But listen, man," I continued, "our own body count is also rising, and the reason we're killing more Cong is because we're running into larger VC forces and more often. Shit, man, we've never had this many spottings since I've been in country. Vechione says he hasn't seen this kind of activity in all the time he's been here. He thinks we might see some mean shit coming. I don't doubt it, but shit man, I don't want to believe that either."

"Hey don't go bumming me out now," said White. "What's headquarters say about all this?"

"Headquarters don't let us know shit!" I spat. "Everything's always hush-hush until the last minute, and then you still don't know if half of what they say is true. I'll tell you one thing though, those grunts out in the boonies have been uncovering large quantities of 120 millimeter rockets. You know, the big ones that Charlie has been using to hit the large bases like Katum, Bien Hoa and Cu Chi. And you know that if Charlie's storing up those big ones, he ain't using 'em to rig booby traps.

"Shit, just look around us man," I continued. "Two nights ago B Battery took a hundred and seventy-five 60 millimeter mortars. We've been mortared every night we've been here, and the Fourth of the Twenty-third has been mortared every night since they moved to this area. And you know the fire base we just left six days ago? Well, they were hit just two days ago and lost seven men. Fifteen wounded."

"Shit man, it makes it hard being down on the guns," White added. "Half the time we don't know what's going on or what we're even firing at. You got it licked up here, man. At least you know what's going on."

"Well, I wish I knew more," I added. "But you know we've been increasing our H & I at night and headquarters is sending us more counter-mortar targets. I don't know if I should say this, I mean, I don't know how much stock to put in it. But, I've got a friend in the Wolfhounds and the last time I saw him he said that their unit had captured some documents that said the Viet Cong felt the time was ripe for a general offensive and that they planned on taking over all the towns and villages through a 'popular uprising.' I mean, do you hear what I'm saying, man? He said they had uncovered other documents which outlined major attacks on Saigon and Pleiku which were supposed to take place sometime before Tet."

"Tet?" White asked. "What's that?"

"Shit, man, you know," I replied. "They talked about it during that jungle training we had when we first came in country. Tet's their big number one celebration. It's like our New Year. It's at the end of the month! Well, I ain't gonna worry about it," I said with finality, wanting to convince myself as much as White. "Command believes the enemy has been moving forces from their border sanctuaries toward Bao Trai and into the Triangle. That's why we're here. Maybe we'll put an end to it before it starts. Still, it's hard for me to believe we've got them on the run when the First of the Fifth Mech suffered the kind of losses they did yesterday. And with sampan traffic on the river continuing like it is, it seems like a build-up of men and supplies is occurring, not a break-down."

By the end of January we had moved four more times and a division posture was beginning to evolve: disrupt the enemy supply channels; search out his weapons, his ammunition, his food; rush his position every time a force tried to gather. By using these tactics command was hoping to preempt battle and save us from having to face any major kind of confrontation that would result in unnecessary deaths of American soldiers or the loss of any strategic location. This meant unparalleled mobility and maneuverability. We were involved in a game of fox and hounds in which the fox knew where all the holes were and we were merely following his scent.

Patrol bases, company-sized defensive positions, were established and moved every couple of days. It was a critical part of division's tactics. The *Stars and Stripes* said that no one had developed the concept better, or used it more, than the 25th.

If the engineers happened to be around during a combined forces operation they would clear the surrounding land of all brush and irregular terrain which afforded the enemy cover. The lieutenant always asked the captain to ask the engineers if they would come over and doze us out a hole so we wouldn't have to dig one, but if they weren't around, the land had to be cleared using other methods. If we were lucky enough to be in one location for over 48 hours, such refinements as fresh water, ice, mess tents and mail were "sortied" in, always by helicopter. We, and a majority of infantry and small artillery units, were spending most of our lives in a series of homes such as these.

9

30 January 1968
FSB Hosecrans
Duc Hoa

I sat quietly inside the dimly lit bunker. The weak glare of the overhanging light reflected my own physical condition. It was late in the evening and my shift was nearly at an end. With it, I hoped, would come an end to a penetrating weariness. I could almost taste the sweet nectar of sleep. Our new firebase was Hosecrans, a rice paddy near Duc Hoa we had occupied for three days. I listened only half-heartedly as Gianettino radioed our weekly sit-rep to headquarters. HQ was sharing our location in the field again, as was B Battery. His transmissions drifted in and out of my thoughts.

"On the 24th at 1137, Bravo Company located 5,000 pounds of unpolished rice, vicinity X-ray, Tango 461-137. Charlie Battery fired 87 rounds on prep in grid X-ray Tango 405-138.

"On two-five January, Bravo Company engaged one Victor Charlie with small arms and automatic weapons fire, negative results. At 0857, supporting gunships vicinity X-ray Tango 422206 engaged one Victor Charlie in sampan, resulting in one Victor Charlie Kilo India Alpha and one sampan destroyed. At 1512 Delta Company apprehended two Victor Charlie Poppa October Whiskeys who were Whiskey India Alphas, and evacuated to Twelfth Evac Hospital. Charlie Battery fireballed to Foxtrot Sierra Bravo Butler and back to Reed.

"On two-six January, Charlie Company provided one platoon for security of Engineers mine sweep operations on Highway 10 to Sugar Mill. At 1145 supporting gunships at X-ray Tango 460 042 received automatic weapons fire, negative results. And on it went, day by day, item by item.

"Two-eight January, Delta Company conducted reconnaissance in force operations in X-ray Sierra 587 971. . . . Alpha conducted same in X-ray Sierra 587 791. At 1923 Alpha detonated a dud round while preparing November Lima resulting in two uniform Sierra Kilo India Alphas. Dud was 105 shell Do you copy so far? Over."

Headquarters repeated Gianettino's transmission, making sure the info was right.

"If I remember right," said Gianettino, "that's the fifth and sixth American killed by booby-trapped 105 duds in the last two weeks. What the fuck kind of fuses are they sending us anyway?"

"Look, we can't help it," said Lee. "C'mon, let's get this report done."

Gianettino finished his transmission: "Three zero January, First of the Twenty-seventh conducted Rome India Foxtrot operations. Alpha Company vicinity X-ray Sierra 590 095. Charlie vicinity X-ray Sierra 572 951 and 567 998. At 1525 Bravo in vicinity X-ray Tango 569 948 received an unknown amount of sniper fire, returned fire with small arms, automatic weapons, negative casualties, Victor Charlie losses unknown. End of copy, over."

Headquarters again repeated the transmission.

"Well that finishes it," said Lee. "Hopefully nothing will happen between now and midnight to change it."

"Amen to that," added Campbell.

I ran my hands through my hair. It was so dirty it would stand up by itself. I wondered when the captain would send for a gook barber. Everybody's hair was getting over regulation length. I hoped, like Lee, that nothing would interfere with tonight's sleep. I just wanted the sun to rise and my shift to end. I hoped the lull would continue in spite of the fact that the Tet truce had been cancelled this morning by division headquarters.

It had been rumored as far back as the 26th that there would be a stand-down in honor of the Vietnamese Tet. Especially since there had been a 36 hour stand-down in celebration of our New Year. I didn't understand what the big hullabaloo was about, but I knew that the Tet holiday was not only a time of revelry, of fireworks and street festivals, but also of worship. For several days the entire countryside was supposed to be on the move as people visited their ancestral homes. All business, even the business of war, was supposed to grind to a halt. The Viet Cong had decreed a truce lasting from January 27 to February 3, but even then there were strong indications that they didn't plan on honoring it. And, they hadn't. Last night, the 3rd Squadron 4th Cavalry came into heavy contact with a VC battalion in the Ho Bo Woods. Even though we had returned fire with all available weapons, artillery, and gunships, we had been unable to disperse the enemy. The 2nd of the 27th finally had to conduct a night assault into the area, one which had continued till early this morning. Spooky, an airplane which dropped illumination flares, had flown over the location most of the night. The Cavalry had lost four men with the wounded. The 27th lost nine, and had 24 WIAs. The only good thing was that VC losses were larger. Luckily, the infantry was able to retrieve some of the Viet Cong's weapons. There were a number of AK-47s, RPG-2 rocket launchers and one 82mm mortar tube.

The 3rd Squadron 22nd Regulars, temporarily assigned to our battalion, had spotted 300–400 Viet Cong last night heading toward Saigon. They were carrying recoilless rifles and 82mm mortar tubes plus small arms and automatic weapons.

When the Regulars called in artillery, the Viet Cong disappeared. This morning, supporting gunships had observed 40 VC near our location and after heavy fighting, killed 24.

Since I had come on duty it had been relatively quiet, except for the eight Viet Cong that had been captured within the perimeter of the 6th Battalion 77th Artillery's base camp. Those Viet Cong had been living in a tunnel under their base and had been caught trying to sneak out early this morning.

I stood in the middle of a sundrenched, baked-clay rice paddy, watching as the area around me quickly became a parking lot for tanks, APCs, artillery, trucks and jeeps. I had snatched only three hours of sleep in the last 29 hours. The sun scorched the top of my head as I labored to fill sandbag after sandbag. My eyes stung from sweat. I could feel a rash starting in my crotch and wished I could take my pants off. Sweat trickled down my chest and arms, leaving streaks in the dirt that blanketed my body. My back ached for relief but I knew none was in sight. Endless hours of continual shoveling still lay before me. Sleep would not come for another day and a half, if then.

The Viet Cong had dropped a shit-load of mortars and RPGs on our position last night, less than three hours after I had gotten off shift. We were in the middle of some kind of large enemy push and with little overhead cover, the evening's assault had been deathly frightening. The 3rd Battalion 4th Infantry was in heavy contact near Tan Son Nhut, northwest of Saigon, and our scheduled ballgame had been cancelled.

The 1st of the 27th was conducting an airborne assault north of Hoc Mon, where intelligence had said a major southward movement of the enemy had begun. The 4th Battalion 23rd Infantry had run into two Viet Cong companies in the Ho Bo Woods but had split its battalion, sending half of its forces to Trang Bang because another two VC companies were destroying the outpost there. Division artillery had sent a red alert, warning everyone to travel armed. All Vietnamese were to be placed under close supervision, including the ARVNs and the Vietnamese peasants who flocked into the major base camps every day to do the washing, ironing, sandbag filling. We had been ordered to check our ammo situation very carefully and to be ready to move on short notice. Intelligence reported that all major U.S. military installations were under siege so while we had convoyed here, headquarters had hurried back to base camp.

The sun was without restraint and its piercing heat evaporated my strength. The blinding sweat hindered my digging. I picked up my t-shirt and ripped it into a long thin shred and tied it around my forehead.

"Hey, look at the fuckin' hippie!" I heard Vechione snarl.

"Fuck you," I said. I felt dizzy. I nearly blacked out when I stood up to toss a sandbag out of our hole, so I stopped to go swallow a salt tablet and get a drink. I had seen others faint under this suffocating heat and go into convulsions, a sure sign of heat stroke. I wasn't going to let that happen to me; it could prove fatal. As much as I hated to wear anything, I stuck my jungle hat back on to protect my head.

In spite of the attack, we had labored all last night to complete the FDC bunker and were now knee deep in another hole, struggling to finish a personnel bunker. Most of the guns had finished their positions. I envied them.

My strength was rapidly ebbing. It's got to stop, I cried silently, I just can't go on anymore. I squeezed my eyes shut. I could feel myself blacking out again. I tried not to betray the fear I felt as I began to feel control of my emotions slip away. I wanted to cry. It was more than I could bear. My muscles ached from exhaustion. I struggled to retain my composure, looking around at the other men to see if they noticed. I wondered if any of them felt like I did. I've got to stand alongside them. I must, I told myself! I've got to do as much as anyone else. I can't let myself lose control. I told myself that again and again, as I struggled to keep on working.

I saw Myers walk out the FDC bunker and head our way. He was buttoning his fatigue shirt as he walked.

"OK gang," he said. "Command just sent down an order that everyone is to have their shirts, flak jackets and helmets on. And, they want us to blouse our boots."

"What!" shouted Lee, almost choking on the word. "What the fuck are you talking about?"

"Hey, you don't mean while we're working?" snorted Vechione defiantly.

"Yes!" Myers replied as sternly as he could. "Even if you're digging! Look," he said pausing, "I don't make the rules. I just obey them. And you'd better too!"

I couldn't believe it! I knew that we had to be on the alert, but having to work in the hot sun with a flak jacket and shirt on was not just dangerous, it was insane! Blousing our pants bottoms into our boots would even increase the chance of the body temperature rising. What the hell were they trying to prove?

"Shit," spat Lee, "I ain't blousing my boots. And, I ain't putting on no vest!"

"An you ain't gonna catch me putting on no shirt till it cools down tonight!" added Vechione.

"These mother-fuckers who come over here and try to pretend this is Basic Training are crazy," Lee said, angrily raising his voice. "Every once in a while we get one of these son-a-bitches. They don't give a shit about anything but impressing their superiors, ordering some dumb ass stunt like this to brown nose someone higher than themselves. I suppose somebody figures that because we're so near Saigon some of the big brass will come out and inspect the troops. The next thing you know they'll be asking us to spit-shine our boots and police the area for cigarette butts!"

I laughed; those memories were still fresh in my mind. Basic and A.I.T. had not been so far off as it seemed. Lee was right. All the dumb shit, the ridiculous regulation that command imposed, was always engineered by some high ranking officer who didn't have to follow his own orders. Officers who sat in their air-conditioned bunkers and offices in the rear. The only time they ever wore their flak-jackets was when they made infrequent trips to the field for inspection or when they posed for some newspaper photos.

The bitching and moaning continued and no one made a move to follow any of the orders. Fifteen minutes later the lieutenant came storming out of the bunker, his thick German accent punctuating his anger.

"Vee can expect the Major to drop in here any time! Vhere are your jackets and helmets? Get those shirts on and button them up! If he shows up here, I vant the area policed before he lands! Is that understood?" he yelled.

"Yes sir!" Lee replied, dropping his eyes.

"Yes sir!" I added quickly when the lieutenant looked at me.

Vechione just looked down and stared at the sandbag he was holding. He didn't respond.

We slowly fanned out to gather up our uniforms. Lee walked over to the cooler and carried it back into the hole. Sitting down near his shovel he dug out a beer, tossing another to Vechione.

"Hey, I'll take one, too," I said.

The beer was lukewarm but we drank it anyway. In a few minutes I started working on another one.

"Shit, you'd better watch out," laughed Lee. "Drinking one warm beer on a day like today, especially working out here in the sun, will get you stoned higher than a six-pack."

He was right. Twenty minutes later I was feeling no pain and we were all laughing, doing our best to keep our spirits up, swapping stories about the Army and its dumb fuckin' officers.

I crouched down and braced myself against the side of the three-quarter, listening to the steady "whup-whup-whup" of the Chinook that was slowly descending above me. It was February 12. We were about to leave the fire support base which had been our home for 12 long days.

The three-quarter was rigged with slings, as were the guns and the rest of the battery's equipment. An airlift was taking place. As the giant Chinook hovered over my position I could see one of the crew lying on his stomach, peering out a rectangular hatch in its belly. I felt like I was about to be devoured. The powerful downdraft from the Chinook's twin rotors beat against my chest, nearly lifting me off my feet. I made a grab for my helmet, but it spun off my head and crashed onto the truck bed. Forgetting everything else, I lifted the sling over my head and tried to drop it over the cargo hook protruding from the bottom of the helicopter. Suddenly the chopper lurched to the right, dropping rapidly. Goddamn, I swore, dropping to my knees, I was about to be crushed. The Chinook righted itself and I sprang upright. I tried again to fasten the sling and get the hell out from underneath.

As the Chinook began to rise, I leaped off the truck and scrambled to get clear. The wind tore at everything around me as the Chinook lifted and sailed away.

I ran over to where Campbell was standing, picking my helmet out of the dirt on the way. As soon as I shouldered my M-16 and ammo belt, we both ran for the next Chinook, about 30 meters away. This time I hung onto my helmet and, ducking my head, tried to shield myself from the sand that stung my face as the wind whipped around us. My flak jacket flapped against my back as I pushed against the downdraft, heading for the back hatch of the helicopter which had dropped to the ground. Grunts were already running up the ramp.

As we hit the ramp, I tripped and stumbled, crashing to my knees. Quickly righting myself, I limped over to one side of the helicopter and sat down. As soon as everyone boarded, we lurched into the air and swung over one of the howitzers.

The hook-up took less than 45 seconds. We lifted again, this time heading towards our new location. I slipped off my helmet and crawled over to the opening. I noticed the fire base beneath us resembled the center of a spider web. The roads, dikes, canals and tank tracks that crisscrossed the area all seemed to intertwine around the circle of torn bunkers and empty pits, all that remained of the barren rice paddy.

February was quickly becoming a blur of events. There hadn't been much time to think about the war or anything else. All my energy was being expended on survival. I had quit counting the number of times we had been mortared. News of the Tet offensive traveled over our radio and from soldier to soldier. The tiny compound surrounding the southern perimeter of Cu Chi had been set afire twice and many ammunition depots, communication centers, mess halls and rear personnel areas had been completely destroyed. Our own rear area had 11 of its bunkers and fighting positions completely demolished.

The VC were all over, attacking every major U.S. Army installation, destroying towns and villages, fighting in the streets of Saigon. They had established ambush sites on all major highways. The bridges were blown and the roads heavily mined. Some areas had been completely shut off from anything but helicopter resupply. What pissed me off was that the Viet Cong were firing mortars and rockets from No Fire Zones, areas heavily populated by civilians. It was always a difficult and lengthy process to get permission to fire into them because we needed clearance from as high up as brigade level in both U.S. and ARVN sources. Although U.S. clearance always came quickly, Vietnamese clearance didn't. And why weren't the Vietnamese civilians stopping the Viet Cong in those areas? Didn't they realize their enemy was launching a major drive to take over their country?

A week ago the 1st Battalion 27th Infantry had suffered major losses during an engagement because we couldn't get clearance to fire support for them. The 27th lost three guys that day, needlessly. One of them could have been Roach. Ten others were wounded. I tried not to let it get me down, but it did. The units we were now supporting had already lost 27 men. The wounded count was skyrocketing. I knew we had killed 151 Viet Cong but balanced against the loss of our own men, it didn't seem worth it.

I was tired of watching an endless parade of men being dragged in to the perimeter each day, lifeless or limbless. I was seeing too many straight lines of body bags, waiting in silence to be picked up by helicopters. There was no escaping the pain etched in the faces of the men who carried in the dead and wounded. I had to harden myself. Yesterday I had watched a group of guys drag a GI with nothing but bloody stumps for legs up to the landing area for dust-off and as they slid him up to the helicopter pad on a plastic poncho liner, his face ashen, I nearly choked. I had to hold my breath to keep from crying. Pain, like a gasp, had lodged in my throat, but I just couldn't allow it. There was so much death. I could easily become immobilized by my emotions. I couldn't afford to waste my strength on the dead. Fortunately, I had been trained from early childhood not to show emotions. I was a man and men never showed pain. Big boys didn't cry!

I looked out the small window in the side of the Chinook. I could see the road the captain had flown over yesterday with the major, scouting it in case we had to convoy. A convoy never materialized because the roads had become too dangerous to travel. I was grateful that the 3rd Division, which had been operating in War Zone C, had committed half of its assets to our area. Hopefully, that would help to ease the pressure we were under. Perhaps they could help us destroy the Vietnamese who were showing up in new blue, pajama-like uniforms. The enemy was now dressed in black and blue. The last two days had been filled with vicious fighting, both for the 1st and the 2nd of the 27th. We had been credited with 179 kills in two battles alone. Things were crazy! In the middle of one of the battles, some ding-dong colonel flew in for an inspection, scouring the base camp for anything out of place. Just before he left, he ordered us to radio his findings to battalion headquarters. I remembered it vividly . . . him stomping in with his shiny, clean, starched uniform, scowling about his findings. Our new captain had to relay the findings personally, to Major Jenkins. I chuckled, remembering the transmission.

"Killer Three Zero this is Killer Six Zero. Over," Captain Ripke had radioed.

"Killer Six Zero this is Killer Three Zero. Over," the RTO answered.

"Killer Three Zero, is Killer Three at your location at this time? Over," Ripke continued.

"Killer Six Zero, that is affirmative. Over."

"Killer Three Zero, would you please put him on the air. Over."

A pause followed, and then Major Jenkins' deep, black voice came on: "Killer Six Zero, this is Killer Three. Over."

"Killer Three, this is Killer Six Zero. Blaster Five has just completed an inspection at our location at this time. He found Whiskey Poppa rounds laying down, loose fuses, pre-cut charges and uncovered ammo. Over."

"Killer Six Zero, let me repeat. . . . Whiskey Poppa rounds laying down, loose fuses, pre-cut charges and uncovered ammo. Is this correct? Over."

"Killer Three, that is affirmative. Over."

"Killer Six Zero," came Major Jenkins' somewhat despondent and angry voice, "is Blaster Five presently at your location? Over."

"Killer Three, that is affirmative. Over," the captain quickly replied. I could tell he was eager to please.

"Killer Six Zero, is there any other transmission that he wishes to convey at this time? Over."

The captain looked at the colonel and the colonel shook his head.

"Killer Three. Negative. Over."

"This is Killer Three . . . Out."

The colonel charged out of the FDC with the captain and the lieutenant close behind. We had to give a temporary check-fire to the guns, stopping cover fire for the infantry, so that his helicopter could leave.

What an asshole! We had been in the middle of a fire mission so of course the ammunition was uncovered. When our artillery fire was repetitious, the guns knew they were going to be using the same charge, so why not cut it? It saved time and human lives. That's what we were trying to do wasn't it? Wasn't that what this war was all about? Shit! I had had it up to my neck with Army rules and regulations! Those bastards in command . . . I didn't see any of those pricks fighting the war. The only time they came to the field was for rinky-dink shit like this. I hated 'em. I despised their hypocrisy and elitism.

Suddenly I felt used up. Had it really only been three short months since I had come in country?

Five days and two moves later, we were on our way back to Cu Chi, this time by convoy. We were going to spend the night in our new location and then head out again in the morning. We were to defend the northwest approach to Saigon and the air base at Tan Son Nhut, on its outskirts. By now there were ten different American infantry battalions operating in our area and we were firing support for three or four of them. Additional units were relying on us for on call missions; some ground pounders, some mechanized.

With unusually stiff resistance from entrenched enemy soldiers we began suffering an even higher death rate. The number of Viet Cong casualties was higher but it was probably because a greater number of possibles were being reported as actual body count. Command was putting increasing pressure on everyone to show a higher rate of enemy loss, so the infantry began falsifying body count and we just went along with it. As far as I could tell that's what was being reported to the press. I assumed it was to assure them that the situation was under control. The only thing was, I wasn't buying that story anymore, and neither were some of the other guys. I wondered how come we were in so much shit when Westmoreland had said the end was in view. I certainly didn't want to believe that the Army was actually fabricating lies about our situation but it certainly didn't appear like we were winning from where I was sitting. After all, Tan Son Nhut was supposed to be a secure position and it had been seriously penetrated by the Viet Cong. So had Bien Hoa, the other major air base. In fact, there wasn't one area I knew of that wasn't being seriously threatened.

More women began turning up in the VC mass graves being uncovered. It was not uncommon to find graves with 30–40 dead bodies. It reminded me of the photos I had seen in a couple of history books my father had kept secreted in the bottom of his bedroom dresser. Books on World War II, his war. There, alongside issues of *Playboy* and *Cavalier*, hidden under pajamas and sweaters, lay a whole part of my father's past that he had never talked about. As a child I had often looked through those books when he wasn't around, wondering how anything like that could have ever taken place. There were photos of human, living skeletons and mass graves that contained hundreds of nude bodies that looked no different from their living counterparts. Jews, gassed and bled by Nazi Germany. I shuddered just thinking about it, telling myself again how lucky I was not to be a grunt.

I stood up in the back of the truck I was riding in and leaned over the roof of the cab. I could see the village of Tan Hoa in the distance. Tan Hoa had finally been retaken after 12 days of fierce fighting. The Viet Cong had fought off the 3rd of the 22nd and the 4th of the 23rd for 14 days before finally melting into the surrounding countryside. Abandoning their familiar hit-and-run tactics, the VC had dug in, fighting from an enclave of bunkers made with concrete and reinforced with railroad ties. The bunkers had been so elaborately connected by a trench and a tunnel complex that I wondered how the hell they had been able to build it without us or the ARVNs knowing about it. Sure as hell the civilians had known about it. When the fighting ended the VC left 219 corpses behind, and, as far as I knew, hadn't accomplished any major objectives. Maybe we were winning, but it was still too early in the ballgame to count their side out. Battalion headquarters had captured documents two days earlier that said Phase III of the Viet Cong's country-wide offensive was to begin yesterday and if it turned out to be anything like phases I and II, we were in for trouble. I tried not to let the fear that gnawed at my stomach get to me, but there was no denying that it was there. Last night we received a dozen rounds of 60mm mortars and even though we had suffered only minor casualties, one of the rounds had hit the three-quarter parked next to our bunker, flattening all the tires. The force of the explosion had shook the FDC, rattling its walls. I wondered when one would come with my name on it.

We began passing an abnormal number of Vietnamese civilians pouring down the road leading west to Cu Chi. I assumed they were refugees seeking safety. With Cu Chi being mortared or rocketed nearly every night, I wondered if the compound there was any safer than their own villages. I had heard that the VC were forcing civilians to carry mortars and weapons for them, so maybe it wasn't. At least they would be free from that. I wondered, though, how many of these refugees were really Viet Cong, trying to infiltrate the cities. There was no way to know. No way to tell them apart. I wondered if we would make it to Cu Chi safely. Convoys had become a tempting target for the Viet Cong.

As our convoy drew near the outskirts of Tan Hoa an explosion rocked the area. As the convoy shuddered to a halt, automatic weapons fire exploded from an ambush site 30 meters off to the right of the road. RPGs slammed into the 2½-ton trucks leading the convoy, setting off secondary explosions which blackened the sky.

A godawful panic tore at my insides as I dropped to the floor of the truck bed and scrambled to its side. I could hear another salvo of explosions near the front of the convoy, this time closer to our position. Over everything else, I could hear the familiar clack-clack-clack of an AK-47. They're assaulting the convoy! Jesus Christ! I don't want to die! I could hear all kinds of shit going off as the convoy began returning fire but I was too paralyzed to move. Suddenly, the gun crew began leaping over the tailgate, bounding out the back. They tore at the howitzer, trying to unhitch it from the truck and bring it to bear on the enemy location. Swinging my M-16 into position and getting ready to fire, I pushed myself up and peered cautiously over the side. I didn't see anything; there wasn't a damn enemy in sight. Two APCs bounded across an open field, firing into a bamboo hedgerow. I didn't hear any more explosions or AK fire.

Although the ambush had been sprung only minutes ago I knew that it was probably already over. I crawled over to the front of the truck and propped my shoulder against the cab. Lighting a cigarette, I kept my eyes and M-16 trained on the ambush site, watching as the APCs sprayed it with fire. In a few minutes the APCs began withdrawing and as soon as they were a safe distance away, artillery began to pound the area. I knew, however, that Charlie had all but disappeared. Still, we kept under cover and waited while gunships swept the area and the APCs and infantry elements cleared the adjoining woodline. Forty-five minutes later I watched the APCs drag in one gook. They had the body tied to a rope and I could see him bouncing in the air as the APC rumbled across the field. I didn't know whether he was alive. Luckily, we had only suffered minor casualties, but major damage had been done to two trucks and one APC. We had to sit tight until two more trucks arrived to replace them. We got into Cu Chi about four hours later.

On February 25, with only 12 hours of daylight remaining, we were frantically racing to reposition our fire support base again. We had barely been in our last position long enough to set up a shower or develop a routine before moving. We started the task of carving out another base called Polaski II. I could feel the eyes of the enemy, watching, waiting, as we worked into the night.

Contact with the enemy was beginning to slow. Infantry elements began penetrating deeper into areas of previous stiff resistance. Infantry elements were now taking along a 105 howitzer on their sweeps to fire directly into heavily entrenched enemy positions, areas which previously resisted penetration by ground soldiers or APCs. Aggressive combat sweeps in the southern portion of the 1st Brigade's TAOI were making little contact so their remaining three battalions joined us.

With deeper penetration into enemy held territory and additional ground troops, we began reporting more findings. There was an increase in the number of dead Vietnamese in NVA uniform.

But the war wasn't the only thing changing. I was too. The ever present threat of death had prompted me to do a lot of heavy thinking, which in turn was causing me to make some difficult decisions. By now, rank didn't mean shit to me. Whether a person was a corporal, a sergeant or an officer meant little; it was whether he knew his job and could do it. That's all that mattered. Rank didn't stop bullets and stripes offered little protection from death. If a person was dependable, reliable under fire, fair and honest, then I respected him. It didn't make a difference if he was black, white, commissioned or noncommissioned. I followed orders, but only if I could see that the person giving them knew what the hell he was talking about. Back in the States I had been held in the grip of fear that extracted instant obedience from everyone. But here, in the face of death, *that* fear was slowly eroding. After all, what could they do, send me to Vietnam? I wasn't openly defiant, but I was becoming more outspoken. I could see I was not alone. There was a growing undercurrent of suspicion and unrest.

Some of the guys had a problem with my attitude, especially Vechione. He had worked hard to get where he was and liked to swing his weight around, and friction between us frequently surfaced. Tempers flared when we were short on sleep. I let most everything he said fly over my head because I found his threats mostly empty. You just didn't fight with someone you might have to depend on to save your life. You really couldn't risk alienating anyone, nor could you go crying to your superiors. If you couldn't handle the conflict yourself, nobody wanted you crying on his shoulder. The inability to command men was just interpreted as another sign of weakness and a detriment.

What bothered me more was the hostility that was developing between shifts. Ill feelings grew whenever there was an inequitable work load, and that occurred often, especially when we had to move. And we were moving a lot. We had made 19 moves in the last two months, 11 of them in February. The night shift, of which I was a part, constantly ended up losing more sleep and had to do a greater amount of the physical labor. Even Vanous, who I had thought was a close friend, became defensive, lashing out at others on my shift because of the way Vechione and Lee rode him. Lee and Vechione, fired by resentment, rarely missed an opportunity to poke at the other shift. It reminded me of high school, where rivalry and that good ole competitive spirit were often an acceptable way of disguising the harsh and vindictive petty jealousies that existed.

I was hurt by the harsh words I was often pummeled with. We stabbed at them, they stabbed at us. It was a demoralizing, petty cycle that we had gotten into and I didn't like it. But there wasn't much I could do about it. I had never been a peacemaker and I wasn't about to launch a new career here.

As February drew to a close it had been six days since a move and things were returning to some sense of normality—if there was any such thing. I finally got the opportunity to wash and change clothes. I had even been catching up on sleep, at least when the enemy allowed it. The Viet Cong continued to harass us, keeping us awake at nights by dropping in two or three mortars, once or twice a night. We never knew when they might precede a major ground assault so we generally stayed on the alert till morning. And I mean "on the alert"! Exploding mortars had the same effect on your system as dropping amphetamines. The adrenalin rush kept me plenty alert. I sure as hell didn't want to get caught napping.

We continued to make daily contact. The VC sometimes put up stiff resistance and sometimes just split up and disappeared. Something was changing for sure, but I couldn't quite put my finger on it. In some areas the VC were renewing strong defensive tactics and in others they were on the offensive again. Cu Chi and other major bases were still being rocketed every night. Captured documents indicated another major assault, but so far it hadn't materialized.

Meanwhile, we were having to make some adjustments ourselves. Division was demanding greater diligence on the part of the infantry. Recent operations were showing that many supposedly unoccupied areas were really not what they had appeared to be. With patient probing of these areas, ground troops were uncovering many concealed tunnels, bunkers and spider holes. Command said that it might be necessary to spend nearly as much time searching for enemy positions as the enemy spent constructing them, because the positions were generally there. D Troop had killed or captured 15 Viet Cong searching the more obvious places such as wells and stream beds inch by inch. In most cases they were not required to fire a shot and suffered no friendly casualties. Almost without exception, POWs stated that there were more VC hiding in the area being searched. Sometimes as many as 60 Viet Cong were in an area where only three or four were killed or captured. They were masters at camouflage.

Our counter-mortar program began changing also. We now laid four of our howitzers on specific counter-mortar targets and used only two to fire H & I's. As soon as we received incoming the guns immediately loaded and fired. Within seconds of our receiving fire, we were returning fire to areas that had been targeted as likely launching spots. Apparently it was working because when the infantry swept those areas in the mornings, they sometimes came across blood soaked bandages or graves near where our rounds had landed.

Harassment and interdiction fires began to be cut down. This was not due so much to their ineffectiveness as it was to an increasingly critical attitude on the part of the South Vietnamese government due to civilian complaints. Up to now the areas established as Free Fire Zones had been unchallenged. After dusk you could fire at anything that moved in them because you were damn sure they were Viet Cong. Now, under pressure from the South Vietnamese, these zones were dwindling and with them our target areas. Most of the guys interpreted division's response as a negative. To us it simply meant greater freedom for enemy movement and some American having to pay for it with his life somewhere down the line. We felt our hands slowly being tied.

Mishaps were also on the increase. There had been at least five instances where artillery fire had fallen on friendly forces. The infantry we supported had alone reported three KIAs and seven WIAs from friendly fire. Like before, some of the mistakes had to do with a breakdown in communications, often in the radio relay of what areas were No Fire Zones and what were Free Fire Zones.

Sometimes infantry elements failed to report their night locations or did so incorrectly and were mistakenly shelled as Viet Cong. Sometimes casualties resulted from shelling which had to be brought down directly on our own men to save their bases from being completely overrun. Either way, with three full brigades of U.S. infantry, artillery, engineers, mechanized armor, tanks and helicopters operating in an area roughly thirty miles square, their zig-zagging, criss-crossing, hopscotching and end-running eventually produced some mistakes. Out of the 400,000 soldiers now serving in Vietnam, I could have sworn that most of them were in the III Corp area. It was hard to believe that less than 25 percent of them were even in the field.

Luckily, only one of the mishaps involved our battery. But even then it hadn't been our mistake. A forward observer who was correcting fire for his unit misjudged his calculations and called in artillery less than 50 meters from his own troops. Anything less than 250 meters produced backsplash of some kind. I didn't envy Myers' position at all. Being responsible for the accuracy of all our fire was a heavy load. It would be his ass if anything went wrong.

By the beginning of March we had absorbed the full force of the enemy's blows and were beginning to move from a defensive posture to an offensive one. The second phase of the enemy offensive had begun to show signs of weakness. We hoped this was an indication that the enemy had deployed its main thrust and was beginning to retreat. It was still difficult to sort out the full impact of what had started during Tet. From all the sources I could gather, the enemy had made deep penetrations into almost every major ARVN stronghold, and in many instances had kicked the shit out of our own forces. But for the most part, we had thrown back the enemy's move to occupy almost all major cities even though there were still some large battles going on in the Northern I Corp. Hair-raising stories of enemy battles began filtering down the grapevine as we interchanged support with infantry and mechanized units in our area. The strength of the enemy had come as a total surprise to all of us. If the end of the war was near, if enemy resistance was being broken down through the new pacification program, I wondered why we were getting our asses kicked.

A credibility gap was widening and I wondered just what the hell command was basing its information on, or if they just really weren't in touch with what was going on in the field. I began to wonder why the body count was purposely being inflated. Heretofore both body count and possibles had been reported as separate figures; now headquarters was demanding they be reported as one. This sudden shift in policy made me wonder if the brass weren't under a lot of pressure to prove that we were winning the war. As far as I could tell, that meant playing a numbers game, to attempt to demonstrate that we were killing more of them than they were of us. As long as their death rate was higher, we were winning. I was grasping a pressing lesson that had been and would periodically be repeated in my life: People in authority couldn't be trusted. The higher the rank, the more the deception, and the greater the abuse of power. I became increasingly cautious about whom I trusted and began paying more attention to the statistics and information that passed through my hands. I figured it might make the difference in my surviving the war.

A decrease in enemy activity also led to a decrease in our moves. I could hardly believe the stroke of luck we were experiencing; we had been in one position nearly two whole weeks.

Enemy activity had by no means ceased, but at least we weren't constantly fearful of running into some large enemy force that would wipe us out. It brought some relief but it didn't obliterate the tension that hung over the base every night.

With three different battalions operating in our area, we were being called on daily to give direct fire support. Only now, contact was mainly with small groups or occasional snipers. Since we were less than 4000 meters from the Saigon River we were often called on to shell sampans. The 3rd of the 22nd Infantry was conducting extensive daylight ambush patrols on the river and if they couldn't knock out the sampans with LAWs—small, lightweight rockets—they called us in to do the job.

The engineers were also conducting Rome Plow operations near us, tearing up VC or NVA base camp areas. They were demolishing about 15 acres a day and often came under sniper fire, or encountered small VC forces when they uncovered bunker complexes or tunnels.

The grunts and the mech had killed or uncovered graves containing 126 bodies, but had paid a high cost in doing so. They had suffered 120 casualties. Six men had drowned just the other day while crossing the river to set up an ambush site. Self-inflicted foot wounds, I noticed, were on the increase.

With routine firing taking place every day I kept close to the FDC bunker and by now had mastered the chart operations and was helping Lee in laying and firing the guns. I became completely familiar with radio operations and communicative language requirements, having memorized all the code words and helped to decode all intelligence data. I observed both the team chief and the lieutenant as they ran the new FADAC computer, but was thankful I hadn't been asked to operate it. My only other responsibility was to maintain the generators. I made sure that we always had a supply of fuel and oil, and did preventive maintenance on them whenever necessary.

Once the brass exhausted their seemingly endless load of work trivia and we had beefed up our security by adding a fourth layer of sandbags to our bunkers, we were on our own, free to do whatever could be done in an area approximately forty yards across. Unfortunately there was very little to do. Boredom quickly set in.

I used the free time I had to empty the ammo box that contained my primary possessions and wash my alternate set of fatigues. I wrote letters to Deb and Diane. Even one to Kim, though she had never answered any of my previous ones. Kim was my secret love. She had stolen my heart the first time I met her, but I had loved her from afar. I had kept my love for her a secret while in Oregon, not wanting to risk rejection from someone who was as obviously popular as she was. But here, the risk seemed much less, so I had written to her often, unburdening my heart. I wondered why she never wrote back. I assumed it must have been because she didn't want to have anything to do with me.

I read all the magazines I could scrounge off others and repeatedly cleaned my M-16. I scrounged up enough ammo box covers to lay a wood floor in my bunker and organized all my belongings neatly, and then simply ran out of things to do.

I slipped off my rubber thongs, pulled my boots on and, cradling my M-16 in one arm, made my way towards White's section. Dust choked my feet as I walked past two empty 105 shell casings that were sticking up out of the ground, improvised urinals. Near them, three holes were dug on top of a rice paddy berm, their openings neatly surrounded with small stacks of sandbags. Our toilets. An inverted can stood upright by each opening, undoubtedly salvaged from the mess tent. They were stamped "Lard" in black. They were excellent for keeping the toilet paper dry. If you needed to shit you hung your ass over a sandbag not ten or fifteen feet from the nearest bunker and like everyone else, bared yourself publicly. There was no privacy in Vietnam. I couldn't help smiling as I walked by. Public defecation had been difficult at first but Nam was providing a number of challenging experiences.

My thoughts flashed back to junior high school. Those days of emerging puberty and self-identity—it seemed like years ago now, but the ridicule I had been exposed to still haunted me. I could still hear the laughter and feel the sting of embarrassment as I thought about how the other guys had teased me about my weight, or about the fact that I had no pubic hair. I could hear the taunts about how short my penis had been. It was still hard for me to bare myself publicly, and especially hard to urinate in public. Sometimes I still tensed up so much I couldn't go, even when I had to. I couldn't count the times I had entered a bathroom to relieve myself and then, when someone else had entered the room, found it impossible. Once a stranger had jokingly asked me if I was "playing with myself" because it was taking me so long. More than once, I had faked going and left, only to return when the bathroom was empty. Here, I had little choice, and it was good for me. I wasn't a kid anymore!

Sweat trickled down my face and neck as I continued walking to White's area. The temperature was in the low hundreds. My salt tablets had become a regular part of my diet, just like the malaria tablets. I wondered if Les would have a cold beer. It had been three days since our last "sortie," and the meager supply of ice that had arrived nearly all went to the Mess Tent. What little was divided among us quickly melted. We hadn't enough to put in both coolers so we elected to mix lemonade in the Igloo. By the time the lemonade had been mixed, the ice had all melted. Still, cool lemonade was better than warm water or hot beer. I was thankful to have it.

I could see White holding on to the end of a huge metal rod as I approached. He and another crew member were pushing it in and out of the barrel of the howitzer, cleaning the bore. Others scrambled around the chamber, wiping it down and oiling the traversing mechanisms. White's face was sweaty and dirty. The muscles in his arms bulged.

"Hey, hippie!" he yelled when he saw me.

I watched as the others turned. Their faces betrayed a mixture of feelings. Les always called me hippie, even though he knew it infuriated some of the other guys, especially the jocks. But he did it because he personally identified with the movement.

I sat up on the sandbagged walls of the parapet and winked at him. "Hey, what's happening? You look like you're enjoying yourself!"

"Hey, man," Les laughed. "You just don't know what it's like to work. You guys have got it made. Why don't you get your butt over here and help me out?"

"No way, man," I replied. "You can handle it. Besides, you're almost done. Why should I get all greasy just to help you get done five minutes early?"

Les laughed. We continued to shoot the bull until he finished.

"Hey, gimme a minute to wash up and then I'll introduce you to our new gun sergeant," White said. He slipped into the personnel bunker. A few minutes later he appeared, dragging a water can behind him. Turning his helmet upside down, he filled it half full of warm water. "Hey, Sarge," he yelled into the bunker, "c'mon out here and meet one of the guys from the FDC."

As the sergeant's head emerged from the bunker, White introduced us.

"Sergeant Rhodes," he said while drying his head with a towel, "PFC Olsen."

Instantly the name and the face connected. I felt a sudden anger rise and then a feeling of confusion.

"Shittt! I don't believe it!" I said. The words just seemed to pop out of my mouth. "What the fuck are you doing here, Sergeant? You remember me don't you?" I asked, drawing my words out slowly.

His face began to turn pink as he stammered, "I, ahh . . ."

"Hell, I know Sergeant Rhodes," I interrupted, turning to White. "We met in A.I.T. at Fort Sill, where I did my gun bunny training. We're old friends," I said sarcastically. "Right, Sarge?"

By now, Sergeant Rhodes had regained his composure. As he looked from White to me, I could see a kind of helpless look in his eyes. He stammered slightly, then spoke directly to me.

"Uh, I remember," he said. "Hey, I'm sorry, OK?"

An apology was the last thing I expected to hear. It took me by surprise. I could see that he really felt awkward. I was sure that our meeting was as much a shock to him as it was to me. I decided to just let it pass.

"Hey, that's all right, man. Everything worked out O.K.," I said. "Things are cool now, O.K.?"

I could see visible relief on his face. It was like he had just been pardoned. Even I felt better. But it didn't mean I had forgotten what had happened.

It had been the latter part of September when our paths first crossed. Our company was just finishing the last two of ten weeks of A.I.T. at Fort Sill,

Oklahoma, when he and two other sergeants were assigned to our training unit as drill instructors. All three of them were fresh out of Vietnam; they stayed drunk most of the time, even on duty.

It had been obvious to everyone in our training unit that most of us would be assigned duty in Vietnam. Few people were anxious to go. Nearly everyone I talked to was hoping for stateside duty or duty in Germany. Any place but Vietnam! A couple of times I had heard some of the trainees asking the Nam vets what it was like over there, but they wouldn't even talk about it. They just made comments like, "It was hell!" or "You ain' coming back man so you'd better write your will." It made me angry to hear that kind of shit. Especially when they said it so flippantly. It was like a joke to them.

I was frightened enough the way it was. I didn't need to hear someone taunting me. I didn't want to go to Vietnam. I was already feeling the fool for ever volunteering for the draft. I hated every minute of the Army and for the first time I began to be aware of the consequences of joining. I was afraid for my life. That same fear weighed heavily on most all of us. As each day drew nearer I wondered how prepared I was to meet death. It filtered into our conversations nearly every day. There were rumors that those graduating in the top percentile of their class would have the best chances of being assigned stateside duty, so I made application for one of the clerk positions that was opening up in headquarters battery of our present unit. I wanted that position badly and was doing my best not to fuck up so I would be considered.

During the last few days of training there remained little for us to do but fulfill our daily routine, part of which was our morning exercises. It had become the responsibility of the new DIs to take us over to the PT Field for exercise. That's where I first met Rhodes.

On one day, what was regularly an hour long exercise began to last not one, but two, and then three hours. As the sun climbed to its zenith and the temperature with it, we were quickly becoming exhausted. We were being forced to run lap after lap around the field. As time went on, the men began to protest. Grumbling intensified. To make matters worse, the drill instructors laughed about it. As we ran past them, they said things like "This will be a good lesson for them, this'll teach 'em" and "Shit, they ain't seen nothing yet." Then, they began riding behind us in the jeep, jeering and egging us on. They were sharing some kind of private joke at our expense.

When the running finally ended they made us fall back into PT formation for "jumping jacks." They were going to work us until we dropped to see if we could take it. From the front of each line they randomly selected four squad leaders to take positions on top of the four large wooden platforms in front of the company, where they could lead the exercises. When they pointed me out, I cringed, but made no attempt to hide my anger. I didn't want to be one of those who would have to set the pace. I had been there before. But there was nothing I could do about it; I simply had to follow orders.

"Get your ass in gear, private!" Sergeant Rhodes screamed at me as I made my way to the platform. Fuck you, asshole, I protested silently. I didn't like what these bastards were up to and I knew on the platform there would be no place for me to slack off or hide.

Sergeant Rhodes followed me up the stairs yelling obscenities in my ear. Taking a leisurely stance beside each of us squad leaders, the drill instructors began calling off cadence. Each of us squad leaders doggedly slapped our hands and feet together, trying our best to keep up with them. The exercise went on and on until I could feel the muscles in my arms tremble and my legs cramp. Then Sergeant Rhodes began calling cadence faster. Most of the men on the field could no longer keep up and had quit completely. Some were on their knees; others were lying on the ground. Some had quit even trying to raise their arms anymore. They just shuffled their feet, trying to keep up. The drill instructors exchanged glances, grinning.

I was filled with rage. What the fuck was life about anyway, was it just a series of injustices? A succession of cruel jokes that people played on one another? How can these guys be allowed to treat us this way! Was I gonna let these bastards get away with this? What happens if I jump this son-of-a-bitch? Will they put me in jail? Probably! Jail time doesn't count against the time I have to serve in the Army. It would mean I would just have to endure it longer. What the fuck was I gonna do? Didn't these guys understand the seriousness? Do they really think they're helping us? I was in a quandary. No matter what I did I was gonna end up on the short side of the stick. Man, what had I gotten myself into? The Army was like one big mind fuck.

All of a sudden the situation seemed more funny than cruel. It was downright ridiculous! In fact, too ridiculous to be true! I started laughing. It was either that or I was gonna cry.

Sergeant Rhodes, who had been standing on the edge of the stage cussing out one of the trainees, suddenly stopped and turned around. "What the fuck is so funny soldier?" he shouted.

I stopped laughing immediately, but I couldn't stop smiling. I tried to, sensing the danger, but I couldn't. I shouted back, "Nothing, sergeant!"

"I want to know what you think is so funny, fuck-head!" he yelled back at me, his face not six inches from my nose.

"I said nothing, sergeant," I yelled, staring out over the formation. I still couldn't stop smiling, but I didn't want to aggravate him further by looking him directly in the eyes. He might see it as a challenge. I was trying to appease him but he wouldn't let it rest. By now the rest of the company was beginning to stop and listen. I stopped doing the jumping jacks, sensing it was ridiculous for me to continue.

"I didn't tell you to stop, did I shithead?" Rhodes shouted.

"No, sergeant," I replied and began jumping again.

By this time the other two sergeants had leapt from their platforms and were heading our way. Now I was in deep shit. My smile suddenly faded. I had a choice of either cowering before these bastards in front of the company, so they wouldn't put me through any more abuse, or I had to stand up to them and possibly get court-martialed for disrespect towards authority. I was cornered. I was going to be the loser no matter what. Shit, I thought, this wasn't even a fair game the Army was playing. The rules were always in their favor! I could feel my heart begin to sink. Here I was, again! Up on stage about to be made a fool of in front of the whole company.

One of the sergeants leapt onto the stage and glared at me, hands on his hips. The other one followed. Another remained on the ground, yelling at the company to get back doing exercises.

"This fuck-head thinks something is funny," Sergeant Rhodes explained, "but he doesn't want to tell me what it is."

"You want to tell *me* what's so funny, shithead?" the other sergeant screamed, "or are we going to have to kick your ass a little bit?"

Cripes, I thought, these guys really mean it. I'm gonna get into trouble whether I speak or keep quiet. O.K., I'll tell you bastards, I thought. I've got nothing to lose. Only when I do, I'm gonna let everybody else know what I'm thinking and saying. If I go down, everybody else is gonna know exactly why. I'm not gonna leave anything I say to chance just in case somebody needs to verify it in the future. Besides, you're always saying you like our responses loud and clear.

"Are you disobeying a direct order, Olsen?" one of the sergeants yelled. "You tell us why you're smiling or your ass is grass. You hear!"

All right, I thought, you bastards asked for it. Continuing my jumping jacks, I lifted my voice. My answer rang out over the parade area. "I'm smiling because of the stupidity of your behavior!" I shouted. "I'm smiling because this is the most asinine thing I've experienced since being in the Army!"

His reaction was immediate, as was the reaction from the rest of the troops — but they were worlds apart. A roar of laughter spilled from the formation, but the sergeant's mouth dropped in surprise! I could see my answer was unexpected. In three quick steps the three of them surrounded me. Sergeant Rhodes had just lost face in front of the whole company and he wasn't about to let it pass. I stopped doing jumping jacks and braced myself.

"O.K., you smart ass," one sergeant said in a low voice, "I'm gonna teach you a lesson you won't ever forget." Grabbing me firmly by both arms, he and Rhodes lifted me off the deck and hustled me off the stage. Down the stairs we went, into the jeep. In an unrelenting verbal harangue, they cussed me up and down while transporting me to the commanding officer's building and had me placed under arrest. While a military guard stood over me, I sat outside the office, waiting while the drill instructors conferred with the CO, explaining the charges.

I was scared but I wasn't about to let it show. I was pissed, too. Their behavior only added fuel to an already smoldering resentment I felt. A few short months ago, in Basic, I had been threatened with an Article 15 under similar circumstances. Fortunately, I had been exonerated but I hadn't forgotten the circumstances.

After the drill instructors left I was questioned by the captain, who explained the gravity of the charges against me. After a stiff reprimand, he placed me under house arrest and restricted me to my barracks room where I was to stay until he could decide my case. I sat inside the barracks, stewing, while the rest of the company finished PT. When the company was dismissed, acting platoon sergeant PFC Moore came into my room and tried to console me. He had called a meeting of all acting platoon sergeants and squad leaders, all men who had graduated from the LPC academy. They had gone as a group to see the commanding officer. They felt I was being unjustly treated and had been since we were assigned to this unit. They told the captain that I had been the top graduate in the LPC school and had been promised the position of acting company commander, but that I hadn't been given it. They told him they felt I had already been screwed over and this was like adding insult to injury. They protested the planned court-martial. The captain had promised to take their protest into consideration and Moore assured me that the group had decided they would do whatever was necessary to back me up on this issue.

"Look," he said, "we don't care whether you were given your rightful position of authority here or not. You proved yourself to us in LPC school and we still see you as the leader of our company. I'm just sorry you got screwed over. You already know how bad I felt when I was assigned acting platoon sergeant and you didn't get it. That's why I asked you if you would take a squad leader's position. It's just this fuckin' Army man; you never know from one day to the next what they're gonna do to fuck you over and you can never take them at their word."

His conversation did little to relieve my anger but at least I didn't feel alone. In fact, I was pleasantly surprised by the willingness of the other leaders to rally behind me. I had never heard of anybody doing what they had. It was really unexpected!

After two days of house arrest, I was ordered to the captain's office. "Olsen," the captain said, "you are really fortunate that your own men and the men of this company seem to hold you in such high regard. I've decided not to press charges against you but it was only because of the strength of the testimony of these other men. There was no excuse for the insubordination you showed! I wouldn't tolerate such behavior by any man toward me and I won't allow any of it in my command. Do you understand? You were guilty of insubordination and not following orders. You're just damn lucky I don't throw the book at you. It won't be that way next time! If you ever pull another stunt like this one I'll bust your ass so fast it'll leave your head spinning, and when you get out of jail you won't pull anything but shit duty for as long as you're under my command. If I was you I would watch your step and keep your nose clean, because we'll be keeping an eye on you. It's unfortunate, because you were being considered for the position of company clerk. Now, am I understood?"

"Yes, sir."

"Then you're dismissed!"

I stood up, clicked my heels together and saluted. Then turned and left. All the time he had been talking I had said nothing. I had sat stone-faced and took it all in. Say your spiel, I said to myself, and get it over with. Nobody believes this bullshit, especially me. You bastards are all alike! Covering one another's asses regardless of whether you're right or wrong. Instead of dispensing justice you make me feel as if you're doing me a favor. Well fuck you! All I know is that I won, motherfucker, and you won't get another chance to have me in this position again.

As I left the office, the only regret I had was that this had blown my chances of being assigned a stateside job. There was little hope now of being sent anyplace but Vietnam. I wondered if I should go AWOL.

That was how it had ended! Now here I was again, face to face with Sergeant Rhodes. But I no longer felt threatened by his presence and decided it would be best for all of us if I just forgot about it. It seemed so long ago now anyway. It wouldn't do me or anybody else any good to hold a grudge against him. I needed his help as badly as he needed mine. Besides, he seemed sincerely sorry for what had happened so I just let it go. Sergeant Rhodes slipped back into the bunker to get a couple of beers. It gave us both a chance to regroup. We shot the bull for awhile, then he left. If not friends, at least we had chosen not to continue as enemies.

That evening White and I walked out to the perimeter. He had discovered that an old stateside friend was serving with the mechanized infantry set up around our perimeter. I made sure I had my M-16 and we set off to visit.

It took a couple of attempts to locate his armored personnel carrier in the dark, but once we were there, the reunion was joyous. We crawled into the back of the APC and he raised the back door. The door had been down to cool the interior so it wasn't bad when we first went in. As soon as the door was secured, he hastily arranged ammo boxes for us to sit on and switched on a night light, bathing the inside in a warm glow.

"Hey, man," White's friend said, "you want to smoke some dynamite weed? We picked it out in the field."

"Far out!" White replied.

"You mean you actually picked it in the woods?" I asked.

"Shit yeah, man," he replied. "We don't often run across it growing wild, but every now and then we do when we get next to the jungle."

"Heavy duty, man," I said.

Within minutes the inside of the APC was filled with the sweet aroma of marijuana. This had only been the third time I had smoked in country, but I was developing a strong penchant for getting stoned. Man, it beat the hell out of alcohol! I had experimented with pot before being drafted, and had smoked it once in Basic and once in A.I.T., and I liked the euphoric feeling it gave. The more I smoked the more easily recognizable were the changes going on. It was easy. I mean, I felt at ease when I got stoned. Relaxed. Happy! Sometimes I simply laughed for no reason other than the joy I felt as my spirits were lifted. Sometimes I even got the giggles! And for that moment, it was easier to forget that a war was raging around me, or sometimes within me. It momentarily relieved the constant tension I felt in these beautiful, yet treacherous surroundings.

As the night grew quiet, we sat silent ourselves, listening intently to a myriad of inner thoughts, poignantly aware of our own inner feelings. The stillness was broken only by occasional whispers, and flaming Zippos.

In Nam, everyone had a Zippo. Personal engravings covered their silver cases with every symbol and phrase imaginable. It was the one thing that was ours, that didn't belong to the Army. We could put whatever we wanted on it, and most people did. Any defacement of Army apparel could be met with strict disciplinary action, but our Zippos were ours. Many of them carried antimilitary sentiments. Mine had a simple peace symbol engraved on one side and my name on the other. If I ever got blown away I wanted them to find at least something that would say who I had been besides my dog tags.

It was close to midnight when White and I left the APC. Walking back to our position, we talked in whispers, commenting on some of the stories the mech guys had told us, wondering what it would be like to serve with them. I thought it was safer than being a ground pounder but I didn't envy them. I felt more secure around six howitzers than around six APCs, at least during daylight hours. Still, there were some definite advantages in being mobile.

Leaving White at his section, I continued on down to the ammo bunker. At their listening post I dropped down and leaned against its sandbagged walls. It was incredibly relaxing just to sit outside and look up at the stars. I had never seen so much unobstructed space . . . so large, so still, so quiet . . .

Suddenly a shadowy figure emerged from the LP. "Hey, Olsen! Is that you man?" exclaimed Wheatstraw, startled by my unexpected presence. "Whatcha doin' out here, boy?" His words rose and fell in sing-song.

"Just takin' it easy. What's happening?"

"Hey, man, c'mon ovah to the personnel bunker. We's got some sweet sounds. That man Johnson, he brought with him some of that livin' sound of the queen of soul herself. Can you dig it?"

"Hey, man, you got it!" I grabbed my M-16 and followed him over to the bunker. Crouching down, I slipped inside. It was pitch black. I propped myself and my M-16 against the wall, and dropped my helmet between my legs.

"Where's Santiago and the Sarge?" I asked.

"They're on guard duty, and it's a good thing," giggled LeRoy. "This brother's got some sweet, sweet sounds from back home, and that's where I be now." Aretha Franklin filled the room.

I was no stranger to the sound of Motown. There were as many hits on the charts by the black Detroit sound as there were by white groups. My taste for Top 40 had slowly dissolved during my junior and senior years in high school when Bobby Ellegard, my best friend, turned me on to folk music, jazz, and rhythm and blues. Through the influence of his older brother's record collection, both he and I were exposed to a world of music that had lain like buried treasure, unopened and unappreciated. It was there that I had first heard the music of Bob Dylan, Pete

146

Seeger, Woody Guthrie, Cisco Houston, Joan Baez, Judy Collins and the like. It was also where I discovered the likes of Leadbelly, Jimmy Reed, B.B. King, Bo Diddley, Elmo James, Bobby Bland, Sam and Dave, James Brown and a host of others who were singing the blues. And then there was this whole other world of music I had never heard called Jazz. I found myself instantly liking the music of Thelonius Monk, Jimmy Smith, Miles Davis and people like Nancy Wilson, who put pop singers like The Supremes to shame. I had been a devout fan of rock 'n' roll, loving Elvis Presley and people like Buddy Holly, but here was where their music had originated. The blacks had it in the bag. Their music had emotional depth. The blues weren't very intellectual, or political, like folk music had become, but they reached an area deep inside of me that I knew was very much alive, though long ago buried. I felt the way Aretha sang, but my emotions were largely kept under lock and key.

Aretha's voice floated through my head. It was like a river to my heart. When she sang "I say a little prayer for you...," I wanted it to be for me. If no one else knew how I really felt, it was comforting to think she did.

It soon became evident that we would be moving again. U.S. forces to the north were experiencing heavy contact. The grapevine was buzzing with rumors of relocation. Bravo Battery had been attacked last night and was involved in a battle which the Viet Cong had carried into the day. That frightened me. If the VC thought they were strong enough to conduct a day assault on a fire base, then we were really in trouble.

When the orders finally came to relocate, we were already prepared. In two hours the base was stripped and our convoy lined up and ready to move.

As we traveled across the trails and roads which led to Cu Chi, I studied the Vietnamese, watching face after face of brown, wide-eyed villagers. I wondered again how many were simply Viet Cong. Some, dressed in familiar black pajamas, squatted in the ditches relieving themselves. It made me poignantly aware of the cultural differences and the barriers of ignorance and fear that kept us apart. Barriers which kept us from really knowing one another. We often passed ARVN soldiers walking hand-in-hand and I wondered if the insults and accusations hurled at them by GIs were really accurate, or whether there was a difference here that we knew nothing about. Maybe they were like brothers, I didn't know. Their customs and philosophies were still foreign to me. Maybe we were misinterpreting their behavior. After all, what was wrong with showing affection for another man if you really cared about him. The guys I knew never hugged one another. It would be like admitting you were a homosexual. But I wondered if the complete lack of affection that characterized the lives of American men was really the way we were supposed to behave. I ask too many questions, I thought. This searching for answers was becoming confusing. Threatening!

As we passed through the villages I noticed an increasing display of hostility by GIs toward the Vietnamese. More of the guys had taken to throwing candy, shell casings and C rations hard at the women and children. "O.K., Gook!" I heard one guy yell. "So you want some chop-chop, do ya? Here, take this!" It made me sad but I said nothing. Some of the guys laughed. Others joined in the throwing. I was torn, but I knew my allegiance had to be with my own men. Besides, I rationalized, most of them were probably VC. Anyway, these people were just ignorant, backward peasants. They didn't even have toilets. They had no technology, no roads, no telephones, no televisions, no radios, refrigerators, cars or trains. They had to be backward. Years behind other civilizations. We were the ones who were civilized! In spite of all I told myself I could not silence nagging feelings that my rationalizations didn't make any difference. They were still human beings. Their lives had to be worth as much to them as mine was to me. They hurt and cried, bled and died, the same as us. Underneath it all we couldn't really be that different.

I lost track of the passing time. The next thing I knew the convoy was slowing to enter Cu Chi village. As we lumbered through I took my weapon off safety, aware of the danger around civilians. Not allowing eye contact with any of the villagers I focused my attention instead on a panoramic view, looking for any threatening movement. Only when a gook was close enough that I could tell he carried no weapons, did I ever relax my vigilance and allow eye contact. Only then, but not for long.

148

IV OPERATION QUYET THANG

10

11 March 1968
Cu Chi

An overnight stay in Cu Chi made it possible to obtain highly valued luxuries at the PX: magazines, cigarettes, lighter fluid, books, thongs and other delicacies. But the real biggie was the opportunity to replenish our beer and soda supply.

"It burns my ass," I said to Vanous as we finished unloading and setting up the FDC. "We're laying our lives on the line for our country and aren't even good enough to warrant hard liquor."

"It's these pussy-footin' O.C.S. lifers that make the rules," spat Vanous, "and generally only to fatten their own stomachs."

"I don't know why the fuck an officer who is sitting back on his ass doing base duty should be treated any different than we are," I said. "This fuckin' Army has got to be the ideal class system and we're supposed to represent a classless society. What a fuckin' laugh that is. Fuckin' slaves is all we are man! No rights and no rule, and to top it off, led by a bunch of self-serving shitheads who don't give a damn about anything but their next grade."

"Fuck it," said Vanous. "It don't mean shit. There's nothing we can do about it till we get out. Besides, I'm getting short. Only 235 days left," he laughed.

"C'mon," I said, "let's head down to Gun Three. I know a man down there that just might do us a favor."

Grabbing our gear we headed toward the perimeter. Even though we didn't have to carry our guns in base camp, it was now second nature.

"Hey, White," I yelled, approaching his position. "Sergeant Rhodes still around?"

"Yeah, man. He's in a squad leader's briefing, but he should be back anytime. What's happening?"

"Well man, I thought I'd see if he would pick us up some hard liquor."

"Shit, man!" White said, "don't expect him to do shit, especially if it's against regulations. Besides, he can't buy it anyway. Only officers can."

Our conversation stopped abruptly. Sergeant Rhodes was approaching.

"Hey, Sarge," White said flippantly, "these guys wanna ask you a favor."

White stood back, smiling, waiting to see what our next move would be.

"Listen, sergeant," I began, "we were wondering if you would get us a bottle of hard liquor."

"Liquor!" he said. "The only place you can buy hard liquor and take it out is in the Saigon PX."

"Hey, c'mon Sarge, I know you can get it from the top or the sergeant major. All you gotta do is ask. That won't hurt nothing, will it?"

The top and the sergeant major both worked at the Officer's Club—they ran it, and they bartended. For the right amount of money, you could get nearly anything you wanted from them. I knew that Rhodes had connections. After all, this was his second tour here. He knew all the ropes by now.

"All right, what do you want?" he acquiesced.

White's jaw dropped! Vanous and I exchanged glances and then spoke almost simultaneously.

"Chivas Regal!" we exclaimed.

"You guys are gonna drink top of the line, huh? It's gonna be expensive."

"How much?"

"Not less than twenty-five dollars."

"Twenty-five dollars!" exclaimed Vanous. "That ought to be enough for two or three bottles!"

"Shit, just pay him the money, Vanous," I said. "You know the wheels have to be greased!"

"All right! Let's just get this over with," the sergeant interrupted.

"Hey wait, Sarge," said White, dashing into the bunker. "If you're gettin', I may as well get some too. I can always sell it in the field."

"Listen," said Sergeant Rhodes, "I won't be able to get it till this evening. I'm on resupply, but I'll drop over to the club as soon as I get a chance."

Snatching White's money the Sarge took off, heading toward the mess hall. He kicked up dust as he made his way across the parched clay.

"Phew! This place stinks," said White, mopping his forehead. "I can smell the fuel oil all over the place. I sure hope we aren't down wind tonight."

"It pisses me off," I started again. "I know that fat ass top is sitting back here in camp making money off the war! I haven't seen that bastard in the field since late November and then it was only for a few days."

"The sergeant major don't cotton much to field duty either," added Vanous; "he's only in the field when the resupply comes out, but he rarely stays overnight unless he has to."

"You should see those suckers," laughed White. "Why their bellies must weigh two hundred pounds alone. They certainly didn't get that way building bunkers or humpin' ammo."

Both the top and the sergeant major were obese. Their stomachs hung over their belts like potato sacks, and top's arms and buttocks bulged like balloons. While the sergeant major had some muscle it wasn't that way with top. His flesh was soft and flabby, his face puffy and flushed. These were our leaders, the top NCOs. They were just the opposite of everything the Army had said it stood for. They were neither physically fit nor virtuous. What a laugh! All those films we had been shown in Basic, the ones which talked about loyalty, courage, patriotism, honesty, service, morality and responsibility . . . I wondered how they expected anybody to fall for all that jive. It was only bullshit and propaganda. Noble words to help entrap the soul into slavery. Well, I wasn't gonna be trapped.

The *Stars and Stripes* lay in the corner and I got up to retrieve it. I needed something to read to help pass the time. It was nearly 0300 hours. I had been on duty since midnight and still had three hours to go.

The yellow light which hung from the ceiling bathed the FDC in a soft glow. Shadows danced on the floor and ceiling from the bugs darting around it. The evening shift had been quiet, almost too quiet. It was hard to stay awake. I thought about flicking on the radio, but I knew there wasn't anything on. Hell, there wasn't much worth listening to any time of the day. There was only one military station. The rest were all gook channels. If I got really bored, I would turn to one and listen to their strange music and try to pick out some of the words – but I had to be pretty bored. The only two programs worth listening to were "GO Radio," which played top 40, and the "Cris Noel Show," which had a female announcer. It was great just to hear an American female. Listening to her soft husky voice rekindled visions that were both sexual and emotional. Visions of past embraces, lingering kisses, the warmth of someone's touch. I never missed her program if I could help it but in the field it wasn't always possible to tune her in, especially with night discipline. Besides, I didn't own a radio. Dangerfield, who had one, listened mostly to country-and-western and kept it with him off shift. I thought about picking one up.

Glancing through the *Stars and Stripes* I scanned the headlines looking for any information about our division.

"Second Brigade Has Rich Rice Harvest" captioned the lead, showing a GI in fatigues humping a bag of rice on his shoulders. "The first major action of the Tet offensive for the 25th Division troops sent columns of cavalry streaming down Highway 1 towards the heavily besieged Tan Son Nhut Airbase. In brutal fighting the cavalry, aided by air strikes and artillery, pried the enemy away from the vital base and left more than 3,000 enemy bodies counted. Meanwhile the 2nd Brigade was drawn into the cauldron of fire near Hoc Mon as the enemy approached Saigon. There the 2nd Battalion 12th US Infantry Warriors killed twenty-two Viet Cong in a sharp fight. The same day, the 3rd Battalion 22nd US Infantry Regulars killed thirty enemy near Ap Cho. The Third Regulars also figured in a ten day battle to prevent 'Charlie' from cutting Highway 1. The Regulars won. Charlie lost among other things, 219 of his best fighters.

"Contact continued almost daily with well armed and disciplined Viet Cong and NVA soldiers, but, when the operation ended, Tropic Lightning forces had claimed more than 3,000 enemy soldiers. In the course of Operation Saratoga,

Tropic Lightning forces also captured a quarter of a million rounds of small arms ammunition and nearly nine tons of rice. They identified huge enemy tunnel complexes and generally destroyed much of the enemy's combat effectiveness. A new enemy, the North Vietnamese Army, had appeared on the scene but with courage and professional skills, the Tropic Lightning soldiers again won the day."

I stopped reading and looked at the front of the paper to read the date. It was current. Shit, I thought, I'd like to know who writes these stories. It sounds like a sequel from the Lone Ranger.

I looked back at the article. It had said Operation Saratoga, the operation we had finished a few days ago. What a line of bullshit.

If I remembered correctly, the total statistics the lieutenant said he had read while visiting division headquarters were slightly over 2,000 and those were from combined operations with the First Brigade. The 2nd Brigade had only reported a total of 876 KIAs and 184 of those were only possibles. I wondered who they were trying to fool, themselves or the public. But still, the lieutenant had said that command felt the large quantities of arms, ammunition and other supplies captured by 2nd Brigade units were rendering sustained enemy offensive operations in this area extremely difficult. There was talk the war would wind down now unless the enemy received a major resupply. In addition, the large number of documents captured would enable us to target their future operations. With the vast destruction of tunnel complexes and caches, command said the enemy had few secure base areas left.

Maybe it was true, but our statistics sure weren't meshing. I didn't have time to reflect on it though. Division accuracy wasn't my responsibility. They could make the figures say anything they wanted to; it still wouldn't change reality for us.

To keep Charlie on the move and deny him rest, the division had begun Operation Quyet Thang. We were expecting to end up in the Ho Bo Woods again since the operation would cover both the Hau Nghia Province and the western portion of Gia Dinh. Quyet Thang could be translated as "resolved to win" and was supposed to be billed as the largest combination of Free World forces since the war had begun. We were expected to work alongside ARVN forces again, and maybe even some Australians. Both the 2nd and 3rd brigades would be operating together to sweep the entire III Corp area. All I could see was that it would mean another series of endless moves, and exhaustion. The value of our running back and forth all over the area, first securing one place and then leaving it, only to return again made little sense.

I leafed through the paper looking for any news about the 9th Infantry Division, and Glover. They were apparently in the Mekong Delta. I had heard the shit was plenty deep there.

I wondered if Glover was all right. I really missed him. I could feel the loneliness and although I tried to shrug it off, I couldn't. It was nearly 0400 hours so I cracked open the cooler and sifted through the Ballantine Beer looking for a

Pabst. I couldn't stand the Ballantine. Neither could anyone else. Somebody high up must have been getting a kickback on the contract to supply it, because we always had more of that than anything else. You couldn't even give it away unless it was cold, and then you had to give it away on a hot day. Finding a Pabst, I pushed an opener through the top and sat back down.

I could see Lee looking at me out of the corner of his eyes. He was laying two of the guns on counter-mortar targets. It was against regulations to drink on duty but I didn't care. There was nothing going on and I'd be off shift in two hours. Besides, I knew that when a bout of loneliness was setting in, depression generally followed. I wasn't looking forward to being down in the dumps again. I wanted to get high.

I listened to the muffled cracks of the two guns as they fired six rounds into a suspected mortar position. A short time later, when everything became deathly still again, my thoughts wandered back to Glover, remembering how it had been at Fort Sill.

A cool breeze had been blowing that evening, beating back the heat of the day as Glover, Carr and I walked back to our barracks from the E.M. club. LPC school had finished earlier that day and I had graduated at the top of the class, receiving higher marks than anyone in the previous eight schools. My selection as acting commanding officer came during graduation. While I had struggled through the course like everyone else, I was surprised at my own ability and potential. But, it was a good surprise, like receiving a birthday cake. My old man had never been satisfied with my performance, no matter what I did. Now here I was, graduating at the top of my class. I had even finished in the top 10 percent in Basic and had been one of the few that got promoted. Maybe I had more on the ball than my old man ever led me to believe.

That evening all the trainees had been released from LPC and we were able to leave the barracks area for the first time. We had headed straight for the E.M. club and spent the evening listening to live music, shooting pool, and drinking pink champagne. I had become slightly inebriated, as had the others, and walking back to the barracks I was experiencing this deep affection for Glover and Carr. I really appreciated their close friendship. It was the kind of evening in which the right combination of friends and alcohol melts walls of mistrust and releases inhibitions and feelings and emotions that men rarely show toward another.

As we walked, laughing and joking, our arms intertwined, our movement slowed as if to say that none of us was in a hurry to get back to the barracks nor to let this evening end. Something unlocked the door to our emotions, and we began to tell one another our deepest secrets, exposing things about ourselves that perhaps we had never revealed before.

"Listen," I said. "I feel closer to you guys than anyone I've known for a long time. Man, I never felt I could get closer to anyone than I did to Bob Ellegard. He was my best friend in high school. Man, it was hard for me when he left for California after graduation. I don't think I've ever told anyone that, not even Bobby. I don't know, Glover, but there's something about our relationship that's

155

even deeper than that. Something special. I've only known you for a few weeks and I can already sense a deeper trust and affection for you than I had for Bobby."

Glover smiled, then laughed, his deep baritone voice filling the night. I could see it made him feel good, but at the same time it embarrassed him slightly. "Oh, it's nothing, Olsen," Glover said. He put his hand on my shoulder and laughed. "I gots to stay close to you anyway, boy, cause you're on your way up. Besides, I'se got to protect you from those black niggers."

We all laughed. We knew he was making reference to the incident between Marshall and me but it sounded ridiculous coming from him because both he and Carr were black.

I raised my arms in the air and ran forward about ten feet, letting the cool night air caress my arms and face. I loved it. There was nothing like a cool evening breeze to wash away the day's heat. "Hey, can I tell you guys something that might be a little weird? You won't laugh will ya?"

"Naw, go ahead," Carr said.

"I talk to the wind," I said. "Can you understand that? I think the wind is like a spirit, a personal friend that I talk to when I need to talk about things that I just can't say to anyone else. Especially when I get really lonely. Many of the nights we were in training I sat outside the balcony door on our floor after lights out and just talked to the wind. Man, I'd get really lonely and depressed, and I needed someplace to get away, someplace private. I would just sit out there, thinking, letting the cool evening breeze blow over me. A lot of times I would catch a scent traveling in the air that reminded me of some other place I had been, and I could immediately sense and feel the things that took place there. It was like being back there. Remembering those times, the good times, made LPC school bearable for the moment and made me feel better afterwards. I believe the wind brings those scents to me, carrying them from faraway places to help me get along. That's why I look at it like a friend. Can you understand that? I mean, do you think that's crazy?"

"It's no mo' crazy than some of the things I do," Glover said, laughingly.

I wished they were here with me now. I wanted to walk outside with them, to catch the cool evening breeze, to embrace the warmth of their companionship and to escape this hell hole of insensitivity. I hated the authority men had over me. This power to control, to enslave, to defile and abuse. Although my quiet defiance and sarcasm reflected these feelings I often struggled to control my anger toward those who derided me. I often fought to keep from committing the unpardonable sin, that of striking an officer. The threat of a jail term was the only thing that kept me in line, but now, I *wanted* someone in authority to say something. Something that would tick me off. I wanted to unleash this tormenting frustration I was feeling, and I didn't much give a damn on who.

Sitting on my cot, a recent acquisition, I bent over and unhooked the clips that fastened the lid to my ammo can. I dug inside for a pen and paper. It had been nearly three weeks since I had written any letters and I knew that the more letters I wrote, the greater chance I had of getting letters back. Letters still remained my only touch with the real world. Moving back and forth against the rough surface of my bunker wall I tried to scratch my back. It itched from sweat and dust. Dirt that always seemed to be there.

To whom should I write? I hadn't written Lois, Mike Finn's mother, in over two months. She had been like a mother to me but I wasn't in the mood to write superficial commentary. I thought about Deb and Diane. Our letters grew deeper every time we wrote. Although it was always a struggle to expose my true feelings, I was gradually learning to trust them both and to accept their care for me as genuine. The more we conversed, the more free I felt to share some of the conflict and confusion I was feeling. Even when they didn't understand the things I wrote, they always encouraged me in their letters and let me know they cared. Their letters made it possible for me to endure the crushing weight of loneliness.

"Dear Diane," I began, deciding to write her. "It's impossible for me to describe to you what's going on over here. It's like a crazy world. It seems like it takes crazy men to fight wars and if they're not crazy to begin with, war makes them crazy. In the last three weeks we've been in three different locations. At our last position we were mortared four nights out of the eight we were there. All this action went on right next to an ARVN Ranger Camp where we had set up. I think that the reason they don't get hit and we do might be because their camps contain Viet Cong sympathizers. I wouldn't doubt it if some of them crawled out of camp at night and switched uniforms, mortaring us with the very same weapons we've provided for them. If they were out doing their job, the whole area around this base should be secure.

"Sometimes I wonder just what the heck is going on. I don't want to end up mistrusting the very people we're supposed to be helping, but when your life is on the line, the stakes get pretty high. Who wants to take chances? As far as I am concerned everyone could be Viet Cong, every last one of them. I can't see any difference between the VC and the farmers who clutter the countryside: they're all in black pajamas, and a hidden weapon is probably within shouting distance of every one of them. Shit, the only people I ever see are the ones too old to fight or the mama-sans and baby-sans. I rarely see any Vietnamese male civilians. They're either in the countryside fighting for the VC or in an ARVN uniform, but you can't always tell by the uniform whether they're on your side. The only problem is, if they're all VC or sympathizers, then where are the people we're supposed to be liberating? Are they the ones who beg and scramble for our money and food? And, if they're *all* the enemy, then what the hell am I doing here?

"On our last move, one of the Chinooks that airlifted us into position dropped one of the howitzers and the ammo that was slung underneath it. They had to send an infantry platoon in to blow it in the place because it was so badly damaged, we were one gun short. . . .

". . . I think one of the hardest things for me is to be separated from my friends, completely cut off from everything that was once familiar, cast into a land

157

where we are deprived of nearly everything that I once took for granted. There ain't nothing here that ain't bad; the living in dirt day in and day out; the weight of the sandbags when you're struggling to fill your hundredth one; the diarrhea; the warm drinking water; the mosquitos; the rain; the torrid heat and the mud; the loss of sleep and the tasteless food; and the worst thing is being deprived of your freedom, your rights, your dignity and your friends. I hate it. I hate it all. Encourage anyone you know not to go into the Army. Tell them to write me first and I'll tell them myself. . . ."

I stopped, thinking about what I had written. I wondered if I was being un-patriotic. Or if patriotism wasn't just a scam, a word that people beat you with to make you do what they think is right. If this was the price of patriotism, I wondered if it was worth the cost.

I wondered if she would think I was exaggerating the situation, or if she would even, could even, understand what it was really like. I wondered what, if anything, the people back in the States thought was going on over here. If they could even imagine it. But it didn't do any good to moan about it.

As tasteless as the food was, at least it was almost always hot. We had it better than the grunts who ate C rations all the time and rarely saw a mess hall. When-ever it was tactically possible the mess crew had always tried to get hot chow out to the field. Even if they couldn't set up the mess tent they tried to air-lift hot food to us. It was only after we had secured a new position that the mess hall could be loaded up and sent to the field, but we had to be in position two or three days for that to happen, and that wasn't happening much lately. Still, I knew it was just as much a hassle for Wheatstraw and the other cooks to pack up and set up as it was for us to move. They had to set up a huge canvas tent and assemble large amounts of cooking utensils, and food supplies. And they needed gasoline to operate their stoves. And it was a hassle keeping dust and dirt out of the food, not to mention the hordes of flies and mosquitos. To top it off, they always had to watch out for raiding parties from rifle companies as well as our own men. Even though most of the food seemed to be powdered or dried, occasionally we got fresh meat, but that had to be prepared immediately upon arrival to prevent its spoiling. Often as not, the iced tea served in garbage cans was the only cold drink available. I was learning to like it, or at least I appreciated the fact that it was cold. But enough of that. . . I returned to my letter.

". . . A team of volunteers from our artillery battery had to sweep the new area we are in because of a lack of ground troops. I was on duty and unable to go, but I'm not sure I would have even if I had had the opportunity. They uncovered some mines and booby traps and found some documents and clothing in a fortified trench position not fifty meters from our location. But they didn't find any Viet Cong. We never see the enemy; that's the frightening part. There aren't any boun-dary lines where we know we're safe except those we establish each evening at our perimeter. We continue to search the same areas again and again but they're different every day. Charlie seems to be able to crop up and disappear at will, and more often than not, to our unexpected surprise and demise. There isn't a safe place, no neutral ground, no area where we can go and relax for a minute without fear of being killed. The safest place I've been is our rear area at Cu Chi, but we rarely see that. I can't wait to go on R & R.

"To top it off, it's so crazy here that there are even times when we can't defend our own men. Last week the 2nd Battalion 14th US Infantry, whom we supported, got into heavy contact in a populated area. It took us four and one half hours to get permission from ARVN sources to fire in their support. By then they had lost 11 men, more than half of them after their initial contact. I just can't believe it. It just burns me up....

"...I'm not sure what to believe anymore, or even who to believe. Command tells us that the Viet Cong are on the run, but at the same time, we've had contact with small forces on a daily basis and more recently with even larger forces. The captain said that the documents we found indicate that the VC and NVA forces are rebuilding and reoccupying old base areas and that they're moving large amounts of supplies from Cambodia by truck toward Dau Tieng, just north of us. The infantry guarding our perimeter says that just two weeks ago they took some POWs, one of whom had said there were four companies of NVA troops who just entered our area. Villagers said there had been over 400 VC soldiers in the area last week. Most of them had recently returned from North Vietnam where they were being trained. It's hard to say whether it's getting better or becoming worse. It's scary, not knowing what the hell is really going on....

"...At least some of the good things are, that I've met a couple of heads. Most people here are juicers, and although officers take a real tolerant view of alcoholic indulgences, they really frown on anyone who smokes pot. Sometimes I feel like an alien around others. I have to keep most of my political views to myself...."

I could hear someone approaching my bunker so I stopped writing. I glanced at the entrance to see who was coming.

"Olsen, you in there?" a voice asked.

"Yeah," I replied, recognizing Myers' voice.

"I'm just supposed to tell you that no one is supposed to be buying anything from the gooks, o.k.? Bravo Battery just had to dust-off one of their men. He said he had bought a drink off the local economy and was reporting severe stomach cramps—probably got a coke with battery acid in it."

"Roger," I said, watching as he left.

I leaned my head back against the wall, feeling a wave of heaviness. How long had I been here? Had it really only been a little over four months? Had I just turned twenty? Somehow I just didn't feel that young anymore.

I looked back down at the letter. I wanted to write that this was not only a year of isolation, but of deep introspection. I was trying to discover who I really was, learning in the midst of battle. I wanted to write that my identity was being forged in the fires of combat, beaten and shaped by death and fear and by the tragedy that surrounded me, but somehow it seemed too pretentious, too emotional, overly romanticized. I felt uneasy exposing that side of my character. I wasn't really sure I wanted it to be there. I wasn't really sure I wanted to admit to myself it was there.

V OPERATION TOAN THANG

11

21 April 1968
FSB Harrison
Hoc Mon

Concentrating on the steady drone of the helicopter blades was relaxing. Their steady, chopping, humming song made me want to sleep. But this was no time for sleeping. We were on our fourth fireball mission out of FSB Harrison and the shit was hot. Fireballing was a relatively new tactic for us and was mainly an air mobile operation. Instead of moving to permanent overnight locations, we now simply airlifted or convoyed out of our fire base in the morning, set up a minor secondary bunker system and then tore it down and returned to the fire support base at night. Generally, the infantry unit conducting the sweep around us then occupied the abandoned base at night and continued search and destroy operations the next day.

In the past we had relied upon the infantry to first secure an area but now we were going into those areas with them. Today, we were taking two howitzers. The other four were deployed to support yet another infantry unit and remained at FSB Harrison. This Eagle Flight, a heli-assault, was the first of its kind.

I was with the advance party again and I hoped the LZ would be cold. I dreaded the thought of taking fire even before we landed. I could sense the fear but I pushed it aside. I had to be cool. I couldn't let fear rule me. I wondered if this was how the grunts felt every time they airmobiled. I wondered if you ever got used to it. This was the way I felt at night, waiting to see if we would be mortared.

Mortars by night, and two if by day. The redcoats are coming; they're coming our way. I'm a poet, and I know it, I said silently, but I hope I don't blow it. I quit rambling, knowing I had to concentrate on what was at hand. The helicopter pilot notified us that the LZ was two minutes away and that we were to make ready. Gripping my M-16, I shifted my flak-jacket, adjusting the magazines stuffed in its pockets. I glanced over at the helicopter gunner.

Going down in the Huey was drastically different from landing in a Chinook.

163

The helicopter dropped to within two feet of the ground and hovered, rocking back and forth. Like bounding antelope, we scrambled out of the helicopter and scurried out to enlarge the perimeter. Some of the men dropped to their bellies, others positioned themselves to fire. We tried to keep from bunching up. Because the helicopter forced everything loose into the air, I ran as much to get out of its downdraft and a whirlwind of debris as to secure cover.

Although we had landed in a clearing, it was barely 50 yards across. The woods towered above us on every side. As soon as we secured the area we began blowing down trees, not only to enlarge our defense, but to clear a path of trajectory for the howitzers. Jeez! I thought, I'm sure glad we don't have to spend the night here! We would be sitting ducks for sure.

The LZ was cold and the day went without mishap. Although the infantry discovered traces of Charlie's presence, we didn't find him. Instead of a body count, we retreated with a few weapons and supplies, leaving behind one sprung booby trap and a dismantled tunnel and spider-hole complex.

I finally broke down and wrote Lois, but even as I wrote I struggled with what to say. Would anything I say change the hell I was in? I knew she at least wanted to hear that I was all right. Maybe she wanted to hear the war was all right too?

I closed my eyes to think. Two weeks ago we had left the Ho Bo Woods and headed south again to protect the western approach to Saigon. Another major enemy offensive was supposed to take place and our job was again to prevent infiltration into Saigon. We began yet another major operation. This one was entitled Toan Thang, or "complete victory," and it, too, was supposed to be the largest combined forces operation ever assembled. Since then, we had moved six times, conducted one over-nighter and five fireballs before finally settling in at Hoc Mon at FSB Harrison. This time we had set up within an ARVN compound.

Each evening we returned through guarded gates into what was supposed to be a secure area, within touching distance of the Vietnamese army. A large wire fence around the compound separated us from them, but still, we could see them playing cards or talking, huddled in groups, all down on their haunches. Some of them had bunkers less than 15 feet from ours. As I sat and watched them I felt a mixture of contempt and curiosity. I had little respect for them and their army seemed to operate on a system entirely different from ours.

I tried to make contact with some of them but they didn't speak English. Only ARVN officers spoke English fluently enough to communicate and they rarely associated with regular ARVN troops, so I couldn't find anyone to translate. I finally gave up trying. I had learned from the Sarge that ARVN units were territorial. Each unit maintained its own recruiting forces or supplemented government draftees with its own acquisitions. In either case, it meant the majority of their soldiers were being pressed into service, the same as ours. Only here, most soldiers were drawn from the local population. These local ties were further reinforced by the traditionally close social and economic relationships that existed between Vietnamese soldiers and their families. Something I was finding common in Asia, unlike the United States. For the Vietnamese, the security and well-being of the soldiers were personal responsibilities; the soldiers themselves often depended upon their families for income and for the performance of domestic duties as well. I had heard that the pay for draftees made it impossible not to be without additional support. Most of their bases were surrounded by ramshackle settlements of women and children, families who either visited or lived with the soldiers. It reminded me of what I had read Army life was like at Valley Forge, when Washington was commanding the Revolutionary Army. It sure was different when you were fighting in your own land.

Although this arrangement was ideal for the ARVNs it made it impossible for them to achieve the same mobility we had, or that the NVA and Viet Cong units had. When the ARVNs moved around like we did it often triggered desertions. Rumors of corruption among ARVN soldiers abounded. The ARVN outposts remained mostly defense-oriented and they never ventured far from fixed locations. It made me wonder. Why didn't the South Vietnamese troops have as much motivation as the VC did? Why did the VC sacrifice so much, and the South Vietnamese army so little? If they didn't care about winning the war, then why were we here? If they wouldn't support their own government, why were we? I really wanted to talk to them but we were under direct orders not to initiate or maintain any personal contact with them. I wondered why.

I felt tired just thinking about it. I put my pen down and laid down in my cot to try and sleep. I needed some rest but I had too damn much on my mind! Soon after our arrival at Hoc Mon, the lieutenant informed me that I was to be the new section leader. It came as a complete surprise. I had automatically assumed it would be either Lee or Vechione. I had never heard of being promoted over higher ranking men. When they informed me of my promotion, they made certain I knew I would be given the rank of specialist fourth class, retroactive to the end of March. The captain knew I would have difficulty commanding the others if I didn't have at least equal rank, and Lee and Vechione were already E-4s. Well, maybe they felt that Vechione and Lee would take it better but I noticed their hostility and resentment right away. Vechione initially shrugged it off, pretending that it didn't matter. He said he knew the brass weren't going to give the position to him anyway since he was so short. Still, I could tell he was disappointed. He said he didn't give a shit because he only had three more weeks to serve, but just the same he was deeply bitter about not making E-5 and felt that he at least deserved the rank before leaving.

Lee too had only a couple of months left to serve, but I knew that he had expected to be in charge until he left and had looked forward to getting his E-5 rank before his DEROS. Yet he never said anything. I think it was as much a surprise to him as it was to me. I don't think that he wanted the responsibility but there were times when it was evident that he was disgruntled. Apparently the decision had been made at battalion level during a review of our records. The brass had thought that I was the best qualified of those who would be there the longest and, therefore, the most productive to train.

165

With Myers getting ready to leave in two weeks, he and the lieutenant began a crash course to prepare me to assume command. Personally, I resented it and at first refused the promotion. I didn't want the others hostile toward me; my life depended on their performance. And I just didn't feel qualified. I hadn't received any formal training in intelligence operations. I had been trained as a gun bunny, not in fire direction operations or communications. I didn't want to be responsible for the accuracy of life and death decisions. I had only been in the FDC a little over four months. What the hell did I know?

Shit! It was just like Basic all over again! Just thinking about that experience left my stomach churning.

"Bivouac," our simulated field experience, had just ended and we were returning to camp on foot in what was referred to as a forced march. For 15 miles each of us would have to carry an M-14 rifle and a 60-pound pack. There were no rests, no stops, no breaks. We either ran or we marched; there was no walking. As a squad leader I had been expected to lead my squad, to be in the forefront all the way. In addition, my squad was placed at the head of our platoon, and our platoon was placed second in relationship to the rest of the company. It was a company foray. I was responsible not only to set the pace for our platoon, but to maintain the same pace as the platoon ahead of me. I could not allow a distance of more than ten feet to come between us. To top it off, the strong sense of competition that pervaded the Army drove our drill sergeants to push us to be the first platoon back in camp.

After 12 grueling miles of blistering heat, mixed double time and trotting, I was wiped out. I mean I was totally exhausted! My whole body ached under the strain of the weight I carried. My arms were limp and shook from having to carry the M-14 out in front of me. Pain shot through my feet with every step I took. Blisters covered my toes, heels, and arches.

I watched soldiers slowly, methodically, stumble and drop behind, only to hear their drill sergeants scream at them mercilessly, calling them candy-asses and cry-babies. Some fell to their knees, others on their faces, their eyes in silent agony. I didn't want to be one of them, so as I gasped for breath and tears streamed down my cheeks, I struggled to keep ahead of my platoon and a hundred and thirty others. I fought desperately to keep pace with the platoon ahead of me, but finally I could hold on no longer. I knew I was destined to fail. All hope of my leading the platoon slipped away.

Suddenly the order came to "double time" and our speed rapidly increased. Within minutes I began slowly falling behind. I struggled to keep up as first one row then another, slowly edged by me. I watched them come out of the corners of my eyes. Many of them stumbled into one another, too tired to watch where they were going as they lunged by.

"Oh, God," I cried out in desperation. "Help me! Help me! Help me not to fail."

Seconds later, Sergeant Kiefer, the assistant drill sergeant, was running alongside me. Leaning over he whispered in my ear. "Olsen . . . Olsen," he hissed between clenched teeth. "Olsen, you can't quit now!"

His words came out slowly, emphatically, like there was no other solution . . . no other alternative. "Pull yourself together and get back to the front of that line. You're the leader of this platoon. I want you out in front! I won't have you finish in any lesser place! Do you understand! You can do it! I know you can. I've never expected anything from you that I didn't think you could do. Don't let me down now. Get going!"

Then he was gone. I could hear him behind me shouting, urging the platoon to keep up, yelling at those who lagged behind. I was in a turmoil as the things he said bounced back and forth in my mind. Then I began to get angry. "Why?" I screamed in silent frustration. "Why do I have to finish first? Why do I have to be the best? I'm doing the best I can right now! Can't you see that? I'm doing all I can!"

The physical pain I was feeling began to ebb. It barely shadowed the indignation, anger and frustration I felt. By sheer will power I began struggling with renewed determination. I gained first one step, then another. I shut out everything in my mind. I fixed my gaze on the helmet of the last straggler in the lead platoon. Pushing and heaving, I called forth every fiber of strength in my body and soul.

By the time we neared the outskirts of Fort Lewis, we were running down hill, slipping and tripping on the deeply rutted gravel road that led out of the woods. First one platoon, then another, broke rank. Every platoon was racing the other to see who would reach the gates first. Now we would determine who was the best. By the time our platoon reached the gate I had not only regained my position, I had led my platoon alongside the lead platoon. When we finally broke stride, I could barely stay up on my feet. I gasped for air. People fell out all over. The drill sergeants began barking orders to get the platoons back into formation, but I didn't care. I was jubilant!

Now here it was again! The mantle of leadership. I wanted nothing to do with it. I didn't want to have to set the lead ever again.

Shit, I couldn't sleep! I just couldn't quiet my mind. I turned on my cassette/radio and gently pushed the earplug in. God, what a surprise this gift was. It was still hard for me to believe. Doc Thornberg, one of the guys from White's gun, a guy I hardly knew, had brought it back from R & R for me. I couldn't remember the last time anyone had given me a gift. Especially someone I hardly knew.

I had been down visiting White's position. Doc returned on a resupply chopper and had plodded across the hot, dusty rice paddy to where we were digging and we stopped filling sandbags long enough to yell our greetings and then resume work. Everyone who hadn't taken an R & R yet wanted to find out where he had been in order to decide where they should go. They were anticipating the stories he'd tell. As Doc stepped into the hole we were digging and started to fill us in, he handed a cardboard box to me and told me it was mine. I remembered how White had squealed in mock protest, teasing Doc for not bringing him back something. I opened the box and found the radio inside. To go with the tape recorder, he had given me four cassettes. Two of them were blank. One was by the Supremes and the other by Mantovani, although who that was, I didn't know. Doc knew I dug soul music, but he thought I might appreciate something new. I had hardly known what to say. I managed to thank him deeply. He never said anything about it other than "you're welcome."

I sat up and began to scribble some words on the letter, trying to write something to Lois that for now would make sense.

"...Brigade says that our unit, the Eighth Artillery, has fired its 500,000th round since its incursion in country. A week ago some top brass showed up in the field for a short ceremony. B Battery, which is now set up next to us, fired the 500,000th round. A brigadier general, somebody named Gleason, strutted all over both battery locations, stringing a line of officers behind him like puppets.

"This is the first time I've ever seen a general in the field. I saw a lieutenant colonel once, and occasionally we see the major, but not a general. I wonder where they're fighting the war from?...

"...I thought it was bad when we had to fill over 1300 sandbags to cover the roof of our bunker, but S-2 and S-3 rear command have unexpectedly moved to our field location, and the peons over there have had to fill over 3000. Their bunker will be three or four layers thick when they're through, and no doubt, if Headquarters does it, they will make us do it too. Since HQ has moved into the field, we've had to start wearing boots all the time and be dressed in full fatigues, even when we're off duty. What a bunch of Mickey Mouse crap....

"At least this time we didn't have to pick and shovel our way through the brick-hard clay to make our bunker. There was an engineering company close by and they sent a bulldozer over to dig us one. It's completely underground except for a couple of layers of sandbags to provide circulation. It's big enough for all off-duty personnel to sleep in the back. I really appreciate those engineers...."

I wondered if I should tell her that I was beginning to question what we were doing here. I wondered if she would think I was being unpatriotic or worse yet, a traitor. I was taking a hard look at what was going on around me and I wondered if some of the atrocities we committed wouldn't be considered horrible crimes under any other circumstances. But then again, what was an atrocity? Was it any more atrocious to kill a man than to mangle his body? Wasn't killing atrocious itself? Was war really an expression of civilized behavior? Was my life more important than someone else's? I thought about it, and thought about it, and thought....

The guilt I felt was doing me in. It saddened me to look at the countryside and to see it slowly deteriorating. I remembered the first time I saw the Boi Loi and Ho Bo Woods. I had been stunned by its grandeur. How magnificent and beautiful those jungle woods had stood, yet when we last left them, thousands of acres had been completely laid to ruin. Many of the remaining trees were merely stumps, their limbs turned and disfigured—crippled by artillery barrages, Air Force bombs, sorties of napalm, and bulldozer blades. The forests had been raped and strangled by repeated applications of herbicides and defoliants, what our

168

captain lovingly referred to as magic dust. But, when I thought about it in terms of survival, I wouldn't have had it any other way. The woods lost their beauty and appeal when they were threatening and dangerous. Nobody wanted to be digging in where Charlie could crawl up to the perimeter and start offing guys with sniper fire. I was grateful every time those helicopters flew around our perimeter, dusting the trees to widen our area of defense and prepare the area for sweeps. The farther out they sprayed, the farther out that I could see. The more they cleared, the safer I felt.

Sometimes I felt like two different people, each holding opposing views and feelings. They seemed to be battling for the right to control my behavior. Inside, I knew that I really wasn't this hard person I had become – but to be more compassionate and gentle, well that scared the heck out of me. What if that meant I wasn't a man? God, what if I was a homo? I just couldn't be one of them!

I knew that sometimes my tough exterior only masked my real feelings. It had been that way most of my life; always trying to be the macho man. Mostly, I was just fighting to protect myself from being hurt. I had been bullied around a lot in grade school, mostly because of my size, and had quickly tired of it. No one respected someone who didn't stand up to others and I hated being called a coward. I wasn't! My first real fight, which I tried to back out of, left me bloodied, disgraced, and emotionally wounded. But, egged on by others, I had made up for it later, by catching up with the same guy and slugging it out again. Still, even as I stood over him, beating him in the face, tears streamed down my face. I had felt no sense of victory afterwards, only a deep sense of shame. It had hurt me far more to hurt him, but little boys just couldn't be that way. It was unmanly. I soon learned to fight simply to protect my image, to ward off the nagging doubt that I was less than a man if I didn't. I had never known any heroes or role models who had done anything less. There were no men in my life who turned the other cheek, that is except Jesus, and he wasn't real. He was just a story book character.

I hadn't fought much in grade school because I was more of a ladies' man, at least until the sixth grade. It was then that I was brutally beaten up by a gang of fifth graders my age. The humiliation I suffered made a much deeper imprint on my life than the bloody nose and torn clothes. I had made a vow then that I would never allow anything like that to happen to me again and swore vengeance on every one of those boys. It took me three years to do it, but by my freshman year in school I had caught up with and beat up every one of those kids, forcing them to suffer the same kind of public humiliation I had. By then, other events in my life had deeply reinforced the walls I had built around my heart and I had become a completely different person. Some of the girls I had gone out with in high school had said that they really didn't believe that I was this real tough guy I put on to be, and that underneath, I was really tender-hearted. But I soon convinced them. I had painstakingly done cruel things to others in their presence to prove to them that there was not one bit of softness in my life. In the process, I had destroyed most of those relationships. I wouldn't even admit to myself that there was any softness in my life and if somebody else could spot it, well that only meant I was still vulnerable, and I wasn't going to be vulnerable ever again.

Now, I was sure I had had my fill of fighting and I wanted it all to end, but I was finding it impossible to lay aside this hardened mask and I really wasn't sure where it started or where it ended.

Sitting on the top of the FDC bunker, I eyed the tasteless food that lay heaped on my paper plate. I was having serious misgivings about mailing the letter I had written last night. I wondered if I would sound to Lois as confused as I sometimes felt. Maybe she'd think I was crazy or going a little berserk. Regardless of what I had thought my true feelings were, I just couldn't let them interfere with the job I had to do in Vietnam. I wanted to survive. I wanted to live even if nobody cared. It was better simply not to think about those things. I had more important things on my mind.

Myers had received an early out and he had packed his gear and grabbed the resupply chopper back to base camp this morning.

I was happy for him. Not only was he going back to the world, he finally got rid of his responsibilities and the conflict and struggle that had gone with them. As team chief, he had had few friends, but in many ways, he had been to blame. He had availed himself the privileges of rank and I was vowing never to do the same.

The thing that was foremost on my mind now was how Lee and Vechione would respond to me. The shift hours had been unfair to everyone and that was the first thing I was going to change. I wondered how the crew would take it. Maybe Vechione would just ease off. After all, he only had a few weeks to go. But would Lee obey any of my orders? What would I do if they challenged me, the way they had done to Myers?

I thought about the division artillery message that had been recently distributed. There had been a disciplinary incident in Cu Chi involving injuries to a number of people. They were looking into it because they thought it had been the result of discontent, but they were also interpreting it to be an act of subversion. Apparently that "incident" had been the "fragging" of an officer. Someone had been discontent enough with an officer to roll a grenade into his sleeping quarters. All section leaders were ordered to pay particular attention to any indication of discontent in the field, such as troops failing to perform duties properly or disobeying orders, and to report them. But I sure as fuck wasn't going to turn anyone in and I wasn't going to side with officers. Captain Ripke had addressed this particular issue in battery formation upon his arrival. Maybe the strong stance he had taken would have some kind of effect on Lee and Vechione.

I wondered how the monsoon season would affect my job. Myers had said he was glad to be leaving before it began. I wondered what that meant. A change in the weather had been rumored to be starting soon, sometime in May, but I rarely heard people talk about it except to say that we would have to begin building above ground again. Nobody seemed to think that it would start this soon but as a slight precaution we had stretched our ponchos over the air holes we had for ventilation, to keep out any rain. Both Myers and the lieutenant seemed to think there was nothing more we needed to do.

I was standing outside when the rain first started. It fell gently in trickles. Ah great, I thought, this is going to be a welcome relief from the intense heat. Might even be refreshing!

Suddenly, a gust of wind whipped my hat off. As I bent over to retrieve it the rain began pelting my back. By the time I stood up it was falling so hard it blocked my visibility. I was instantly soaked. I had never experienced rain like this except in a tornado. Damn! The rain began falling in sheets and by the time I reached the FDC bunker, water was already cascading down the steps and onto the floor. Lieutenant Voss had a definite worried look on his face as he glanced in my direction.

"Plug up the doorvays!" he was shouting.

Vechione was already moving out the back of the bunker, carrying his poncho. He had anticipated the lieutenant's command. Vechione might have been an ornery bastard, but one thing was for sure, he knew his job!

"Campbell!" I shouted. "Get your poncho and as many of the others as you can find."

I headed off to the back to help gather them up as Vechione took off up the stairs. As soon as I had an armful, I headed outside. The rain and wind tore at my fatigues and face as I rushed to Vechione's side. He was struggling with sandbags at the front entrance, trying to hold down the poncho and stretch it across the opening at the same time. The wind whipped the poncho around in a frenzied dance. I threw down those I was carrying and grabbed one side of his. Moving across the top of the bunker, I stuffed one end under a sandbag to hold it in place. It held.

"I can take care of this!" Vechione yelled. "Get some covering over the windows and the back entrance."

I picked up the ponchos and threw one at him. "You'll need this one too!"

I could see Campbell at the far side of the bunker. At least I assumed it was Campbell. The rain was falling so hard I could barely make out a figure moving about. I headed for the far side and began removing sandbags from the top of the bunker and stuffing ponchos over each window opening, covering them back with sandbags to hold them in place. But, even the ponchos wouldn't hold back the rain. The wind ripped the ponchos out from under the sandbags. Rain streamed through the windows and poured down the doors. I ran around to the front again and began stacking sandbags in front of the entrance, hoping they would stop the water from coming in.

"Vanous! ... Vanous! Take these sandbags," I yelled from the entrance, throwing one down the steps. "You and Gianettino start stacking them at the foot of the stairs!"

But even that didn't stop the torrent of water that rushed down the steps. Ten minutes later we were all standing knee deep in water in what was rapidly becoming a muddy swimming pool. Nothing was working to keep the water out. The lieutenant was in a frenzy. Fuckin' Lee was as calm as if nothing was happening, and I didn't know what the fuck to do. For a moment, we all stood around looking at one another and then someone cracked a joke and suddenly everyone but the lieutenant was laughing. Man, the situation was ridiculous! But the levity was quickly squashed when the captain's voice thundered down the stairway.

"Lieutenant!" he yelled. "Get this goddamned equipment over to the mess tent before you get flooded out!"

There was a sudden flurry of activity. Lee and Gianettino grabbed the radios and, sloshing through the water, began carrying them up the stairs.

"Vanous, you and Dangerfield grab the chart tables," I said, looking around for Vechione. "Campbell! Get Vechione down here. You and him grab the FADAC!"

The lieutenant, who was scrambling to pick up data sheets and maps, looked over his shoulder. "There's no time for that!" he screamed. "You and I will have to take it over!"

By the time we both reached the FADAC I could feel the water at my crotch. Slipping and sliding on the wet floor, the lieutenant and I grappled with the weight of the FADAC, which was now partially submerged. I knew we weren't going to be able to handle it. Suddenly the captain slid through the doorway and waded over to help us. With the captain's help we were able to get it out the doorway before it became completely submerged. By the time we got all the equipment transferred to the mess tent, everything was a mess.

We had managed to keep our communications from shorting out, but everything else was a disaster. The chart tables and maps were completely soaked—many of the markings and locations were washed off. A grease-like mud covered nearly everything else. It was obvious that all the computations would have to be redone. Scrambling to salvage the FDC section from ruin, we had completely neglected the other half of the bunker; our sleeping quarters, now ruined.

On my last trip I had noticed a couple of ammo boxes floating near the surface but the water in the bunker was now over our heads. Blankets, clothes, and air mattresses, all floated in a sea of mud. Somewhere beneath it lay my M-16. I didn't know what to think of first! I determined that it must be the FDC, and in the dimly lit refuge of the mess tent, I began to try to put the center back into working order.

The lieutenant was nearly hysterical. He knew that the axe was going to fall someplace for this disaster and he was the one who was in charge. He was rushing around the mess tent, his face flushed, his voice near panic.

"Olsen! . . . Olsen! . . . Do something!" he demanded. "Get this place back into shape. . . . Immediately!" He raced from one thing to another as he yelled, trying to do it all himself. He was causing such a commotion that the new guys didn't do anything. But I saw Vechione and Lee just going about their business as if he weren't there, so I did the same. I kept my mouth shut and did what I could.

The lieutenant was still barking orders when the tent flap lifted and the captain slipped in.

"Lieutenant!" he said coldly. "Just what the fuck happened here?" The room grew quiet. No one looked up. I could tell that every ear was attentively pitched to hear his explanation. The lieutenant tried convincing the captain that everything was all right but the panic in his voice wasn't very reassuring. In spite of the fact that communications had been reestablished and the charts were now in working order, the captain wasn't buying it.

"How did you allow yourself to get in this kind of predicament to begin with?" he demanded. "You're not a damn greenhorn. You're supposed to be a seasoned veteran. This had better not ever happen again. Do you understand me, lieutenant?"

"Yes, sir," the lieutenant replied weakly.

Whew, I hope it's all over now, I said silently, breathing a sigh of relief.

"Olsen!" the captain said sharply. "I want to talk to you!"

My stomach tightened. Approaching him, I drew myself to attention, snapping a quick salute and a "yes sir!"

"Olsen!" he blasted, "What the fuck's wrong with you? How come you weren't prepared for this rain?"

Gritting my teeth, I dropped my eyes to the ground, trying to avert his angry stare. What the fuck was I supposed to say? It wasn't my fault. I hadn't designed the bunker. Why all of a sudden was I being made the scapegoat? Was I some kind of a seer who could predict the future? I hadn't been the one in charge!

"Eyes front!" he demanded, his hard stare piercing my flesh.

I lifted my head and stared straight ahead, past him. The last time anybody had spoken to me like this and got away with it was when I was a civilian. Then, it had been a large, fat lady who headed the clerical department at Northwestern Bancorporation where I had worked as a delivery boy. Her face had been red and puffed up just like the captain's was now. A week after her chewing out I had walked off the job, but there was no leaving here.

"What the fuck is wrong with your thinking! What would you have done if we had been in the middle of a fire mission? There are soldiers out there who are depending upon you for their lives. You had better get your head on right, mister! Do you understand?"

"Yes sir!"

"And another thing, the safety and responsibility of the FDC is yours. Just where the hell is your cover if we get mortared now? You'd better get it clear that the firing ability of this battery rests squarely on your shoulders and I never want to see this place inoperable again or as long as I am in command, you won't be. Is that understood?"

"Yes sir," I replied. I wanted to say, fuck you, sir! You can take this job and shove it up your ass, sir! But I didn't.

"I'll be back here in twenty minutes," the captain continued, "and when I do, I want to see this place fully functional and everything cleaned up. Is that understood?"

"Yes, sir," I replied emphatically, watching him walk away.

I could feel the eyes of the whole crew on me and I wished the ground would swallow me up. But there was no place I could hide. I would have to swallow my pride and face them. I stole a quick glance around the room but every eye was on the ground. That is, except Vechione's. He was kicking his right foot at some nondescript place in the dirt, making no attempt to hide the sheepish grin that covered his face. That's what it's like, he suggested with a shrug of his shoulders. We all get ours in due time!

"Look, Lee," I said, trying to circumvent my anger, "just what is it that has to be done?"

Everyone pitched in and as the work progressed silently I stewed over the things the captain had said, wondering why the lieutenant hadn't bailed me out. He knew it wasn't my fault. Why hadn't he stood up for me? It was supposed to be his job to protect those who were under his command. I knew from then on, he wasn't a man to be trusted. It was clear that the safety and the responsibility of the crew were now mine and mine alone. The firing ability of the battery rested squarely on my shoulders. I wondered if I could handle the weight. I could feel the anger and hurt boiling within me. The lieutenant was supposed to be the one in charge! This was supposed to be his responsibility, not mine. He was the one in command! That bastard, the captain, why did he have to put me down in front of all the men?

12

25 April 1968
FSB Pulaski II
8 Klicks N.W. of Saigon

With a deep sigh, I plopped down on a paddy berm behind our bunker, juggling a tray of chow. I was completely fucking drained. I welcomed the opportunity to take a break when the mess crew announced that chow was ready. It had been 54 hours of backbreaking labor since I had last slept, and we were still laboring in this brick-hard clay. I had been struggling with the fear of failure ever since we left the ARVN compound at FSB Harrison. I had resolved to do my best.

"Hey, man, you mind if I sit here?" I recognized LeRoy's voice. I stretched the muscles in my neck. "What's happening? he asked, sticking a spoon full of food in his mouth.

"Fuck, man," I said bobbing my head, "the same thing that's happening with you guys. We're working our asses off!"

"Sheee-it man, we ain't slept in over forty-eight hours. Now ain't that a mother-fuckin'-shit?"

Something struck me funny about the way he said it, either that or I was so tired I had gotten the giggles. "Man, you oughta be in my shoes! I just can't seem to get my guys to work as fast as the lieutenant wants them to, and that goddamned prick thinks I ought to take charge of the situation and kick some ass! When I told him that the crew just refused to work any faster, he really jumped into my shit. He said that if I don't get them to work faster, he'll have the captain come and talk to me. Shit, man, I can imagine what that would be like. What the fuck am I supposed to do, man? If they didn't respond to him, what the fuck makes him think they'll respond to me? He's the fuckin' lieutenant!"

"Shit, man," LeRoy said, "I sure am glad I'm not in your motha-fuckin' shoes!"

It was now my responsibility to see that the bunker got built, even if it meant no sleep for the crew. But, if I didn't force them to work harder, I was gonna get the axe. I could threaten Lee with an Article 15. That's what the lieutenant had threatened me with. Lee was the most outspoken. Damn him anyway! It was a good fuckin' thing Vechione was gone. Reprimanding Lee meant incurring the disdain of my own men, though, and I wasn't sure I could handle that!

Suddenly I was aware of a loss of feeling in my hands. They felt cold and clammy. The numbness and tingling rose to my wrists. My forehead began to sweat profusely, even though I was sitting in the shade. I was suddenly aware of an acute pounding in my chest, my heart was racing! All my muscles started tensing as if I were suddenly preparing for combat. I could feel my jaws tighten, my teeth hard against each other. My hands began to tingle again, and then started shaking. What's going on, I wondered. Suddenly the mess tray slipped off my lap and crashed into the dirt. Confused, I turned to LeRoy. I tried to keep my voice under control, but I was scared!

"I can't feel my hands! Shit, man, what's going on? My whole body's becoming numb!"

Before LeRoy could answer, I began to cry. I hadn't cried in over eight years, but suddenly I was sobbing like a child. I don't know why, but my situation seemed hopeless. It seemed useless for me to even try to figure it out. I felt myself slipping into despair! It wasn't right! We weren't prisoners! Wasn't I an American? Where were my rights!

Tears ran down my cheeks. A crowd was beginning to gather. I could see they were wondering what was going on, but wasn't I too? I tried to say something. I wanted to give an explanation but the words wouldn't come. There were no words to convey my feelings. My mind was awash with a torrent of thoughts. I tried to grab one but it slipped through my fingers, and I couldn't seem to find just the right one to explain. How queer this is, I thought.

It was the funniest feeling! I was standing two feet from my body, looking down at myself!

How could this be? I laughed! That's me sitting down over there crying my head off.

Only now I wasn't sitting down, I was standing up, laughing my head off! It was all so funny! So unreal! What was I crying about? Why did it seem so ridiculous? This was war! It seemed perfectly natural to return hurt for hurt, injury for injury, pain for pain, life for life. Maybe we were all insane! I laughed. We were all insane! I wept for us all. If we were all insane, then it stood to reason that those who sent us here were insane as well. That or we were the victim of a hoax. But, if Vietnam was all a hoax, then they've got to be insane!

The resupply convoy was lined up outside the gates of the ARVN compound, its last stop before returning to the field. They were drawing water at one of the pump stations nestled among the ramshackle huts of Hoc Mon. The afternoon was already unbearably hot, and humid. It was hard to tell that there had been a rain storm less than a half hour ago. But that was how it was.

Dust curled up between my legs as I walked. My boots scuffed the earth. It had been two days since my breakdown and I had just finished visiting the shrink.

I was heading back out to the field, still trying to make sense out of what had happened. I had been sedated and had slept for nearly two days. I didn't remember much, only the doc's being there and his saying to me that it would be all right. I remembered lying on a cot in the back of the mess tent. At least that's where I thought I was. I didn't remember being awake for long.

As soon as I had recovered sufficiently, arrangements had been made for me to take the supply convoy back to the ARVN compound at Hoc Mon to see a doctor there. They couldn't spare me for the length of time it would take to return to Cu Chi, so they sent a doctor to the field to see if I was still fit for duty. I had heard the captain tell the doctor over the radio that I was to be sent to base camp only under the most urgent circumstances. Otherwise, I was to return to the field. We were short of men the way it was, and with Lee leaving, I was the only one with sufficient training to run the place.

Not fully understanding what had happened myself, I had been hesitant to see the doctor, especially a shrink! I didn't want anyone questioning my sanity! I didn't want to question it myself. But the captain had insisted I go in for the checkup. I refused, but when he asked me if I was going to disobey a direct order, I went. It didn't mean I had to trust this guy they were sending me to.

I decided at the beginning of our conversation not to say anything revealing. I was cautious, careful not to make myself vulnerable. You never knew what a shrink might say. At first I warded off his probing, but as our conversation lengthened I began to open up. I was tired of playing this game with myself. With unusual boldness I told him how I felt about the killing that was going on; that it was just about breaking my heart. I told him I didn't know what we were doing here and I asked him to explain. But the doctor just evaded my questions concerning the war and turned the conversation instead to my past. He wanted to know about my relationship with my parents, my behavior in school. Shit, I didn't want to talk about those things! Those weren't the issues I was trying to face! Finally I resigned myself to answering only his questions, skeptical that anything would be resolved. When he finished his interview with a lecture on cowardice and patriotic duty, and on what it meant to be a man, I knew that he hadn't heard a word I had said. He sounded exactly like a filmstrip I had been shown in Basic, twisting words like honor, duty, liberty and fairness to fit his own purposes. Why, the Army no more believed in moral integrity than it did in Constitutional rights! This officer was no different from the rest. He didn't give a fuck about me, he just wanted the war machine to go on. He had decided beforehand that I was going back to the field, whether I thought I could handle it or not.

Anger and resentment filled my heart as I approached the convoy. I felt nothing but disdain for military professionals. For anyone who would actually give the Army his life. They didn't give a shit if I survived or not. I was just suffering from exhaustion, he had said. Exhaustion and a lack of sleep. I had to be a man about it! I needed to pick myself up by my bootstraps and go back to the field!

O.K., I thought, nearing the convoy, if this was what it was all about, then I would play the game. I would see to it that I never had to face this kind of embarrassment again. I would never again allow myself to crumble under any pressure or emotional strain! I would betray no weakness, no pain. I wasn't a coward and would show them so.

I felt my muscles tense. Fuck it, I thought, these people don't mean shit. Don't let 'em get to ya! Only seven more months and you'll be going home.

I knew that if I cracked up again I would only be a fractured piece on their assembly line. If I didn't make it they wouldn't shed a tear. I could be replaced like any other expendable piece of equipment. That just didn't set well with me! I was trapped in a system where human lives were being used like toilet paper, and I hated everyone responsible—them and the whole fuckin' system that let them get away with it.

These bastards, I thought. They think they can use me like rags, but one day I'm going to spit in their face.

I could play the game as long as I had to. Pretend that nothing really mattered. I just had to push down a little harder on my feelings and keep them back where they belonged.

I spied Sergeant Ramos talking to some mama-san and headed in his direction. We weren't supposed to be talking to civilians. I wondered how he got away with it.

"Hey, Olsen," Sergeant Ramos called, "c'mon over here, I want you to meet mama-san."

I headed for the opening in the hut that framed her tiny, frail figure.

"Hey mam-san," I said, "what's happening?"

"No what's happening me, G.I." she spat. "You talkee numbah one Englees!"

"O.K. mam-san," I laughed, "me talkee numbah one Englees."

"This here mama-san runs the water station," said Ramos. "We stop here to resupply nearly every day. She says she knows where she can pick up some weed. 'Thuoc la,' she calls it. She can get just about anything else you need, too," he added, grinning. "Right, mama-san?"

The old lady's face broke into a wide grin, revealing a mouth full of decaying teeth deeply stained from chewing on betel nuts. I wondered why anyone would chew those things when they left your teeth that way. Someone on convoy had once said it was because the juice of the nut contained a substance that numbed pain. Pain probably caused by teeth that had rotted.

"Ya want thuoc la?" she said, smiling. "It be five dollah!"

"How soon can ya get it, mama-san?"

"In five, maybe ten minute. Yo pay five dollah!"

"We got that long before the convoy leaves?" I asked Ramos.

"Sure," he said, laughing. "I'm in charge of the convoy! It's one of my new duties."

"O.K. mama-san," I said, "I give you fifteen dollah MPC, O.K.?"

"O.K., G.I." She stuck out her hand.

I pushed some crumpled bills in her hand. She turned and called a small

178

brown-skinned boy from behind a curtain. She handed him the money and said something in Vietnamese, and he ran out of the back. The mama-san hobbled to a straw chair near the wall and sat down to wait.

"Hey, is it all right to go in here?" I said to Ramos. "I mean, is this like a store, or is this her home, man?"

"It's her house. They all sleep in the back, behind that curtain. She's got two baby-sans living with her and a couple of kids. I don't know if the kids are hers, or the baby-sans."

I peered into the shadowy interior, speaking to the mama-san as I did. I kept outside the entrance. After all, it was her house, and she hadn't invited me in. "You get numbah-one deal, mama-san," I teased. "You get beaucoup MPC and I get ti ti tokla, huh!" I knew that our military currency was worth more on the black market than their own piasters. Undoubtedly she knew it too. But I didn't care if I was getting a good deal. If there was anything that I could use right now it was a joint. When I was stoned all the anxiety and pressure lifted. Right now I needed that. Who cared how much money it cost? What the fuck good was money over here anyway? It sure couldn't buy me happiness, and it couldn't buy me freedom. I couldn't eat or drink it. It couldn't make my life last one minute longer — and smoking the money sure wouldn't work. Smoking dope would though.

In five minutes the boy was back, carrying six plastic bags of marijuana, about two ounces each. Shit, I had never seen so much grass. I would be set for life! I scooped up the bags and stuffed them into the large pockets of my fatigues. "Thanks, mama-san," I said. "You numbah one mama-san; me beaucoup happy with this deal."

Sergeant Ramos laughed, and we turned and headed for the convoy. I could see two or three blacks sitting in the back of the lead truck, so I headed in their direction. As I drew closer I could see that one of them was LeRoy. A white film of dust blanketed his body. It was odd how on him, the dust looked white, but on me, it looked black.

"Heyyyy, Olsen," LeRoy yelled.

"Heyyyy, Pearson."

"You O.K.?" LeRoy asked as I climbed aboard.

"Yeah, I'm O.K. It's not me that's fucked up, it's the Army!" We laughed.

"I thought I'd sit back here," I said, moving closer to LeRoy, "so I wouldn't have to lick everyone else's dust on the way back."

"Shee-itttt, ain't no where you can sit and not get dusty. You can help us man this new .50 caliber machine gun we're totin'. We are the new pro-tec-tors of the convoy. They done mounted a machine gun on this truck just in case we get hit, on accoun'-a we have such light security. But you know where Charlie gonna be slinging his shit once he spots this fifty, don't you? Right at us. Now ain't that the shits?"

"Hey, it don't mean nothin'," I said. "Charlie ain't gonna tangle in our shit anyway. Listen, ya wanna smoke some weed? I picked some up at mama-san's just down the block."

"Who-ee! Man, we picked ourself up some too! We be rolling in the stuff!"
"All right! I can dig it! Let's light up!"

As our stay at FSB Pulaski II lengthened, I began spending more time reflecting on my life. I had thought a lot about leadership since being thrust into the position of FDC chief, and I had lots of time with nothing to do but think. With life as spartan as it was in the field, once we were settled it could become extremely monotonous.

I gave a lot of thought to people who had been in positions of authority in my life, dissecting their behavior, looking for characteristics that I could use to command the respect and obedience of my men. I had never wanted anyone reigning over me; how, then, was I supposed to reign over my men? I searched the past for clues.

Of those in authority, I could think of only three men I had ever trusted. One of those had been a high school teacher, Mr. Glynn. It was his encouragement and concern that kept me from dropping out. I still remembered the day he took me out of his class, upset by my continual disruptions. He had repeatedly warned me about my behavior in his class, but I hadn't paid him any mind. Instant obedience, to me, was a sign of fear and weakness. I didn't obey anyone I didn't want to or wasn't forced to, and I had done pretty much what I pleased in his class. At least until that day. I was sure that my removal would mean another pink slip and a return visit to the principal's office, but it hadn't turned out that way. This teacher let me know in no uncertain terms that my behavior would no longer be tolerated, but when his anger abated, he also told me something I hadn't ever heard from an adult. He told me I had talent, brains and potential. He didn't understand why I was screwing around in school and wasting my life. He knew I had a reputation for being a hood and a troublemaker but he didn't think that was the real me. He liked me. He just didn't understand why I was continually testing him in class, pushing him to the limit.

I could sense he was sincere, and it made me feel ashamed of my behavior, though I couldn't let on that anything he said had touched me. Here was a teacher who hadn't immediately passed me off as bad. A teacher who, unlike the other jerks, maybe could even be trusted.

Three months into the school year I was expelled for drawing a picture on the wall of the auditorium— a picture which somebody else had already drawn and to which I had added a nose. And, while most of the other teachers and coaches joined the administration in blackballing me, Mr. Glynn stood by me, believing that I was guilty of nothing more than bad public relations. He knew the incident had just been an excuse for the administration to throw the book at me for other things I had been suspected of. After a two-week suspension and a plea by my parents, I was allowed to come back to school. But in a private session with the principal, I was told I would have to make up time-and-a-half for all the hours I had missed in addition to my make-up work. That meant detentions after school, forty-five minutes every day for nearly five months. It meant being kicked off the football team and the loss of my high school letter, after I had worked so hard to earn it. It meant no other sports for the remainder of the year and no extra-curricular activities. It meant being kicked out of the three clubs I belonged to and the resignation of all offices I held. But mostly, it meant putting up with being treated like a scab for the rest of the school year by coaches and teachers whose slightest report could repeat my expulsion. It didn't seem worth it to me, but fortunately Mr. Glynn was the detention hall supervisor, and his constant encouragement made it possible for me to stick with it through the many times I wanted to quit.

Thinking about him, I realized how important his concern for me had been. I wondered if I had ever thanked him. I determined that if I made it out of here alive I would.

Another one of the three had been Sergeant Kiefer, the assistant drill instructor in Basic. It was Kiefer who had run alongside me on the forced march from bivouac, encouraging and pushing me to see it through when I had fallen behind. Though Kiefer had demanded and extracted rigorous obedience from all of us recruits, there had been something different about his behavior that set him apart from all the other instructors. When he led physical training, he just didn't count cadence; he performed all the exercise right along with us. When we had to run the obstacle course, he didn't stand back and yell and scream at us; he led us through it. When our company had to run fifteen miles, he was there running right alongside us, not riding in a jeep or waiting back at base camp like most of the others. Although he was never required to carry a pack, a rifle, or a helmet, he deliberately chose to on many occasions. He never asked us to do anything he couldn't or wouldn't do himself. None of the other sergeants did that! In fact, most of them would have had a hard time crawling through the obstacle course. Their biggest obstacle was getting their belts to fit around their bellies.

Sergeant Kiefer rarely, if ever, berated us trainees. He never called us names or put us down. If someone needed an additional push, he might have been there yelling encouragement in their ears, but he was never yelling obscenities.

In the middle of Basic, I had become totally disillusioned with military life, tired of taking verbal and physical abuse. I was tired of being told what to do, what to think, how to feel, when to shit and what color of paper to wipe it on. I had never taken shit from anyone before, and swallowing the abuse I was taking in the Army made me feel like less of a man. There were times when I would have gladly gone to jail just for the privilege of striking those bastards if it hadn't been for the fact that jail time didn't count against your service time.

In a roundabout way, the way I felt about the Army resulted in a personal relationship with Kiefer.

I had become close friends with Daniel Merril, a young trainee from Portland, Oregon, who was also kind of a hippie. Like me, he had experimented with drugs shortly before his induction. One day he received a letter containing a small supply of Darvon and a couple of joints, and we ended up sharing them. I had never taken any downers before but I figured anything that would change the way I was feeling was worth a try. I took three or four of them one evening. Sitting on my upper bunk in the squad leaders' room, I felt the heaviness of the drug slowly envelop my consciousness as I struggled to control the anger I felt toward the military, a system I was beginning to see was fraught with injustice. I found that concentration on pleasant memories, coupled with the numbing effect of the drug, enabled me to create a fantasy world of good feelings. The weight of despair slowly drifted away. Somewhere along the line I simply decided to stay in this condition. I knew that if I concentrated hard enough, I could close out all reality and remain in this state. God, it was so much better than returning to the suffering I was going through.

The men whom I had bunked with gradually noticed that I was acting mighty peculiar and began to ask me questions. I heard them at first, but their voices were faint, as if far away. Although I could hear them calling, I made no effort to answer. A couple of them got frightened and began a vigorous attempt to bring me out of my trance. I paid them no attention, denying to myself that they were even there. But they wouldn't give up. While one of them scrambled to get a doctor, another one climbed up on my bunk and began shouting and slapping me back to reality. I finally chose to return from my fantasy world, tired of his slapping, although I felt no pain. As soon as I came around they sent a squad leader to tell the doctor that it had been a false alarm. They didn't want me to get into trouble.

Two days afterwards, Sergeant Kiefer called me into his office for a private talk. "Olsen," he said, "I've had my eye on you from the beginning. From the time they stood you in front of the hair cutters, I've remembered your face. Now, I'm not like a lot of the others. I'm not holding the length of your hair against you. I figure that once you're shorn of your hair you've left the past behind. I don't care what you did before, once you get into the Army you're a new man. I'll give every man a chance to prove himself, and I make my judgments on what they do now, not what they did before. As far as I can tell, Olsen, you've got a lot of moxy and you're far from being stupid, although sometimes you act pretty dumb. It was my suggestion that you be made squad leader when Englebrook couldn't handle the slot, and, I think you've done an outstanding job. I've looked over your tests and you've scored higher than any other man in this company. I know they wanted you to go to Officer Candidate School, and I don't blame you for refusing; I wouldn't be an officer either. But you've got a lot going for you. I don't want to see you screw it up.

"Look . . . I don't know what kind of problems you're having, but I'm willing to listen to you if you want to talk about them. As far as I'm concerned, you've given an excellent performance in everything you've done. You're generally the first person to get an assignment done and you generally end up doing it the best. That's why I count on you when it comes to platoon competition, to set a standard for the rest of these men to follow. Now, maybe none of this means anything to you—and you can take or leave whatever I say—but I want you to know that I am you friend. I'm not saying that you can get chummy with me in the field, because you can't. But it's only because I'm in a position of command. If you ever need anyone to talk to, however, my door is always open. You think about it, O.K.?"

After that conversation Sgt. Keifer began calling on me with even greater frequency. He asked me to demonstrate correct procedures during training drills. Whenever competition surfaced between platoons in our company, he would call me to represent our platoon. Whether it was memorizing nomenclature or dismantling and refitting a rifle, I generally came out on top, not only to his pride but to the cheers of my own men. The recognition and respect I earned made it possible for me to combat an enemy I knew was trying to break my spirit: the Army.

It was during the last three weeks of Basic that another incident helped to cement my trust in Kiefer. It was by no means a small one either.

Our head drill sergeant was a tall, lanky Southerner whose crisp demeanor clothed a vile tongue and an explosive temper, which he used to keep us subject to his every whim. He was not above sending us on long extended exercises in the care of Sergeant Kiefer while he lounged in the comfort of the E.M. club.

One afternoon, wanting to spruce up our appearance, he brought it to our company's attention that although the other platoon leaders in the battalion wore training stripes, ours didn't. He felt that wearing those stripes, black armbands with corporal's stripes sewn on them, would help polish our appearance. Unfortunately, he said, there were none available. But, by chance, he knew a set of stripes existed in a desk drawer in one of the unused barracks. And if they should all of a sudden be gone, no one would miss them, and no one would be the wiser. Of course, he added, it would be against Army regulations to steal them and he certainly wouldn't want to influence anyone to do that.

It was obvious that he was indeed asking someone to get them. So after much discussion between platoon leaders, another leader and I volunteered to slip into the barracks under the cover of darkness and retrieve those stripes. I was only too quick to volunteer. The challenge excited me. It was a chance to prove my bravado to the rest of the guys. I was sure that I would even win the respect of the sergeant, and it might put me on his better side. I even volunteered to be the one to give them to the sergeant, to say that we had just sort of "found them."

Unfortunately, things weren't quite what they seemed.

A couple of days later, as we were passing the rest of the companies in review, one of the drill instructors from Bravo Company noticed that our platoon leaders had gotten new stripes and wondered where they came from. After checking his desk in the old barracks, he quickly ascertained that they were his. Now the odd thing about it was that he was the best friend of our drill instructor, and when he began an investigation into the matter, it didn't take long for him to come up with my name.

Confronting me in front of our company, he yelled and cursed and threatened me and anyone else involved, with an Article 15. I didn't admit to anything. I certainly wasn't going to turn the other platoon leader in. But under constant pressure from him and, surprisingly, our own drill instructor, I finally admitted to being the one who had taken them and openly apologized. The funny thing about it was that our DI was enjoying the spectacle as much as the other sergeant was.

All of a sudden, the pieces of the puzzle came together. The stripes had been the bait and I had fallen neatly into a trap. Both DIs had had it in for me since my haircut. Both of them had ridden me harder than all the other guys. They thought I was a wise ass and told me so plenty of times. They had tried to break me repeatedly, in front of both companies, and I always got a dressing down by Bravo's DI even though I wasn't attached to his company. It was always the first thing he did before matching his company's best man against me in competition.

My immediate reaction was anger. Both sergeants were now openly delighting in the power they had over me, and I began to realize the dangerous position I was in. I was sincerely sorry but Bravo's DI wasn't about to be satisfied with just an apology. He announced to both companies that he was going to make an example out of me and show us what happened to people who broke military law. He was going to give me an Article 15.

For two weeks I fretted while the drill instructors debated my fate. The fear that I was going to jail was punishment in itself. When the DI from Bravo Company finally decided to drop charges against me, he let me know in no uncertain terms what a favor he was doing me. My own DI prompted me to grovel before him on my knees and apologize again. I hated it, despite my great relief.

It was later that Sergeant Kiefer sought me out and explained to me what had really happened. He had gone to a meeting of the drill instructors that had been called to determine my punishment. He had told them that he would personally appeal any charges they brought against me, and that if it came before the company commander and the truth about the incident was revealed, they wouldn't have a leg to stand on. They had backed down. Kiefer let me know that he didn't believe in this kind of shit going on as a part of Basic Training.

I knew he had put his own ass on the line when he challenged the others, and that was no small favor. I would have followed him through hell or high water after that.

The only officer I had ever trusted and respected was Captain Nyberg, our previous commander. Although he could have used his rank to ease his own position, he hadn't. He too, hung right in there with us men, doing what we did, eating what we did. If there wasn't enough ice for everyone, he didn't take any. If we had to go without sleep, he went without sleep also. His personal concern for our welfare made him a rare specimen among officers. I would have followed him against all odds because I knew he would have been point man.

If I wanted my men to follow orders, I knew I'd have to be like the men I admired, and earn their respect. I wasn't about to follow any man blindly, and I knew my men wouldn't either. I knew that I would have to lead by example, not by threats. I didn't fear punishment as much as I feared death, and that was a growing consensus among the GIs. Threats got temporary obedience, but they wouldn't make men follow you to their death. And I didn't want to have to worry about getting fragged, either.

If I wanted to maintain their trust and friendship, there would have to be equality in every sense of the word. That meant sharing the work load and the privileges. I vowed I wouldn't ask my men to do anything I wouldn't first do myself.

I also knew that if I harassed or belittled them, they would resent me for it, and we wouldn't be friends for long. I resolved never to correct or rebuke my men in public. I also made up my mind to fight for what was right for my men, whatever the cost, and to be there for them if they ever needed encouragement or help.

The 25th Division had maneuvered the bulk of its combat forces into the southeastern quadrant of our TAOI and established a screen of protection around the Saigon and Cholon area. We were still sitting at Pulaski II, in the northern Long An Province, hoping to block the main avenue of approach to Saigon. As it turned out, three NVA and VC divisions that were moving toward us were successfully intercepted before they could reach our position, but that didn't mean we weren't constantly harassed by mortar barrages. In place of a frontal assault, the enemy mounted a boastful "one hundred rockets a day" assault against the capital region. In the early morning hours on May 9, they intensified their attacks.

At 0100, Division Headquarters at Cu Chi was struck by thirty rounds of mixed 122mm and 107mm rockets. The rockets, all falling within a span of two minutes, resulted in 7 killed and 28 wounded.

An hour later, FSB Maury came under heavy mortar and rocket attack, followed by a battalion-sized ground assault. We fired in their defense in the ensuing battle, which lasted for three hours. Nine servicemen were killed and 68 were seriously wounded. In addition, two 105mm and two 155mm howitzers were destroyed by enemy sappers who had breached their perimeter. When it was all over the grunts found 14 enemy dead.

When on the same day the 1st of the 27th ran into a large enemy force just southwest of us, we began to be apprehensive about our own position being attacked. That evening, as we lay poised and waiting, the night ambush patrol outside our location surprised an advancing enemy force. All hell broke loose for nearly an hour. In the morning we counted 11 Viet Cong bodies strung out on our perimeter and hanging on the concertina wire. Many of the bodies were in pieces, the result of direct artillery fire.

At the same time that enemy movement was escalating, we received word that North Vietnam was entering peace talks. Still, the battle raged on, and a new wave of enemy assaults began taking place.

By mid-May we still hadn't moved. Intelligence sources indicated that the strong enemy movement toward Saigon, which had begun on May 3, was now reversing. Viet Cong began exfiltrating back to their sanctuaries in the Iron Triangle. That meant that we were still in the midst of it. We were directly between the Triangle and Saigon.

By now, Lee, Vechione, Campbell and Gianettino had DEROS'ed – all the old crew. To replace them the captain had transferred White from the guns and assigned me three new recruits: Joe Gracelli, Elijah Mitchell and Mike Jensen. I particularly liked Mitchell, a tall, skinny black with a rare sense of humor. He looked like he should be a basketball player. His head often grazed the light bulb that swung from the ceiling of the FDC bunker, and he joked that at future sites he wanted the bunkers a little taller.

By the first of June there wasn't a damn thing I didn't know about the FDC and how it worked. I could do my job proficiently and every other job in the center as well. I was making damn sure there weren't any slip-ups!

To combat the extensive rocketing and mortaring by the Viet Cong, the infantry elements we supported began an extensive search of suspected enemy ammunition caches along the banks of the Rach Tra Canal and the Saigon River. We fired sporadically as we covered their movement each day.

The monsoon rains made it more difficult for our mechanized forces to move. The clay roads turned to mud slicks which immobilized our heavy trucks and surface transportation. Even the division's main supply route, Highway 1 (narrow and poorly paved in most places), was often impassable. We were forced to remain in our fire support bases longer, both a blessing and a curse. Even though it meant less work, the longer we were in any one location, the greater the odds of being clearly targeted. We began to be mortared more often and with greater accuracy. Practice makes perfect. The FDC, being the center of communications, was always the first place the VC tried to knock out.

During heavy rainfall we lost our crucial air support and Charlie was well aware of it. It became easier for him to assault our base, especially when we couldn't get needed assistance from the gun ships. They began to come at us on rainy nights.

On the blessing side, longevity gave us unlimited opportunity to put our resourcefulness and American ingenuity to work, and we constructed our first private shower in the field, a teepee-like structure covered with ponchos which had a canvas bag hung from the top. We collected wooden ammo boxes and made walkways all around the FDC bunker, alleviating the need to slosh through the puddles that often surrounded us. Tired of the stench and clutter of the garbage the other guys threw around the personnel bunker, I constructed my own private sleeping quarters. It was a thrill to have my own room; clean, neat, and orderly.

I had the good fortune to meet John Threet, a clerk from Battalion Headquarters. He lived in the rear in Cu Chi and had access to a tape recorder and an ample supply of music. He taped two of his albums for me, favorites of mine: the Doors and Fresh Cream. I spent a lot of my free time listening to them, stoned, burning incense I had ordered out of the back of a magazine.

186

By late May the second enemy offensive was blunted and the division began to move more freely throughout the area. We began to experience slightly more cooperation from Vietnamese civilians. Some of them, after being handsomely paid, pointed out booby traps, supply caches, and small enemy bunker complexes. It seemed the majority of main force NVA positions around Saigon had moved to the Cambodian border, or further north into War Zone C. The division's main objective turned to thwarting enemy infiltration back into Vietnam.

Sometimes we fireballed two of our howitzers, airlifting them to support infantry units crossing into Cambodia, but that was top secret information. The FDC had been instructed not to tell the others in the battery where they were going because headquarters feared that one of them might write home and leak information through their parents. But I talked about it freely with my friends. I wondered why command was trying to hide it, especially from us. It seemed to me a necessary move if we wanted to win the war. I resented the little game of cover-up that headquarters wanted to play, but I was beginning to realize that the war was being fought like some kind of a game anyway. What angered me most was that we were the game pieces. But I was not alone in my feelings; frustration and disillusionment were growing among other soldiers.

Through weekly trips into Hoc Mon I acquired close to a kilo of marijuana. I had even finagled my way back into base camp on a resupply chopper and stashed most of the pot in my footlocker. I was extremely cautious about smoking it, but just the same, I got stoned whenever I was off shift.

The weekly sorties into Hoc Mon gave me an opportunity to get to know some of the Vietnamese people. Even though the mama-san spoke only Pidgin English, she had two daughters, Van and Luan, who could speak English quite well. When they weren't speaking for themselves, shy as they were, they were translating for the mama-san or other Vietnamese, most of them ARVN soldiers.

One day, I had jokingly propositioned one of the young girls, thinking they were just like the others whose brothers, shouting from the streets, offered to sell their bodies. That little episode nearly cost me my relationship with the mama-san. Her eyes had burned with indignation and fury. Her quick, curt reply immediately set me straight. Her daughters weren't prostitutes! She sternly rebuked me for thinking so. Girls who were prostitutes brought shame and disgrace to their families. She didn't want me kidding in the least bit about a deadly serious issue. The other guys thought it was funny, watching her wagging her finger at me and chewing me out in Vietnamese.

As all of the Vietnamese I met spoke some level of English, I often questioned them, trying to draw out their thoughts about the war. Over a period of time I was successful in doing so. Particularly helpful was one ARVN officer with whom I conversed repeatedly. It was through him and other ARVN soldiers that I began to piece together a bit of Vietnam's history. They had told me that since the fall of Diem, in 1963, it had been impossible to separate the military from the political leadership of South Vietnam. Since then, no strong civilian leadership had ever emerged. The morale was low among Vietnamese servicemen just as it was for civilians. The new Thieu regime had not gained popular support either, and these people felt it was particularly full of corruption.

I also began to understand some of the differences I had seen between their army and ours, as well as the similarities. For example, despite American advice to do so, the Vietnamese government would not open the officer corps in their own forces to the lower economic class. Their leadership was a relatively uniform group, recruited primarily from the urban middle class. Potential leaders from peasant origin normally could not meet the educational requirements to be an officer and were thus ignored. As a result, the average ARVN officer was comparatively sophisticated and wealthy and often found it difficult to relate to enlisted men, who almost all came from rural areas. One ARVN told me all of this apologetically. He was an officer, but even he didn't think that the government was right.

Another problem stemmed from Vietnamese social tradition and the political orientation of the army. Traditionally, family ties and personal loyalties were much more highly valued than experience or ability, and promotions and assignments were often based on such bonds, rather than on merit. Ambitious officers often shunned combat, seeking instead to rise through the ranks by whom they knew rather than by what they did.

Not once in the course of our conversations was patriotism or liberty mentioned. I thought it odd.

Although the officers' views seemed sophisticated or maybe just complicated, the views of the mama-san were quite simple: she was just tired of war. To her, it didn't make much difference who won or who ruled. Either way, she knew she would have to pay taxes to somebody, and neither form of government would give back to the people anywhere near the measure that it took. It had been that way all of her life. She had resigned herself to it. Over eighty years old, she had seen many governments come and go and was quick to point out that not one of them had been dominated by the Vietnamese. Nor had any of them given more than they took. All of them had exacted a price that left the people poorer.

One day, while I was listening to her dispassionate conversation about "foreign invaders," she looked directly in my eyes. The sudden embarrassment and guilt I felt caught me off guard, and I dropped my eyes to avoid hers. It was as though I had suddenly become aware of a secret that lay hidden in my heart, and I was disarmed. I quickly changed the subject, wanting to avoid the implications of her statements, but the questions I had been asking myself had resurfaced. Much of what she said had the ring of truth, but I didn't want to believe it. I needed to believe that we were here fighting for liberty and justice. How could I be the oppressor if I was an American?

I sat on the bunker line, watching the sun set, passing a joint back and forth with LeRoy. My helmet sat crooked on my head; the sweat band in my liner was soaked and felt clammy and restrictive. I wished I didn't have to wear the helmet at all, but I wasn't taking any chances. The discomfort was well worth the protection if Charlie started dropping in mortars.

The sun slowly set. It would cool off now, but I knew by the small swarm of mosquitos that were gathering that I'd better cover myself with repellent soon. As the sky turned a pale pink and a shadow began forming in the tree line a hundred yards to our front, the muscles in my face began tightening. I strained to catch a glimpse of any movement. I readied my M-16, fully loaded, safety off. I felt LeRoy's gentle nudge as he handed me the joint. I smiled at him, watching his face as I sucked smoke into my lungs. I was grateful for his companionship.

"Hey man, how you doing?" I said softly. "I really dig you, man, you know that, right?"

LeRoy smiled as he drew in another toke, nodding his head. He handed the joint back to me but I waved it off. I didn't want any more. I was stoned enough. I just wanted to relax and concentrate on the woodline. It was becoming harder to see. There was something about dusk that made the horizon sparkle, and if Charlie shot a mortar round off it was incredibly difficult to see the flash. Once it was dark, the flash from the mortar tube was clearly visible, and that was why Charlie liked to drop three or four mortars on us at dusk and then split. Then maybe he'd come back later at night and bomb the shit out of us. You never knew. Night settled. All lights went out or were covered. Everything dropped to a whisper. It was remarkable how well sound traveled at night! I became aware of the sound of crickets. In spite of the accompanying threat, night was one of my favorite times. I loved the intense quiet. It was as if life was pausing and something unique was taking its place. Man seemed suddenly shrunk as a whole other world around him awakened. This world, so huge, I had hardly noticed most of my life; yet it surrounded me. It was a limitless canopy of sky, an ever-extending forest that breathed with a life all its own. My concerns seemed so small in relationship to the world I could now see. Why had I been so slow to pay attention?

As June drew to a close, we had been in our position a little over two months. This amazing longevity was mostly due to the weather, but it was also the result of a change in strategy on the part of command. During the whole first half of June there had been few significant moves or operations other than a concentrated effort on the Saigon and Tan Son Nhut DARMA program. We had entered Phase II of Operation Toan Thang and were still in direct support of the division's 2nd Brigade. Division Arty Headquarters had been redeployed from Tan Son Nhut to Cu Chi Base Camp, where established communications facilities provided better control of the situation. Most fire support bases had been deployed in relatively stable positions. Most, like us, had been stationed around Saigon in the same configuration used during Tet, as intelligence had expected a mini-Tet uprising the first of June, but it had been relatively quiet. Intelligence wasn't getting good information; possibly it was being fed deliberate misinformation. One thing was sure, though: tactics were changing. Trying to risk fewer American lives, we had begun a policy of no contact. That is, we had decided to use more heavy bombardment. If we made contact with the enemy, unless directly assaulted, we pulled our troops back and riddled the area with air strikes and artillery fire instead of assaulting the area with ground troops. That policy was probably best illustrated by a fire mission we had gotten from C Company, 4th/9th, just recently. Their commander had refused to go into a previous area of contact until clearance was obtained for artillery fire. He wasn't going to risk losing men like he had the first time he went through the area and hadn't been able to get ARVN clearance right away. But Battalion Headquarters again refused him prior clearance. When they ordered him into the area anyway, he just called in a fire mission for 92 rounds of heavy explosives, describing Viet Cong in a bunker complex when in reality there were none. He was just taking precautionary measures. I didn't blame him.

We had completely stopped H&I fires. We could no longer get Vietnamese clearance for nightly interdiction targets in spite of the fact that we resided in heavily rocket-infested areas. Tan Son Nhut, Saigon and Cu Chi were still coming under periodic heavy rocket fire.

Reports of accidental woundings in the feet, thumbs, and hands were on the rise again, and I knew they were being self-inflicted.

13

I pushed my air mattress into the personnel bunker adjacent to the FDC and slid in behind it. I cared little that my fatigues were soaked with mud. The bunker stank, but that didn't matter either. All I cared about was that it was overhead cover and I could finally get some rest. Crawling on my hands and knees, I was careful not to bump my head on the PSP that supported the roof. There was no room to lie down; everyone but a split shift had hit the sack four hours ago. I stretched my air mattress out near the entrance. I didn't care to sleep in the open but at least there was a barricade in front of the entrance. That would protect me from any direct hits. I'd take my chances just to get some sleep.

We had set up next to a Vietnamese village not three klicks from our last position. We had dug in off the road near the edge of the village. The area to our north was completely open for a hundred meters while a swamp and rice paddy covered the area to the east. I didn't like being so close to the swamp; there was too much cover for the Viet Cong. We trained two of our guns in that direction and laid them for direct fire. To our south and west not thirty yards from the edge of our perimeter was the village, a collection of thatched huts and paths, deeply bordered in brush. A thick woods was directly behind it, but I felt unconcerned. If Charlie tried to sneak up on us, he would have to attack from the village and that seemed improbable because he knew we would blow it away if he did. As if in foreboding, however, the people who lived in the village had deserted it at dusk. Still, I thought, nothing will happen. At least not tonight. I soon convinced myself and fell asleep.

It took a little while before I realized that the explosions I was hearing were not a part of my dreams, but when one landed directly alongside our bunker, I was suddenly thrust into reality. The fog in my head immediately cleared. I shot abruptly to a sitting position. Adrenaline pumped into my system through a needle of fear.

"We're being hit, we're being hit!" I yelled to the others, kicking at their bodies to shake them from sleep.

I heard the perimeter suddenly burst into fire. I knew I had to get inside the FDC where I belonged. Fear knotted my stomach and groin as I rolled to my knees and grabbed my helmet. I pushed it firmly on my head. There was no time now to put on a flak jacket. I grabbed for my gun. Without hesitation I threw open the poncho that covered the entrance and slid out behind the barricade, racing for the entrance of the FDC. An explosion shook the bunker, knocking me to my knees as I ran through the doorway. The lieutenant charged out the door, M-16 in hand.

The situation inside was completely out of hand. One chart table lay collapsed on the dirt floor and the second was tilted on its side. The electric light bulb normally hanging from the ceiling was dangling two feet from the floor. Gracelli was hunched against the back bunker wall, his helmet and rifle in hand. Mitchell was huddled next to him, struggling to put on his flak jacket with one hand while trying to lift the chart table with the other. Mike, the radio microphone still in his hand, had fallen backwards off his chair, spilling underneath the remaining chart table. His eyes were wide with fear. "We're hit, we're hit," he kept yelling.

Crawling to his side, I peeled back his fingers and wrenched the microphone out of his hand. "Killer Niner, come in, over," I began. "Mitchell! Get that chart table operable and get to your feet! Gracelli, you do the same!"

Grabbing the phone that led to the guns, I shouted into the receiver, "Guns! . . . Guns!"

By now all hell was breaking loose on the perimeter. I knew from the small arms and machine gun fire that we weren't just being mortared; we were under ground attack.

"Where's the fire coming from?" I yelled to the guns.

"Directly in front of Gun One, sir," came a voice.

"Gun Six, Gun Six, you laid on direct fire?"

"Yes."

"Then fire the damn thing, don't wait to be told!"

While the guns were firing, I heard Command come up on the radio.

"This is Killer Niner. Please give your call signal! Over."

"This is Killer Six Niner and we're under attack," I said.

"What's your location?" Right away I recognized the major's voice.

What the hell were they asking me that for? They already had our position. "Mitchell," I said, "give me the coordinates for our battery center."

I relayed the coordinates as Mitchell called them off. Leaping to my feet, I checked the azimuth that the enemy fire was coming from. It was directly to our south.

"The village," I said. "The god-damned village!" I grabbed the mike again. "Killer Niner, we are coming under fire directly to our south on an azimuth of three-two hundred. We are receiving fire from inside the village and request permission to fire, over."

"Killer Six Niner, this is Killer Three. Permission not granted. I repeat, permission not granted! We have one-five-fives laid in counter-mortar targets for your area. Those rounds should be landing in less than two minutes. Tell your personnel to keep close to cover. Cobra Gunships should be arriving at your location in one-zero to one-five minutes, to give you a hand. Over."

"Killer Niner, this is Six Niner. Thank you. Out."

Fuck him. I knew that we had received previous clearance for some targets in case we came under attack, so I grabbed the clipboard to see what they were.

"Gun Three . . . Gun Four . . . fire mission," I said.

I could still hear RPG and mortar rounds falling all around. Between rounds, I could hear a number of the guns shouting anxiously over the external speaker on the phone.

"FDC . . . FDC . . . this is Gun One. We can see the flash where they're firing from, sir. It's right in front of the ammo bunker's perimeter post."

"FDC . . . this is Gun Three. We're ready."

"O.K.," I shouted. "Gun One . . . lay on counter-mortar target number four . . . Gun Two . . . lay on counter-mortar target six and fire when ready . . . Gun Six . . . Five . . . keep in direct fire and prepare to load . . . Gun Three . . . Four . . . azimuth three-two hundred . . . deflection . . . one-two-niner-six . . . height . . . one-two-niner . . . charge, one . . . fuse, time . . . time 1.3 seconds . . . let me know when you're ready to fire." I was going to fire into that village whether I had permission or not.

Just then the radio began to crackle as Killer Niner broke over the air.

"Killer Six Niner, this is Killer Niner, over."

"Killer Niner, Six Niner over," I replied.

"Killer Niner, you have permission to fire on previous check fire, over."

"Killer Niner, permission to fire, right . . . out. Gun Six . . . fire."

The intensity of the battle lasted nearly twenty minutes before coming to an abrupt end. As quickly and as quietly as the enemy had arrived, he withdrew. Mortars stopped falling; the perimeter grew quiet. As far as we could tell, Charlie had been unable to penetrate our perimeter defense. After getting a sit rep from all the guns, I was able to ascertain that we had suffered no casualties and only minor wounds.

As soon as I was sure it was all over, I radioed command, letting them know so that a cease-fire could be given.

Four hours later I slipped quietly out of the bunker door. In a couple of hours it would be daylight. I was sure nothing would happen between now and then. The crew inside had calmed down a couple of hours ago, and with Lieutenant Murphy (Audie, we called him) back on duty, I could afford to get some rest.

The lieutenant hadn't returned until the gunships departed, nearly twenty minutes after we had given cease-fire. He was new with us, having replaced Lieutenant Voss when Voss left to become a forward observer with B Company, 1/27th. He had been with us nearly five weeks and still hadn't been able to adjust to his new responsibilities. He was still a grunt at heart, infantry all the way. It was his responsibility to command the FDC, especially whenever we were in contact, but as soon as we came under fire he was out the door, M-16 in hand, headed for a defensive position. Each night he still set out his own claymores.

As long as he knew I could handle things inside, he was going to be outside where he could see what was going on. If Charlie was coming in after him, he wanted to see him coming. He wanted room to maneuver. He didn't want to be some sitting duck in a penny arcade. I knew that he felt defenseless inside the bunker. So did I. But we had to trust that if we stayed inside and did our job, the people on the outside would do theirs and keep the enemy from penetrating this far. But Lieutenant Murphy couldn't trust, and he couldn't concentrate on what was going on. Invariably, he was out the door. I didn't see his actions as blameworthy, but I knew that Command would. Up till now, I had been able to cover for him, but I wondered how long it would be before the captain said something.

During late night hours Audie and I had frequently sat up and rapped, and more than once he had mentioned how bad he felt about not being with his old company in the field. Often as not he felt guilty, as if he had deserted them when he had been transferred to the artillery. But that was the way the system worked. The lieutenants spent half their tour with the infantry as forward observers and half with the artillery, providing cover fire. With exposure to both, they would better understand what each situation was like, and they could perform their duties in a more efficient way.

I finally got back to sleep, only to be rudely awakened less than two hours later.

"Hey Olsen," Mitchell said, shaking my arm. "Olsen! Headquarters wants a situation report on last night's contact. You're gonna have to do it, man, 'cause nobody else knows how!"

"All right," I grumbled, "I should be in there in a minute or two."

Turning over on my side I struggled to keep awake. My eyelids felt like metal plates. All I wanted to do was sleep for a hundred years. I staggered to my knees, abruptly aware of the putrid smell coming from my own body. I could sure use a toke, I thought.

Laying my M-16 on the roof of the bunker, I made my way to the water tank and filled the steel pot of my helmet. I carried it back and balanced it on two sandbags, careful not to spill the water that sloshed inside. Lifting the cover of my ammo can, I dragged out the small canvas bag that protected my soap and razor, and after splashing my face with cold water, began to shave.

Shit, I thought, this is ridiculous! Shaving just because of Army regulations. Another horseshit rule that doesn't fit the circumstances, and the Army's too fucked up to make a change. Still, I scraped my face in obedience and then went inside.

As soon as the sit rep had been channeled to headquarters, I left the FDC and headed for the chow line, actually looking forward to powdered eggs and dry toast, anything that might give me a boost. I was sitting on top of the personnel bunker eating when Vanous stuck his head out the FDC and yelled, "Hey, any of you guys interested in going out on patrol this morning? The infantry is short of men and we need to sweep the area where we made contact last night." There were no volunteers. Ten minutes later White came walking out of the FDC, his helmet and flak jacket on, M-16 cradled in his arm.

"Hey, Olsen," he said excitedly, "I'm going out on sweep. Why don't you come along? It'll be a lot of fun."

"Fun like last night, huh!"

"C'mon, we'll get a chance to sweep the village and check out the hootches. Maybe we'll find us some young baby-san!"

"Yeah, or we might get our shit blown away!"

"Listen, c'mon! I know you're gonna come! I'm gonna fill up my magazines and then I'll be back to getcha, O.K.?"

He disappeared inside the personnel bunker. I was apprehensive. To me it wasn't worth the risk. But then, White was surely going, and if something happened to him I wouldn't be able to live with myself, especially knowing I could have been there. Besides, I thought, maybe it'll be like Les said. We'll find something interesting, and I'll have the chance to pick up some souvenirs. I wasn't anxious to get shot at, but on the other hand, I was thinking that maybe I'd get a chance to see Charlie out in the open. I relished the chance of getting into his shit the way he'd been getting into ours.

I strolled over to the FDC bunker and stepped inside.

"Hey, lieutenant," I said, "I think I'm gonna go out with White on sweep this morning. Do you think you can handle things while I'm out?"

"If you see Charlie, give him one for me!" he replied.

"O.K., lieutenant." I went to pick up my rifle and a sling of magazines.

The lieutenant had no gripes about my going out on patrol; in fact, he was chomping at the bit to go himself, but since he had deserted his post last night, he knew he'd better hang tight and stay on duty today. He was clearly disappointed, though, that we were going out and he had to stay behind. I was slipping on my flak jacket when I saw him come out of the bunker. "Hey Olsen, hold up a minute," he called as he walked. "Take a couple of these with ya . . . pin 'em to your vest." He handed me some grenades. "Ya got enough magazines?"

"Yeah . . . I'm O.K. Take it easy, O.K., Lieutenant? I know you'd like to be out yourself, but maybe I can take your place and help out. All right? . . . I'll see ya later. You take care of things, O.K.?"

"Hey, Olsen, let's go," White yelled impatiently. He had been waiting about fifteen feet away. I turned and walked toward the ammo bunker where the patrol was gathering.

"Hey man, that lieutenant's all right, huh?" said White.

"Yeah, he's O.K. I feel sorry for him, though. He sure doesn't like being stuck in the artillery."

"Yeah, sometimes I wonder what it would be like to be out in the bush. At least those guys aren't having to spend most of their time filling sandbags or humping ammo. It's got to be a lot more exciting than this."

"Well, if it's excitement ya want, you've come to the right place," I answered, doing a Groucho Marx imitation. "Only this kind of excitement I need like a hole in the head."

I spotted LeRoy and Lusk as we approached their bunker. They were dressed to the hilt, also ready to go. "Shit, looks like the whole ammo detail turned out for this one," I yelled. "Hey, what's happening, LeRoy?"

LeRoy turned, smiling. His flak jacket hung loose and open. His deep black skin glistened in the sun. "Hey, brother! Ya going on this gig, too?" He laughed. "I sho' 'nuff didn't expect to see you here."

Before I could answer, the infantry platoon sergeant stepped up on some sandbags and started talking.

"Listen up! We're gonna be sweeping the vil' and about 500 meters surrounding it as well. You guys who haven't been on patrol before, listen up! Make sure you keep your eyes open for trip wires and don't go searching any place on your own. When you're checking out these huts make sure you've got a backup. Team up with someone; don't go it alone! Hey," he added as two guys drifted up with only their jungle hats on. "Nobody goes out on patrol without their helmet. Ya got that, you guys!"

Minutes later we were lined up, waiting our turn to cross through the barbed wire that lined our perimeter. A tingle swept through my groin as I stepped over. I could sense both excitement and fear with each step I took. My body breathed fresh life as my senses quickened. I pushed my fears aside. Who cares anyway? If those two RPGs that hit our bunker last night didn't do me in, why should I worry about getting knocked off today. Some guys get it and some guys don't! It just seems to be luck. Lady luck! Well, lady, you've been with me so far; I hope you don't desert me today.

As we made our way through the concertina wire the men up front pointed to a patch of ground about two meters off to our right. When I approached the spot, I saw what they were pointing at. There, snagged in the wire, were small bits of torn clothing, deeply stained in blood. Charlie had gotten closer than I thought. I wondered where his body was now.

We cautiously plodded our way through the village. Not one villager had returned this morning. I could certainly guess why. We should have blown this village to smithereens like we did that Buddhist temple the VC tried to hide behind when they attacked us at our last location. At least then we would know Charlie wouldn't be using it again tonight.

I wondered how I would feel if someone came in and destroyed my home. Shit, if they wanted to keep their homes safe they should have been here last night to keep Charlie from coming in. If they didn't want to protect their village, then why the hell should we? If they weren't sympathizers, or VC themselves, then why didn't they stay and fight!

White and I stepped quietly up to the open doorway of a bamboo hut, pressing our backs against the wall like they did in all the movies. What a dumb move this is, I said to myself. These bamboo walls wouldn't even stop a knife, much less a bullet. Charlie could be right on the other side and stick a knife in my back.

I stepped out from the wall and waved White off too. Leveling my M-16, I stepped in front of the doorway and cautiously peered inside. My eyes darted across the room. It was empty.

Why the hell don't they have floors in these places, I thought. What the fuck are they doing living in the dirt?

In one corner, some army issue mosquito netting hung over a flat bamboo mat. "I wonder where he got that," I whispered to White, pointing at it with my M-16. The stark simplicity of the hut reminded me of the small clubhouses we built from scrap lumber when I was a kid. The only interesting feature was a small mud-caked bunker occupying one side of the room. A few planks rested on top of its sandbag roof. They were covered by another thin straw mat. Somebody's bed, I guessed.

"Cover me," I whispered to White as I approached the bunker.

A small dark opening pierced one side of the bunker, like the entrance to a dog house. I wondered how anyone could squeeze in there, much less a family. Leaning over the top, I stuck the end of my M-16 inside and poked it around. "Anybody in there?" I asked, laughing.

"Shit, there isn't anybody in this village," said White. "In fact there ain't anything in these houses at all."

"Well, no spoils to the victor," I joked, but it did seem odd. White was right. These huts didn't contain anything. No beds, blankets, cooking utensils, stove, tables or chairs. No furniture of any sort. No nothing! A rickety set of wooden shelves had been built on one side of the hut, but all it contained were some stained ceramic saucers and some sticks of incense. I stuck the incense in my pocket. I wondered if they had carried all their personal belongings with them when they left, or if they even had any. Did these people live like this all of the time?

We left and continued searching the village, making our way toward the southeast corner where we were to regroup.

"Hey man, look here," White said, pointing to a spot on the ground near the rear of a hut. "They must have fired some mortars from here. You can see where the ground has been packed down from the impact of the base plate!"

I decided to look inside the hut. I had seen two GIs coming out of the place, so I knew it had already been searched. Stepping inside, I looked around. One corner of the wall had been completely blown apart and blood was splattered all over it.

"Not much cover in here last night," I called out to White. "We might not find any bodies but you can bet your ass we got at least one last night."

Having satisfied my curiosity, I left, following White to the outskirts of the village. I could already see some of the soldiers gathering. Cigarettes were quietly being lit as we approached and silence hung in the air with gently curling smoke.

As soon as we had all regrouped, a corporal in charge of our squad gave us directions.

"Now be on the lookout, especially in those bamboo hedgerows. If Charlie's got a spider hole there he could pop up, do you in, and disappear forever. Be especially careful for trip wires there. Keep your eyes open for any disturbed spots on the dike tops, 'cause that's where we'll be walking and it's a good place to plant mines. Follow the point man and watch where he's going, he'll signal if anything happens. If something should happen, don't dive into the rice paddies; they have bamboo stakes underwater planted near the edge. If you jump down you might get a stake up your boot, and if you fall down, you might get one up your ass!"

"Shit, corporal," someone blurted out. "Where the hell we supposed to go? There's only the berm and the water!"

"Spread yourself flat on top of the berm," the corporal answered, "then slide quickly over the edge and keep your head down. Chances are, if the point man doesn't run into anything, then neither will we. All right? Saddle up!"

We filed slowly down a trail that led out of the village, passing through thick bamboo grass. As soon as we broke into a clearing and began to hike the dike, I felt easier, though my active imagination battled my desire to relax. We kept our eyes and ears alert, constantly scouting the horizon for any sign of movement.

Four hours later we returned to the base. The two sticks of incense I had lifted seemed an unfair exchange for the apprehension and tension. I had learned to live with a sense of expectancy in the base, but being on sweeps was completely different.

Later that evening, I noticed Mike Jensen leaning against the outside of the FDC bunker. His shift had recently been relieved, so I hadn't expected him to be hanging around. He seemed preoccupied.

"Hey Mike," I said, "what's happening? You all right?"

"Yeah, I've just been waiting to talk to you. You got a minute?"

"Sure. What's on your mind?"

"Well," he began, his head bent down, "I just wanted to apologize for what happened last night, I mean, about the way I acted. I don't know what happened! I just freaked out."

"Hey, listen, it don't mean nothing. You're not the only one it's happened to. There's nothing to be ashamed of. There isn't a one of us who doesn't understand the meaning of fear and no one holds it against you or thinks any less of you because you freaked. You gotta understand, man, you're just new in country. We all were at some time. You'll get used to it."

"But I let everybody down."

"Look, man, let me tell you something. Covering for one another is what this gig is all about. There ain't none of us who isn't willing to go beyond his duty when it's necessary for the survival of the battery. We all need each other if we want to get out of here alive. You aren't the first one who's been scared to death, and you won't be the last. Just stick in there and pull your weight. As long as you don't let it play on your mind and get you down, no one else will either, O.K.?"

198

"All right," he said sheepishly. "Thanks."

"Forget it. Now take it easy and get some rest."

Two days later there was renewed life in the village and with it came the young children and baby-sans selling coke and trinkets. Although we weren't permitted to have any contact with them, I knew that the back of the mess tent straddled the wire fence that stood at the village entrance and behind it, hidden from view, you could make contact with any of the vendors you wanted. It was the responsibility of the mess crew to make sure none of the guys went back there to chase the gooks away, but since Wheatstraw and I were tight, he let me go back and see what they were selling. He kept an eye out in front of their deuce-and-a-half while I walked around behind it to talk to the Vietnamese.

I bought marijuana from a baby-san, who called it *"can-sa,"* and shared most of it in the ammo bunker, where I had begun spending most of my free time. It was becoming a haven for me, a place where I could get away from the responsibilities I shouldered most of the day. There, I wasn't a Specialist Fourth Class; I wasn't a section leader. I was just Olsen, a soul brother.

I had changed the rotation of shift hours so that each crew spent eight hours on and eight hours off. That way, every other day the shift reversed itself. No one crew had to pull night duty all the time or be stuck with the work load whenever we moved. This didn't relieve me when I was off duty, as I spent most of my time training the new crew. But at least with the new shifts I was fairly free six hours of each day, unless, of course, there was a complicated fire mission. I was on duty then, whether I was off shift or not.

White, Mitchell, and Vanous frequently accompanied me to the ammo bunker: Mitchell, because he was black and liked the company of the brothers; White, because he was a stone head, like most of the brothers; and Vanous, because he smoked occasionally, too.

One afternoon LeRoy told me to take a walk with him. He had a surprise to show me. Shouldering my M-16, I followed him out toward the perimeter. We headed toward a corner where the resupply Chinook generally dropped its sorties. The deuce-and-a-half used by the mess hall was parked there, and as we drew closer and approached its far side, I could see a small string of GIs lined up outside the cab.

"Hey man, what's happening over there?"

"Just wait and see, man." LeRoy giggled. "It's part of that surprise I was talking to you about."

We walked to within ten yards of the truck and stopped. The guys standing in line were talking and laughing excitedly, although some of them were glancing around with obvious apprehension.

"Hey, c'mon man, hurry up in there," someone said. "We want our chance too!"

"Shee-ittt, you gonna get nothing but sloppy thirds anyway," someone else said. Laughter rippled through the line.

"Hey, I don't give no shit, man," another man said, "I just wanna get mine."

Suddenly the door of the cab swung open. I saw a poncho lift and a soldier slid out of the cab, his fatigue pants still wrapped around his knees. I suddenly understood what the commotion was all about. I saw the poncho rise again, revealing the sweaty face and arm of a pretty young Vietnamese girl.

"Shit man, how the hell did she get in here?"

LeRoy started laughing. "The mess hall sergeant brought her out here this morning. He must of snuck her into the truck through the back gate. He's charging twenty dollars a hit and probably paying her one-fourth of that."

"Man, he could really get his ass in a sling if the captain found out. He's sure taking a big chance!"

"Shee-ittt, he'll probably clear a few hundred dollars today. These guys in the field don't ever get a chance to get themselves a piece. Why, half of those men in line are infantry grunts. They're bound to go back and pass the word! You'd better get in line, Olsen, before it really gets sloppy!"

"No thanks! I wanna go home with my dick in one piece. There's no telling what she's got. By the time these other guys are through, the risk is gonna be even greater!"

"Well, I'm gonna get me some," LeRoy said, smiling, walking toward the line. "Wheatstraw was supposed to save a place in line for me; it looks like my turn is coming up soon."

"I'll wait for ya! But you'll be lucky if your dick doesn't rot off!"

LeRoy laughed. Undaunted, he trotted over to the front of the line.

I sat down against the edge of a rice paddy berm to wait. As far as I was concerned it was no laughing matter. Campbell had picked up a case of VD before he left and they had held him at his point of departure, shooting him up with penicillin until he was cured. Worse still, the news was circulating that guys were picking up a strain of VD that even penicillin couldn't cure, and you couldn't get back to the States if you didn't get cured. I wasn't gonna let anything stand in the way of my getting back.

The door of the cab swung open again. Tiny, the cook, a huge man weighing over two hundred pounds, climbed into the cab. Unbuttoning his pants, he pulled them down to his knees. Everyone laughed at the expression on the girl's face as he climbed in. Holding the poncho back, she exposed her tiny frame as he climbed on top of her and then shut the door. A stream of wisecracks and innuendo followed as the poncho rose and fell above the truck cab window.

The spectacle was disgusting and sad. I wondered how the guys could expose themselves like this, taking part in ruthless copulation as if it were some big joke. Didn't they feel any shame? How could this Vietnamese girl allow herself to be used like this? I felt embarrassed and ashamed for these men, and for this woman as well.

Lifting the tent flap that covered the bunker entrance, I let the cool morning air sweep over me. I left the flap up and watched as the sun began peeking over the horizon. A soft red glow softened the retreating darkness. It was 0600, time for the shift to change.

"White," I said, "why don't you go shake those people out of bed again. I'll watch the radio while you're out."

"O.K." His unshaven face accented the shadows beneath his bloodshot eyes. I watched him as he disappeared around the corner of the bunker, his rumpled fatigues giving him the appearance of some bowery bum. I was glad that he had transferred to the FDC. I liked having him near. I enjoyed the hours we pulled shift together, rapping into the wee hours of the morning.

I was glad my shift, which had stretched exhaustingly long, had finally come to an end. I was anxious to hit the sack. The fresh morning air seemed to lift my spirits and I could feel a second wind coming on, but I was glad that I didn't have to endure another sleepless day. Still, this war was teaching me that I could do anything; and I could do it 24 hours a day if necessary. I had never been so stretched in all my life. Never had so much been demanded, and never had I given so much. If I had never known before just what I was physically or mentally capable of, I knew now! But it had left me tired . . . tired all the way through, as if I were rapidly aging.

I leaned against the door frame and looked out over the camp. Everything was calm. I could see a few men silhouetted against the dawn sky, walking between geometric bunkers which jutted up on the horizon. Everything was picture perfect. I loved it like this. Why couldn't I have seen this country under other circumstances?

I walked back inside. Picking a clipboard off the table, I reviewed the figures. I'd better get the guns up and get them laid, right.

Stepping over the chart table, I checked the infantry locations again, just to make sure. A Company of the 4th Battalion 9th Infantry was conducting an air mobile combat assault at 0745 hours near the Saigon River. We would be on call in case they ran into any shit. I wondered why they weren't prepping the area beforehand. Checking the map again, I could see that their LZ was in a heavily populated area. That was why! Well, if there were a lot of civilians in that area, they shouldn't have any problems. It should be just another routine sweep.

Slowly, the other crew staggered on shift. First Vanous, then Dangerfield, finally Jensen.

"Hey, why don't one of you guys go over and see if the lieutenant's up?" I asked. "The Manchus have got an assault planned around 0800 this morning; he should be wide awake by then."

"All right," grumbled Vanous, "Mike, go over and get him up!"

"Hey, why don't you?" whined Jensen.

"Hey Mike, just do what you're told, O.K.!" I said. Downcast, Jensen rose and made for the door. Mornings weren't good for anybody's disposition.

The morning silence was broken by the crackle of a message coming in on the radio. Dangerfield reached for the mike.

"This is Killer Six Niner, over," he said.

"Killer Six Niner, this is Alpha Red Alert. Our sit rep is negative at this time. We have negative findings at night Alpha Sierra, over."

"Alpha Red, you report negative findings, over," replied Dangerfield.

"Killer Six Niner, that is affirmative, over."

"Alpha Red, roger, out."

"What was that all about?" asked Dangerfield.

"He's talking about their night ambush site," I said. "They sprung an ambush last night. They thought they spotted some movement on the river."

"Is that what the firing was about last night?"

"No, we were firing DARMA targets. Saigon was taking rockets last night, but nothing more. If Charlie was supposed to be mounting another major attack on Saigon the first of June, he's a little bit behind schedule. Hey listen, I'm gonna get some hot chow and then hit the sack. You know where to find me if you need me. The guns are already laid on target, and the firing information is on the forms. O.K. Vanous? You'd better familiarize yourself with them before the LZ comes up!"

After explaining everything that was going on, I left. I'd check back in once more after chow and then hit the sack. The lieutenant would be on duty by then and I wouldn't have to worry about anything going wrong.

As soon as I had eaten, I stuck my head back into the FDC, to make one last check. It was 0730. "Everything O.K.?"

"Yeah," said Dangerfield. "They just finished dropping CS gas into the area in preparation for the LZ. The infantry should be going in there in ten or fifteen minutes."

I could see the outside of the perimeter from where I stood. Like a swarm of insects rising from the earth, a flight of helicopters began lifting, raising clouds of dust. Just then the radio crackled and I could hear the infantry CO reporting that their troops were airborne and on their way.

"Hey, Olsen," said the lieutenant, "show me exactly what's going on here before you leave."

"Hey, lieutenant, I already explained everything to Vanous; he can tell you what's happening."

"No! You took the information last night; you show me what's happening!"

"O.K., lieutenant," I answered wearily.

Lieutenant Voss was again acting as our temporary fire direction officer. Lieutenant Murphy had asked for a transfer shortly after leaving our last position; the artillery was just not for him. Command had sent Lieutenant Voss back until a permanent replacement could be found. Only now, it was First Lieutenant Voss; he had been promoted. Since he was now anxiously bucking for his captain's bars, he didn't want anything going wrong. Still, he spent most of his time in the captain's tent, drinking, and had delegated all of the FDC's responsibility to me. I didn't mind. As far as I was concerned Voss was an alcoholic and bumbling idiot. Things worked smoother if he kept out of the way. I simply did my best to appease him and to assure him that everything was all right. He trusted my judgment fully, so that wasn't hard to do. For me, it was just one less person to have to take orders from.

I was going over everything again when the radio suddenly erupted with an urgent, commanding voice.

"Killer Six Niner . . . Killer Six Niner, this is Alpha Red Alert. We are under attack . . . I repeat, we are under attack; the Lima Zulu is hot, over."

Dangerfield shot upright in his chair. He grabbed a note pad and pencil in one hand and the mike in the other. "Red Alert, this is Killer Six Niner, sit rep and position, over."

"Mike," I shouted, "get to that chart; I'll take the other."

Jensen leaped to his feet as I crossed over to man the other chart. Vanous picked up the telephone to the guns, twirling the handle to ring each one. "Guns prepare for a fire mission," he shouted.

The lieutenant pulled his chair up by the FADAC computer, handing me a slide rule to check the computations coming out. As soon as I heard their location being relayed, I plotted it on the map . . . "from cigarette, left one-five-zero meters" . . . and began relaying the information to Vanous. "Azimuth zero seven hundred, range . . . five four three zero meters. . . ."

"Killer Six Niner, we have two helicopters down and are receiving small arms, automatic weapons and rocket fire. Enemy size unknown. Request gunships and artillery fire, over."

The fighting raged for hours, the enemy breaking contact sporadically only to re-engage the infantry repeatedly throughout the day. It was dark before the enemy finally slipped away. As I prepared the evening's situation report to headquarters, I looked over the log of the last few hours:

. . . 2000 Casualties for 4/9 as of 1830: A/4/9 has 1 US KIA, 11 US WIA, 3 US MIA. B/4/9 has 1 US KIA, 5 US WIA. All casualties dusted off except MIAs.

2145 4/9 have recovered 1 MIA, change status to KIA.

2215 A/4/9 reports recovery of other 2 MIA, both dead. Inf. elements will pull back and use more arty, will check out area in morning.

I slumped down in my chair. It was 2300 hours and we were still firing sporadically to cover the infantry's night location. The 3 MIAs had been reported at 1305. All day I had been hoping that they would be found O.K., and now a heaviness lay in the pit of my stomach. We had been credited with 10 VC body count, as had B Battery, but numbers on a sheet of paper didn't make up for the loss I felt. Were we fighting merely for an enlarged body count? What did these people die for today? Was it for a government riddled with corruption? Was it for these peasants who didn't even want us here? What was the sense of losing lives for land we occupied one day and left the next? We had spent months crisscrossing an area no larger than fifty miles square, and it didn't seem to make a damn bit of difference. We were like a fox in a field of gophers. As soon as Charlie appeared in one place we ran after him, only to have him disappear and reappear at the other end of the field. No matter where we went, he always came back. No matter how much we destroyed, he always rebuilt. We couldn't control any area larger than our own base camp! Fuck! Why, we weren't gonna win this war unless we occupied every square inch of land—or destroyed it all.

I was angry. Not only because of the senseless way the war was being fought; not only because we'd have to move an entire population over here to dominate, or decimate, this country; but because we were now fighting a war where winning wasn't the goal. I wasn't even sure that we were fighting on the right side. We were losing American lives for nothing! We were gaining nothing! Not liberty, not honor, not freedom and certainly not victory. The only victory we saw every day was our own survival. We were still alive. We had made it through another day. All except for the soldiers for whom there was no victory at all.

Why did I believe those people who told me that we had come to set captives free? Shit, we were the ones being held captive. As far as I could tell, nearly everyone was against us! We seemed to be fighting the whole population. If the majority of these people were against us, then where were these people we were supposed to be setting free? If it wasn't for freedom and liberty that we fought, then just why the hell were we fighting?

I pushed my chair back and stood. It had been over forty hours since I had slept.

"Vanous," I said, "why don't you send in the sit rep? Make sure you include the number of rounds so they can send out a resupply . . . and tell them we don't have total body count as of yet. I'm going to sleep! Wake me in the morning if they send down a prep so I can check it before we fire."

I could feel my heart pounding as I stepped out into the night.

Loading the last of my personal belongings on the back of the three-quarter, I turned to survey the FDC bunker, which now lay in shambles. As my eyes darted around the area, looking for any unfinished business, I tried to decide which of the new recruits I would assign the responsibility of driving and maintaining the truck. Not one of them looked old enough to have a driver's license. Not that it mattered over here. Joe seemed the most capable. He also seemed a bit older than the other two, Mitchell and Jensen. Maybe it was just his dark complexion and the shadow of stubble that covered his chin everyday. It seemed to grow as fast as he shaved it. He could do the job all right, but I had something else in mind for him.

Jensen was probably the logical choice; Mitchell still seemed like a boy. Besides, an earlier conversation with Mitchell led me to believe that he hadn't much experience driving. So, Jensen it would be. "Jensen, come over here for a minute!"

"Yes, sir!"

"Don't call me sir!" I snapped. "I'm not an officer. And I don't want Charlie singling me out as a leader."

"Yes, sir," he stammered, then quickly apologized.

White and Dangerfield picked up their ammo boxes and crammed them into the back in preparation for the move. Leaning against the three-quarter's side, they both took a breather and listened.

"I want you to take over responsibility for maintaining the truck," I continued.

"That means that you'll not only do preventive maintenance, but you'll drive on convoy as well. You think you can handle that?"

"You bet," Jensen replied. "Does that mean I'll be driving on this convoy as well?"

"No better time than the present to start learning."

"Whewww, shit," teased White, "I'm sure glad I don't have your job!"

"Shit, man," said Dangerfield, "if we run over a mine, you're gonna be the first one to get it."

"Hey, ya never been on convoy before, have ya, boy? Lots of times those front APCs won't set off a charge or will miss it. Sometimes one of the heavier trucks will run over a mine with a delayed fuse and it won't go off immediately."

"Shit, that's not so bad, 'cause those big trucks can take it. All a mine will do to them is blow the tires. There's too much steel between the ground and the driver to cause any serious injury. But it's different with this three-quarter. Any mine explodes under that and you'll lose both your legs, and maybe your balls!"

I listened as the guys teased Jensen, really laying the bull on thick. I laughed along with them as Jensen took it in. It wasn't long, though, before I noticed some genuine concern on his face. "All right, knock it off, guys," I ordered. "He's had enough!"

"Is that really true?" Jensen asked me, his voice full of apprehension. "Is what they've been saying how it really is?"

"Hey man, don't pay mind to those guys," I said. "You'll be all right. There's no need to worry!"

Jensen's hurt look quickly changed to anger. He yelled at White and Dangerfield who were now departing. He didn't like being the butt of their jokes. I didn't blame him. What the hell, I knew it was no use kidding him about the truth, either. Our convoys had been stalled many times because of mine clearing operations, but I didn't see any sense in causing him to worry about it. If it happened, it happened. Besides, it was his responsibility to drive. Every other man had done it, and he would have to do it too.

When the final word came to tear down, we rushed to load the remaining equipment into the three-quarter, anxious to get into place before the convoy moved. By the time I made sure everything was taken and radio contact was still in place, everyone else had boarded the three-quarter or a deuce-and-a-half close behind. As I leaped into the truck I could hear Lieutenant Anthony and Jensen arguing. Anthony was our new fire direction officer.

"Get into this truck and drive!" the lieutenant said sharply.

"I don't want to be the one to lose my legs," Mike pleaded. "Why can't someone else drive?" He stood outside the truck, his hand on the open door.

"Are you disobeying a direct order?" the lieutenant demanded. "Get in this truck and drive!"

"No, I'm not going to do it."

"Hey, c'mon, Mike, do your duty," I said. "There's nothing to be afraid of. These guys were just pulling your leg!"

"Goddammit," the lieutenant screamed, "we've got to get this truck into the convoy! We're holding up the move!" Cursing, he began sliding from the right side of the cab toward the driver's position.

"If nobody'll drive this son-of-a-bitch, I will myself. Your ass is gonna be grass, though," he spat at Jensen. "You stinkin' coward! I'm gonna see that the book gets thrown at you!"

I was disgusted with both of them. Why the fuck did it have to be this way?

"Hold it, Lieutenant," I said, leaping over the back rail of the three-quarter into the passenger side.

"How do you start this fucking thing?" the lieutenant said, raving. His face turned beet red as he tried to locate the ignition switch and starter button.

"C'mon, lieutenant, I'll drive it." But it was too late; we lurched into gear.

"C'mon, lieutenant," I urged as we drove, "you let me do the driving. It's the responsibility of my men!"

But the lieutenant, still furious, would have nothing to do with me. He continued to drive, at least until the minesweepers halted the convoy to remove two mines from the road. Then he switched positions with me and I took over the wheel.

As the monsoon season continued, ushering in skyrocketing temperatures and persistent humidity, changes were taking place. Not only in military strategy, but in my behavior.

Although the major enemy movement forecasted by intelligence never materialized, we were consistently encountering small enemy forces. Even though there was a clear indication that Charlie was moving troops and supplies through free fire zones at night, the Vietnamese government had begun putting pressure on us to abolish the zones. Civilians were complaining. First it had been the squelching of H&I fire, now this. Someone in the government seemed intent on giving the enemy every advantage.

It was becoming harder for us to get Vietnamese clearance for air strikes and artillery fire as well, even when our troops were in direct contact. In July, three such incidents had occurred. I remembered them all quite vividly. One infantry element had gotten into heavy contact and the S-3, who was flying in a minicopter above them, had called us for artillery support. We had stood by helplessly, unable to fire for thirty minutes, first awaiting U.S. Army clearance, then ARVN clearance, and finally political clearance from the Vietnamese provincial authorities. The S-3 had circled helplessly making repeated requests; first for armed helicopters, which were delayed because of a commitment of all available assets to simultaneous operations, then for artillery fire, which didn't come. He had to watch a barrage of RPGs and small arms fire explode through his men, killing or severely crippling most of them. By the time we received clearance the enemy had withdrawn and disappeared. It was difficult for me not to believe that the provincial authorities had deliberately taken their time, working in sympathy with the enemy.

Infantry elements were becoming even more cautious about risking contact and began using artillery and air strike coverage more frequently. Some infantry elements would call in air strikes just to dislodge one Vietnamese sniper.

As more restrictions were lumped on us, the Army began a more aggressive attempt at "Vietnamization," an effort to reverse the military role that the South Vietnamese Army played, with the one we were playing. I couldn't have been in more agreement with their plan, although I could see that it hadn't been working. Even though we were arming the Vietnamese with every available conventional weapon, increasing their firepower, their mobility and their logistical support, we were still playing the major role in the war effort. As far as I was concerned, this was a war the Vietnamese had to win for themselves. If they didn't want to fight it, even after we had given them military superiority, then fuck 'em, the Cong could have the country. If the Cong were willing to fight the hardest for it, then it belonged to them. I knew they wouldn't be fighting their hearts out if they didn't believe in what they were doing. If the ARVNs didn't want to die for their country then screw the war! I just wanted out!

I began protesting the war and the Army's regulations with small rebellions. I began wearing jewelry next to my dog tags. I was also growing my mustache and had refused to shave. Although that had met with considerable resistance from the authorities, I had gained the support of enough other people with similar intentions that the brass backed down. I was finally allowed to wear it as long as I kept it clean and short. Others quickly followed suit. I began writing and drawing protest symbols on my helmet cover, sweatband, and flak jacket. "Peace," "Love," "Short," "Fuck You," and a peace symbol covered those articles. In addition, I began wearing peace tags—red, white and blue plastic dog tags that had a dove and a peace symbol stamped on them. I had decided that this was going to be my statement of patriotism. As a loyal American, I was going to make a stand for what I thought was right, even if it went against the grain of the majority. I had learned that simply being in the majority didn't necessarily make you right. If being a patriot meant fighting and dying for one's countrymen, I was willing to do that, but I wasn't willing to do that for the Vietnamese. Patriotism meant doing what was best for one's country, and it seemed to me that what was best for us was to get the fuck out of this war and let the Vietnamese decide their fate among themselves. I knew that I wasn't alone in my opinions. More and more symbols of protest were beginning to emerge, most markedly in soldiers' attire. You could simply read the discontent.

I knew it wasn't likely that I would get by wearing my peace tags without some kind of confrontation with the brass. By some, maybe most, my actions might be interpreted to mean I was a traitor. But I had reached the point where I wasn't afraid of being categorized or labeled. I had been labeled most of my life. I had been an outcast before. What difference would rejection make now? I had to stand up for what I believed.

I wasn't surprised, then, when one evening the field staff sergeant stopped in to see me.

"Hey, Olsen," he began, sneering as he stood behind my chair, "you know that it's against Army regulations to wear any jewelry but your dog tags, don't you?"

"Gee, I didn't know that, Sergeant," I said calmly, not turning around. It was late and I had a prep to work out for the guns. I didn't have time to get into a confrontation, and I wasn't in the mood for it. But the shuffling of feet and the squeaking of chairs let me know that he and I were becoming the center of attention in the small bunker.

"White, you got those figures?" I said.

"Range, 7000 meters," said White.

"Check," drawled Mitchell.

"O.K., left three-hundred meters, drop five-zero."

If this confrontation had to be carried out in my bunker the sergeant was going to be sorry, 'cause I wasn't backing down, not in front of my men. I had already decided that if I got my ass in hot water for wearing these tags, I would probably take them off. Everybody pretty much knew where I stood anyway. But if I was pressed now, I wasn't going to back down.

"Well, the captain has asked me to point out to you the Army regulation that prohibits you wearing any jewelry but those dog tags," the sergeant continued. "Now why do you suppose that is?"

"Well, it must be because he thinks I'm wearing something against regulation."

"I'm not looking for any smart ass answer from you! You got that, soldier?"

"Sure, sergeant." I didn't want tempers flaring because I knew I would end up on the short end of the stick if they did.

"What he's concerned about is some tags he's heard you're wearing that aren't Army issue," he continued. "Do you want to show me what he's talking about?"

"I guess he means these." I unbuttoned the top of my fatigue jacket and pulled out my chain.

"What else you wearing that is not Army issue? I still see one chain too many around your neck."

"Well, this one's got a tiger's tooth on it," I said, pulling out the other chain.

"What are you, some kind of sissy? Wearing all kinds of necklaces around your neck. Or are you one of those fuckin' hippies—those peace-niks like they got in the States!"

I turned around and went back to work. "Give me those numbers," I said to White and Mitchell.

"Range nine-zero-one-zero," answered White.

"Check," said Mitchell.

"Well I'm not gonna talk any more about it," the sergeant said, "I want those things gone by tomorrow. The next time I see you, you won't be wearing anything but Army issue tags! You understand that, Olsen?"

I didn't reply. I called out a new set of numbers while the sergeant made his way out the door, a satisfied smirk on his face.

208

"Whooeee," said Dangerfield, after the sergeant left. "That boy was gonna jump all over your shit. It's a good thing you kept your cool, Olsen, or your stripes would have been down on the floor!"

"Fuck him. They're not giving me enough stripes to take this position anyway."

"Hey, what you gonna do?" said White.

"I don't know, man. But I'm not afraid of that slob. I'll be damned if I'm gonna let him shove me around!"

"Whew," giggled Mitchell nervously, "you'd better have your shit together if you're gonna take on that man, boy!"

"Now, why don't you just do like the staff sergeant said," the lieutenant interjected. "Just go by the book!"

I turned and looked at him. His face betrayed his nervousness. I could tell he was still a bit insecure about his position, hesitant about taking authority, not wanting trouble right off the bat. His voice had held a mixture of assertiveness and apology. Army regulation! To him, that was all that mattered. Fresh out of the States with less than one year of officer's training. How could I expect him to see it any other way? I turned and went back to my work, wanting to get this paperwork out of the way. I decided right then I wasn't going to take them off.

Three days later I was stopped by the captain's driver, a clean-cut, freshly shaven kid in new fatigues. I didn't care much for him. He was new, and from what I had seen of him in the field, he didn't pull his fair share of work. Yet he enjoyed privileges that nobody else did. He reminded me of the brown nosers I had known in high school.

"Hey, Olsen," he said, in a voice full of self-importance, "You'd better take those dove tags off if you know what's good for you."

"Now just why should I do that," I shot back defiantly. Startled, he took a quick step back.

"Well, I was in the captain's tent this morning, and he and the sergeant major were saying they were going to write up court-martial papers on you."

"Court-martial!" I responded, caught by surprise.

"Yeah," he said, the swagger returning to his voice. "They say you're a traitor and that the tags you're wearing represent the colors of the NVA flag. They're gonna bust you for not taking them off. For disobeying a direct order!"

"What the fuck are they talking about?" I said, anger flaring. "These tags are red, white and blue! The Cong flag is red, blue and yellow. Do you see any yellow on these tags?" I waved the tags defiantly in his face.

"Listen, punk," I said, "you go back and tell those bastards to do whatever they want to. You tell them to either shoot shit or get off the pot. They ain't paying me enough money to take this job and if they want my stripes, you tell 'em they can have the job right along with it."

The driver made a hasty retreat. I watched as he made a beeline for the captain's tent. I knew that my ass was in hot water now, but I didn't care. I had meant what I said! If they were gonna take my stripes, they could have my job as well. I knew they would be in a bind to replace me. It angered me that they were so narrow-minded they thought my tags represented the Viet Cong flag. Why couldn't they just see them for what they were—a protest against this war. A cry for peace! A call to stop this endless slaughter of human lives.

Fuck 'em, I thought, I don't care what they do. I turned on my heels and headed on down to the ammo bunker. I was gonna get stoned and talk this up with the brothers.

The second week in July, Captain Ripke left. I never heard anything more about my tags, and I had never taken them off.

VI OPERATION TOAN THANG II

14

Grabbing my M-16, I hurried on down to the ammo bunker. I patted a shirt pocket on my fatigues, making sure I had my cigarettes. I had carefully shaken all the tobacco out of two of them, and stuffed them with finely cleaned grass. I now had filter-tipped menthol joints.

My not-so-recent change to menthols had been out of necessity. Smoking two-and-a-half packs of Marlboros everyday had made my throat raw. Smoking the same amount of menthols didn't. In addition, fewer people in the battery smoked menthols, so when the Red Cross packages were distributed, I generally got a carton and a half of cigarettes instead of two or three packs. An added advantage was that the gooks really loved Salems and I could trade them for nearly anything.

I was now getting stoned during all my free time and sometimes even went on duty high, though I never smoked on shift. I was discovering that getting stoned not only helped me to relax, it always gave me an added lift, a surge of energy when I was exhausted. Some of the guys in the battery were using whites, but pills were definitely not for me.

I reached the ammo bunker as the day faded. I saw Sgt. Ramos and another man I couldn't identify climbing into the LP bunker a few meters in front of the personnel bunker. They were manning the .50 caliber machine gun inside. Ramos had been recently decorated at an open field presentation for wiping out the mortar position in the village near Quoi. Since then, he had determined to be behind that .50 caliber every evening. I think he was looking for another medal. I sure hoped it wouldn't cost him his life.

Since no one else was outside, I figured the rest of the crew must be in the personnel bunker and slipped inside. "Hey, what's happening?" I said, crawling over to a corner and sitting down.

"You wanna smoke some weed?" LeRoy said. We got a bunch rolled here an' we's just thinking of startin'."

"Sure, man," I answered, "I got some here too. I got them rolled up in Salems, and man, if you want to try a real cold smoke, I can put some stuff called Bai-loc on 'em. That'll really make 'em mentholated."

"What's that you say?" asked Lusk. Lusk was a greenie.

"Bai-loc, man," I repeated. "I picked it up from a friend in Battalion Head-quarters the last time I was in. It's a green liquid that comes in a small bottle. John says the Vietnamese use it as a medicine – kind of a cure-all, like a medicine man's potion. I've been using it on my joints and sometimes on my cigarettes. Want to try it?"

"Sho' man, why not," LeRoy said.

I applied just a dab of Bai-loc to my joint. By the time I finished lighting up, five more were circulating like peace pipes at an Indian council, and the bunker was engulfed in smoke.

"Hey man, that's some decent shit!" volunteered Johnson.

We sat shoulder to shoulder, sweat mingling with sweat as a deep silence fell. Slowly, with eyes closed, we withdrew into our private worlds. Eventually we began talking about our lives back in the States.

Ray, from a small Midwestern community, bragged about what it had been like for him before he came in the service. "Man, I had me a fine momma and some real clean clothes. I was sitting back, and it wouldn't of been long before I had me a shiny new car. Shee-itt, the Army done take that away from me, but when I get out that's the first thing I'm gonna get. A shiny new Cadillac!"

"Shit, man," laughed Johnson. "You didn't have no Cadillac before you came in, and you ain't gonna get one when you get out. Least ways not on no Army pay! Whata you jiving us for, man? Man, you jiving yourself!"

Johnson, who was from a New York ghetto, was deeply cynical of every-one. He especially hated whites. To him, all whites were the same, not to be trusted.

"Hey, man," Williams said, calm authority in his voice, "don't be puttin' him down. You don't know what he did before he came in. It could be just like he said. He's got a right to his own dreams, same as you and me. If that's how he wants to live his life, who are you to be putting him down? Just be cool!"

"Whew!" giggled LeRoy. "Lean and Mean Johnson. You gotta watch out for that cat, he's a hard one."

I had seen a pained expression on Ray's face when Johnson put him down, but now he was smiling and everything was cool.

Pretty soon Johnson was bragging himself. "Man, whoee!" he whispered. "If those Viet Cong try to mess with us tonight I'm gonna really kick ass! I got duty tonight on that .50 caliber and if Charlie tries sneaking his head up I'm gonna blow it off. Man, he'd better not mess with me! I'm one hot motha-fucka' an' I ain't in no mood to be messing around tonight, so he'd better not mess with me!"

"Why don't you cut the bullshit, man," Williams said flatly.

"What do ya mean bullshit!"

214

"I mean bullshit! The kind that smells! We don't need anyone flapping his gums about how macho he is. If you're really as brave as you say you are, we'll see it when the shit starts happening. Either way, afterwards you won't be flappin' your jaws so free."

"Hey, brother! I'm a mean mutha-fucker," Johnson repeated. "When Charlie comes in to try and do me in I'm gonna kick some ass. I ain't afraid of no fuckin' pipsqueak gook!"

"Bullshit!" I whispered, shaking my head. "Man, you're no different from the rest of us. When Charlie tries to come through the wire in front of your position you're gonna be shittin' tacks like the rest of us. You're gonna pucker up and do what has to be done, regardless. You could be as mean as you say you are, man, but like Williams said, we'll see when it happens."

"Yeah, and I'll show you too!" he said angrily.

"Hey, fuck man, wha' chu angry about anyway!" LeRoy said. "We just saying how we see it. You got a right to say how you see it. Well, we got that right too!"

Johnson quieted down.

"Hey, Olsen," LeRoy whispered, "tell us what's happening! Anything new coming down?"

"Naw, nothin' that I know of."

"Hey, c'mon, man. You be in the center of what's happening! Ain't you heard nothing about how long we gonna be here or when this war's gonna end?" said Lusk.

"Hey man, if you're asking how long we're gonna be in this location, I ain't heard nothing yet. As far as how long we're gonna be here in this country, this war ain't never gonna end."

"Hey, what you mean, man?" said Johnson.

"I think he right," said LeRoy softly.

"Yeah, me too!" said Williams.

"God damn, it makes me sick," I whispered. "I don't know what we're doing here, but we sure ain't here to win no war!"

"Right on, brother," Williams said softly. "Man, it's hard for me to believe that I am here doing something for my country, which I love, but I just don't believe that jive about us fightin' to free these people. This is just some small under-developed nation. These people are fighting us with sticks and stones when we're supposed to be the most technologically advanced nation in the world. How come the United States, supposingly standing for world peace, is releasing such colossal destruction on a small underdeveloped nation like this? These people don't even want us here!" He paused. "Man, I was brought up in poverty, but these people are worse off than I was. These people got to be struggling just to have enough food to eat. My family back home is doing the same thing. Man, I don't wanna be killing these people; they're just like my family."

"Shit, man," spat Johnson, "they talk about freedom when that's something I didn't even have at home. Man, you got these guys telling me I'm supposed to be fighting for the rights of others when they deny them to me, just 'cause I'm black!"

"Yeah, it seems odd," LeRoy agreed. "They don't give you no rights in the Army, yet they want us to fight for someone else's."

"Look man, we're just being used," I said, "we're just pawns in their game. This whole Army trip is a line of bull. It was based on deception from the start."

"Yeah, man," laughed Ray, "I sure bought that recruiting sergeant's pitch. My choice of a career, he said. Any kind of training I wanted! Join now, pay later. Fun, travel and adventure, he said. Shit, man, did I get roped in."

It was the same for all of us. No one had gotten what he had signed up for. When I volunteered for the draft, they promised me that I could work in the Arts. What a fool I had been!

"Hey, you R.A.?" Lusk asked incredulously, directing his question at Ray. "Man, you got to be dumber than you look. Why, you crazy to join the Army, man, everybody knows that. I'll be warming my ass in the back seat of your car two years before you even get out of the service. You probably lifer material, man!"

"Hey, you'd better hope the Army doesn't change the tour in 'Nam to two years before you get out!" I said.

"Hey, they can't do that!" Ray protested.

"Like hell they can't, and you know it. The Army does what it damn well pleases."

"Shit, how come that is?" asked Lusk. "How can they get away with what they do? Don't the Army have to answer to the government, or somebody?"

"As far as I can tell, either they got those in the government conned, or the government is playing right along. I mean look at what's been going down. Do you suppose anybody in the States really knows what's going on over here? Man, they just know what the authorities tell them. You remember that battle we were in up near Co Dau Ma, the time that A Battery got their shit kicked, up near Tay Ninh? Well, I read about that battle in the *Stars and Stripes* when I was in Cu Chi. What they got in there ain't what went down at all. This is far out, man. I mean we got our shit kicked, and they got it in the paper as a victory for our side. They had the VC body count inflated nearly six times what we reported, with hardly any mention of the Americans that lost their lives. Man, and that's the Army paper. If they're trying to pull the wool down over our own eyes, what the hell do you suppose they're telling the American people? All the people know is what's in the press. And the press only knows what the Army tells them. And the Army only releases what they think is best for them to know. Man, the military ain't only trying to decide how we should think or act, it's trying to do that for the whole American nation!"

"Yeah, man, but you can't hide what's going on from the American government," Lusk countered. "After all, the President is the head of the military, ain't that so?"

I thought about it. That had to be true! At least the President and his advisors must know what's going on. The President was the supreme commander of the military. I had been made to memorize that in Basic, time and time again. He was the head of the military chain of command. But if the government knew what was going on, why didn't they tell the American people? Man, the President and the military had to be in on it together.

"Shit, Lusk," Williams said, "if I was you I wouldn't put much stock in the government. There ain't no government that ain't corrupt and doesn't use its power to oppress the people. If you think there's oppression in the Army, man, you should have grown up in the ghetto where all the power is in the hands of the white man. You don't see too many black men in power in government, do you?"

"Right on," a small chorus of voices replied.

"It's the government that has been keeping black people down. It ain't no different in the Army. Most people in power are white, and blacks are treated just the same."

I knew what Williams was saying was true. I wasn't blind to racism. Even in a small secluded Minnesota town, I hadn't been entirely unaffected by the civil rights movement. But it didn't take being black to relate to oppression. The rich used the poor. Bosses in business used their employees. Teachers and administrators used fear and violence to keep students in line. Parents used punishment to make their children think, act and dress as they did. The whole system of authority stunk. The abuse of power was everywhere.

"Hey, mon," Santiago said, "it's not just the black man that's getting screwed. We Puerto Ricans are getting screwed as well! You know where me and the sergeant are, humpin' ammo! Sheet, man, I could have served my country in a better way than this. We're not even Americans and here we are serving in the Army. It's not because we wanted to; it's because we had to, mon."

"Our only problem was that we weren't rich enough to go to college," whispered LeRoy. "If we had of been, we wouldn't be here."

"College?" I said. "Why the fuck would you have wanted to go to school? Shit, man, school was where I was told we were fighting communism in Viet Nam. Man, if they hadn't fed me that whole line about communism, and my duty to serve, I probably wouldn't be in this mess. If they were telling me lies all through high school, what do you suppose I would have learned in college?"

"Hey, man, you don't believe in patriotism?" asked Ray.

"It's not that I don't believe in patriotism, I'm just not sure what a patriot is. I'm an American but that doesn't mean I have to believe what everybody else does, does it? I'm just saying what I think! Isn't that what an American is supposed to do? Isn't that what we believe in . . . freedom of speech? Hey, I'm no communist. I don't even know what a communist is. It just seems to me that we are doing more destruction here than anyone else. Where are these Russians we're supposed to be fighting? How many Chinese communists have you seen lately?"

"Yeah, but shit, man, don't you think we're fightin' for freedom for the Vietnamese?" Ray asked.

217

"Freedom! Just what the fuck do you mean by freedom? That's just something people talk about. I don't think I've ever really known freedom. I sure as hell don't have it in the Army and I'm not sure I really had it in the world. If it wasn't my parents trying to run my life, it was the school. When I finally left home the fuckin' corporations and businesses took over! Freedom! Freedom for who? For us? For the Vietnamese? Just who the fuck is it that's free over here? You tell me!"

"Well, that's why we're here, ain't it, man? To help the Vietnamese get free from the Viet Cong."

"Yeah, and after we set them free from VC taxation and oppression, then are we also gonna set them free from taxation and oppression from their own government? Or from the ARVNs and G.I.'s that have been raping or killing them? After all, it is freedom we're talking about here, isn't it? Well, you ain't free until you're free from all oppression. Fuck, man, I think you know that as well as I do. Just look at how you were treated in the States. Can you say that you were truly free?"

I stopped. No one said anything for a long time.

"Yeah," Williams said finally, "I think it takes a long time sometimes to get the slave mentality out of our heads. We ain't been free for so long we've forgotten what it really is. What it really costs. It's hard to get some things out of your head when they're pounded in there daily by society."

There was a heartbreaking heaviness in the way he said it. It was as if he was feeling the weight of sorrow of his childhood, or maybe of generations of black people who had been living in chains.

I understood too clearly how easy it was to let yourself be bound and chained. I had let fear, especially the fear of rejection, keep me from saying what I truly thought, truly felt, for years. Suddenly, I wanted to cry. For him, for me, for all the oppressed people in the world. Now, suddenly, all the anger I had felt as I talked about freedom disappeared. Who was I to judge? Freedom was nice to talk about, but even I wasn't willing to face the consequences to attain it.

"Fuckin' heavy duty," I finally said.

"Right on." LeRoy added softly. For the first time in a long time, LeRoy wasn't smiling.

"Yeah, it ain't just patriotism we're talking about, is it?" I said. "We're talking about human rights. It isn't right to oppress anyone whether they're white or black ... or yellow for that matter. The Vietnamese want to live as badly as I do. Shit, man, being American doesn't automatically make everything right. And man, I'm just not sure what we're doing here is right."

"Hey, Ray," Williams said, "do you write home and tell your family what's going on here—like where it's really at? Are you getting letters from people in the States encouraging you to represent them like you're doing, telling you that it's O.K. for you to be killing these people, or it'll be O.K. for you to be black when you get back? I got brothers writing me who are getting an idea of what's really going on over here, and they want to know what I'm doing over here fighting poor people when the poor are fighting their own battles back home. Now wha' chu gonna do man? How is it that we gotta be fightin' for human rights over here, when we don't have any of our own back home? What you suppose that says, boy?"

"Hey, brother, I ain't your boy, and I ain't nobody else's," Ray shot back. Then he dropped his eyes. "Your fight ain't with me, brother," he said, "and I'm hearing what you say."

It grew quiet again, till our conversation took a new course. We continued to speak honestly. After all, what was there to keep us from opening ourselves to each other? None of us wanted to meet death without ever being really known. That urgency gave me the courage to be honest with myself and others. I had approached these rap sessions cautiously at first, but I was surprised at the liberty they brought. Maybe the greatest chains weren't those you could see.

At 0200 I dismissed half the crew, letting two men go to sleep. White and I would keep watch through the night. Half-shifts, that was another policy change I had fought for and got.

The bunker was unbearably hot and stuffy, which made it difficult to stay awake. When conversation lagged, so did our alertness. "I'm going out for awhile to get a bit of fresh air," I said after about an hour. "Can you handle things O.K.? I should be right outside the entrance. I'll keep my ears tuned into the radio."

"Gotcha."

I lifted my flap slightly and quickly slipped out so as not to expose any light. I stretched my arms and walked back and forth on our walkway. Sitting down, I pulled a cigarette out of my pocket. I needed something to keep me awake. I looked out over the base camp area; there wasn't a soul in sight. Man, I thought, what I really need is a joint. I put my cigarette back and took a joint out of the back of my cigarette package. Cupping it in my hands, I struck my Zippo and inhaled deeply. A couple of hits and I was no longer tired. I snuffed the joint, tossed it into a puddle of water that lay close by and lit a cigarette, keeping it cupped and down between my legs. I didn't want to set us up for some VC mortar squad. The word "wasted" slid into my mind. How appropriate it seemed as a synonym for "killed." If I were to get wasted by some sniper, that would describe my life to a T. In the twenty years I had been alive I hadn't accomplished anything. Twenty years wasted, and on what? On boozing and partying. On trying to get laid. On jobs that I hated. On life that seemed empty and boring, lonely and painful. What made life worth living anyway? Was there nothing more to it than self-gratification? Did I really value anyone's life outside of my own?

I would stoop to anything to survive in Vietnam. Kill or be killed. All I worried about was my own life. I could think of very few things that I had done for others that hadn't benefited me also. Why had I become so callous? In my attempt to keep others out, had I locked myself into a prison of my own making? Had I hardened myself only to become like those I despised for their own hardness of heart?

I slipped out my billfold. Squinting in the dark, I studied the worn photographs in my hands. Debbie and Diane had written repeatedly to me. Kim hadn't written at all. They had been on my mind a lot, but they weren't the only ones. I had been thinking about all the people who had ever cared for me. Those who had encouraged or befriended me, especially when I had felt discouraged and alone. I had spent hours and hours of slack time extracting those memories from my past. I wasn't sure why, but those times were taking on new importance in my life. They were threads I was hanging on to when I thought I might lose my grip on life itself.

What seemed to be missing were the love and acceptance of my own parents, especially my father. Even now, thinking about him made me angry, yet I also had tremendous feelings of sadness and loss because our relationship had been so distant.

I wondered who had sent the letter I had received last week in the mail. I was still puzzled about its meaning and slightly miffed by its formality. It had been a form letter containing what looked like an advertising brochure from which a tiny gold cross hung. The brochure contained a printed message about God's love and someone's prayers. What did that mean, someone's prayers? This was the kind of mail that was addressed to occupant, yet it had been addressed to me. If someone was praying for me, why didn't he at least have the courage and decency to sign his name? It turned me off! It reeked of the brand of Christianity I had grown up with, a message void of personal commitment. I had tossed it away angrily, but I kept the gold cross. Since then I had been unable to get the letter off my mind. I kept trying to imagine who would have sent it. Was there really someone out there who honestly cared? Someone who was actually a practicing Christian? Shit, I didn't know any real Christians. Were there really any people who actually lived and acted like Jesus Christ? I thought about Merle Kupitz and his wife, the youth advisors and teachers in my Sunday school. They had always been friendly, open and loving, and had even hugged me on occasion. They knew my reputation in town yet it didn't make any difference to them. Not once did they interfere in my life or put me down. They always seemed to have understanding and cheerful hearts, and the times we had spent together in youth fellowship were good times. Their religion was filled with laughter. I couldn't remember either of them ever sermonizing me, yet we had deep discussions, and they never seemed threatened by my unbelief. I wondered if they might have sent the letter? But surely they would have signed their names.

By now it was beginning to grow light outside, and I went back in the bunker.

Through the height of the monsoon season we continued our chase for the elusive enemy. Though limited in mobility by the heavy rain and mud that clogged an inadequate transportation system, we managed to move at least once a week, carried to and fro by Chinooks. Although a constant rumor persisted that the war was nearing its end, we were beginning to see that the rumor was a light at the end of the tunnel that could be turned on as needed.

The credibility gap between command and enlisted men widened, but there was not much open rebellion. The Army was quick to single out men who were even slightly hesitant to respond to orders, making them examples and that threat was enough to keep most in line. From induction on, every act of independence had been dealt with severely. The Long Binh stockade, referred to in hushed tones as LBJ for "Long Binh Jail," was a testimony to that. The fact that the initials were the same as the President's was no accident. People looked at both him and Long Binh as perpetrators of a sentence. The guards at LBJ were all Marines. Rumor held that command had hand-picked them for their toughness and sadistic behavior. The cruelties they imposed on prisoners made Basic Training seem like a playground. It was said that they especially liked to get ahold of any peace-niks, people who claimed to be conscientiously opposed to the war. Conscientious objectors were placed in isolation, and supposedly, savage beatings and denial of food accompanied their incarceration. I had no reason to doubt it. We had all been sufficiently indoctrinated in the code of conduct and how it applied to war times. Refusal to follow orders in a war zone could be punishable by death in front of a firing squad. If direct disobedience warranted death, surely any lesser punishment was fair by their standards.

With the monsoon came a rapid decimation of materials and supplies. The heat and humidity made their way into every duffel bag and ammo box. Moving made it almost impossible to keep things clean or dry enough so they didn't rot. Although fatigue replacements had been requisitioned by nearly every section chief, we rarely saw any come to the field. What fatigues did come were always distributed to the gun sections first, just like promotions. It was only after repeated protest that the FDC received what promotions and supplies it did. It was always the captain's justification that the guns worked harder and therefore were more deserving, or that the people on the guns were short and had to get their promotions before they left. My men, I was always told, were all longtimers and their chance would come later, maybe with the next allotment of stripes. Even I couldn't get my promotion and I had been holding an E-5 slot for over three months. But promoted or not, we needed clothing. Finally I decided that if my men were going to get any new fatigues I would have to go into the rear and bring them out myself.

I talked the lieutenant into letting me take the resupply chopper in one morning, promising to return when the Class IV sortie was brought out that afternoon. Once I arrived at the chopper pad in Cu Chi, it took another thirty minutes to hitch a ride over to our battery location. I walked most of the way to headquarters. When I entered the Quonset, the rush of air conditioning hit me like a cold slap. "Hi, Top," I said.

"Whatta you doing in the rear?" he growled. I could see my reputation had preceded me.

"I came in to see the supply sergeant. Can you tell me where he is?"

"He's in the back, typing. How long are you supposed to be in for?"

"I'm taking the resupply back out this afternoon, if I get what I came in for."

"Well, the chopper's scheduled to leave at seventeen hundred. You make sure

221

you get on it. There'll be a jeep leaving here at sixteen-thirty. You can catch it to the landing pad!" He lowered his head and went back to shuffling papers.

Fuck him, I thought. He may be the big boss back here in the rear, but I wonder how long he'd last in the field.

I went through a door leading to another small office and leaned against the counter. "You the supply sergeant?" I said to a soldier sitting behind a typewriter.

"Yes, what is it you want?" he said, lifting his head only long enough to glance in my direction.

"I'd like some new fatigues for my men."

"All right," he answered with a note of irritation, "but you'll have to wait!"

Hurry up and wait. Army policy. I sat down and waited, annoyed. These people had the easy life. Air conditioning, hot chow, clean mess halls, mattresses and clean sheets on their beds, plenty of beer, movies at the E.M. club—no worry about Charlie's sneaking up behind their backs. You'd think the least they could do was be responsive to the men in the field. Tapping my chair, I looked over at the supply sergeant. He just acted like I wasn't there. I watched him. He had a buzz hair cut and clean, freshly pressed fatigues. His figure was beginning to show signs of excessive drinking and eating and lack of exercise. I wondered if it was true what they were saying about him in the field. Rumor had it that both he and Captain Ripke were queer and that the supply sergeant had been seen entering the captain's hootch late at night and not leaving till morning. Shit, they must be kidding, I thought, Captain Ripke was married. What the hell would he be doing with some queer? Besides, they didn't let homosexuals into the Army, and if one did get in, he sure as hell wouldn't be in Vietnam.

The supply sergeant finally finished typing his order and rose from his desk. Grabbing his fatigue hat from a hanger on the wall, he made for the counter. "All right," he said in a pussy kind of voice, "we can go now!"

He walked by me, his big hips moving in kind of a waddle. He didn't even look at me or acknowledge my presence. He just opened the door and left. I followed him to a nearby jeep and climbed in beside him, and we drove over to the supply Quonset.

The walls in the Quonset were lined with shelves and boxes. Everything smelled new. The sergeant stopped to unlock the door to a huge wire cage separating the shelves from the small entrance area. Entering, he latched the door behind him. Then he swung the top half open so he could hand the stuff out.

"All right," he said, sitting down at a desk and putting a requisition form in a typewriter, "what size do you wear?"

"Medium."

"And did you bring in your old pair?"

"What do you mean, my old pair? I want fatigues for all of my men!"

"Well, we can't issue fatigues without the old pair being turned in."

"Hey, what the fuck is this? I just came in from the field! I need new fatigues! I didn't bring any requisition in! What kind of shit you guys operating back here, anyway? My men need fatigues! That's all I know and I don't expect to leave here without them!"

"Well, it's against regulation," he said prissily. "I have to account for everything that goes out of here, and if it's a replacement, I've got to have something in return."

"Well then don't issue them as replacements. Just issue them as new fatigues!"

"You can't have more than two sets of fatigues. That's all that you were issued when you came in. If you want new fatigues they have to replace old ones and to replace old ones, you've got to turn them in or have a requisition sent in from the field."

"Hey, look," I said, "we've already sent a number of requisitions in from the field, and you haven't sent us diddly squat."

"Well, we're only allowed to issue so many new fatigues per month, and we're only supplied as many as we return."

"Are you trying to tell me that you're sitting here with boxes and boxes of new fatigues while my men in the field don't have shit to wear, and you won't send them out?"

"Well, I'm only following orders."

I shook my head. What the fuck kind of war was this anyway? I leaned on the bottom half of the door and looked at the supply sergeant. It wasn't his fault. Like he said, he was just following orders. "So how about if I hand them in?" I said.

"All right," he said hesitantly, evidently hoping the confrontation was over. "Why don't you hand them in?"

Leaning my M-16 up against the fence and dropping my helmet to the floor I began to take my fatigues off.

"All right," he said, rushing over with his hands outstretched, "hold it. I'll issue you one new set of fatigues and you can send the old ones in later!"

The supply sergeant loosened up after that. By the time we finished talking, I had two additional sets of fatigues in my possession, and a new fatigue hat. I also had a promise that I would receive a box of fatigues marked FDC on the next day's resupply chopper. I had given him the sizes for all my men.

It wasn't as though we had become friendly; it was just that after I gave in to his authority, he had a change of heart. He relished the knowledge that my fate was in his hands, and as soon as I saw where he was coming from I made a big show of letting him know that I understood the authority he had. The more I played up his position, the more responsive he became. It also became obvious in the course of our conversation that he held no more love for those in authority than I did, so in the end, I led him to believe that by using his authority to benefit my men, it would be a kick in the pants to those in authority over him!

Here we were in Vietnam, supposedly the best equipped Army in the world, and I was having to scheme and manipulate just to get necessary clothes. Not only that, we were richly supplying the ARVNs with guns and materials we wouldn't even supply for our own men. The ARVNs dressed better than we did. We had problems replacing malfunctioning equipment or rifles, yet the ARVNs had an abundance of both. Why was it that our government seemed to have an abundance for them but couldn't supply our needs?

As we drove back to headquarters, I thought about how I would spend the rest of my time in the rear. The supply sergeant cautioned me about remaining in the battery area because the top liked to put every available man to work. I thought about heading down to the PX, but I doubted if I could make it there and back before the chopper left. Besides, I hadn't gotten permission to go there and I was not about to ask the top. I thought about John Threet at Battalion Headquarters; maybe he would be around. I knocked at the screen door and waited.

I opened the door and stuck my head in. Some soldier was sitting in his briefs shining his shoes.

"I'm looking for John Threet," I said. "Is he around?"

"Hey John," he shouted, tilting back his head, "are you around?"

"Yeah." The voice rose lazily over a partitioned wall.

"Some guy to see you." The soldier looked back at me. "Go on in. His bunker is on the right, third one down."

Making my way slowly down the hall, I checked out the sleeping quarters that lined the Quonset. I couldn't believe it. Each man had a living area separated from the others on both sides by tall metal lockers. Within each area was a metal bed with mattress, sheets and blankets, all neatly made and tucked in with forty-five degree corners. Around each bed hung a large mosquito netting, lifted in the front by strings, pulleys, and weights. There were rugs and chairs and a concrete floor. Some of the areas had small refrigerators and desks, and almost all of them had huge stereo set-ups with reel-to-reel tape recorders and headphones. Some of the lockers had huge colorful posters on them with rock groups like the Jefferson Airplane or Grateful Dead. Others had large neon beer signs or posters of John Wayne. All the conveniences of home.

"Hey Olsen!" John said, sticking his head out in the hallway. "What brings you in from the field?"

"Hey, nice to see you," I said, grasping his hand and locking thumbs. "What's happening here, the place looks like the PX!"

"You ain't seen nothin'. Have a seat and I'll turn you on."

With an air of excitement, John showed me all his gadgets, including his smoking paraphernalia and water pipe. A huge poster of Jimi Hendrix covered his locker.

"So, you wanna smoke some dope?" he asked. "We can do it in my water pipe?"

"You don't mean right in here, do you?"

"Sure, it's cool. Some of these guys are just juicers but most of 'em smoke. Everyone figures it's his own business what he does, so nobody freaks."

"All right." Seemed cool to me.

We toked up until we got wasted. Then he plugged in a second set of headphones to his tape recorder, and we lay back and listened to the Jefferson

Airplane, the Doors, and the Jimi Hendrix Experience. We rapped for what seemed like hours. Before I headed back to the chopper pad he gave me four more bottles of Bai-loc and promised to pick me up a 20-pound bag of marijuana on his next trip into the Vietnamese village outside the compound. It cost me eighteen dollars. All in all it had been a very profitable visit.

15

The monsoon must have begun taking its toll on the Viet Cong as well, for as July dragged on, we began to experience a lull in enemy activity. The weather could slow anyone down. Days were a nightmare of slow motion, in which it took great effort just to lift your feet and walk, let alone to lift sodden, mud-caked boots or push spades full of muck into sandbags.

I dismissed the temptation to count the days I had left. To do so brought only despair. Yet, each day was being marked off in my subconscious. Slowly, painfully, my prison sentence was shortening.

The isolation was by far the most crippling hardship. Still it provided a suitable environment for reflection. Except for brief periods of active contact with the enemy, I had several hours each day to do little but read, visit or think. With my essential physical needs provided, there was little to distract me in the pursuit of meaning. This pursuit had occupied my mind the last few years, and being so far from everything familiar challenged my earlier perspectives.

The need for companionship weighed heavily on my mind. I began to see the value of my relationships with others in a new light. Because my relationship with my parents had been so distant, I had always relied heavily upon my peers to provide emotional support in my life. As early as the seventh grade I had formed a kind of extended family with a gang we later called the Keemos. Their friendship had provided me with a sense of belonging and identity that I lacked in my home. When the Keemos finally disintegrated during my junior year, I was left floundering until I met Bob Ellegard. His companionship and the support of his parents enabled me to survive my last two years in school, especially when stormy conflicts with my own parents finally led to my leaving home. When Bob left town after graduation, I found myself alone again, and this time I was also in the middle of a confused search for my own identity. Though I had maintained social contact with others, I found myself slipping into frequent episodes of extreme depression, times which led to even further isolation. I also began to experience a growing alienation from my peers as the things I believed in gradually caused others to withdraw from me. Finding someone who understood what I was going through became a rare experience indeed.

A year and a half after graduation I left Minnesota for the West Coast. I had withdrawn to a point where I confided very little in others, even with friends. I found myself talking less and less, just as a method of survival.

In Oregon, I was a stranger in a different world, and Mike, a one-time member of the Keemos, was the only person I knew. He had moved to Hillsboro three years earlier, and it had been at his insistence that I had ventured there. I moved in with him and his folks, went where he went, did what he did. I rarely spoke. His friends began calling me "Mike's Silent Partner" or "the Silent One." I didn't mind. I didn't feel compelled to act in any particular fashion for his friends and at least I was getting some kind of recognition. My silence even produced an air of mystery that drew some people to me even while it provoked others. But the truth was, at this confusing time in my life I could think of little to say with any conviction. Discarding the things I had been brought up to believe in left a large void in my life and I was looking for something to fill it. New ideas were forming every day as I struggled to lay a foundation in my life based on what I believed, not just on what others said was true. Some days I didn't know what I believed. When people talked about their beliefs, I listened, and tried to sort fact from fiction. As I followed Mike through a life of college parties, I could see that the ideas I thought were valid were rarely in vogue, and one thing I didn't want was to be an outcast again. So I kept my thoughts to myself.

But in spite of, or because of, my long hair, Beatle boots and wildly colorful clothes, I did find a small group of people who eventually became my friends. Slowly, I weaned myself from Mike's group and began spending time with my own.

Here in Vietnam, thinking about those friendships, I realized that I had experienced a number of affectionate relationships with males. Yet I had suffered from a cultural standard that inhibited my showing it. I thought of the Vietnamese soldiers I had seen holding hands. I compared them to the male images I had grown up with: John Wayne, and Randolph Scott, Marlon Brando, James Dean. Men who touched only women, sometimes with tenderness and affection, but always with sexual overtones. But were all expressions of affection only motivated by sex? I wondered why it had to be that way in America. It didn't seem right.

One day White entered the FDC with the mail in his hands. "Hey, Olsen! You got a package from Hawaii and guess who it's from?"

"You got me," I said, taking the package from his outstretched hands. "I don't know anyone in Hawaii."

"Shit, it's from Captain Ripke!" he exclaimed.

"Captain Ripke!" I said, laughing. "Now what the fuck would he be sending me a package for."

I looked at the return address, thinking that White was putting me on. He wasn't. But what would Ripke be sending me anything for? This was the man who was going to court-martial me a few weeks ago.

By this time the whole crew gathered around. "Hey, ease off," I said. "Let me look at it first." I cautiously began tearing off the brown wrapping paper. Was this some kind of joke? Was there some kind of indictment inside?

Slipping the flap out of the top of the box, I peeked inside. There was a black string or something like that. Pulling on the string, I brought the object out of the box. It was a necklace with a small, black, wooden, hand-carved woman attached. The woman was dressed like a native; her two hands caressed an enlarged pregnant stomach.

"What the hell . . ." I said.

"Hey . . . let me see it," said White, snatching it from my hands and passing it around the crew.

"Shit, what do you suppose that's all about?" said Mitchell. "That ol' man crazy or something."

"Hey, Olsen, check to see if there's a letter inside," demanded Mike.

"Hey, just hold on," I replied, digging into the box.

I pulled out a sheet of paper that had been folded inside and began to read it to myself.

"Hey Olsen, c'mon, let us read it too," laughed Mike.

Mitchell reached out his long black arm and snatched the paper out of my hands, giggling as he ran for the other side of the room. "Hey listen guys!" he began, "Who-eee, that captain's a crazy ole shit!"

"'Dear Howard, I thought you might like another necklace to add to your collection. This one's from Hawaii, and it's called a fertility goddess. I picked it out especially for you. I'm on my way back to the States. My tour in Vietnam is now over so I'm finally free to speak out on issues as I couldn't have done before. I wanted you to know that I respected the stand you took. It took courage for you to speak against the odds you were facing. I haven't made up my mind about Vietnam yet, but I am hoping that you will live a long and fertile life and come out of it yourself. Captain Ripke.'"

The room grew quiet. No one, including myself, knew quite what to say. I felt good inside but wondered why he couldn't have said those things here. Why did he threaten to court-martial me if that was how he felt? Sometimes I just didn't understand people at all, but today, I didn't care. I took the necklace and slipped it around my neck, then stood up and walked out of the room.

As we continued to search for the enemy we began moving farther north. The 25th Division's boundaries were enlarged to include the Hoc Mon Canal, and the area from the Saigon River to the Pineapple, generally considered the TAOI for the 3rd Brigade. In an intensified operation to halt a threatened enemy third offensive, we began operating with the 2nd Battalion 14th US Infantry. It was during that operation that my path again crossed Lt. Murphy's.

I was sitting inside the FDC working out an upcoming prep when Lieutenant Anthony walked into the bunker. Throwing his helmet into a corner, he shook the water off his poncho, muttering under his breath about the rain.

"Hey, Olsen," he said, "I want to check those computations before we do anything with the guns. I don't want to take any chances on this prep. The major's supposed to be observing this operation in the air."

"O.K., lieutenant," I replied. "You generally do anyway."

"Well, it's supposed to be my job!" he snapped.

The lieutenant was a bit uptight, but that was nothing unusual. He was overly cautious about everything and a stickler for detail. Everything by the book! He lived under the constant fear that something was going to go wrong and he'd get into hot water over it. He meticulously checked everything, not once, but twice, and usually made me do the same. I wondered if he hadn't gotten his ass chewed sometime or another for screwing up, so he was just making sure it would never happen again. I tried to tolerate his behavior as much as I could but we clashed often, especially concerning procedures. I kept telling him that this wasn't some stateside exercise and that sometimes operating by the manuals just didn't work, but he wasn't the type to take any advice, especially from someone lower in rank. Particularly someone who hadn't been through Officer Candidate School. I tried to pass most of it off on him being a fuckin' greenhorn.

We were going over my figures when Dangerfield got a radio transmission.

"Killer Six Niner, this is Red Fox One, over."

"Red Fox One, this is Killer Six Niner, over," Dangerfield replied.

"Killer Six Niner, would you put on your Fox Delta October over."

"Red Fox One, roger, over." Dangerfield handed the mike to the lieutenant.

"Red Fox One, this is Killer Six Niner, go ahead, over," the lieutenant said.

"Killer Six Niner, in regard to our previous conversation, our Lima Poppa will be leaving the location in eighteen hundred hours, over."

"Red Fox One, roger that, will you send us their designation for marking rounds? Over."

"Killer Six Niner, our Charlie Poppa will have that information. Why don't you send a runner over to pick it up? Over."

"Red Fox One, roger, will do. Out."

"Hey, Olsen," the lieutenant said, "send one of your men over to the infantry command post to pick up the night locations for the infantry's ambush sites. Their bunker's located on the eastern side of our perimeter, about fifteen meters to the left of the ammo bunker. Lieutenant Murphy is in command. I talked to him earlier and he remembers you. He said to say hi for him."

Lieutenant Murphy! Great! I would pick up their data myself. It would give me a chance to visit with him.

"Here, these are all finished, Lieutenant," I said. "I'm going out to the CP to pick up those locations myself. You can reach me on their radio if you need me."

"All right, but don't be long."

I thought about Lieutenant Murphy as I made my way through the puddles

229

and greasy mud that covered everything. I had really missed him. He was the only FDO I had gotten close to. I wondered how he was getting along . . . how he liked it back with the infantry. I had worried about his getting hurt, but I tried not to think about it; worrying only brought you down. I was really looking forward to seeing him again. I had a hundred questions to ask.

As I neared the perimeter I saw some grunts struggling in the rain, trying to erect a makeshift shelter to keep out the wind and rain.

"Hey, can you tell me where the command post is?" I shouted.

"It's over there. The one with the large antenna coming out the top!"

The bunker they indicated looked as if it could hold no more than three men at a time. Sandbags covered the front and sides, but it had no overhead cover. A large poncho stretched over the top kept out the rain. Hurrying over, I looked for the entrance. It seemed completely shut in.

"Lieutenant Murphy," I whispered.

"Yeah," came a reply from inside.

"How do you get into this thing?"

"Crawl in under the back."

I lifted up the rear of the poncho and slid underneath. The inside was fairly dark. Mud and water covered the floor. The only light coming in was from the open portholes to the front.

"Hey, lieutenant," I said. "How's it going?"

"Olsen," he said, surprised. "Cripes, it's nice to see you. Did you come to pick up the night locations?"

"Yeah, but it's just an excuse to come and visit you. How have you been?"

"Olsen, meet Corporal Dragill," he said, nodding toward the other soldier in the bunker. "Draghill, this is the FDC chief that I used to work with from Charlie Battery."

"Hi," I said, "nice to meet you."

"Sorry about the accommodations," the lieutenant said. "It's about the best we can do for now. We just came in this morning and have taken over Delta Platoon's old positions. Apparently, they didn't spend too much time working on their bunkers before they left, but we're trying to make do. It still tends to leak, particularly where we've buttoned our two ponchos together."

"Listen, lieutenant, can you use some ammo boxes and plastic? I'll go back and pick some up for you! In fact, I'm sure I can get some at the ammo bunker. If not, I'll pick some up from the guns. I'll pick you up some sandbags, too. You ought to be able to stretch one piece of plastic over this whole bunker, and you can build up your wall in the back and put sandbags down to keep the roof from blowing away. If you lay the boxes on the floor, you can get out of the mud."

His face lit up and so did his radio operator's. "Thanks, we'd really appreciate it."

"Listen, how's it going in the field?" I asked.

The lieutenant glanced at the RTO and then over at me; he grew serious. "Things are changing. I'm not sure what's going on but it's not the same kind of war it used to be."

230

"What kind of things?" I asked, adjusting my poncho to keep the water that dripped from the ceiling off my pants.

"Well, we just don't seem to have the same kind of control over who we're fighting anymore. . . ."

I could detect a note of bitterness in his voice as he talked about some contact they had a few days ago.

". . . and by that time they had already split," he was saying.

Somehow that whole story seemed mighty familiar. "What's your call sign again?" I asked the lieutenant. I had an idea in my mind that we might have been involved in that particular skirmish.

"Red Fox One."

"Red Fox One!" I said. "It's no wonder that incident sounded familiar. I didn't know you were the ones who were calling in for help. Listen, let me tell you what happened. We tried to get clearance to fire for you, but it was slow in coming. That's not too unusual anymore. First, we couldn't get U.S. clearance, and then when it finally came, we couldn't get ARVN clearance. They said that the people you spotted were probably civilians since it was close to a populated area. When you radioed that they were carrying weapons, they wanted us to have you check again, just to make sure, and by that time, it was just like you said, they were out of range. Shit, lieutenant, I feel the same way about it you do. All of a sudden we're getting all these rules. It's like they don't even want us to fight the war."

"Well, look," he said, "I wouldn't let this get beyond you, but we're not looking for permission to fire on the enemy anymore. We just do whatever we find necessary and say that they opened up on us first, or that we walked into an ambush; because once contact is made we can get cover fire as soon as we need it. The fewer there are of them, the better chance more of us will survive. We plan on keeping it that way."

Our conversation continued for nearly an hour before I had to go.

"Hey listen, lieutenant," I said as I was leaving, "when was the last time you had a hot meal?"

"A hot meal! Shit, man, we've been out in the bush for over a month eating nothing but C's."

"Well listen, I'll bring you out a couple of hot trays from the mess tent at noon, O.K.?"

"Far out," Dragill said excitedly.

"Yeah, that would be great," said the lieutenant.

That afternoon I had a chance to visit with him again but by evening his platoon was replaced by another and out he went, back to the bush. I was sad to see him go.

It was fifteen hundred hours. Less than an hour ago I had gotten off shift but was now back in the FDC, frantically scrambling to come up with the necessary data to fire a prep that had been moved up two hours. The lieutenant was checking my information as fast as I could feed it into the computer. With the phone cradled on my shoulder, I was trying to set the guns at the same time. We had only ten minutes' notice to set up the battery before the prep would be fired. Battalion had changed its mind about the LZ site because of intelligence reports and had set up another air mobile assault to take place in thirty minutes. We had to set the guns and fire a 60-round prep before the infantry helicopters arrived. The last round had to be on the ground before their choppers came into the area.

"Guns," the lieutenant yelled, grabbing the phone off my shoulder and shouting in the receiver. "This prep has got to be fired in less than eight minutes. Let's get the lead out! The major will be watching this prep and I don't want any screw-ups! Is that understood? Now report back in one at a time!"

"Hey, take it easy, Lieutenant," I said. "They're doing the best they can. They'll get it done. Just don't push 'em or it'll make it even worse."

"Olsen!" he said, "who's in charge here?"

"You are, Lieutenant."

"Well, then, I'll do this the way I think it needs to be done. Now, you get them laid and ready." He shoved the phone back at me.

Shit, I thought, I might as well not say anything. The lieutenant's so hyper that nothing I say is gonna change him anyway. Why the fuck does he always get this way?

A radio transmission broke the silence.

"Killer Six Niner, this is Killer Three, over."

I immediately recognized the voice of Major Jenkins, and so did the lieutenant.

"Killer Three, this is Killer Six Niner, over," answered Mike.

"Killer Six Niner, is your battery laid and ready to fire? Over."

"Hand the mike here," the lieutenant snapped, but before Mike could do it the lieutenant had leapt out of his seat and snatched the mike from his hands.

"Killer Three, this is Killer Six Niner. The battery will be ready to fire in zero five," he answered.

"Killer Six Niner, this is Killer Three. Out."

"All right, Olsen, get those guns on the phone!" he demanded.

"Guns!" I said, lifting the phone off my shoulder and pressing it to my ear. "Guns!"

"Gun One," "Gun Six," "Gun Four," "This is Two," they answered.

With resignation I handed the phone to the lieutenant, who had stretched out his hand impatiently.

"Gun Five," he shouted, "Gun Five, where are you?"

"Gun Five," a man shouted.

"Report when you're ready!" the lieutenant bellowed.

"Gun One has already reported, Lieutenant," a voice said. "Gun Six ready," came another. The rest soon followed.

The lieutenant breathed a sigh of relief. He looked over and smiled at me. Everything was O.K. now. We were buddies again. The pressure had been lifted.

232

"O.K. guns, prepare to fire," the lieutenant said.

"Killer Six Niner, this is Killer Three, over," the radio interrupted. "We have changed the Lima Zulu; we are going in one-zero-zero meters to the west. There is too much area cover at the present site. Over."

"God dammit!" the lieutenant erupted, jumping to his feet. "Guns! Guns!" he shouted into the phone, "unload your pieces and stand by for new directions."

I could hear the grumbling and swearing coming over the phone as the lieutenant set down the receiver.

"Left 100," I snapped at the chart operators, "you should have had that information by now!"

"Azimuth 0700," shouted Mitchell, "range nine-seven-two-zero meters!"

"Check," shouted Gracelli.

I fed the information into the computer as fast as I got it, checking the data on my slide rule at the same time. As soon as the lieutenant confirmed my computations, I fired the changes down to the guns—and waited. The seconds ticked by.

"Killer Six Niner, this is Killer Three. Are you ready to fire? Over."

"What the fuck does he expect?" I said to the lieutenant as he made a beeline for the mike.

"Killer Three, Killer Six Niner, not at this time. Over," he replied, his forehead deeply set.

"Gun One ready." "Ready on Three," the guns shouted over the phone.

"Two, Six, Four, Five, how are you doing?" I asked.

"We'll be ready in a minute," someone shouted.

"This is Gun Four, we have a round stuck in the chamber," a voice cried frantically.

"Well get your rod and push it out," I said.

"They're working on it," replied an angry voice.

"Gun Two ready," another said.

"Killer Six Niner, this is Killer Three," came the major's impatient voice. "What's the holdup down there?"

"Oh shit!" shouted the lieutenant, then spoke into the mike. "Killer Three, this is Killer Six Niner, we're ready at this time. Over."

"Lieutenant," I cried, "the guns aren't ready. What the hell are you doing?" It was too late.

"Killer Six Niner, this is Killer Three. Fire. Over."

I was still waiting for the guns to report in ready when the lieutenant reached out and grabbed the phone from my hand. "Fire! Fire!"

I could hear four of the guns exploding, their firing scattered and uneven.

"FDC ... FDC ... we weren't ready," called Gun Four as another gun exploded into action.

"Well, fire as soon as you can," shouted the lieutenant.

I held my breath, waiting to hear the last gun fire. Five—ten—fifteen seconds went by. Ka-boom! They finally got it off.

I knew that we were gonna get our ass chewed on this one, and so did the lieutenant. That first volley was supposed to be fired as a single unit. A battery was judged by its ability to fire in sequence, and unison of volley was a mark of excellence. We had just made one pisspoor showing!

"Killer Three, this is Killer Six Niner, last round fired, over."

"Killer Six Niner, this is Killer Three. You can fire for effect, over. Put your Fox Delta October on the horn."

Here it comes, I thought, and sure enough it did! I turned my attention to the guns, making sure the prep was being fired in order and marking the guns off as they finished their rounds.

As soon as we finished firing, the major radioed a check fire and I relayed the word to the guns. I pushed back my chair and put down the phone.

"Lieutenant, I'm going outside!" I said flatly, not waiting for a reply.

The air outside was heavy with smoke and the smell of sulphur. I walked to the end of the walkway, downwind from the bunker, and sat down. Shaking a joint from my package of Salems, I lit one up and got stoned. I was angry as hell!

It was the first of August before we moved again, this time farther south, to FSB Keene II, near Ap Tram Lee.

We had been set up two days just north of Bao Trai when I got news that one element of the 2nd Battalion 27th Infantry would be coming in to provide base security. I radioed the infantry CP to see which company it would be. It was Charlie, the company Roach was with. I vowed to get out and see him as soon as I could.

By 0800 things had cleared up enough for me to leave shift, and I headed on out to the perimeter. The whole battery was out milling around—washing, shaving, changing their fatigues. Battalion headquarters had radioed us earlier that we would be visited somewhere between 0900 and 1000 hours by a couple of Doughnut Dollies, so almost everyone was preparing for their visit. Doughnut Dollies was the name given to the Red Cross girls who sometimes visited fire support bases that were considered safe, creating one-hour audience participation programs to entertain the men. Headquarters had issued strict orders that the battery area would be entirely policed and spruced up and that all men would be clean shaven and in clean fatigues—full uniform and bloused boots! It made me sick. I wasn't putting on a full uniform or blousing my boots for anyone. Especially just to see some American broads come out in scanty clothes and shake their boobs around and then leave. Was this supposed to be some kind of special treat? All I could see was a tease, a carrot hung out on a stick safely out of reach. Man, the whole thing just turned me off!

I was halfway to the perimeter when I heard the helicopter approaching. I could tell right away that it wasn't a Chinook. That generally meant something special. I stopped alongside one of the bunkers behind Gun Six and watched its descent. They're coming early, I thought.

234

And so they were. As the blades on the Huey slowed to a halt, two men in freshly starched uniforms jumped out. Soon afterwards, two girls took their hands and were helped out of the chopper. They were followed by two other men, both of them in freshly starched uniforms. I could tell by the caps, haircuts and aviation glasses that the two men were officers, even before I made out the cluster of leaves on one man's hat. Like a herd of cattle the men in the battery began heading toward their location, pulling on their fatigue shirts and struggling to blouse their boots. Ahead of them ran the new battery commander, Captain Cindric, followed closely by Lieutenant Anthony. Crisp salutes and handshakes were extended and the show got underway. Jiggling butts and smiling faces, stupid games! Before long they would be leaving, I thought, their asses pinched and caressed by the lily white hands of someone in command . . . another privilege of the officer class.

I turned and left. What a bunch of fools! Today they'll write home and tell their moms they actually saw a white woman in the field, even though all they could do was ogle her from a distance. Among themselves they'll talk about what a nice ass she had and, "Boy oh boy, wouldn't she have been great in bed," but it was nothing but a dream . . . just another ploy to keep the troops happy on the road to their deaths.

It didn't take long to locate the infantry position. They stood out like a sore thumb. After questioning some of the men, I was directed towards some high jungle grass where a couple of metal culverts had been dropped. Pushing my way through the dense, wet grass, I made my way over to one that looked inhabited and peered inside. There he was, two weeks of whiskers on his face and his hair hanging over his ears. A bandana was tied around his forehead and a towel lay draped over his neck and shoulders, partially hiding the thick, matted red hair that covered his chest.

"Shit, you're nothing but a fuckin' hippie," I spat. "You'd better clean up your act, soldier, or it's gonna be your ass!"

Roach's head jerked upward, his mouth dropping. It took a few seconds for him to recognize me, and then his face turned quickly to a smile.

"God damn you, Olsen! You son-of-a-bitch! You scared the shit out of me."

"You'd better watch your shit then," I said, laughing. "There's some real brass just landed, and they won't like what they see if they come snooping over here!"

"Fuck, just let 'em. We'll grab those mutha-fuckers and push an M-16 up their ass!"

I had the feeling he meant what he said.

"Hey, where's the big guy?" I said, crawling inside.

Roach's head and eyes dropped; he didn't say anything. I knew better than to pursue it. For awhile, we both sat quietly, saying nothing. After all, what could be said? Pushing myself up against the steel corrugation, I began emptying my pockets.

"Hey man, I thought you might like these," I said, pulling a couple of cans of cold soda out of my fatigues. His face lit up. I pulled a small bag of weed out of my pants and tossed it in his lap. "I thought you might like this, too."

"Shit, man, is this Christmas?"

"You wanna smoke some?"

"You bet."

I shook a couple of cigarettes from my package and began rolling out the tobacco. In a few minutes they were stuffed with marijuana, and the sweet smell of burning pot filled the inside of the culvert and spilled out into the grass.

By now the heat and humidity felt like a vise, so the shade from the culvert offered sweet relief. Still, beads of sweat broke out on my arms and trickled down my face. Ten or fifteen minutes passed, what seemed like an eternity. Then something caught my eye.

Through the tall grass I could see two men in starched, pressed fatigues, cameras hung around their necks, approaching the area. Every now and then they stopped, pointed around, and took pictures. I wondered what was going on?

"Hey Roach, you'd better stash that grass some place. It looks like we're going to get company."

The men approached our position and stopped. I couldn't hear what they were saying, but I could hear their laughter as they shook their heads and pointed in our direction. I recognized them as two of the men who had accompanied the Doughnut Dollies. They took a couple of pictures and then slowly moved on.

"Shit man, don't worry about those guys," Roach said. "They're just a couple of base camp warriors. We see 'em in the field every now and then. They come out in their clean, custom-tailored uniforms and take pictures of the real war. They come out to look at the freaks or photograph the dead bodies and then write home to their moms and dads and tell them that this is what it's like, or that this is where they're at."

I understood the bitterness in his voice. The soldiers in the rear probably felt they had it bad, but to us they were on one long R&R. They didn't know shit about the real war! And then there were guys who had it a lot worse than I did. Roach was one of them. I knew that regardless of how bad it was for me, there were comforts I had that he rarely experienced. 'Nam was like Dante's Inferno, a multi-level hell. Each step into the bush led you deeper into torment. I was glad I wasn't a foot soldier; they seemed to have it the worst.

I sat and talked with Roach long after the Doughnut Dollies had departed. When the time came for us to part, it was an emotional separation. I didn't know whether I would see him again, and I had an uneasy feeling in my stomach. Perhaps someday I'd get word that he never made it out. It hurt too much to even consider the possibility. It made me angry . . . angry because it just didn't seem there were enough people who even cared.

I told myself that he would make it. He had said that they were starting to avoid contact with the enemy whenever they could, even letting VC patrols pass by that they could have ambushed. He was just as alarmed as I was by the fact that we didn't seem to be fighting to win anymore. He couldn't see wasting any more American lives if there was any way they could avoid it. I was behind him 100 percent.

As the days progressed we found ourselves participating in a large reconnaissance in force operation north of Bao Trai, and as we convoyed back and forth between FDS Meade and FSB Keene II, I became increasingly aware of the mounting devastation. Rice paddies and countrysides once green with vegetation were rapidly becoming stark dirt piles.

Everywhere we went, there were huge caverns left by exploding bombs and artillery shells. Pagodas lay scattered over nearly every traveled road, burnt and bullet-ridden like beached hulls from savage shipwrecks. Piles of straw, bamboo and corrugated metal lay where small hamlets and villages once stood. Forest and jungle alike were crushed and raped, nature retreating from advancing bulldozers and explosives. It was a different kind of destruction than my father's World War II books had depicted, yet it was all part of the same force. I wondered what it had been like for my father. I wondered if I would leave a similar heritage, or any heritage at all.

As we traveled the countryside I searched for the people that we were sent to protect. I found them nowhere. Nor could I find the hordes of communist aggressors. Where was the destruction that had accompanied *their* invasion?

I found myself asking the same old questions. How did we get into this mess in the first place? Here I was, in the middle of this war, hating it, yet unable to get out. I felt like a murderer, but at the same time I felt highly victimized. I was vividly aware of the destruction I helped to generate everyday. I wanted it to stop, but I was helpless to do anything about it. I wanted someone who had the power to make it all end. Didn't anybody care? If only there was some kind of benevolent power beyond man's, a being who had greater power than people did.

Something deep within me was quickened by those thoughts—something struggling to break out of the cramped quarters of my subconscious. At times I experienced just the slightest flicker of hope. At such moments it seemed there just might be a power that could liberate man from senseless destruction.

The truck lurched to the side and slowed down, shaking me from my thoughts. I could see a small village up ahead, and I watched as the lead tank slowed, churning up clouds of dust as it approached the outskirts. I swung around facing the edge of the road and leveled my M-16, letting it rest on the ridge of the bed. I fashioned a comfortable seat on the duffle bag I occupied and prepared myself for the unexpected. The village was a little larger than most we passed through. Store fronts lined the only road that passed through its center. It reminded me of a Hollywood western movie set.

As we lumbered through the village, I looked down at the six or seven children that ran alongside our truck trying to sell cigarettes, Cokes and trinkets. My younger brother and sisters hadn't been much older the last time I had seen them.

237

"Hey . . . tokla, you got tokla?" I yelled down at them. Observing their puzzled expressions, I tried another name. "Gung-sa! . . . you got gung-sa?"

From the smiles on the older boys' faces, I knew I had gotten through.

"Can-sa, can-sa," one shouted, panting as he ran alongside the back, "me got . . . 500p."

"No . . . 200p," I yelled back down at him laughing as he raced to keep up.

"No . . . you cheap Charlie! Me do 300p, O.K.?"

Suddenly the truck slowed down and stopped. I turned quickly and stood, lifting my M-16 and looking up front to see what the holdup was. We didn't normally stop in villages.

The children, who had at first backed away when we stopped, now began crowding forward.

"Hey get back!" I said sharply, pointing my M-16 at them as they crowded around the base of the truck. "Di di mau! Di di!"

The children were hesitant to move, so I leveled my M-16 at them and released a round into the chamber. A loud click sounded as the bullet slammed forward.

"Hey, take it easy," yelled one of the guys who had climbed on top of the cab to get a look at the front of the column. "They're only stopping to let another convoy of APCs pass down at the crossroads. We shouldn't be here more than a minute!"

I sat back down, relieved but still guarded. Shit, I thought, this should be an excellent opportunity to pick up some weed. I scanned the faces of the children and spotted the boy who had been racing alongside the truck.

"Hey . . . you . . . baby-san, you get gung-sa! Two bags," I said, holding up two fingers. "Five hundred p."

"O.K., G.I.," he yelled, turning to run. "You wait. Me be back chop chop!"

As soon as he left, the whole group began to push toward the truck again, yelling and begging.

"Hey, di di!" I warned them again, leveling my M-16. I wasn't going to take the chance that one of these kids might be carrying a grenade.

A couple of the other guys began hanging over the side of the truck, buying Cokes, encouraging even more of the young girls who had crowded the storefronts to come over with their trinkets.

The front of the convoy was slowly beginning to pull out when the young boy carrying my grass came racing out from behind a straw hut. I dug five 100 piaster bills out of my pocket, and as he caught up with the truck, I leaned over the side and quickly exchanged the cash for the bags. At the same time, I saw a young girl step out of the crowd and walk toward me. She was carrying a baby on her hip. In the baby's hands was a long, beaded necklace of small gray and white shells.

"Hey, baby-san," I called, stuffing the two bags of grass into the vest pockets of my flak jacket, "how much money you want . . . necklace?"

"You no buy," she said, smiling, stepping even closer. "Me give."

I was surprised but quickly leaned over, feeling the truck start to pull out. The child slipped the necklace over my helmet and it dropped around my neck. I didn't know what to say! A thank-you was trying to form on my lips, but I couldn't get it out. I just sat looking at her and the baby as we slowly drove away, watching them smile and wave.

"Hey, Olsen!" said one of the men who sat next to me. "We didn't get anything from these gooks. How come you get treated so special?"

I looked down at the necklace, picking it up in my hand. Why had she given it to me?

I didn't know. I only knew that this was the first act of kindness I had experienced from a Vietnamese, and I hung on to that necklace as if it were made of diamonds.

16

17 August 1968
FSB Keene II
Ap Tram Lac

On August 17 the long expected VC/NVA Third Offensive began. Early that morning, the Tay Ninh base camp shook to the sounds of exploding mortar and rocket shells. As troops and reinforcements were directed to that area, Fire Support Base Buell II and the Signal Facility at Nui Ba Den came under heavy rocket and ground attack. Reinforcements from Dau Tieng rushing to their aid got caught in a crossfire of enemy positions deeply entrenched in the Ben Cui Rubber Plantation. The road between Tay Ninh and Dau Tieng became completely cut. As enemy forces launched three human wave attacks against the 1st Battalion 5th Mech "Bobcats" caught in Ben Cui, two battalions of NVA moved into and occupied Tay Ninh East.

After three hours, the combined forces of artillery and infantry at FSB Buell II beat back the determined enemy. Eighty-four men lay dead. As Tropic Lightning forces deployed themselves in blocking positions around Tay Ninh, Vietnamese ARVNs began the slow, arduous process of moving through entrenched enemy positions in the city to flush them out. In the southeast portion of the city, elements of the 4th Battalion 23rd US Infantry and the 3rd Battalion 4th Cavalry fought house to house among the burning ruins.

For six hours the 1st of the 5th Mech fought off repeated enemy assaults. When the 3rd of the 4th Cavalry began moving east to assist them, they ran into heavily entrenched forces along Hwy. 26 and were forced to battle through six hours of heavy fighting themselves. Before the Cav could assist them, the Bobcats beat back the combined Viet Cong and NVA forces that had them pinned down. However, as the Bobcats continued to move through the Ben Cui Plantation, they ran head on into another enemy battalion. This time, assisted by artillery, gunships and airstrikes, they killed 182 in a battle that lasted ninety minutes.

The enemy began launching attacks at Cu Chi and the main supply route between Cu Chi and its surrounding territory. All the fire support bases in our area began experiencing attacks by mortars and rockets, often followed by light ground probes.

Anxiety crept over our base every evening. The chances for observing the enemy dropped significantly despite the use of such highly sophisticated night viewing devices as the Starlight Scope, and even though we relied on every possible early warning device, laying out trip flares and concertina wire as far as eighty meters in front of our position, nothing seemed to ease the tension. Charlie had a reputation for penetrating even the most sophisticated defense systems with special sapper squads, suicide squads with explosives taped to their bodies. A squad of VC had recently made their way right up to the bunker line of a unit of the very elite 101st Airborne troops and had slit the throat of every man on the line. The guards had been drinking and had gotten careless. Orders on a division level quickly followed, banning all use of alcohol on the perimeter at nights. It became a court-martial offense. We couldn't help thinking about those mishaps, and we all struggled against our own imaginations.

My eyes searched the area below us as the Chinook descended, carrying our three-quarter and crew. I could see the netting that held the PSP, sandbags and ammo boxes, swaying below the chopper. I made a mental note of the infantry foxholes that dotted the open area below us, noticing that very little had been done to secure the area. Luckily, the LZ had been cold, so I felt more secure.

Enemy activity had finally subsided and the last three days had been relatively quiet. The VC body count was at 900, an indication of the fierce fighting that had taken place the previous two weeks. Perhaps their loss was the reason for the lull. I wondered whether the enemy was regrouping, as he always had, to attack again. I didn't even want to think about it. I just wanted to lie down and sleep. I wanted to rest my head against the skeleton of this Chinook, close my eyes and wake up a week later, somewhere else. The strain of being constantly on Red Alert had robbed us of strength and sleep. I hoped that it would soon be different. There had been a rumor that with heavy rains starting again, we could possibly be in position for a number of weeks. I hoped it was true. We all needed rest and we needed it soon.

But in seconds we would be hitting the ground and it would start all over again: the building, the sleeplessness, the wretched back-breaking digging. I had to prepare myself for it. It was my responsibility to see that it got done.

With less than ten hours of daylight remaining we began the frantic race to carve out another patrol base and establish a secure perimeter of defense. We wound up directing fire for the 2nd Battalion 14th US Infantry most of the day, and had to send one man to hump ammo for the guns. Fatigue was taking its toll on my men and I wondered how they would respond tomorrow after another night without sleep.

The following evening, tempers began running short. Grumbling and complaining increased.

Although we had completed the top three layers of sandbags required by regulation, and a third layer of sandbags waist high around the FDC walls, we were still struggling to complete a second layer of sandbags on the personnel bunker. A stricter standard had been imposed by headquarters because we were considered to be in a high risk area, so we were having to fill a lot more sandbags than usual.

At 2200 hours it was time for my shift to take over the job. I had finished passing all necessary information on to Vanous and was walking out the door when the lieutenant spoke. "Olsen, I want you to stay on shift."

"It's my turn to fill sandbags, lieutenant."

"Look, Olsen," he said sharply, "you can let the men do the physical labor. You're team leader and that means you're the ranking NCO here and don't have to do common labor. The operation of the FDC is more important than filling sandbags. I want you in here watching over things while I get some sleep."

"Lieutenant, Vanous can handle anything that comes up. Besides, I'll be right outside the door if you need any help."

"Olsen, are you arguing with me again?"

"Lieutenant!" I said, my voice rising. "I'm not gonna let the men work and not do my share. There isn't anything you guys can't handle in here. I'm sorry, I've just got to do what I think is right!"

I slipped out of the bunker and walked to where my men were filling sandbags. I stooped and picked up a folding shovel, screwing the blade into place.

"Hey, Olsen," Gracelli whispered. "We wondered if you would be coming to join us tonight!"

I said nothing. Sticking my shovel in the ground I pried up a chunk of sticky clay and tried to shake it off into the sandbag that hung between his knees.

"Whooeee!" said Mitchell softly. "That lieutenant, he sure is a honky muthafucker, ain't he?"

They must have overheard the conversation.

"You keep on doing what you do, and you're gonna end up in hot water one of these days," warned Gracelli.

"Yeah ... maybe," I replied. "We'll wait and see."

"Shit," said White, "you can't take on the system by yourself and beat it, and you know it. Sooner or later you get swallowed up by it or put in jail, and then you're just doing double time. It ain't worth it."

As work progressed, conversation died. We were simply too tired to talk.

This wasn't the first time the lieutenant and I had clashed, but it was the first time I had disobeyed a direct order. It felt good! Not because I had disobeyed him, but because I was doing what I thought was right, and hadn't given in to fear. I was tired of living my life afraid—of punishment, of rejection, of dying. As long as I was bound by fear I could never be free in any situation, and I was determined to die a free man.

As the hours stretched, Danny and Mitchell nodded off as they sat holding their sandbags. Danny had just come in country. I swore that he couldn't have been more than sixteen.

"Hey, Mitchell! Wake up!" Gracelli whispered, poking Mitchell's shoulder with his shovel.

Mitchell bolted up, startled. "Shit! You mutha-fucker!" he snapped at Gracelli.

"Hey, knock it off, Mitchell," I said sternly. "He didn't mean anything. He's just trying to keep you awake. You know the rules."

"Fuck the rules," he cried. "I'm shit-ass tired! I can't keep awake any longer. What the fuck these people trying to do anyway! Fuck 'em! I want some sleep!"

"Hey man, I know it!" I said, trying to calm him down. "We all want to get some sleep, but you know the rules. If someone comes out here and reports you, you could get an Article 15. If you go to sleep that only means we have to stay up and do your work. The best thing we can do is work at it together until it's finished. It'll get done faster, there won't be any hard feelings, and then everyone can get some sleep."

Their mumbling continued and I didn't try to stop it. They had every right to be unhappy. I thought we already had plenty of overhead cover and felt we should have the right to determine for ourselves what we felt was safe. It was enough to be fighting Charlie besides having to struggle against exhaustion.

A half-hour later everyone's movement had deteriorated to slow motion. Gracelli had stopped shoveling and had fallen asleep, standing. Mitchell and Danny, their heads hanging, were asleep again in their seats. Only White and I were awake, and even he was now nodding his head.

I looked around the battery area, scouting for any officers. I couldn't see anyone around the captain's bunker, and I didn't hear anyone stirring inside the FDC. Maybe the lieutenant was asleep. If he was, he wouldn't be coming out.

"All right," I whispered, shaking White and Gracelli, "we'll split the shift. White, you and Gracelli hit the sack for two hours and then you can get up and relieve Mitchell and Danny. O.K.?"

"Shit," mumbled Mitchell, waking, "I need some sleep *now*, Olsen! How am I gonna make it two more hours?"

"If I can do it, you can do it!" I replied.

A half-hour later Mitchell was fast asleep again, his arms stretched out on his knees, clutching a sandbag. I looked down at Danny. His head jerked upright as I dropped a shovelful of clay into his sandbag. I tried to rouse Mitchell by shaking his shoulder, but couldn't. I heard Danny mumble something to me. I could see the pleading look in his eyes as tears ran down his boyish face. I stood up, my heart heavy. It just wasn't right for him to suffer like this. Fuck it.

"Go ahead," I whispered to Danny, avoiding his eyes. "Hit the sack! I'll fill sandbags with Mitchell."

Danny dropped the sack and crawled toward the FDC bunker. Curling up against a pile of sandbags, he fell fast asleep.

I reached down and picked up his sandbag, grunting as I tossed it out of the hole. Picking up another one, I awkwardly stuffed a shovelful of wet clay into it. Thumping it on the ground, I made it stand up by itself. I forced the top open with another shovelful of clay. I looked at my watch. It was 0420.

Forty minutes went by before my thoughts were interrupted by approaching footsteps. I looked up at the figure towering above me. I could barely make out who it was in the pitch black, but when he leaned down there was no mistaking the lieutenant's figure and voice.

"Olsen, where are the other men?"

"They're sleeping, lieutenant."

"Well, get them up! No one's supposed to sleep until the personnel bunker is covered!"

"Shit, lieutenant, these men can't even stay awake, much less build anything."

"I don't care if they're sleeping on their feet! I want them standing!"

"Lieutenant," I countered, "these men haven't slept in nearly three days. They're exhausted! They've reached their limit. You can't push them till they drop. They're not animals!"

We argued back and forth until finally the lieutenant tired and began to give ground. He must have sensed it was no use. Rather than becoming angrier, as he often did, he gave up. I felt sorry for him, but I felt more concern for my men. I struck for a compromise.

"C'mon, lieutenant," I said, "at least let half the men off. If we keep two on, at least we can say that we worked all night on it."

"All right," he said grudgingly, yet obviously relieved. "Let half of the crew out here sleep, and I'll let half of the crew inside. But if the captain comes around they'll have to get up, and you'll have to take the responsibility for disobeying orders. I won't!"

Straightening up, he walked back to the FDC.

Since Danny was the new recruit, I woke him up first, though I hated to do it. I told him to hang in there one more hour. It was the best I could do, but I felt a little better knowing that again I had refused to let fear influence my actions. I had fought for my men, and the lieutenant had backed down. For the second time that night, I tasted freedom.

Shortly before the 6 a.m. shift one morning, Dangerfield rushed into my bunker, rousing me from sleep and telling me that I had better get inside because there was going to be some shit flying any second. I pulled on my pants and shirt and made my way hurriedly to the FDC. The lieutenant was already angry when I arrived, sweat beading up on his forehead. He was anxiously awaiting the arrival of the captain, who had also been summoned. The lieutenant explained to me that the night crew had received a fire mission for a prep that was supposed to be fired in the morning. They had figured the data and had laid the guns, all without waking either the lieutenant or me to check their data. The lieutenant had assumed the prep data had been checked by me, so he fired it. The white phosphorus marking round, which was timed to explode in the air directly over the target, exploded right above the position of our own troops. Though no one had been killed, the prep had been observed by Major Jenkins, who had been flying over the area. Now he was on his way here to find out who was responsible. The tent flap lifted as Captain Cindric entered.

"The major wants you to go up on push four-five, sir, on your own radio. He wants to talk to you privately!" Dangerfield said.

"What the fuck is going on?" Captain Cindric asked, his face flushed with anger.

The lieutenant explained the situation. The captain quickly turned to go back to his tent. "This won't be the last of it," he hissed as he left. "I'll want to talk to you lieutenant, as soon as I return."

But instead of returning, he sent for the lieutenant. As the lieutenant hurried to the captain's tent, I could hear the major's bubble chopper approaching. I sat down hard in my chair, wondering what the fuck would happen now. I was angry at my crew for not following safety procedures and upset by their arrogance, particularly that of the new Spec Four recently transferred to us, Ed McCoy.

"What the fuck were you guys thinking?" I demanded of Dangerfield. "Shit, you know better than that. Why didn't you get me or the lieutenant up to check your data?"

"Well, the lieutenant was asleep and we didn't want to wake him," Dangerfield protested. "He said only to wake him for something important and we thought we could handle it O.K."

"Yeah, we figured we could handle it without you, Olsen," McCoy put in, exchanging a wink with Dangerfield. Though he spoke in a jesting tone, there was a rebelliousness behind his words. The smile that covered his face reflected the obvious pleasure he was getting from the whole incident.

I looked at them, surprised. These two Ozark Mountain boys were like two peas in a pod, each defending the other. Trying to laugh this mistake off as if it didn't mean a thing. But I could see that they were tense, probably wondering what was going to happen to them. I knew that McCoy had been transferred out of his old outfit for insubordination. I hadn't expected him to be insubordinate here.

"Besides," McCoy added, "what can we do about it now, anyway?"

That was all it took! "I'll tell you what *I* can do about it," I said, leaning into his face and staring hard into his eyes. "I can bust your ass down to a PFC and you can spend the rest of your time over here picking up paper and burning shit! And if you don't go home with a god-damned nickel to your name, it won't mean a fuckin' thing to me either! You assholes think this is a fuckin' game? Those were American troops you nearly wasted this morning, not some dumb fuckin' gooks!"

Although he stood at least a head taller than me, he slumped back immediately in his chair. His eyes dropped to the floor. I waited for his response but he didn't say anything. I immediately regretted chewing him out in front of the other guys, but I still hadn't spent my anger. This wasn't just a case of insubordination; those were our guys out there! I decided not to say anything more until I heard from the lieutenant. Clenching my teeth, I sat down and waited. It was deathly quiet.

245

Ten minutes later the lieutenant returned. "Olsen, the major wants to see you!" he said sheepishly.

See me! God damn, what was going on now? I pushed myself from the chair.

"He's holding you personally responsible for the incident," the lieutenant said quietly. Embarrassment crossed his face.

Me? I hurriedly left the bunker. What the fuck for? I wasn't the one who fired the guns! The lieutenant had final responsibility for checking all the data. Why hadn't he done his job instead of just assuming I had done mine? Up till now I had been proud of the fact that the lieutenant had not seen it necessary to check my data anymore, having never found a mistake. But now I wished he hadn't had so much confidence in me.

Reluctantly, I entered the captain's tent and snapped to attention. Standing stiffly, I looked straight into the major's glaring eyes. He began to chew me up and down.

". . . and I hold you totally responsible for every bit of information that comes out of the FDC," he finished, "and from now on there will never be another incident like this. You will see to it that there isn't . . . is that clear?"

"Yes, sir," I answered. I wanted to protest but I didn't. He was steaming and I wasn't going to take any chances.

"And to see to that," he continued, "you will go on shift every morning, two hours prior to sun-up, to insure that all night data is checked before any infantry operations begin. Is that understood?"

"Yes, sir!"

"Now," he said, "I'm finished."

I understood immediately that I was dismissed. I saluted, turned and left.

The infantry assault operation had been pushed back to allow us time to recheck our data and by now the guns were firing. I made my way back to the FDC and slipped inside. Pulling up a folding chair, I sat down between Dangerfield and McCoy. I leaned on my knees and hung my head down, waiting for a lull in the fire mission. When everything was quiet, I began.

"I don't want anything like this to happen again," I said. "And to insure that it doesn't, you'll get me up two hours prior to shift change everyday. Is that understood?"

I looked directly at Dangerfield and then at McCoy. They nodded their heads in agreement, not looking up from their hands. I stood.

"Lieutenant," I said, looking him straight in the eyes, "do you have everything under control here?"

"Yes," he said, blushing.

"Then may I be excused?" I walked out the entrance without waiting for a reply.

I had decided on my way back from the captain's tent that I would spare my men the same experience I had just gone through. I could have chewed their asses the way mine had been chewed, but what good would it have done? Still, I felt deeply betrayed by both Dangerfield and McCoy. I wouldn't make the mistake of trusting them again.

As September ended we began experiencing an increase in enemy activity and a rise in significant contact. With it came a rise in "speculation" from so-called "intelligence." Captured enemy documents revealed another major offensive. The Viet Cong's principal objective was now to destroy Tropic Lightning forces deployed across the northwest flank of Saigon; then they hoped to penetrate the capital again. Leaflets found among captured supply caches were proclaiming a devastating attack from NVA forces to be conducted to our west and calling for a general uprising of the people. Our contact was supposedly with units who were being sent in advance of that strike. They were trying to position themselves in strategic locations. I didn't like it! The rumor was there was going to be another Tet, and many times, information on the grapevine was more reliable than that from intelligence.

We had already been heavily mortared five times in our new location, FSB Keene III, and the likelihood of our being hit again increased every day. The longer we stayed, the more we risked the chance of Charlie's plotting our exact position. Still, if we had to move again now, the demand would literally extract its pound of flesh. I didn't know which was worse! It was a continuing no win situation.

17

24 September 1968
FSB Keene III
Xom Giong Dau

I heaved a sigh as beads of perspiration broke out on my skin. I sucked the hot air in and exhaled slowly. I could feel the weight of the heat on my chest. I tugged at my poncho liner and adjusted my position so that the sandbags I was lying on would be more comfortable. I wondered how long I would be able to stand it, but I wanted to have a dark tan when I got back to the States.

I could feel myself changing, and wondered if my getting short had anything to do with it.

How many days would it be, now that I had extended my tour? I counted them off. Eighty! Eighty days left to serve on the big rock. I could have been going home in 37, but then I would have had seven more months of stateside duty, and I knew there was no way in hell that once I got out of 'Nam, I could stand to finish my time. The Army had recently begun offering a program to drop service time for people who were drafted if they would extend their tours in Vietnam, and I took them up on it. I knew it meant stretching my luck an additional forty-five days, but what was forty-five days compared to seven months? I extended one and one-half months, they chopped five. The risk seemed like a small price to purchase my freedom.

I punched out my cigarette and tossed the butt in the tall grass that edged my bunker. I looked out over the base camp. With no officers in sight, I shook a joint out of my cigarette pack and lit up. I didn't have to go on shift for another six hours so I could get plenty high and still be in good shape when I came on. Besides, by now everything had become so mechanical that I could function as well stoned as not, and did most of the time. What's more, I had begun smoking dope openly, except in the immediate presence of the captain or the lieutenant. There were few others so bold, but I didn't care. More than half the battery experimented with marijuana and I would guess by now a third were stone heads. I had little to worry about from my peers. Even the lieutenant knew I was smoking. One night he had confronted me about it shortly after I had built my last bunker. I had built it as a lean-to on the rear of the FDC and since he slept in the rear of the main bunker, we shared one wall. Whenever I got stoned the smoke would drift right through the openings between the ammo boxes and over his cot.

"Olsen," he had said one night when a full crew was on, "what was that smell coming from your bunker last night?"

"What smell was that, Lieutenant?" I could see eyebrows rising on the faces of the crew.

"Olsen, you know darn well what smell I mean!"

"Oh, that. That was incense, Lieutenant."

My men began to grin. They knew I was putting the lieutenant on.

"That wasn't incense I smelled last night, Olsen! I know what incense smells like!"

"No, Lieutenant, I'm sure you're wrong. This is some new stuff that I sent for from the States. I burn it all the time. You want me to bring some in here so you can see?"

I was enjoying myself, making light of it. I didn't care if he knew that I smoked dope.

"Olsen," he said angrily, only slightly less sure of himself this time, "I think I know what it was and it wasn't incense. You had better watch yourself or you're going to get in trouble."

Not satisfied to let it drop, I continued. "Well gee, Lieutenant, what do you think it was if it wasn't incense?"

By now the rest of the crew was finding it hard to keep from laughing, and the lieutenant realized it.

"Well, just don't let me catch you smoking it!" he said curtly. "And I don't want you doing it on duty."

That had been the end of the subject. I hadn't cared. His threats or anyone else's meant little to me any more. I had had it with regulations. I let my hair grow longer, I let my mustache grow, and some days even went without shaving. I smoked openly and wore whatever I wanted. After all, what did I really have to lose? I knew they could strip me of my rank and pay, but I had told the lieutenant if they did that then I simply wouldn't take the responsibilities. He had told the captain, and after that, the harassment ended. I knew they wouldn't put me in jail simply for my appearance, because then they would lose my service. The position I held was one of the most important in the battery and they didn't have anyone who could replace me. I always did my job extremely well, and they knew it. My skills were necessary for the efficient function of the FDC; the battery depended on the effectiveness of the FDC for its survival; and the infantry depended on the battery for theirs.

Stretching back down on my poncho liner, I kicked my thongs off and adjusted my sunglasses. I was going to hit the coast looking my best. I had started doing sit-ups every night, determined to get rid of the extra fat I carried. I was also watching my diet. I began eating less mess tent food to try and drop a few pounds. I wanted to be standing tall and looking good when I got back to the States.

I smeared another handful of suntan lotion on my arms. I was thinking about the Vietnamese vendors I could see out near the perimeter wire. I wondered where they came from. There wasn't a village within two or three thousand meters from here. Shit, they must have had to walk an awful long way just to sell their crap out here. I didn't like the fact that the perimeter guards let them hang around. I was sure that every time they left, they were counting off their steps, measuring our exact location and then feeding the distances to Charlie so that he could mortar us more effectively. We had been mortared seven times and each time the explosions were closer to the main bunkers. Their rounds weren't just falling randomly any more; they knew what they were looking for. Still, here were the Vietnamese, some of them children, outside the wire.

It was a curious thing, these children. They seemed to raise one another. It was common to see three-year-olds carrying their baby brothers and sisters around on their backs, and just as common to see three- and four-year-olds carrying water in buckets suspended on long poles. I had never seen children so young with so much responsibility. Children forced to labor at an early age so their families could survive. Still, they hardly seemed as stunted by their work as they had been by the war.

I had come to view the plight of the Vietnamese as cruel and unjust as mine, only theirs was never-ending. I was beginning to feel more sympathetic, realizing the suffering they endured. I felt a growing shame and embarrassment for the way we treated them. At least I would be going home some day and for me all this would end.

I thought that I had become thoroughly hardened to the violence that surrounded my life, but I wasn't. In fact, that violence had been slowly whittling away my self-esteem until I could see only a skeleton of my humanity remaining. I tried desperately to justify my part in the violence but could not. I wasn't even sure I could justify taking someone else's life just to preserve mine anymore. That rationale now seemed the ultimate in selfishness. In seeking to know the truth about the war and myself, I didn't like what I was finding. Still, I deeply resisted the truth because I knew in my heart that I couldn't face it ... not here ... not now.

"Hey, Olsen." I recognized White's voice. "Look at you, man! You think this is Hawaii or something? You ain't on R&R here! You'd better get your shit together!"

"Hey, what's happening," I said, turning and propping myself up on my elbow.

"Miller is back from the bush. You wanna go down and visit him?"

"Sure, just let me get my shit together," I said, slipping down off the roof.

Miller was one of White's close buddies from his old gun section. We were friends, but not like he and White. Not long after White had transferred to the FDC, Miller had volunteered to be an RTO for the 1st of the 5th Mech. Since the FOs generally wanted their RTOs to understand the radio language used by the artillery, they had begun recruiting gun bunnies from artillery units, training them for the job. Miller had been out with the Mech over three months.

As we walked down to the gun section, we talked. "Hey, man," White said, "I'm seriously thinking about volunteering to go out as an RTO."

"Listen man, don't do it!" I said.

"Shit, it's just too boring working in the FDC, and I don't want to go back to humping on the guns; that's even worse. I want something exciting in my life. Man, it might be really a trip working out there with the infantry. At least I'd get to see the enemy! I'd like to see who the fuck it is I'm fighting!"

"Man, you're crazy," I said, "it just ain't worth it. You could get your shit blown away easy. For what . . . some cheap thrill? Fuck, man, I'll put up with the boredom. It's a lot safer in here than out in the bush, I don't care what the grunts say. How many times have you heard of an artillery battery being overrun? I admit it happens but shit, look at what happened at Pope last week. The Viet Cong left behind 104 KIAs. Even though they penetrated the perimeter and blew up some of the guns, they didn't totally overrun them. Man, if that had been some infantry night location, they would have been gutted. I don't know, man. When I weigh the odds, it don't look good to me. Shit, we're short, man! Why you wanna go fuck with your life when you've made it safely this far? There's always some guy who really gets short and then gets his shit blown away, and I ain't going back in no body bag!"

We both lapsed into silence. I wanted desperately to talk White out of making any kind of rash decision. I couldn't stand the thought of his going to the field and possibly getting blown away. We had become too close. I knew I couldn't stand losing him. What would I say to his parents? But I knew I couldn't pressure him about it either. He had to make up his own mind.

When we arrived at the gun section White darted into the personnel bunker looking for Miller. In a few moments both of them emerged. I walked over and hugged him.

"Hey, Olsen," said White excitedly, "he says he's back for good this time and that they're looking for two replacements!"

It was obvious what he was hinting at.

"Hey, let's sit down over here," said Miller, pointing to a cluster of ammo boxes. Drawing his jungle hat down over his eyes, he squatted down against the parapet. We dragged out two more ammo boxes and sat down next to him.

"Did White tell you he's thinking of volunteering?" I asked.

"No," Miller replied, casting a glance at White's face. "Is that true?"

"Yeah, man," said White excitedly, "man, you did it and you came out O.K.! It can't be that bad."

Miller just shook his head. "Hey, don't do it." A heaviness hung on the edge of his words that I hadn't noticed before. I looked in his eyes. I could see that some kind of change had occurred since I last saw him. He didn't have that restless enthusiasm or humor I remembered his having. There was a sobriety about him that was new; a quietness and a reserve that hadn't been there before.

"Why not, man? You did it," White said.

"Shit, it was O.K. in the beginning," Miller replied. "But it just turned bad!"

Leaning back and resting his head back on the sandbagged wall, Miller looked off into the distance. When he spoke again he seemed even more distant.

251

"Look, man, we're friends, right! Just don't do it, O.K.! It ain't worth it. It just ain't no good!"

He shook his head sadly as he spoke. "Man, they're fucking crazy out in the bush. Some of those guys are like animals! Man, I've seen 'em cut the ears and fingers off gooks and wear 'em on their belts! It's like some of these guys have gone insane!

"I don't hardly blame 'em though," he added, dropping his voice. "If you could see some of the things the VC have done to our guys it would make you sick to your stomach."

"Hey, like what?" White probed.

"Shit, you just don't wanna know," Miller replied. "Anyway, it ain't no good to talk about it!"

"Aw c'mon," White pleaded.

"Shit, man!" I interjected. "C'mon, White, you heard the man. Why go bringing us down?" I had already heard plenty of horror stories while visiting the grunts out on the perimeter. I didn't want to hear any more.

"Hey, speaking of being down," Miller grinned, pulling a pack of cigarettes out of his pocket, "how'd you like to smoke some stuff I picked up in Saigon, down in Soul Alley? This stuff is laced with opium."

An explosion shook me from my sleep! Is this real, I thought, or am I only dreaming? Another explosion shook my bunker and the blast knocked me off my cot and onto the floor. Oh God, no! It's really happening!

My heart pounded as I sprawled face down on the floor. My fingers clawed the dirt, digging in. I tried to pull myself closer to the earth. *Wham, wham, wham!* Another explosion shook my bunker. Panic gripped my chest. I pushed my cheek hard into the dirt.

Pop! Pop! Pop! Pop! I could hear the small arms fire. A series of pops . . . automatic weapons! God damn, its raining death! I could hear mortars and RPGs exploding all over the base. Suddenly I heard it: a burst of AK-47 fire roughly fifteen meters from my position. Oh my God, I thought, they've penetrated the perimeter! They're coming in, they're coming in!

I knew they would try to knock out the communications center first thing. Maybe a gook carrying a satchel charge would drop one through my bunker window any minute.

Explosions, machine gun clatter, and small arms fire filled the air with deafening volume. I identified the direction of Charlie's assault from the distinct sound of the AK fire which rose above everything else. It sounded like we were going hand to hand.

A thousand thoughts raced through my mind as I fought back paralysis. If only I could dig deeper . . . shrink to the size of a mouse . . . oh God, don't let me die . . . was this my time . . . would it happen now . . . how would it happen . . . would it be a grenade . . . was he out there now . . . where was my gun . . . would he get to me first?

Almost by reflex I stuck out my hand, found my helmet, and slapped it over my face. The chin strap hung down in my mouth and I blew it away. It landed in my eye. I began to make a slow turn for my M-16.

Suddenly I heard Dangerfield yelling at the rear entrance of my bunker. "Olsen, Olsen! We need you inside . . . now!"

Jesus, I thought, I don't want to move from here. But I stuck my feet in my boots, and crawled out of my bunker, leaving my pants behind.

While the lieutenant called in artillery fire from Cu Chi, I worked frantically to pinpoint the Viet Cong and to provide defensive fire for ourselves and the listening posts outside our perimeter. I could hear machine gun fire and screaming over the radio as an infantry outpost radioed its position. They were fighting for their lives as the enemy swept over them.

The ambush patrol to our north was also in the middle of a fierce fire fight. I immediately shifted two of our guns in their direction to lay down blocking fire.

Heart pounding, adrenaline pumping, I raced to compute data to fire the guns. While the lieutenant shouted additional infantry positions to me, the crew split the data off the charts. Punching numbers into the FADAC, I double checked its information on my slide rule.

A large explosion shook the side of the FDC bunker, sending a shiver up my spine.

"God damn it," I shouted, "we've been hit!" I wanted to run outside and see what the hell was going on, where the enemy was, but I couldn't. I forced myself to stay put.

". . . Two . . . Three," I shouted into the phone. "Are you ready? Then fire!"

After devastatingly accurate artillery fire, the first wave of Viet Cong to our south fell on the perimeter wire. Fire! Fire! Fire! Claymores, M-16s, M-60s, grenades, M-79s, howitzers, M-50s, small arms, RPGs, mortars, AK-47s—all of them smoking the area like hell's gate. Yea though I walk through the valley of the shadow of death. . . .

The assault to our north began crumbling. Sappers on the west side, explosions, screams, insanity and your worst fears. . . . Turn the guns, fire point blank, hope for it all to end. Tracer bullets and red skies, bulging eyes and frightened cries . . . lungs forgetting to breathe . . . another explosion rocks the bunker! . . . The enemies repulsed on the northern side. The assault is breaking . . . Huey slicks are raking the southside amidst the continuous thumping of artillery rounds. . . .

After two and a half hours the assault finally collapsed.

Three hours later the first light of dawn revealed the dirt, sweat and exhaustion on our faces. With light would come respite from fear. The enemy would fade away. He would be gone before we could search the area, but I welcomed his escape with relief.

Standing outside, stretching my arms, I focused my attention on the thick gun smoke still hanging in the air. A misty silence permeated the morning air.

Soldiers sat staring blankly into the distance, waiting for the warm smell of coffee and breakfast. Waiting to fill their stomachs before they drifted off to sleep. A deep sense of weariness prevailed over the combined smell of sulfur and blood that soaked the battery area.

Few of our men had been injured in spite of the rain of mortars and RPGs that had fallen. Most of the devastation was borne by our bunkers and overhead cover.

The lull was soon broken by light infantry teams assembling their gear and gathering, preparing to search the perimeter with the first good light.

Danny rounded the corner of the bunker, his hand holding down the helmet which bounced on his head. He headed my way.

"Shit," he exclaimed. "Did you see the hole on top of the personnel bunker? That fucker must have been an 80 millimeter mortar; it blew a hole through two layers of sandbags and opened the third!"

"No," I said, "but I heard it last night! Where you off to in such a hurry?" He was scurrying off, dragging the butt of his M-15 in the dirt.

"I'm going to get my camera," he said without stopping. "I'm going with Dangerfield. Somebody said you could see gooks hanging out on the perimeter. We're going out to see them with the infantry."

I kept myself busy inside, figuring up data for a prep on a proposed landing zone near our area. Saddened, disgusted, even curious, I thought about the guys going out to take pictures of the dead. But I couldn't take the time now to sort out my feelings. Battalion had just notified us that they wanted to conduct an air mobile assault in our area as soon as possible and I was rushing to get it set up and obtain clearances.

The telephone land line rang and the lieutenant quickly picked it up.

"Yes, sir . . . no, sir," the lieutenant repeated. "Yes, sir!" He slapped the phone back down.

"Olsen," he shouted, "do you have any men out on the perimeter?"

"Yes, sir," I replied, "I think Dangerfield and Danny went out there."

"Well, the CO in charge of the infantry says there are a whole bunch of guys out there. He wants them out of there, now. Telephone the guns and give them the word! They don't want anyone in that area until it's been thoroughly searched for booby traps and weapons. And they don't want any picture taking!"

A few minutes later, Dangerfield burst in to the FDC. "Wooooeeee!" he said, sounding like Gomer Pyle. "I done got me some real pictures! Wait till you see these suckers come back! Shee-iit, Olsen. Them VC were hanging all over the place, and blown to pieces!"

Danny burst through the rear entrance, a Polaroid dangling from his wrist. He clutched a handful of photographs.

"Look what I got!" he said, thrusting the photos toward the center of the room. The crew and the lieutenant quickly gathered, passing the pictures back and forth.

"Whew . . . shit! Look at that one!" they said. "God damn . . . holy shit . . . whew, mother fucker!"

Revulsion churned my stomach, but I didn't want anyone to know. I was disgusted by their morbid curiosity to view the dead, yet I wanted to see them too. I wanted to see the enemy beaten and still, victory written on every photograph. But I hung back. I had already seen my share of dead men. These pictures couldn't possibly be anything new.

"Hey Olsen, you want to see?" Danny asked, thrusting the photos in my face.

I took them and shuffled through them quickly. A small gasp lodged in my throat. Oh my God, no! It can't be! I fought for self-control.

"They're just children!" I said. A wave of nausea rose in my throat. There they were, there was no denying it! I numbly slid each photograph over the other again and again. This one had no arms, only bloody stumps. Another only half a face. Another only half a chest. Another only one arm and one leg. Here a severed arm, a dismembered leg. A dismembered head, eyes frozen open, mouth grimacing in pain. Grotesque forms of once human life. Most of them couldn't have been older then twelve. I stared at them, fighting back the tears. Only the strong survive, only the strong survive, I repeated. My mind raced to find an excuse for this horror. Yes, there it was; I saw it. They all had on green uniforms. Some of them still wore slings of ammunition. I could see an RPG round only inches from a dismembered hand. They had all been the enemy! It was either them or us!

I shoved the pictures back in Danny's hands. "Here you go," I said flatly. "There's nothing here worth looking at. They're just dead gooks!"

Turning aside, I quickly resumed my work. I was lying to him and myself, but how could I show sympathy for the enemy? Who would understand?

"Shee-iit," Mitchell drawled, "they ain't never gonna let you keep those pictures! They gonna snatch those things outta your hands as soon as you leave country!"

"That's right," the lieutenant agreed. "They confiscate any pictures of the dead at the DEROS Center. It's against regulation to bring or to send them out of the country."

"Well, I'm gonna send them home, just the same," Danny said defiantly. "They're mine, and I'm gonna keep them!"

"Shit, I'm gonna send mine home too!" added Dangerfield. "There ain't no way they can tell what's in the mail!"

"They probably won't even develop your pictures," said the lieutenant, "not over here."

"Well, then I'll just send the whole roll of film back," said Dangerfield.

"Hey, let's get back to business," I said. "You can worry about your pictures some other time."

The hot afternoon sun penetrated my jungle hat and I pulled it on tightly to keep it from blowing off. The thick stench of diesel fuel filled my nostrils as dust rose from the back of the three-quarter. We were hurrying in the direction of the PX. I should have been excited but I wasn't. I was angry.

255

I had persuaded the lieutenant to let me return to the rear on the morning's resupply chopper to replace my M-16, which had been damaged during last night's assault, and to have my knees checked at the base hospital. I had crawled back into my bunker this morning, anticipating a well-deserved rest, when I noticed that the whole lower end of my mosquito netting had been torn apart. Below it, on the floor, my rifle stock lay splintered and pitted. How the hell did this happen, I thought. Examining the netting, I could tell by the pattern of holes that it had been torn apart by shrapnel, and that the spray had come from the top edge of the wall. But there weren't any holes, only the six-inch space where my air vents were. Backing out, I checked the outside, trying to locate where the shrapnel had entered. There, where the roof and wall met, I found a piece of iron channel which supported the roof, crumpled and bent. Upon closer examination I saw that it had stopped an RPG round, causing it to explode into the bunker through the upper air vent. Below it, a large chunk of the wall had been blasted away. Looking back inside, I could see that if the RPG hadn't struck the overhanging channel and exploded outside the wall, both of my feet would have been blown off. So that's what had knocked me to the floor!

Suddenly the realization hit me. My feet . . . I could have lost both of my feet! Checking the area again, I saw that two more RPGs had landed within five feet of my bunker and another mortar crater was less than ten feet away.

Why was I spared when so many around me were dying? Was it more than luck that spared my life? Could there really be a God? Shit, there had to be a God. What hope was there at all if we had to depend on the nature of men?

But why me, I thought again, why was I spared? I didn't have an answer to that question.

When I checked my M-16 I found that it was still operable but I didn't care for the look or feel of the stock. Maybe here's a chance to get back in the rear for a few days, I thought, or even one day, who cares!

Though the lieutenant had first refused to let me go, my persistence had worn him down. Now here I was, still holding the same rifle. The supply sergeant had refused to issue a new one because it was against regulations! As long as it remained functional it didn't make a difference what shape it was in. "Far out!" I had shouted at him. "What the fuck kind of Army we got? What's the matter? Are we short on weapons? We have enough to supply the Vietnamese Army, which hardly ever uses them, and can't even spare a new one for me!"

I had stormed angrily out of the supply depot, slamming the door and cursing both him and the Army. Riding down to the PX, I was still outraged!

Now I could see the gates of the PX and the growing line of Vietnamese shops at its entrance. I'd better just forget it, I thought. So what! Don't let it get to ya. At least I'm gonna get the chance to spend the night in Cu Chi. I'd better take advantage of my vacation while I can.

The truck braked to a squeaky halt and I scrambled out the back. My boots kicked up dust as I made my way to the gate, walking alongside LeRoy, who had come in for a dental exam. We debated whether we should go through the

Vietnamese shops. We decided not to waste our time, having heard that the PX had built a fast food shop where you could actually buy hamburgers, french fries and cold drinks. We wanted to check it out.

The PX compound had become a fairyland. There were new miniature golf grounds, an enlarged PX store, a new swimming pool, and a budding post office. There were palm trees and flowers, white picket fences and even a pond stocked with fish. (Invariably one or two GIs ended up splashing around in it, fully dressed.) To us it was like seeing Paris or London.

As we neared the hamburger joint we saw a line that trailed over two blocks. With no more than one glance at each other we knew we needed to find an alternative.

"Hey, let's go down to the steambaths," LeRoy said. I quickly agreed.

The line of GIs waiting to get in the steambaths was short, so it only took a few minutes for us to get inside. Depositing 500 piasters with the head mama-san, we collected our towels and received permission to enter the dressing rooms. We stripped, stuck our fatigues and boots in a locker, and made our way to the steam room. Towels around our waists, our cigarette packs and Zippos in our hands, we pushed open the heavy doors and stepped into a dense cloud of moist heat. We could barely make out the people a few feet away. LeRoy and I found a secluded corner and sat down on the wooden bench that lined the walls. Basking in the wet heat, I let myself relax. I shook a couple of joints out of my cigarette pack, and we both lit up so we wouldn't have to pass it back and forth, making our smoking less noticeable. Though the smoke was heavy in my lungs, the combination of heat and marijuana felt good. It was odd, but for once, I felt secure, not really being able to see anybody and knowing that no one could see me. I rarely felt that way in the field.

We sat in the steam room nearly forty-five minutes. When we stepped out of the room, the mama-san in charge quickly called two of the young baby-sans to come and escort us to their cubicles for massages. The rooms were separated only by thin wooden partitions with curtains hanging over the entrance.

I concentrated on the pretty young Vietnamese girl who massaged my arms and shoulders, walked on my back and squeezed my thighs. I had heard that these girls were also whores, selling certain favors along with their massages.

"Hey baby-san," I asked coolly, turning over on my back and watching her face, "you do short-time?"

"No can do," she said quickly, slapping me on the stomach, "mama-san cat-mau!"

"Hey c'mon, baby-san," I teased, "you numbah one short timer, I bet."

"You crazy G.I.," she laughed, "mama-san, she be beaucoup angry. No can do!"

I watched her quietly as she continued to massage my legs. As I let my imagination roam, an erection soon lifted the towel which lay across my waist. I felt slightly embarrassed but was more interested in how she would react. She looked at the rising hump and giggled.

257

"Me do hand job," she said quietly, "only fifteen dollah!"

"Fifteen dollars!" I said. "Hey, I can do hand job myself, it no cost me fifteen dollars!"

"O.K., twelve dollah," she said, "numbah one deal!"

"No way, sister," I said, laughing. "You're crazy if you think I'll even give you twelve dollars."

"O.K., G.I.!" she snapped, slapping me on the leg. "You done!"

"All right."

"You give me ten dollah now, O.K., G.I.," she said sweetly, a smile on her face.

"Ten dollars? What for?"

"Me give you numbah one massage!"

"Hey, I already paid for the massage up front," I answered, swinging my legs over the table.

She grabbed my knees. "You give me ten dollahs!"

"Hey, forget it, baby-san."

"You numbah ten," she spat, "you beaucoup cheap Charlie!"

I began to get angry. I didn't like no fuckin' Vietnamese putting me down. I wanted to haul off and hit her one, but I controlled my temper. Jumping down off the bench, I pushed open the curtain and walked down the hall. I could hear her mumbling under her breath.

"Hey, LeRoy," I yelled down the hall as I walked, "I'm splitting. I'll be up front, O.K.?"

A second later he emerged and followed me down the exit. As we left, the baby-san who had given me a massage stuck her head out the cubicle.

"You numbah ten, G.I. You numbah ten!"

"Hey, what's that all about?" asked LeRoy.

"Man, it's nothing important. All these fuckin' Vietnamese want from us is our money!"

We finally ended up in line at the snack bar, enduring the wait for hamburgers and fries. It was more than food that kept us there. It was an attempt to recapture a part of our life in the States.

By the time we finished going through the PX and made it back to the battery area, the E.M. club had opened. Night had fallen and we decided to continue our R&R at the club.

The first person I recognized in the club was John Threet. He was sitting at a table in the back and waved me over as soon as we entered.

"Hey John, what's happening!" I said.

"Not much," he answered, standing up to take my hand. "This is Frank Falcone," he continued, referring to another GI at the table. "I don't think you've ever met."

I introduced LeRoy. We shook hands all around, and Frank went to the bar for us while we sat down.

"Shit, you guys really look rough," John said. "How long you been out in the boonies anyway?"

258

"What has it been now, LeRoy?" I asked. "It's been something like a month, I think?"

"Yeah, if you count passing through at the end of July. It was about three and a half months before that."

"So, how are things in the rear?" I asked.

"Not so good," John said. "I've been busted for possession."

Frank returned, setting the four cold beers he juggled down on the table.

"Well shit man, tell me more," I said to John.

"Yeah, they came in one day and searched the whole barracks. They found my water pipe and then did a thorough search of all my belongings. Shit, man, I only had a quarter ounce on me but the brass has decided to use my case as an example of their hard line against drug use. They said they're going to court-martial me. Shit, those bastards! I wasn't the only one caught. I'm just the only one being singled out for punishment."

"Yeah," Frank added. "If they were really serious about it, they'd try all of them."

"Yeah, I know what you mean," I said. "When justice is selective, it's not justice anymore."

"And look at this bullshit!" John said, unfolding a sheet of paper and handing it to me.

It was a photocopy of a confidential report that was to be distributed throughout the Division. I read it aloud.

"*Item*: The use of marijuana is hazardous to the health of the Troops.

"*Discussion*: There is reason to believe that the Viet Cong may be behind the program to increase the use of marijuana. For example, it is known that up to three "sticks" are routinely made available free to U.S. soldiers in some areas. This encourages experimental trial, usage, and endangers both the health and security of our forces.

"*Observation*: Use of marijuana decreases to some extent alertness, caution, and the ability to detect and respond to sudden danger. Experimental trial of marijuana frequently results in repeated use. Relaxing with the use of marijuana can be the first step toward the use of even more potent drugs which have markedly dangerous psychological and physical dependence and complete ruination of the individual. Other diseases such as venereal disease are probably prevalent in the establishments where marijuana is processed and used.

"The product itself may be dirty. The lack of caution, sharing of a butt, etc. can give rise to disease."

We all laughed.

"What a crock of shit!" I said. "This is ridiculous. I wonder if the people who wrote this shit actually believe it?"

"Oh yeah, they do," John said seriously, reaching out to take the paper back. "I need to be careful. If I get caught taking confidential information out of headquarters, it'll be a hell of a lot worse than smoking marijuana."

"With all the kinds of rank injustice and corruption that's going on over here,"

259

I said, "I just can't see why they'd pick on something as small as having a quarter ounce of weed. Why don't they stop the fuckin' murdering? Why don't they investigate Top, or the First Sergeant? They've got a fuckin' black market going on and they're getting away with it. These people have just got their heads screwed on wrong. In all this shit they're singling out the use of marijuana as an important moral issue. I just can't believe it!"

The table grew silent.

"Hey, how about another round of drinks?" John said finally.

"Fuckin' A!" I shouted. "Let's get loose!"

We tried our best to cheer John up, and as the beer cans stacked higher, his troubles receded. By the time we were on our second wall of cans, the club had become loud and rowdy.

"Short!" somebody yelled above the noise.

We continued talking.

"Short!" the person yelled again.

Another GI stood up at the bar. "Short!" he yelled. Pretty soon the air was filled with "Short! Short!"

I stood up.

"Seventy-four fuckin' days!" I yelled. Eyes looked in my direction.

"Sixty-six!" another man shouted.

"Forty-four!"

"Twenty-two," LeRoy said quietly.

I felt a twinge of pain. Yes, that was right, that was why he had come in. He was getting his medical papers in order before he had to ship out. I had forgotten. Damn, I just didn't want to see him go. On the other hand, I sure didn't want him to have to stay.

"Three fuckin' days!" someone finally shouted.

The crowd grew quiet, waiting. Nobody spoke. Suddenly the place exploded with cheers. People clapped and stomped and hooted!

Not everyone was clapping, though. On some faces I saw only stony silence. On others, anger. Some of these guys had beaucoup time to serve.

Sitting in my bunker one night, smoking grass, I looked at the log book I had recently begun using as a diary. I read over the first entries, wondering again why I had felt compelled to start writing these things down.

"I feel almost prompted by an unfamiliar source. It seems to be nudging me from deep within myself. It seems complicated, sometimes confusing, and I wonder if it is not my own soul! Maybe it's my subconscious wrestling with my mind. But whatever it is, I am engaged in a battle for the truth, and I'm not sure that in every situation I know what that is. Maybe it's the mind of God I'm wrestling with. I wish I could have some evidence of that in my heart. . . .

"After twenty years of agnosticism, atheism . . . I sense the possibility of the reality of some kind of God standing beside me. I feel I must embrace it. . . .

". . . I can see the need for love . . . and understanding. I can see a need to know the truth. I can see the need for hope, if only to combat despair. But hope in what? I see the need of some power greater than man's, simply to harness the will of man, if mankind is ever to survive. Especially if we continue to believe in survival, at any price. If there is a power outside of man, it needs to show itself— here and now. Whatever God is, I see the need for God now.

"*September 28:* . . . meditation, whether upon my dreams and aspirations, or on the most complex issues of life (purpose, meaning to my existence, moral justice and human values), is beginning to consume more of my time. It occupies a permanent niche in my behavior and supplies a valuable need in my life.

"I am faced daily with issues that require a most passionate response and have been struggling in turmoil and conflict for such a long time. Often, when I discover what is right, I do not have the courage or conviction to stand up for it. It seems that I am still imprisoned by fear. The longer I refuse to speak out and walk out my beliefs, the stronger the sense of shame I feel. I am trying just to hold on. To let it all pass. For me the war will be over in such a short time. I simply can't afford to blow it now."

I put my hand over the page and stopped. I didn't even want to see what I had just read. The weight of it seemed too much to bear. Staring out into the shadows that surrounded my bunker, I caught my breath and pushed back the ache in my throat. Tears slowly ran down my cheeks. I could feel them landing, hot against my chest.

I just can't let this happen, I thought, grimacing. I've got to stay strong if I want to survive. I can't let myself feel pain. Concentrating, I held my breath and pushed back the tears. Down . . . down . . . till they were finally gone.

18

1 October 1968
FSB Keene III
Xom Giong Dau

I could feel my chest constricting as I tried to resolve the conflict that raged within me. I was being forced to make a decision that could endanger my life. I had been struggling with the issue for hours; maybe days, even months. Having peeled away so many of my masks, I was left with the fact that the values I had discovered in myself were incompatible with my behavior. The conflict was tearing me apart. Any kind of peace eluded me. It didn't help to get stoned. I just couldn't put up with it any longer! Only fear kept me from resolving this conflict, which hovered over me like a guillotine blade.

I knew that a direct refusal to continue killing would only be construed as treason and cowardice and would undoubtedly result in my being sent to Long Binh Jail. But I didn't know what else to do! No, I knew what to do, I was just afraid to do it! Either way, a type of hell awaited me.

If I continued to kill those whom I now recognized as fellow human beings, I was guilty of murder, the highest form of insanity. Even though the government of the United States condoned it, I knew I could not. I couldn't live with the guilt. The distorted faces of dead children haunted my dreams. Lifeless faces of GIs haunted my days. I didn't want to lose my freedom, yet I could not shake my torment. I hated the Army, my oppressor, but I was angrier still at my own cowardice. I didn't know which was worse: to be branded a coward by the Army or to see myself as one. To be branded a traitor by my country or be a traitor to my own conscience.

Putting my elbows on the FADAC table, I cupped my head in my hands. I had to stop the battle raging in my mind. I was grateful we had finally finished our fire mission; it was becoming difficult to concentrate.

I closed my eyes and listened to the body count being relayed over the radio. I felt a numbness in my finger tips that was beginning to creep slowly up my arms. I could feel them tingling as if they had been asleep. I noticed I was breathing

262

harder, almost hyperventilating. There was something all too familiar about this. Then I had the sudden, sickening realization that these were the same symptoms I had had during my first nervous breakdown. That sent me straight up out of my chair and onto my feet.

I had sworn never to let this happen again. I made my decision. Pushing my chair back, I turned, eyeing the lieutenant, who was sitting next to me. Involuntarily, I tightened my abdominal muscles like a fighter anticipating his opponent's blows.

"Lieutenant," I said as calmly as I could, "I want to talk to you, sir, privately."

We went over to the corner of the bunker, as much privacy as one could have in a ten-foot-square cubicle where normal conversation could be heard easily.

"Sir," I whispered cautiously, "I can't go on doing this!"

"Doing what, Olsen?" the lieutenant responded, puzzled.

"Killing people, sir."

"What? ... What did you say?" he answered, as if not quite believing what he had heard. "What are you talking about? What the hell's wrong with you, Olsen?"

The lieutenant gripped my shoulder with his left hand and straightened me up. I could see the bewilderment on his face as he stared deeply into my own. He quickly shifted his body and drew closer to me, trying now to shield our conversation from the rest of the men.

"Look, Lieutenant," I said, in an attempt to make him understand, "if I go on killing people like this, I'm gonna have a breakdown! It's just not right! Killing these people is just not right!"

My voice began to rise. Fuck it, I thought. I'm not going to hide what I'm feeling or plead for understanding. I was determined to make a stand. I wasn't going to beg for anything. I wasn't going on killing, and that was that!

"Olsen, let's go outside."

"Look, lieutenant..."

"Outside!"

"O.K., sir!" I snapped. Grabbing my helmet and M-16, I followed him to the entrance where he waited, his eyes blazing. I pushed past him and he followed me out. I knew he was moving as quickly as possible to avoid any confrontation in front of the men. He knew I didn't often back down once we butted heads, and he wasn't about to lose this one in front of the crew.

Moving quickly to the west side of the FDC bunker, outside of hearing range, the lieutenant started in. His voice had softened.

"Olsen, think about what you're doing," he said. "This just isn't rational. You can't just stop doing your job in the middle of a war because you're against killing! Look at what you're throwing away! You know you're looking at a court-martial offense. You'll be thrown in prison for what you're considering. Get a hold of yourself, man!"

It wasn't any good. I just wasn't going to be talked out of it; the lieutenant needed to see that.

"Lieutenant, this isn't going to work. I'm not going to kill any more people!"

A scowl formed on his face. I could see that he was through talking.

"Olsen!" he barked, shaking a finger in my face and then grabbing both of my shoulders. "You're going back on duty! Now! Furthermore, you'll do what I say, and whenever it's needed. Do you understand? . . . Now get back inside!"

That was it! A silent stream of curses filled my mind. Why did it have to come to this? Why did they insist on forcing me to do something against my own conscience? What was wrong with these people; did they have no consciences of their own?

I saw clearly their power, and my vulnerability. I knew I was without hope, yet I just wouldn't, just couldn't give in. Something inside me snapped!

"No," I shouted, "I'm not gonna do it!"

Grabbing my M-16 by the barrel, I wheeled on my heels. With one quick, powerful thrust, I sent it hurling over the top of the bunker. Tears ran down my cheeks. My voice cracked and broke as between gritted teeth I made my last statement.

"I'm not . . . killing . . . anymore!"

Ripping my helmet off, I stepped back and slammed it into the lieutenant's chest.

I turned and stumbled into the darkness, struggling to keep from crying as I ran. I didn't care what they did to me! I didn't care what they thought of me! I didn't care what happened to me anymore.

I stumbled toward the perimeter in anger and despair, knowing that it was the only way out. Ten yards outside the bunker line I stepped up on a rice paddy berm. This was it! The next step was out! Crossing over the berm meant certain death, if not from the Viet Cong, then probably from my own men. The minute I tripped a flare or crossed a wire I knew I would be caught in a cross fire of death!

I waited, my chest heaving and pounding. I've got to pull myself together, I thought. I've got to settle down. I have to stop this shaking . . . I'm so close to the end. I knew then that I did care what happened: *I don't want to die.*

Crumbling to my knees, I stared out into the darkness. I took a deep breath and held it, then slowly began to exhale. Again and again, I fought to control my breathing, the grip of panic slowly releasing as I did. Finally, I could feel my control returning. I turned and sat on the berm, my back to the perimeter. Shaking a couple of joints out of my cigarette pack, I boldly lit up.

I sat on the berm for over an hour, struggling with feelings of anger, self-destruction, hurt, and despair. I saw that no matter how much I got stoned I could not escape my thoughts or emotions. Even if I could escape these circumstances, there was no escaping myself. Death was the only escape. But I wanted to live.

I needed someone to talk to, someone I trusted to understand. Slipping quietly off the top of the berm, I threaded my way through the battery area toward the ammo bunker.

I knew that I had gotten myself into a mess of shit, yet I was helpless to do anything about it. There was no backing out now; my cards had been laid. I wasn't about to go back and apologize. I had made my decision. I might suffer for my rashness, but I would be a coward no more. I had been right! It wasn't courage that made men killers. Men killed each other out of fear. I knew now that it took more courage to lay down your own life than it did to take another's. They had been wrong, all of them! The Army, the psychiatrist, the movies, the heroes; I wondered if the whole world wasn't led and ruled by the insane.

My mind and body had been enslaved for the purpose of killing. The Army had been nothing more than a long process of dehumanization and brain-washing designed to produce a killing machine. I had gone along with it, bullied by fear. Now I had to pay the price if I was ever going to care about myself again.

A faint childhood memory crossed my mind. Something that I had heard in Sunday school crept into my thoughts.

Greater love has no man than that he lay down his life for another. Was that what Jesus had said? I wondered if I remembered it correctly.

"I'm not a coward," I said, trying to reassure myself. "I've given my all to these men. I've held nothing back."

I could see the outline of the ammo bunker silhouetted against the sky, and I quickened my pace. I reached the entrance, pulled back the poncho that covered the doorway, and quietly slipped in. "Is LeRoy around?" I whispered.

"He's on watch," Johnson answered.

Not wanting to talk to anyone else, I went back outside and walked over to the LP. The back was completely open and I could see the silhouette of two men.

"LeRoy?" I whispered, sticking my head inside.

"Hey, what's happening?" he answered. I could see his familiar smile. I felt better immediately.

"I gotta talk to you, man," I said, making an effort to hide any hysteria. Still, there was a clear sense of urgency in my voice.

"O.K.," LeRoy whispered, "I'll get someone to stand watch for me."

As LeRoy slipped past me, I told him I'd wait for him where the ammunition was stored. A few minutes later I saw him approaching.

"Hey man, what's going on?" he blurted out as he neared. "They been calling all around for you up at the FDC. That lieutenant is pretty upset about something! You want me to tell them you're here?"

"No! I don't give a fuck whether he's upset or not. I'm not going back up there, so don't let them know I'm here!"

"Hey man . . . ," LeRoy said, his voice sobering, "what's happening?"

Slowly, hesitantly, I unfolded my story. We were deep into coversation when Lusk stuck his head out of the personnel bunker. "Hey, LeRoy," he said in a loud whisper.

"Just a minute! I'll be right back," LeRoy whispered. Leaping down from the bunker, he hurried over to Lusk. A few seconds later he returned.

265

"Hey man," he said worriedly, "it's the captain on the phone and he wants to see you. Right now!"

"I don't care!"

"Man, you gotta go up there. You'll get your ass in all kinds of hot water if you don't."

"Hey man, I'm already in over my head. What's he gonna do, sent me to Vietnam? I'm not ready, and I'm not going till I am."

"Well, what you gonna do, man?"

"I don't know," I said softly. "Wanna smoke?"

The warm night air covered me like a blanket. Its gentle touch seemed to cushion the turmoil I felt inside. Nothing more needed saying. My situation lay before me, still unresolved; yet I knew I was not alone. I could sense LeRoy's singular commitment; I knew he was behind me no matter what I did. I also knew I had to come to grips with my struggle myself. I had to subdue my anguish, even if only temporarily.

Twenty minutes passed while I deliberated. Finally, I decided there was little I could do but face the music.

"Shit, I may as well go," I said, pushing myself off the bunker. "Thanks, LeRoy."

As I walked off, I wondered if he knew how much he meant to me or if I had ever told him. How did you tell another man you loved him in such a way as not to be misunderstood?

I have to see this through, I thought. I'll explain what's happening to the captain. I'll honestly let him know what I'm going through and see what he says.

I knew the captain's decision would mean life or death, but I wasn't going to beg. I would simply have to embrace it.

No one was visible around the command tent as I approached. I was relieved. It would be between just the two of us, unless the staff sergeant was in there with him.

I set myself firmly against the fear I felt rising. I would be taking a chance exposing my feelings to the captain. He might ridicule me, or denounce me, but it was a chance I had to take. I wasn't going to let any Army lifer's opinion of me form the foundation of my self-worth.

I knocked softly on the ammo boxes stacked outside the tent entrance and waited.

"Come in."

I lifted the tent flap and stepped in. I stopped just short of the captain's table and stood at attention. A soft orange glow from a dim bulb cast shadows in the corners and on the floor. Traffic was quietly coming over the radio. I looked at the captain. He sat silently behind his folding table, his eyes intently focused on mine. I wondered if he expected me to salute. I kept my hands clenched tightly behind my back. "You wanted to see me, sir."

"Sit down," he said quietly, rising from behind the table. Dragging his folding chair out to the center of the tent, he pointed to another, and I quickly sat down.

"I want to know what's going on," he said, lighting his pipe. I could sense neither malice nor anger in his voice, and he spoke softly, yet I detected a terseness that suggested he was both puzzled and a little upset.

"Lieutenant Anthony says that you threw an M-16 at him and walked off your duties. Is that right?" he finally asked. He sounded as if it was simply too far out to believe.

"Well, something like that, sir," I said shyly.

"What's gotten into you?" he said disbelievingly. "You've always been able to handle yourself."

The captain seemed genuinely interested in hearing my part of the story in spite of his stern questioning. I didn't feel threatened, so I let it all hang out.

"Look, captain," I began, "you've only been with this battery four or five months, but I've been here nearly a year. You don't know it, but I had a nervous breakdown after my first four months in country. The symptoms I experienced then, I was beginning to experience tonight. That's what led to my behavior. I'm not gonna go through another experience like that one, sir. Not now—not ever again!"

Earnestly, I explained to him what had happened, both before and tonight. And I let him know how I felt. In the end he only asked me if I had taken an R&R since I had been in country, and I said no. He said that one was due and asked if I could handle the responsibility for the FDC until he could arrange it.

The next day, after the lieutenant visited with the captain, I was instructed to begin training another person to temporarily take over my responsibilities.

Three days went by without another mention of the incident, and I tried to put it behind me. I had waited expectantly for two days, expecting the hammer of judgment to fall, but it never did. I was beginning to believe it never would.

It was late afternoon by the time I finished going over the second shift's firing data. I decided to go down to the ammo bunker. Picking up my M-16 and helmet, I made my way around the back, past the personnel bunker. Mike was sitting on the top, daydreaming.

"Hey Olsen, where you going?" he asked.

"Down to the ammo bunker to get stoned!"

"Hey, can I come along?"

"Sure. Why not!"

I had seen a noticeable change in Mike, a change I thought was for the good. He had been raised on hatred and bitterness, and his attitude toward blacks was, at best, condescending. I had been forced to take him aside several times and severely reprimand him because of his attitude toward Mitchell. Those two had exchanged bitter words from the onset of their arrival, and that kind of infighting had to be squelched. I knew that I wasn't going to change years of prejudice and ignorance with a few reprimands, but I also knew we needed a crew that trusted one another and operated as a team. Mike had to know that our survival depended upon it. It may have been because of the talk we had following his first exposure

267

to battle that he even listened to what I said, but I did notice a change in his behavior afterward. I wasn't sure his heart had changed, but at least it seemed to have softened. He did work at disciplining his tongue, and there were times when I saw him bite his lips to control his anger. Whatever the cause, the flareups between him and Mitchell subsided markedly. And more often now, he would accompany me to the ammo bunker for the rap sessions. In the beginning, he had been wary, but now he looked forward to them.

I was deep in thought as we approached the ammo bunker. At least here was one place where a sense of unity transcended race. As far as I was concerned it was home!

"Hey, Olsen," Santiago called out, his voice booming. "Wha' chu doing down here again, gringo? We should maybe jas' set you up a bed, huh amigo!"

I laughed, loving his thick Spanish accent. How dull it would be, I thought, if we were all just WASPs.

I leaned my rifle against the wall of their sleeping quarters and slammed my helmet down hard on the top. "Hey, what's going on in there?" I yelled.

In a few seconds Lusk emerged, rubbing his eyes. "Oh, it's only you, Olsen," he said, yawning. "What you mean, man, getting me up like that?"

"Hey man, where's the rest of the crew?" I asked.

"They're probably over in the main bunker."

Just then I saw Johnson and Pearson coming from that direction. With them was a soldier I had never seen before.

"Hey, Olsen, meet our latest addition," said LeRoy.

I looked him over. He appeared to be about nineteen years old. Thick blonde hair hung over his ears and a long drooping mustache covered his upper lip. He was short and muscular and his sleepy blue eyes were covered by slightly drooping eyelids. He gave the impression of being really laid back. I liked him immediately.

"What's your name?" I asked, sticking out my hand.

"Dwight," he said, "but they call me the Viking."

I could see why. He looked just like many of the characters I had seen in Viking movies. The only thing missing was a two-horned helmet.

"Where you from?" I asked. He didn't look like a new recruit.

"I got transferred from the Seven-Eleventh."

"Hey man, what he means to say is that he had no choice," added LeRoy. "It was either a transfer or an Article 15. He got busted for doing dope."

"Hey, welcome to the club," I said, smiling. I knew he was gonna fit in like a well-worn glove.

We all climbed up on the two walls lining the entrance to the sleeping quarters and started rapping. We questioned Dwight about the bust and his background, passing around two or three joints as we listened. As the sun began to set I reached over and pulled on my helmet, just in case. We had gotten mortared last night at dusk.

I had no sooner dropped my helmet on when an explosion shook the earth

268

about thirty meters behind us. Before we could react, another exploded even closer.

"Incoming," everyone shouted, running for their positions and the nearest cover. Since Mike and I were sitting directly above the bunker entrance, we both immediately dropped down and scrambled inside. We dove for cover at opposite sides of the bunker, pressing our bodies flat against the bunker walls. The front of the bunker had been left open for gun ports, and I noticed that the sandbagged wall was barely 6 inches over my head. I wished the floor hadn't been covered with air mattresses. I didn't feel secure in here at all. Explosion after explosion rocked the front of the bunker. Dirt and shrapnel whizzed through the gun port, spraying the inside.

"God damn son-of-a-bitch," Mike screamed, "where's my helmet? God damn, I can't find my helmet!"

Pulling my helmet tight down on my head, I turned slightly in his direction, opening my eyes.

"There's one behind you, it's right by your feet!" I yelled.

"Shit, I ain't moving!" Mike answered, "See if there's one closer to you!"

I felt the roof of the bunker shudder as we took a direct hit. I squeezed tighter against the wall, pulling my M-16 tight against my chest. My eyes darted around the darkening interior, looking for another helmet. Spying one in the middle of the room, I swung my leg out and gave it a swift kick. It skidded in Mike's direction.

"Mike, grab it!" I yelled, quickly pulling myself back against the wall.

Then I heard this frightening sound. It was a long *sssssss*. The air mattresses were leaking. Shrapnel was penetrating the bunker. Mike and I must have heard it at the same time because we looked up at each other simultaneously. We didn't have to say a word. Like dancers in unison, we pushed ourselves to our knees and scrambled out of the bunker, crouching as we bolted out the bunker door. Mortars were raining all over the camp as we scampered inside the main bunker.

It took only a glance to tell that things there weren't right. I surveyed the situation. LeRoy was sitting upright, his back against the wall; Lusk lay cradled in his arms, moaning. Santiago was sprawled on his back, his hand gripping the inside of his thigh, his pants thick with blood. "Mutha-fucker," he said in quiet surprise, "I am bleeding!"

I couldn't see the Viking or Johnson anywhere. Adrenaline pumped through my veins as I tried to calculate the extent of injury. It was clear these guys needed medical attention, but I first had to make sure the FDC had located the direction of fire and was setting up our perimeter defense. Someone had already taken control of the .50 caliber machine gun; I could hear it start to fire.

"Johnson . . . where's Johnson?" I called.

"Yo!" he yelled from the recesses of the bunker. Squinting, I could just barely make him out. He was wedged in a corner near the front of the bunker, his M-16 gripped tightly in his hands. He had positioned himself to provide fire to our front, in case our perimeter was being attacked.

"Viking!" I yelled, trying to pinpoint his position.

"Right here," he said, appearing around the corner of the bunker, dragging himself on his hands and knees.

"Mike, get your M-16 and cover the front . . . Dwight, you do the same! Where's the phone?" I shouted.

LeRoy pointed to the wall. I fell to my knees as we took another direct hit. Grabbing the phone in one hand, I fell to my side and slid my back up against the wall. Every gun had at least one man on the line. I had to break through to get the FDC's attention.

"FDC!" I yelled, "FDC!"

"FDC," Vanous replied.

"This is Olsen. I'm down in the ammo bunker. Is everything O.K. up there? Do you need me?"

"No, I think we've got it under control."

I could hear him asking the lieutenant if he needed me to come up, and the lieutenant's negative reply.

"Where's the doc?" I said, as soon as he was back on the line.

"I don't know."

"Guns! Guns!" I shouted, "has anyone seen the doc?"

"Not on Two." "No!" "Negative!" came their replies.

"He's on Gun One," someone said.

"One," I shouted, "One . . . is Doc down there? We need him up here bad!"

"This is Gun Three, we've got two wounded down here. We need him too!"

"That's affirmative on Gun Six also," someone else shouted.

A chorus of voices yelled their needs.

Damn! It would take him ages to get here! What if he came too late?

"Medic," Lusk moaned, "I need a medic. I'm hurt bad."

Damn . . . damn . . . damn. . . . What if he's dying?

"Hold on, Lusk!" I said. "I'll get the doc and be right back!"

Crouching, I sprinted with all my might, heading in the direction of Gun One. As I scrambled past the personnel bunker I tripped in a hole and stumbled. I flung my hands out in front of me as my chest smashed into the dirt. My helmet went flying. All of a sudden the area in front of me lit up with a blinding flash and chunks of clay and debris bounced off my body.

Pulling my hands off my head, I groped madly for my helmet. I felt the sharp impact of shrapnel and rocks striking my jacket.

"Oh momma!" I moaned, feeling myself on the verge of panic. I found my helmet and slapped it on my head. I forced myself to my knees. I couldn't stay here and get killed, I had to keep moving.

"God-damn, this is crazy!" I said, bracing myself to take another run. Another mortar exploded, knocking me off my feet.

"Oh Jesus! Jesus!" I whispered. "What in the world have I done?"

Pulling myself forward, I scooted through the grass. With each pause in the explosions I pushed myself to my feet and sprinted through the dark. Fear dogged my every step. Another round of explosions and my face was in the dust again; I could taste the dirt in my mouth.

It seemed like hours later when I finally burst into the bunker on Gun One. The doc was bent over someone, fumbling with bandages, trying to stop the spray of blood that spurted from an open wound in his leg. He looked up at me as I crashed to my knees. I could see his face contorted in confusion and panic, and I knew immediately that I was on my own.

"Doc," I blurted, "where do you keep your bandages and supplies?"

He just looked at me, eyes wide, mouth open.

One of the gun crew, a short-timer with curly blonde hair who was helping the doc, turned. "They're probably in the personnel bunker, where he's been sleeping."

I turned around and dashed outside, praying that they would be there and that I would find them without wasting time. Reaching the personnel bunker, I crawled inside, clawing through the pile of ammo boxes and duffel bags that crowded the entrance.

"I think I can find it!" someone said, scrambling in behind me. He pulled over a metal ammo box with a red cross painted on the side. I began to dig through dressings and bandages, gauze and tape. Not knowing what was needed, I grabbed a wad of tape and bandages and a little bit of everything else.

Fifteen or twenty minutes later the mortar rounds had stopped falling. Spooky and another night-lighting aircraft circled our position, illuminating the surrounding area. Debris and dust rose from the artillery rounds still impacting on both sides of our perimeter. We had dragged all of the wounded out of the bunkers where the overhead illumination provided the necessary light to dress their wounds. Santiago had taken a large chunk of shrapnel in the inside of his upper thigh but was joking about it, saying that if it had been an inch higher, he would have lost one of his balls. I did what I could to stop his bleeding. Viking had taken shrapnel in his back, but both he and LeRoy were suffering only minor wounds. I was applying a tourniquet to Lusk's arm when the doc finally made it over. He began treating Sergeant Ramos, who had been struck in the leg. Even though he had been bleeding badly, it was Sergeant Ramos who had manned the .50 caliber, throwing fire in the direction of the mortar sites until the attack had subsided. No one even knew he was wounded until shortly before the doc arrived. He had then limped over to our location and sat down.

As the doc tore open Ramos' fatigue pants, exposing his wound, I glanced over at him.

"Hey, Doc, you O.K.?" I asked, noticing that his hands were shaking.

"Yeah," he mumbled. But I could tell from the look in his eyes that he wasn't. Even Lusk noticed it.

"Hey, Doc," Lusk said quietly, "maybe you ought to take a couple of Darvon. You carrying any with you?"

The doc just shook his head. I finished bandaging Lusk's arm and then his leg, and he was free to move.

"Hey listen, Doc," Lusk repeated, "I got some Darvon in my ammo box, maybe you want me to get you some."

"Is that right?" I whispered. "Where'd you get 'em?"

"From the Doc!" replied Lusk.

"Well, go get a couple and give them to him, O.K.? Make sure he takes them."

Lusk obediently limped off. I crawled over to Santiago to see how he was doing.

It wasn't long before word came down that we were calling in a dust-off and that all serious injuries were to report to the landing area between the infantry command bunker and ours. As soon as the helicopter was in our area a check fire would be called until the evacuation was over. Draping Lusk's arm around my neck and pulling Santiago to his feet, I helped them hobble over to the landing area. Sergeant Ramos refused to leave. In the pitch black it was difficult to make out our surroundings so we moved only when a flare illuminated the area. When we finally arrived at the dust-off area, I lowered Lusk down on a bundle of sandbags and Santiago sat down beside him.

"Hey, what's that?" asked Lusk, pointing to a row of black bundles silhouetted near the edge of the area.

"I'm not sure," I answered tiredly, "but I think they're body bags." In the dark I could only make out faint shapes, but they appeared to be the right size.

"I gotta see!" Lusk responded with a sense of urgency.

"No you don't! C'mon, man!" I answered.

But there was no talking him out of it. Forcing himself up, he made a couple of limping steps in their direction.

"Help me!" he cried.

"O.K., hold on," I answered, "Shit," I muttered under my breath. Santiago didn't say anything but followed right behind me. We walked over to the objects. They were all bodies. Some in bags and some exposed.

The body bags glistened under the illumination rounds. Ghostly shadows danced on faces that stared blankly at the sky. How many was that now, I asked myself, not really counting. I had seen so many dead. I looked over at Lusk. His eyes appeared to be bulging out of their sockets. He stared at the bodies, unable to move. Suddenly, Lusk, the man who played Mr. Cool to the hilt, began to whimper softly. It wasn't as if he were afraid. No, it wasn't fear that was shattering his world. It was the sudden, awful realization of death.

"They're dead!" he mumbled, sounding astonished. "They're dead!"

"C'mon, Lusk," I said, forcibly turning him around. I put my arm around him and pulled him close. His legs buckled as he staggered under the weight of the scene and the loss of blood. Santiago grabbed his other arm as soon as he saw him sag. Slowly we headed for a seat.

Still, Lusk struggled to remain. As Santiago and I lifted him, he arched his back, straining his neck to look back.

"They're dead, they're dead!" he kept muttering.

"I think he's going into shock!" I said to Santiago. "Let's lay him down on these sandbags and get something warm over his shoulders."

I didn't see anything to wrap him in so I stripped off my fatigue shirt and draped it around his chest. "Where's that damn helicopter?" I sighed.

Sometime later I drifted back to the FDC. What a night! Charlie had dropped in three more mortars the minute a check fire had been lifted, just as the helicopter was settling down. We had scurried to get the wounded and the dead on the helicopter so it could depart and had thrown the body bags on like sacks of potatoes, piling them up in the middle of the wounded. I could still see Lusk sitting there in Santiago's arms, pulling away in horror as the body bags were tossed in next to him.

Huddling next to a rice paddy berm to fend off the fury of the rising helicopter and to protect myself from the falling mortars, I had lain quietly, long after the helicopter had left, trying to put it all together.

Now, lying down on my cot, I was still trying to figure it out. I felt hurt and confused. Tears streamed down my face. I picked up my bayonet and stared long and hard at it. I suddenly had this compulsion to stab myself. This is crazy, I thought, what's going on? Then I knew. Somehow I wanted the pain I felt inside to be visible. I wanted my buddies to know that I was hurting too, hurting for them. I just didn't know how to show it. I thought maybe if I stabbed myself in the arm and bled, they could see that I was hurting too.

But I knew that it was wrong. If I injured myself, how would I explain the wound? It was crazy! Their injuries were like a badge of honor and mine would be a travesty. Trembling, I laid my bayonet back down and wept.

It was noon when I heard about the doc. I was down at the ammo bunker checking up on LeRoy and the Viking when they told me the news. Apparently, the doc couldn't handle being in a combat situation and had performed so poorly last night that the captain had to call the infantry medic to come over and help out. The captain was sending the doc back to the rear on today's resupply and had asked headquarters for a replacement as soon as possible. In the interim, he was asking the infantry medic to help us out.

Here was my chance, I thought, making my way back to the FDC. I would ask the captain if I could take the doc's place and assist the infantry medic. I wondered if I stood a chance. After all, I had no formal training as a medic. What would I know?

Both the captain and the lieutenant were standing outside the entrance of the FDC when I returned.

"Captain, may I have a word with you, sir?" I asked.

"What would you like?"

"Sir, I heard that you were sending the doc in. I was wondering if it would be possible for me to take his place until you get a replacement?"

He and the lieutenant exchanged glances. A frown formed slowly on the lieutenant's face, while a puzzled look covered the captain's.

"Please, sir," I said, "you know I'm no coward. I'm not asking to be sent out of the field. I just want the opportunity to help others instead of killing them. It would mean a lot to me to be saving lives instead of taking them."

The captain smiled. I wasn't sure if he understood or if he just thought the situation was comical.

"I'll think about it," he replied, but I could tell he wasn't serious.

Just then I heard someone call my name and I turned to see the doc approaching. His eyes dropped when he noticed the captain standing in the doorway, but he kept on coming anyway.

"Let me look at your back," he said, "the guys at the ammo bunker said that you had a wound."

I turned around, facing the lieutenant and the captain while the doc lifted my sweat-stained shirt.

"Damn," the doc said, "you should have told me about this earlier! It's already infected."

"What's that you got, Olsen?" the captain inquired.

"It's nothing," I said, taking off my shirt. "I got it two days ago when we were mortared. I caught a piece of metal in my back when I was diving into my bunker."

"You've got to have this cleaned every day," the doc insisted, pulling some alcohol from his satchel. "In these conditions, if you don't, it could take months to heal and the infection will only get worse."

"Ouch! Damn, take it easy, Doc."

"Well, it's got to be cleaned," he said, reapplying the alcohol.

"Hey, Olsen," the captain said, smiling, "do you want me to put you in for a Purple Heart? You can get one, you know, for any wound taken in action!"

I looked up at the captain. He and the lieutenant were smiling at one another. Bastards!

"Forget it," I snarled. I brushed Doc's hands from my back and stuck my hand in the sleeve of my shirt. I wanted to scream, "Fuck you, bastards." I gritted my teeth just to keep my mouth shut. At that moment I hated the captain with a passion. I hated him for the mockery he made of me and of every man who ever suffered in combat. Did he think that he could pass out Purple Hearts like popsicles, like candy to soothe the wounds and fears of children? How dare he belittle the sacrifice and courage of men who truly suffered in combat by offering to put me in for a Purple Heart? That medal was supposed to mean something! How could he cheapen it? Did they think they could appease us with medals? A medal for an arm, a medal for a leg. A medal for a stubbed toe, an angry soul. A medal for anything and everything, as if that would make everything all right.

It was senseless, all senseless, I thought. I reached for a joint as I walked away.

A tiny wisp of smoke rose and then danced around the Buddha's stomach, then vanished as it climbed higher toward the ceiling. The sweet smell of incense tickled my senses. The odor reminded me of more pleasant times, when burning leaves, autumn nights, and potatoes wrapped in tinfoil provided a feast and a childhood festival. Those days were far behind me now.

As the music of the Cream slowly faded I reached over and pressed the stop button on my cassette player. It was late. Only God knew how late it was in my life. It was coming to an end and I could see it happening.

I removed the earpiece and set it on the tape recorder. Sitting erect, tucking my legs, I let my arms fall limp across my groin and closed my eyes. My mind was not at rest and was tired of pushing questions aside. I knew I needed some answers if I was to carry on. What was it that would give my life meaning?

The war had stripped me of the life I had been familiar with. A life I had taken for granted. What remained important to me? What had been important about the life I had left behind? Was there anything that mattered in the one I was living now? What was I seeking? It sure wasn't modern conveniences, though I knew I would never again take them for granted. It wasn't prestige or power, or anything that money could buy.

Of all the things I left behind, it was the people I missed most. I yearned for their affection. It was this separation that caused my incurable ache. But it was more than that, and I could see it in a way I had never seen before. It wasn't so much those who had loved me I missed; it was those that *I had loved*.

Suddenly, unexpectedly, it all became clear. For the first time I understood what it was that I had been so actively pursuing. It was the truth of love. Loving was the purpose of living. The happiness and fulfillment of life were found in love.

What before had been murky was now incredibly clear. I was astonished at how simple it seemed. I needed to capture every thought! I opened my diary and began writing.

I had had some kind of mystical revelation, an experience foreign to me. Even as I sought to understand what was happening, I knew that this experience was somehow outside the realm of my own imagination. It strengthened a growing conviction that there was, in reality, a power outside of my own that I had never touched. And this power was somehow connected to the existence of some kind of God. What kind I still didn't know, but that he or it existed, I was sure.

As I turned this revelation over in my mind, I began to see events in my own life in a new way. My perspective suddenly changed. Some of the things I never understood began falling together like missing pieces in a puzzle.

I had gone through life believing that no one really cared about me or loved me, when all along people had. In my flight to avoid injury and rejection, I had simply removed myself from them. It had been my unwillingness to trust or believe in their love that had separated me from them. But while my aloofness had kept many away, it hadn't really fooled those who really cared. And my defenses had really never effectively kept me from loving others, only from showing it. Though I had created an effective mask, those emotions remained intact; they were just deeply repressed. I had repeated a pattern of rejecting others whenever I found myself caring too much, unwilling to face the pain of possible rejection.

Yet there had always been those who through patient perseverance had penetrated those walls. Those who had made themselves vulnerable for my own sake. The Kupitzes had been like that, and so had Pat Glynn. And Bobby Elle-gard and Sergeant Kiefer and Glover. Debbie and Diane immediately came to mind.

I began to see that if the love of others had played such an important part in my own salvation, then it was important for me to begin giving the same.

I found myself posing a situation in my mind and asking myself some ques-tions. If I was in a room full of people and across that room, at an opposite wall, stood a girl who was madly in love with me, and if I didn't know it, would her love bring me happiness? No! Because I would be unaware of it. Then what is it that brings joy to a relationship? It is the *giving* of love. That love need not even be returned. If I truly wanted to experience the joy of love, I could do it by giving, without waiting to receive. Love was active, not passive! I resolved to make such a change in my life.

I was suddenly filled with a longing to be back in the States, back among the friends I deeply missed. Yet I knew that if I wanted to experience the fulfillment of loving, I didn't have to wait to go home; I was already surrounded by a battery of people I could give myself to. With a new sense of purpose, I committed myself to becoming a friend to every man, especially to those people whose lives were burdened with the same loneliness and rejection I had experienced.

Even though I felt propelled by this new sense of purpose I wondered if I even knew just what real love was. I had heard that word so often and used in so many different ways. Either I had some misconceptions, or the word was truly abused. Still, I had a good idea of where I might learn about love. I knew from my own experience that it was something more than romance. It was intrinsically woven through personal relationships and was a part of brotherhood. It was also the underlying theme of many of man's religions, and though I knew little of religion, I knew of two figures to start with: Jesus and Buddha. Both had taught a life of brotherly love. I vowed to learn more about what each of them had said. Perhaps that would enable me to practice love more fully in my own life. And because these individuals also taught about God, I knew that discovering just who or what God was, would also lead me to a deeper understanding of love.

On my twenty-first birthday, I felt I was coming of age.

19

26 October 1968
Cu Chi

Night fell quickly and the shadowy landscape created a monolithic picture of fallen ruins. Night discipline had obliterated all lights expect those in the heavens, which I was glad were out of man's control. The destruction of Vietnam was so complete that I wondered if anything would ever rise from the ruin. Yes, it was a good thing the heavens were out of our grasp.

The rear was empty now, as if it had been deserted. Only a scant remnant of personnel ran things in Cu Chi because everyone else was out in the field. By now the top would be mixing drinks and stories, or lying in bed with some whore. The supply sergeant and the few other men would be gone too, lounging at the E.M. club or safely retired in their quarters. I liked it that way, my being all alone. There was no one to hassle me. No enemy to fear. No one asking silly questions or demanding my time.

I sat quietly, listening for the enemy. I had to remind myself that this was the rear; there was nothing to fear. Force of habit. But it had been that way even on R&R.

I put my hands on the wall of sandbags that ringed the edge of the roof and looked down. I liked this. Maybe this was how we should build our bunkers in the field. High up, out of reach! No, that would just make them easier targets for rockets and RPGs. It was safer having them halfway underground.

I leaned back against the sandbags that shielded the mount for a .50 caliber machine gun, empty now. The sandbags were tattered and rotting. I lit a joint. I wondered what they were doing tonight in the field. I was sorry I had to go back tomorrow but R&R was over.

With forty-nine days left I was experiencing short-timer's fever, a slow, creeping anxiety about dying when I was so close to leaving. But I was also excited about returning to the battery. I had constantly worried about my crew while on R&R and I wondered how they were doing. I hoped they were all right and that nothing had happened during my brief absence that would cause me any regret.

I couldn't shake the feeling that I had deserted my men. I knew I would feel like shit if anything happened to them while I was gone. I still felt personally responsible for their welfare and their safety. I felt I owed it to them to keep them alive by doing my job, just as they kept me alive by doing theirs.

A new operation was about to begin. "Toan Thang III," headquarters had called it. I laughed, reflecting on the translation, "Complete Victory III." Complete victory for the third time? It was just a continuation of the same fuckin' program. New and more encouraging statements! Lies and propaganda!

The 1st Brigade was continuing its operations in and around Tay Ninh City, so we would keep bouncing around the southern half of the 25th's TAOI. The new-old word was that the main VC/NVA forces had withdrawn into sanctuaries in War Zone C and Cambodia, to regroup, refit and retrain. They were "on the run again," or so Top said.

"We're beating them back" was another good one. Why did the brass always see these retreats as victories when as far as I could see they were simply runs for fresh troops and supplies? It didn't seem like victory to me.

When I was in grade school I had a bully neighbor. Even as an eight-year-old, he was foul-mouthed and mean. He would come out into the dirt street that separated our houses and when we played in our front yard he would swear at us and throw rocks. When we got angry and chased him, he simply made a beeline for home. We could only go after him as far as his yard because his mom and dad would come running out the door and yell and cuss at us to leave him alone. The only time we could ever get back at the kid was if we could catch him on the run, but he always maintained a safe distance. We never caught him although sometimes the chase was close. Once, frustrated and enraged, I had chased him back across his property line. His father came running out after me and as I scurried back to the safety of my own yard, he gave his kid a brick to throw at me. Somehow, that game was being replayed here, only the neighbor's property line was the Cambodian border.

As I scanned the perimeter once again, I had a sudden feeling that something had just gone wrong. It sent a shiver down my spine. Instantly alert, I peered into the darkness. Nobody was there. It must be this new battery area, I said to myself. It's just unsettling to be in unfamiliar terrain. The battery had just recently moved here, abandoning the old perimeter location to rats and layers of dust while the Vietnamese peasants made repairs.

The Rest and Recuperation program had enabled me to get out of the country, if only for a short time. And while it had been enjoyable, it had proved to be disquieting as well. I had chosen Hong Kong because it was known for its night life and fine tailored clothes. Doc Thornburg had been there, and to me it sounded good! I had heard that you could go to Bangkok and buy all the drugs you wanted, and that the women were beautiful and crowded the streets, but what I had in mind was getting those custom-tailored clothes.

The experience was still strong in my memory. I had gotten off the plane only a few hours ago.

278

I could still see the taxis that had clamored for our attention, the sound of their screeching tires vividly etched in my mind. I remembered the excitement as our taxi raced dangerously through narrow streets. It had been a safe kind of excitement, not terrifying like war.

I had learned at the hotel desk that every convenience was within walking distance or in the hotel itself. A restaurant, a bar, and a tailor were at my disposal, even overnight "guests" I could conveniently check into my room.

I had found my room small, but adequate, certainly larger than any bunker I had slept in, and a hundred times as clean. The first thing I did was open the little refrigerator at the foot of my bed and lie down in front of it, letting the cool air spill over my face. I felt like a child with a new toy. Finally, I reached in and drew out a small bottle of vodka from among the variety of miniatures that filled the inside. Pouring it in a glass, I sat down crosslegged against my bed and watched the inside of the refrigerator, sipping my vodka slowly.

An hour later I unpacked my bags, spreading out the men's fashion pages I had torn out of *Playboy* magazines. I was going to put the house tailor to work.

For the first four days I wandered through the crowded, noisy streets, investigating the wall-to-wall stores and dim-lit bars, buying clothes and looking for companionship.

I knew that I could buy companionship but that wasn't what I wanted. I wanted to be with someone who was attracted to me, not my money. I didn't want some whore who would just take my money and run. I wished I could find someone who would care about me. I spent my nights searching the clubs and bars, but the only single women I found were hookers.

My fourth night in Hong Kong I pushed my way into what seemed like my fortieth bar. It was like all the rest. A thick haze of blue smoke hung over the dim interior, appearing in the lights that swept the room, then dissolving in darkness. It was crowded and noisy; a stereo blasted in the background, drowned out occasionally by the din of conversation. Sailors in whites, grunts in greens, gyrenes in browns, flyboys in blues, they were everywhere. And so were the hostesses. I squelched a sudden impulse to flee, resigning myself to the fact that I would find nothing new. Besides, I encouraged myself, I'm feeling good. I'm stoned and I'm happy. What more could I want? I knew what more, so I convinced myself to hang in there a little longer and sauntered up to the bar.

The sailor to my right was feeling no pain. He was involved in an intense conversation with his hostess, whispering in her ear and laughing. His face was flushed, dripping with sweat. Slipping his hand around her well-formed buttocks, he rubbed them as if polishing a car.

I slid up on my stool, signaling for a drink. I had never been any place where there were so many whores. Everywhere I looked, couples were engaged in conversation, exchanging kisses in the dark, swaying together on the crowded dance floor. I felt left out!

A soft touch on my shoulder startled me and I swung around in a defensive posture. Standing next to me was a slim, beautiful Oriental woman. Her hand covered her mouth to stifle her laughter.

"Oh, I am sorry!" she said, "I did not wish to startle you."

"It's O.K., I'm just jumpy," I answered. My eyes locked into hers.

"You are new here? I no see you before."

"Yeah. I've just been here a few days," I answered, "and I'm already getting ready to go."

"Where you from?" she said, taking the stool next to mine.

"Vietnam."

"Oh. I'm sorry! You please buy me drink?"

"Sure, why not?"

That was a dead giveaway. This was no stranger as I had hoped it might be. She was just another hostess with the same thing in mind. What a pity, I thought. She's so god-damned beautiful too. There was something about these Oriental women that knocked me out. Their thick, straight, shiny black hair framed exquisitely formed faces. Their eyes were huge, open, emotional pools. They could twinkle and sparkle with laughter but in a flicker could change to unquestionable hate. It was impossible not to be drawn to them. I had never seen anyone communicate so clearly or so easily with their eyes. It was like they had been taught to use them instead of their mouths. I looked at this girl sitting next to me, her hands raised so gracefully as she sipped on her drink. Her mouth, so red and vulnerable, wondrously poised.

"Five dollar," the bartender repeated, snapping me out of the spell I was in.

"Yeah, O.K.," I said, reaching into my pocket and pulling out change. Almost twice as much as my own drink had cost! A lot of money for what I knew was just soda, or watered down tea. Here I was, already paying the price for conversation. It didn't set well with me.

"You want to go my place?" the hostess asked, running her hand up my thigh.

"No thanks," I said casually, looking her straight in the eyes.

"O.K., G.I.," she replied softly. "You have a nice night."

She slid off her stool and into the crowd, putting her arm around another man.

Well, at least she didn't push it, I thought, finishing off my drink. I was on my second cocktail when a live band hit the stage. I decided to stay and listen. The band played American music, but it was terrible. A far cry from even the most mediocre American band I had ever heard. What did interest me, though, was the singer. Her husky baritone voice could have melted an icicle, and I became enamored with her as I listened. I felt myself strangely defenseless and drawn to her charming smile. As the minutes turned into hours, I wondered if she was aware of my presence. I had not taken my eyes off her since the band started playing. Occasionally, I allowed myself to believe that the smiles she cast in my direction were for me. After I had been there nearly three hours I got up the courage to send her a note, asking if she would visit me during her break. I watched her face as she opened my note on stage. She seemed hesitant as she read it. I held my breath as she glanced up in my direction. She gave no indication of what she had decided, but when the band took its break, I saw her hand the note to the bass man. When he nodded in approval, I saw her leave. I was unsure whether she was coming to see me or had simply been excused to leave the stage, but minutes later I saw her make her way through the crowd to my left. My heart thumped as she walked up to the bar. I think she must have seen my enthusiasm, because she giggled just slightly as I leapt from my seat. As soon as she had seated herself, I climbed back on my stool.

"Hello, my name is Lin To," she said in remarkably good English.

"Hi," I answered, not taking my eyes off her. "My name is Howard, can I buy you a drink?"

"Oh no," she said smiling, "I'm sorry. I am not allowed to drink with the customers, but thank you anyway."

I could see the bartender eyeing us as we continued our conversation so I chose my words carefully, not wanting to blow my chances.

"How long have you been singing?" I inquired.

"I have been singing in this club three years now," she answered. "I enjoy it very much."

"I love your voice," I said. "I've been listening to you all night!"

"Yes," she giggled, "I have noticed you at the bar. You have been looking at me all night."

That caught me off guard and I felt a little embarrassed, but I really didn't care.

"I can't help it," I said, "I think I've fallen in love with you."

At this, she was caught off guard, but she laughed, deliciously, and I knew it was all right.

"I suppose you hear that from all the guys though," I continued, "but with me I think it's really true."

"You're such a sweet boy," she said, letting her hand fall on mine and leaving it for a moment. "You also say the sweetest things."

"I'd love to have dinner with you tonight," I said. "Is it possible that I could see you after the show?"

"Oh I'm sorry, but it is just not possible. Please excuse me, I have to go now. It was really nice to meet you." She slipped off her stool. "Please enjoy yourself and stay for the music." With a smile she turned and quickly melted into the crowd.

The band was already warming up as she returned to the stage. She turned her back to the crowd to talk to one of the players. In a moment, the band started to play.

"This song is for a member of the audience," she said, "and I dedicate it to him with all my love."

While the band played, she sang "Misty." I sat in silence, watching from the bar.

I spent the rest of the evening at the bar, hoping that she would change her mind.

Tiring of the bars, the booze and the prostitutes, I spent my fifth night looking for something new. One of the GIs at my hotel had recommended a new club that was referred to as a "disco," so I took a cab, following the directions on a card he had given me, to a place called the Purple Peanut.

As I climbed the stairs to the second floor, I could hear the music blaring into the hall. Whatever this was, it was no Chinese band. The music they were playing was American, through and through. Even before I pulled open the heavy double doors, I could see lights flashing on and off through the textured glass. As I stepped inside I was greeted by flashing strobe lights and acid rock and I knew I had walked into psychedelic heaven. A dance floor stretched from wall to wall. A small bar, perhaps forty feet long, was stuck in one corner of the room. Nine or ten tables surrounded the bar. Colored lights blinked on and off across the dance floor, which vibrated from the huge speakers covering the wall. The crowd was small, but most everyone was dancing as Arthur Brown screamed "Fire." It reminded me of places in San Francisco. I felt right at home.

I walked up to the bar and ordered a drink, then turned to watch the dancers. There was something else about this place that was different. I noticed it as soon as my eyes adjusted to the dark. Most of the couples on the floor were Asians. There were some soldiers with Orientals on their arms but there were also white skinned civilians with white girls. The place was evidently minus the many whores.

I noticed a thin young man with blonde hair and a smartly tailored suit excusing himself from the table to my left. I watched as he made his way to the bar. He picked up a drink from the bartender, walked straight over to me and introduced himself. "I am Peter," he said, "co-owner of this bar. You're American, aren't you? Won't you come over and join us?"

"Sure," I said, surprised. "Thank you."

Peter introduced me to his other companions, interrupting a heated conversation. To my surprise, both Peter and the other owner, Lars, were Swedish. Neither of them looked over twenty-five. Their female companion, a pretty young Asian, was the only woman in the group. Another American had arrived shortly before with a friend.

I introduced myself and sat down while the other two Americans carried on by themselves. The two Swedes seemed genuinely interested in knowing more about me, especially after I told them I was serving in Vietnam. As our conversation lengthened, it became politically oriented and very intense. They began telling me about the small number of Americans who were deserting, flying to Sweden by way of Hong Kong. They volunteered the information because it was evident by my conversation that I had a distaste for my involvement in Vietnam. Their increasing contact with American and Australian soldiers, and the stories they had heard, were leading Peter and Lars to question the war as well.

I had heard rumors about desertions on my flight to Hong Kong. Here, it seemed very real. Lars, who had met some deserters personally, said he agreed with the stand they had taken. Taking a newspaper clipping from his pocket, he read, "We ex-soldiers who have come to Sweden have refused to contribute to the military arm of destruction of Vietnam. We have refused to participate in any way with an organization which has carried on all the death and destruction in Vietnam. We choose to live in exile rather than to be used as pawns in the deadly game of world imperialism. We have found that our duty to the rest of mankind and to the Vietnamese people far outweighs our duty to the U.S. Army. A choice of loyalties had to be made. We chose to be loyal to our fellow man and therefore to ourselves. And each day that more men come to Sweden, motivated by the same loyalty, there is one less man that can be used for the futile aggression in Vietnam.

"Isn't this what you're saying?" he asked.

"Sure, but deserting is another thing altogether," I replied.

As our conversation continued, I thought back to the pamphlet stuck up on the wall at Bien Hoa, our point of departure for Hong Kong. I didn't remember all it had said but some of the phrases had stuck in my mind. Things like:

"...AWOL is a serious offense, as much as larceny, fraud or robbery. If you go AWOL, notification that you are a fugitive or outlaw wanted by the Army is made to: your family, police in your hometown, the sheriff of your county, FBI, Military Police, and the Commander of the Army in which your home is located.

"As a prisoner, you will be locked up, guarded and watched. You will be thought of as part of a group that includes: persons of low intelligence; mentally and emotionally unbalanced persons, criminals, alcoholics, deviates; anti–American and unpatriotic soldiers; ignorant 'know it alls' who say 'I have nothing to lose.'"

I thought about those things as our conversation lengthened and found myself losing interest as the night wore on. It wasn't that the conversation was boring; it was just that I had come to Hong Kong to get away from the war.

I could see that Suong or Suan (I couldn't quite remember which, her name had sounded like Sue-Ann to me) was also tiring of the conversation. She had asked Lars to dance with her a couple of times but he had waved her off, engrossed in conversation. But I was ready to dance. I had come here for a good time.

"Would you like to dance?" I asked, without addressing her by name.

"Oh yes, I would love to!" she replied.

"Excuse us, will you guys," I said, setting down my drink and rising.

Peter just turned his head and smiled, acknowledging our intentions. The rest continued their conversation.

I felt relieved to be out on the dance floor, pleased to be in the company of this woman. The music, loud and driving, shook the dance floor and filled my senses. Amidst the flickering, colored lights, I closed my eyes and let myself be swept along in the current of sound. Twisting, turning, rocking, I drove myself deeper into the beat. I felt free and alive and unencumbered by the weight of war.

At length, we drew closer to one another, and raising our voices above the music so as to be heard, we engaged in casual conversation.

"Do you come here often?" I inquired.

"Oh no, this is only my third night here."

"Do you live here then? I mean, are you Chinese?"

"Oh no." She laughed. "I am Korean, I am only visiting here."

I wondered if she laughed because she had known what I was thinking. All Orientals looked the same to me. Sue-Ann's face was a little broader and seemed a little flatter than those of the Vietnamese I had seen, but the rest of her features looked the same.

We stopped dancing as the record changed, and on an impulse, I reached out and took her hand. I was hungry for affection and she didn't seem to mind.

As if the disc-jockey had anticipated my desires, a slow song began playing, Dusty Springfield's "The Look of Love." When I pulled her close to me, she put her hand on my shoulder and pressed her face against my chest. We danced silently, moving slowly through the shadows and soft-flickering lights. It was an electric, emotionally charged moment. I could almost taste the perfume that lingered in her hair, and I let my lips brush softly past her ear. She pulled me closer.

"Have you known Peter and Lars long?" I asked, pulling back to look in her eyes. I had to determine what her relationship was with them.

"No," she answered softly, "I met them on the boat I was on."

"The boat?"

"Oh yes, the boat. I am traveling on a ship. I am headed back for school. I met them on the boat while traveling here."

It was safe then, I thought. If she just met them on the boat then she wasn't either one's girl.

"Would you care to go some place else with me tonight?" I asked cautiously. "I mean after a while."

I saw a flicker of regret in her eyes, but then she smiled, squeezing my hand.

"I think I would enjoy that very much," she responded, "but I can't. I am Lars's companion. That is, I came with him tonight."

"Oh!" I said, trying to hide my disappointment. "I'm sorry, I didn't know."

We continued to dance, holding one another, not saying a word.

That evening, alone again in my hotel, the question of desertion crossed my mind continually and as much as I tried, I could not sleep. In the hours of silence, I weighed the cost. Lars had told me he knew where air passage to Sweden could be arranged and even volunteered to help with the cost. I knew I risked death returning to Vietnam. Here was an opportunity for me to choose life. But it would mean never going home again and I would have to turn my back on my own citizenship. More precisely and more importantly, it would mean closing myself off from the very people I was longing to see. It would also mean turning my back on my brothers in 'Nam. I owed them a debt I could not abandon.

I wondered if the political influence I could have in Sweden would be any greater than the influence I had on my fellow soldiers right now. I was already speaking out against the war. Everyone in the battery knew where I stood. What more would I accomplish in Sweden? The soldiers there already agreed with my stance.

Finally, I determined that deserting so close to my departure just wouldn't be worth it, and I laid the question to rest.

The few hours I slept that night were haunted by scenes of dismembered bodies, faces of children that couldn't be patched. When I awoke, still fully dressed, I determined not to spend my last night alone.

Walking through the narrow, crowded streets, I forced my way through a steady flow of bicycles, motorcycles, cars and pedestrians. I paid no attention to the pleas and invitations from salesmen that hung in every doorway. I relentlessly continued my search for that one encounter. I didn't care if it was a one-night stand, as long as it came from the heart. But as night approached, I was no closer to finding someone than when I had started. In the back of my mind was the nagging reminder that I would be leaving the next morning, returning to the hell of Vietnam. Maybe a hell from which I would never return.

Spying the flickering neon lights of a saloon, I trotted across the street and made my way inside. It was early and the barstools and booths were still full of slender young women. I ordered a drink at the bar and scanned the bodies that waited in dull passivity. Bored and lethargic, they looked like worn-out shoes. Their faces were hardened by indifference and sadness that no mask of make-up could soften. Occasionally a light would flicker in their eyes when they noticed me looking, and they managed a seductive smile with what sincerity they could muster, but other than that they were lifeless and sad. I saw a few young faces, still soft in their innocence; and on some, a remnant of beauty. But most were demoralized, stricken with age.

I looked around at the choices that confronted me. Any of these could be mine, whatever my income could afford. Pleasure could be bought here so cheaply.

God, I thought, what am I doing here? I wondered if I shouldn't just pick up and leave. Then the slowly approaching, slender young woman helped me to decide.

After agreeing on a set price for the evening, my hostess was willing, as she said, to "get it on." Her only question was whether I wanted to have sex with her right off, or go out and dance for a while first. I elected to dance, hoping for more than a casual encounter.

Following her suggestion, we returned to the bar where I had previously spent an evening. While we lingered at the bar, drinking, I probed her with questions. Even though I had bought her, I wanted to know something about the woman I was going to sleep with.

She parlayed my questions like a politician and would reveal nothing personal—nothing more than her name. Finally, she tired of my probing and coaxed me out on the dance floor, reminding me that it was I who had wanted to dance.

Out on the dark, crowded dance floor we embraced, and slowly the music carried us around the room. As we swept past the stage, I looked up at the band and saw Lin To. At that instant her eyes locked on mine. I knew she recognized me and I felt deeply embarrassed, almost ashamed. But she only smiled a long-knowing smile, winked at me as if laughing, and continued to sing. My heart sank as I saw myself through her eyes; how deplorable I must have looked.

My hostess hugged my leg against her crotch as we danced, sliding indiscreetly up and down, whispering that we should go and make love. Her words sounded hollow and cheap and I was bothered by her persistence. After all, I was paying her for her time.

Finally, she insisted that we go. By then a warm, alcohol-induced glow permeated my body, making me feel amused and encouraged. Why not?

Upon entering my room, she quickly called the desk clerk to register, one of the house rules that prostitutes had to obey if they wanted to be allowed in the hotel again. She made no effort to hide the fact that a payoff was involved. She demanded cash in her hands before we started, so I dug out 250 Hong Kong dollars. It was all that I had left. I had reserved it for the end. She insisted that we both shower before we had sex so I took mine first, taking pleasure in watching her undress while I toweled myself dry.

I turned off the lights and sat down crosslegged between the foot of the bed and the dresser, blocking the narrow passage between them. Pulling open one of the dresser drawers, I took out my stash, placed a piece of newspaper on the carpet and proceeded to roll up a couple of joints.

A soft light illuminated the room as she opened the bathroom door and stepped out. She stood there for a moment, letting her eyes adjust to the dark. Her long black hair, no longer in a bun, cascaded down her back and shoulders, shiny against her bronze skin. My eyes followed her hair to her small, firm breasts and then down to the black net panties that covered her hips. I could feel my anticipation rising, heightened by her graceful movements as she entered the room.

Slowly lowering herself to her knees, she looked up at me with a softness I had not noticed before. "What are you doing?" she asked quietly. But it became evident to her even before I answered, and she sat back and laughed. She didn't seem to be laughing at me; it was a childlike giggle. For a moment I sensed her letting her defenses down, and I felt a strange kind of kindred, as if we were friends.

I lit up a joint, sucked the smoke into my lungs, and then extended it to her.

"Oh no!" she responded, putting me off with a wave of her hand. "Oh, you are crazy!" Still, she smiled, looking intently into my face as if trying to discover something there. Then she picked up a hairbrush and began stroking her hair, quietly observing me as I smoked.

"Why is it that all Orientals say 'oh,' before almost everything they say?" I asked.

"Why is it all G.I.'s always say you know after everything they say?" she retaliated.

I laughed, coughing and spilling smoke out of my lungs. "O.K.," I said, "I think I understand."

I suddenly felt as if this were a different woman here, someone I wanted to know.

"Why do you do this for a living?" I asked quietly, stubbing out my joint.

"Oh, you wouldn't understand. You're too young and innocent!" she said with a smile.

I could tell there was something different in her voice. It had a ring of sincerity. Pressing on, I asked her more personal questions. Very hesitantly she opened the door a little, letting me catch a glimpse of her life. But she soon took the offensive and turned the conversation around by asking me questions about myself.

"It must be very hard for you being in Vietnam," she said quite seriously. "You are so very young."

"I'm no younger than most people over there. There are some younger than me."

"Oh, it's very tragic," she continued, "the war I mean, with so many young people losing their lives."

She must have seen the smile fade from my lips because she quickly changed the subject. "You have a nice girl at home?"

"No, not really," I answered, trying to smile. It was hard to forget about what she had just said.

"Oh, you butterfly then!" she teased, poking my hand.

"Butterfly?"

"Oh you know," she said, making waving motions with her hands. "You fly from flower to flower, picking the pollen, but never stay long in one place after you land."

I laughed. She was right! I was definitely a butterfly. How well she had known.

"But what about you? Do you have a boyfriend?" I asked.

"Oh no, I have no room for a man."

"What about your family? Do you live with your parents?"

I tried to draw her out, but the more personal I got the more edgy and irritated she became. Finally she would have no more of it. She grabbed my hand and led me to bed.

Crawling under the covers, I stroked her body, telling her how beautiful I thought she was. But the more I tried to draw out some kind of emotional response the more hardened and businesslike she became. She became insistent on my getting an erection, drawing me down on top of her, trying to push me inside.

"Take it easy," I said. "Let's take our time. Let's spend some time holding and touching one another. I want us to care." I thought it could be that easy; it seemed easy enough for me.

Finally, in exasperation, she pushed me off. She had had it! She was leaving! She kicked the covers aside and, in a quick twist, leapt out of bed.

"You're crazy," she yelled. "You see life through a pair of rose colored glasses! Life isn't the way you want it to be. It's not full of love or compassion. It's full of hard reality and poverty. Come and see the boat that I live on! Come and see my

287

two children! Who will feed them if I don't? You are so naive and innocent. You live in America where everyone's rich. You are crazy to think that life will ever be the way you want it to be!"

I was surprised at her outburst, but as I listened, watching her expressions, I knew for a moment her mask had been stripped. Her defenses were shattered by anger. For a brief moment, I saw her again as she really was.

I pleaded with her, telling her that it was truly possible to care and to love strangers and people of every race. That there was room for compassion for all mankind and that we were missing an opportunity we would never again have. She would have none of it.

She quickly gained control of her emotions and I sensed immediately that I had lost her. As she quietly dressed in her businesslike manner, I sat back, fumbling with my defeat. I had a deep suspicion that more was being lost than just sex and money. Her life was being lost, abandoned without hope, and I felt powerless to do anything about it. Here was someone who truly lived in despair, and who really needed help. Yet she could count on no one to help her but herself. I felt embarrassed, perhaps because I so deeply empathized with her plight. I was desiring her emotional involvement in my life, yet I wasn't committed to involvement in hers. I had wanted her to really care for me. But would I then, in return, really care for her? It wasn't much of a bargain for her.

Sorrowfully, I lowered my eyes, staring at the bed covers. She must have noticed how I looked because her anger suddenly abated. With genuine compassion in her voice, she spoke to me again.

"You're just a crazy young boy," she said softly. "Too young to be involved in a war. . . . Here," she said tossing $125 back on the bed, "that's my share. You can have it back."

She quickly turned and left the room, but not before I saw a tear running down her cheek. Long after the door had closed and the room had grown silent and still, I was still sitting in bed, searching my heart once again for the truth about love.

Late that evening, I pulled my khakis back on and went down to the hotel restaurant. If tomorrow I was to be a condemned man, at least I would have my last meal.

I ordered orange duckling and ate in the quiet of the restaurant since very few patrons were left at this hour. I noticed two young Oriental women in conversation near me, and I watched them intently as they talked. Finally, one of them noticed me staring and smiled. I smiled back but quickly dropped my eyes, slightly embarrassed at having been caught staring. A few minutes later they both came over and introduced themselves, apologizing for disturbing me.

The two women were students, one of whom worked in the hotel, and were close friends. The bolder of the two engaged me eagerly in conversation, asking about the war, and why I had come to Hong Kong. Eventually, I found myself talking about my experience with the prostitute and I found myself opening my heart to two perfect strangers, something I had never done. As our conversation lengthened, I discovered I was face to face with a young woman who, although she had shared a similar background with the prostitute, had chosen a completely different path to solve her own poverty. Yet she held no contempt or criticism for her peer. She knew only too well the hardship of poverty, and she knew what it could make a person do. She had only understanding and compassion for her countrywoman; she wanted me to have the same. She explained that she had received her education in a Christian Missionary School and that somewhere along the line, she had grasped the lesson of forgiveness and love, not only in her head, but in her heart as well. I had very few kind things to say about churches or about the people who frequented them, and I told her so. Still, there was something real, something different in what she felt and believed. Before they left, she encouraged me not to let my experience with my church harden me to the teachings of Jesus Christ, but to study them and judge them for myself.

That night, as I lay in bed, I opened the Gideon Bible I found in the top dresser drawer. Leafing through the pages, I read verses here and there. Some passages seemed to confirm how I felt about killing and violence, but there were others I could not accept. Some of it was simply too supernatural to believe. Some of it seemed to require too great a change in my life. Discarding what I couldn't accept, I concentrated on reading the words that came from the mouth of Jesus, trying to grasp what he said about love.

The early morning hours found me hurrying to buy another suitcase to carry my custom-tailored clothes home: four new suits, one knee-length Nehru jacket, silk monogrammed shirts, a brightly colored ascot and a custom pair of tan, suede, knee-high boots. For sure this time, I was going home in style. I was going to make sure I fit in when I got back. A year had passed and I was worried that I might be out of the mainstream. Everything was changing so rapidly, at least from what I could piece together about what was happening back in the States.

Now here I sat on the roof of a bunker in the rear, writing about my R&R in my diary. It was close to midnight when I stopped writing and quietly climbed down from the roof. Noticing a crack of light coming from behind the shutters at headquarters, I made my way over there. I knew somebody had to be on duty all night and wondered who it was. I wanted someone to talk to and hoped I might find someone willing to listen.

The supply sergeant, Pirren, was standing night watch. He looked up at me for a brief moment when I entered and then went back to reading his book. I could see the disinterest in his face so I didn't even consider starting a conversation. I slouched back in a chair and looked around. It was quiet and warm. It felt safe. It reminded me that I had to go back to the field. Forty-nine days left—only forty-nine! I didn't want to die with only forty-nine days left.

"Hey, Pirren," I said, breaking the silence. "Don't they need any more personnel back here?"

"You should be so lucky, sweetie."

Shit! Why was this guy such a prick! He never had a kind thing to say about anybody.

"Hey man," I said, "what makes you so self-righteous?"

"You got a lifetime to listen, sweetie?"

"Hey man, I'm not here to hassle you," I said softly. "If you're carrying some kind of chip on your shoulder, I don't think it's because of me. If you want to be left alone, fine, but don't go laying a lot of your crap on me. I'm not the enemy. I don't think any more of the military than you apparently do, but I'm not some fuckin' peon that you can take your frustrations out on either. And your rank don't mean shit to me. Now do you get where I'm coming from?"

"I'm sorry," he said in mock amazement, "I didn't mean to step on your cloud!" Still, his voice softened. He even tried forcing a smile. When it faded, it left a tired, sad look on his face.

"Maybe I'm just tired," he added apologetically. "It's been a long, hard day, and I've had it up to here."

We began to talk—really converse—and to my surprise his hostility seemed to slowly vanish. When his shift ended, he invited me over to the supply building where he had a bottle of Scotch.

Rather than sleeping in the personnel bunker with all the other enlisted men, Pirren had fixed up private quarters behind the locked cage that contained all the Class IV supplies. The room, larger than most sleeping quarters, contained a cot with a mattress, a refrigerator, table and chairs, a throw rug, a stereo, and all the modern conveniences. Under the soft electric glow of an overhead light we sat in the shadows of the wire cage and drank and rapped.

"You may not see it," Pirren said, leaning over the table, "but there's an underground network of protestors growing all over Vietnam, especially here in the rear. A lot more people than you and I are tired of this military fiasco. Something stinks and we're beginning to do something about it. Man, I hear more and more grumblings all the time. I think it's gonna rise up and bring a halt to this war and to the military system itself."

Leaning back on his chair, he continued, "We're tired of this crap. Of being treated like shit. Like second class citizens, like dogs on a leash . . . let me tell you, I'm seeing more and more signs of direct disobedience. Of outright rebellion. There's a revolution going on. It's here in the making, and it comes closer to the surface with each day we remain."

We talked for two or three hours about the way things were changing, about the political climate both at home and in 'Nam. As we exchanged observations and experiences, they seemed to confirm deception that was going on. We talked about the rising drug use. Each of us could see a growing subculture of heads and peaceniks. Our feelings about the war and the Army were almost the same, at least until he began talking about the increase in fragging.

I could understand fragging taking place, all right. I knew what a pleasure it would be to waste some of those smart ass officers and stop their endless fucking with your mind. But still, to kill one, well that wasn't something I could do. Pirren told me about a couple of soldiers who had rolled a grenade up to the side of a lieutenant's bunker one night, and after the explosion, when the lieutenant was wide awake, shouted out that the next one would be his. It pained me to believe that it was coming to this. That we were deliberately killing our own men.

The more Pirren drank, the less inhibited he became, and he began exposing his personal life. He strayed back and forth from his past to his present, revealing bits and pieces. I was beginning to get a picture of the pain and loneliness that filled his life, and I felt an empathy building in my heart toward him. Strangely, he seemed unaware of my presence, and let his head slump slowly on the table as he talked. Then, without warning, he suddenly jerked upright, straightening his back. It was as if he was suddenly aware that he had become naked and vulnerable, and now needed to cover up. He stared at me intently, wondering if he had crossed some invisible line or had revealed too much and now needed to withdraw. He seemed to be searching my face for a clue.

Slurring his words, he leaned on the table and with a look of genuine puzzlement, stared into my face. "Why do you sit here and listen to me, Olsen? Can't you see I'm drunk? . . . Aren't you afraid?"

"Afraid?" I said. "Why should I be afraid? No . . . I like you."

"Like me!" he snorted. "How can you like me! You don't even know anything about me."

"Look, man, I know enough to know that we're a lot alike."

"You . . . like me!" He shook his head. "No, you're not like me, you're kind! I can sense that about you. You're kind and you're gentle, not like me at all."

"Hey man, you're O.K.," I said, trying to encourage him. I could see he was getting depressed. At the same time I was becoming uneasy. I wasn't quite sure I liked where the conversation was heading, but I wasn't sure why. I began to remember what I had heard about Pirren's being queer and I sensed a small red flag beginning to wave inside.

What if he is queer, I asked myself, feeling a small twinge of fear. Is he getting ready to make a pass at me? What the hell will I do then, deck him? Suddenly, I wished that I had never gotten myself into this situation.

What if he wasn't queer? What if they were wrong? What if it had been nothing more than something the guys spread just to have something to joke about?

"I like you, Olsen," he said almost apologetically. "There's something about you that makes me want to trust you. I almost feel as if you really care. But it's hard for me to believe it."

"Why is that?" I asked softly.

"For one thing," he said, his voice suddenly hardening, "you don't know that I'm a homosexual!"

He spit the words out, thrusting them to the surface with great effort. I could sense him immediately retreating. I knew he was preparing for the worst.

Damn . . . why was this happening to me? Now what was I supposed to do?

Suddenly I was confronted with a whole mixture of emotions. I had never personally known a homosexual before. I would never have allowed myself to even get close to one. They were the antithesis of manhood. They were "queers" and "fairies," something to be despised. Complete degenerates! Still, here was this . . . man, and he seemed nothing like the monsters I had thought homosexuals were. What the hell was going on? Had everything I'd been programmed to believe been a lie? This man obviously suffered pain and loneliness. In many ways he was just like me. He was a sensitive and intelligent person. We were similar in more ways than we were different! How was I to respond to that?

"So what?" I finally said, trying to sound convincing, but unsure of what I really believed. "It doesn't make any difference to me."

He crooked his head ever so slightly, turning away in disbelief. Suddenly, the corners of his mouth quivered and he began to sob. His whole body heaved as if wracked with pain. He lowered his head into his arms and wept, and wept.

I didn't move. I watched, spellbound. This was embarrassing! I didn't know how to respond. I had never seen another man cry like this. I wanted him to stop because I could feel his pain. I felt so sorry for him, but I didn't know what to do. I wanted to be able to comfort him but I didn't know what to say. I wanted to reach out and hold his hand, as I would with a crying child, but I was afraid of what he might do. I didn't want to do anything that would make him think I was a queer.

Finally, his sobbing grew quieter. I reached over and put my hand on his.

"Hey man," I said, "I don't know what you're going through, but I do know how you feel. It's O.K., man, I've been there before . . . just don't go letting it get you down."

He slowly raised his head. His eyes were red and tears ran down his cheeks. He looked like a lost, hurt child. There was an appeal in his eyes, but I didn't know what for.

"Look," I said. "As far as I'm concerned we're friends, O.K.? Your being a homosexual doesn't change that. If this is your thing, then fine. I don't understand it, and I sure don't agree with it, but if you think it's O.K. for you, then fine. But, it's not my thing. I'm not that way. As long as you understand that, things will be cool . . . O.K.?"

He nodded.

Even though I was being somewhat defensive, I knew that for me I was making a courageous statement. I could have bolted from the room in fear or reacted by threatening him if he dared touch me, but neither of those responses showed evidence of love, and I was trying to do the loving thing. I was trying to behave in a way that would show I cared, because I did. However strange the situation had been, he had truly touched my heart.

"Look," I said after a while, "I've got to catch the resupply chopper back out to the field in the morning. I'd better go hit the sack."

I felt slightly embarrassed standing to leave, but he thanked me for being who I was. As I walked to my bunker I wondered myself who I was. I certainly wasn't the same man I had been when I came into country, but I still found it hard to believe I was the same person that others seemed to think I was.

20

I could see smoke rising from the fire support base long before I could distinguish the guns that were firing. As the Chinook began its slow descent, in back of the line of fire, my mind buzzed an alarm. I wondered what was going on. By the time I reached the FDC the firing had stopped. Was it the end of a prep, or was a contact mission on?

I stepped from the hot sun into the cool, dark interior of the FDC.

"Hey, Olsen!" came a trio of voices.

"Hey, what's happening?" I replied excitedly. "How's everything going, is everyone here? Where's the lieutenant?"

"He's over at the captain's," replied Vanous, busy with the work at hand.

"Shit," shouted White, "you left just in the nick of time. And you're not coming back a day too soon. If you'da been here yesterday, you'd know what I mean!"

He was smiling because he was glad to have me back, but the seriousness in his voice let me know that he wasn't kidding around.

"What do you mean? What happened?"

"The 2nd of the 14th was sending out its night ambush patrol yesterday when Charlie rained down pee. The point man was the only one to clear the perimeter. Everyone else was out in the wire. They got pinned down when a sniper opened fire and wasted the point man. Before we could get the guns going, the VC were dropping 60s all over the place. They walked them right down the gap where the patrol was lying and every one of them was hurt bad! Not only that, one of the mortars fell into Gun Three's parapet and blew off both of Miller's legs!"

I felt a sudden stab of pain in my chest. "Miller!" I grabbed a chair to sit down. Why the fuck had it happened to him? He hadn't been touched out in the bush!

I could hear the hardness in White's voice as he continued, but it was like I

293

was shutting up my mind, not wanting to hear. Damn, I thought, and he was really short too!

The room grew quiet as White finished his story. I hung my head, not wanting to look anyone in the face. I wondered if I had made the right decision in coming back. Somehow, my being here made me a part of everything that was happening, and I felt particularly responsible for Miller's legs. Maybe if I had been here it wouldn't have happened.

The eerie silence was broken by the sergeant major's entrance. I glanced up at him.

"Sergeant," I said.

"So you're back, huh?" he said. "You get all the ass you wanted on your trip? Boy, I heard there was plenty available on the streets of Hong Kong!"

I immediately resented his coarseness. I was ashamed of the fact that I had picked up a whore in the first place. It made me feel like one of them and right now I detested having to identify with this warmonger slob. I didn't say anything, and the sergeant major changed the subject.

"Well, I thought you might want to know about your friend, Lieutenant Murphy," he added. "He's in a base hospital in Japan. The command trac' he was riding was hit by a rocket grenade between Dau Tieng and Tay Ninh. It blew off one leg below the kneecap, and apparently his right arm. They had to evacuate him to Japan immediately, but he was lucky. They saved his life."

Lucky! What the hell did he mean . . . lucky? I could feel my anger rising uncontrollably, engulfing the pain.

"How can you say he's lucky?" I asked in amazement. "What the hell is so lucky about losing an arm and a leg? He's going to be crippled for the rest of his life!"

The sergeant major backed off a little in the face of my anger. "Look," he said seriously, "it's just like Miller down on Gun Three. Now there's a lucky guy. All he lost was his legs, and only below the knee. He's still alive! Now the Army is gonna take care of him for the rest of his life. The Army takes care of its own! From now on it's easy street for him. Shit, I've got seven years to go before I can retire and start enjoying my pension, and who knows if I'll even make it till then. But these guys are out now . . . and they're out on easy street."

I couldn't believe my ears. He actually, wholeheartedly believed what he was saying. Was that what he was living for? Waiting to get his lucky disability so he could retire and live on easy street? Was life so bad in the real world that he couldn't hack it and had to hold out for something like this? What kind of mentality was this?

Suddenly, I hated him. I despised him for his selfishness; for his commitment to war as a profitable vocation, where his type fed off the blood of dying young men; for causing wars to continue and suffering to grow, like a dangerous cancer.

"Excuse me!" I said, livid with contempt. I grabbed my duffel bag and fled the room.

With 45 days left and November starting, the 2nd Battalion 14th Infantry continued to work out of our fire support base. Even though the VC/NVA main forces had withdrawn into their sanctuaries, battalion-sized units and smaller forces continued their harassment, trying to interdict our main supply routes. They seemed ready for this war to drag on for years if needed.

We, in turn, were continuing to provide strategically located bases for extensive daylight reconnaissance and heli-borne assaults against suspected enemy bases. At night, we continued to send out platoon-size ambush patrols and listening posts, trying to monitor the principal trails and suspected routes the enemy stalked.

We continued to uproot enemy supply caches and small base camp complexes. As always mines and booby traps posed a critical problem for elements conducting the search.

Though the 2/14th was limiting its operations to the My Hanh, Duc Hoa and Bao Trai complex, their operations proved profitable, without heavy losses.

At the close of the first day, D Company, sweeping 5 kilometers northeast of Duc Hoa, apprehended two VC suspects and A Company apprehended one. Later they found three dead VC with two AK-47 rifles in an area where a helicopter had previously engaged a small group. One VC turned himself in as a *hoi chahn*.

On the third, the infantry engaged in sporadic enemy contact, and we spent the day firing for them. The only serious incident happened in the morning when one of the grunts with A Company was wounded by a booby-trapped hand grenade.

By the fourth day we had picked up 26 detainees, but had lost six men.

In spite of what they were saying back home, the war continued with very little change. Even though I was sympathetic to the peace movement I was confused by L.B.J.'s recent halt to the bombings of North Vietnam. That son-of-a-bitch was not only deceiving the American people by lying to the press, he was now going to leave us here and stop bombing the supply routes from North Vietnam. How could he? Didn't he give a damn about the loss of lives that would result from an uninterrupted flow of ammunition and soldiers from the north? Damn, you couldn't even trust the President. That our lives could be so easily disregarded churned at my insides.

LeRoy was gone now. I really missed him, but I was grateful that he was at last able to escape this place.

I tried not to, but I felt myself slipping back into a pattern of withdrawal. I began spending most of my free time, what little I had, alone. I wasn't interested in developing any more relationships. I was tired of going from a place of knowing and caring about people to a place of remembering them. Perhaps it was just because I was getting short; I wasn't sure. I still hadn't gotten over the shock of finding out about Miller and Murphy. But, no matter what the reasoning, I was becoming a recluse.

I slipped a blank cassette into my tape recorder and plugged in the microphone.

Setting the cassette to record, I turned on the mike. "November, on a Thursday night. Tonight is the night we are supposed to be hit and our position overrun in a ground attack by two Viet Cong battalions. I'll leave this tape set up and if something should happen we'll click it on and see what goes."

Adjusting a couple of sandbags, I set the tape recorder on top of the personnel bunker and slipped back inside. To lessen the risk of someone's being killed by having to run outside to get from the personnel bunker to the FDC, I had had a portion of the wall removed between the FDC and the adjoining personnel bunker. Now, by pushing aside the poncho that covered the hole, we could crawl into the FDC. If we got into any heavy shit tonight, all I had to do was dash from the FDC out to the hanging microphone and turn it on.

Finally, I thought, I'm going to have a chance to really capture the kind of hell we've been living through; some of the reality of this experience that will be more vivid than my writing. Maybe it'll give me something to remember when I try to tell others about it. I wondered if I might also be having a premonition of my own death. Maybe I was never going to make it back and that was why I was recording my experience. Pushing that thought out of my mind, I went back inside the FDC and took a seat by the FADAC.

Even if I didn't record a battle tonight, I would probably be able to sometime soon. After all, we had been hit or mortared eleven times since setting up FSB Keene III. This place should have been called "Sitting Duck."

The extensive daylight reconnaissance operations were turning up a surprising number of Viet Cong, especially considering intelligence had said that all main NVA and VC forces had withdrawn from the area. As usual, I wondered where they were getting their information! True, most of our recent contact had been with small patrols, but that's the way it had been since I had gotten in country. There had been continual small harassment, interspersed with full-scale attacks.

I knew that contact with the enemy was increasing despite what the brass said. All the data that I could put together was pointing to another Tet. After all, next month was December; then came the new year!

I had been able to trace the enemy's movement through periodic confrontations. They were heading in our direction. This morning B Company had engaged over fifteen Viet Cong four kilometers west of Duc Hoa. That put them less than two kilometers from us.

The phone to the guns rang and I picked it up. "FDC."

"FDC . . . this is Gun One, Wilson speaking. Do you have anything planned for us tonight?"

"I've got a couple of counter-targets for you to lay on, but they only have to be fired three times during the night," I replied.

"You got the firing data with you now? Then we won't have to bother with getting it tonight."

"Wait one," I said. "Lieutenant, is that O.K.?" I asked.

"Tell them they can wait till tonight; that way there won't be any screw-ups!" he said.

"C'mon, lieutenant, they'll be able to set it up quicker if we give it to them now. Besides, they can call in their settings before they fire and we can check them then."

He hesitated. "Oh, all right."

"O.K., One," I said, "you prepared to copy?"

"Go ahead," Wilson said, obviously pleased.

"Azimuth one-six-zero-zero. . . ."

After I relayed the data, a couple of other guys who had been on the line asked if they could get their data too; so I called all the guns up and relayed the information to those that had targets.

"Hey, Olsen," Gun Three asked, "what's the sit rep?"

"Yeah, what's going on?" another person asked.

"Nothing's changed," I answered. "We haven't heard anything more from headquarters or you'd know about it too. You know that whatever information I get goes down to the guns."

"Anything more on the Victor Charlie we fired on this afternoon? Has the infantry made contact with anyone else?"

"Nothing."

"Well screw headquarters! What do you think is going on?"

"Yeah, c'mon, Olsen, you seem to always know what's going down. What are we supposed to be in for tonight?"

"Well, if I was you, I'd sleep awful light," I joked. "Those Victor Charlie that the infantry have been running into all week have been headed toward our position. The skirmish we fired today was only a couple of thousand meters away. You check the odds out for yourself."

"Shee-it," said one of the guns. "He'd better hope he don't tangle with us tonight!"

With that, the lieutenant reached over and grabbed the phone.

"I'll have none of that kind of language over this phone," he said angrily. "Now if you don't have any more business to take care of, let's cut the chatter!"

The lieutenant handed the phone back to me, then sat back in his chair.

"Fuck, when you gonna stop being such a hard-ass, Lieutenant?" I asked. I wondered what he was so uptight about.

Caught up in the excitement, I nearly yelled into the microphone. "We have just received AK four-seven fire, numerous RPG 2s, and RPG 7s fired in by Victor Charlie." I took a deep breath, trying to calm myself.

At the most, only ten or fifteen minutes had passed since a heavy barrage of mortars, rockets and RPG fire had rained down on our base. At first, fire seemed to be coming from everywhere. We thought we were totally surrounded, but we finally narrowed it down to two locations.

It had come as no surprise this time. Throughout the evening our listening posts had detected movement to our south and east, and I had trained the guns in those directions. Now our howitzers were zeroing in on the enemy's likely avenue of retreat, and we had radioed gunships to lay down heavy fire across the woodline to seal off any attackers that might try to make it across the open plain.

As soon as I had determined that the on shift could handle anything that came up, I rushed outside and turned on my tape recorder. Now, nestled down behind the waist-high wall that covered the entrance to the personnel bunker, I made sure that my M-16 was on hand before I continued to record.

"The contact has been broken at this time," I recorded in hushed tones, "as you can tell. Otherwise I probably wouldn't be doing this. I would be hiding in a hole."

A series of deafening explosions shook the perimeter.

"The rounds you just heard go off were fired by one of the new Huey Slicks called a Cheyenne, a gunship which we now have patrolling our perimeter with two others. The perimeter is lined with flares. The Victor Charlie hit us from an azimuth of approximately two-eight hundred and went from there to a northern direction of about one-six-hundred to one-eight-hundred. He was spotted crossing from one area to the other. Both artillery and gunship fire have been brought to bear on Charlie's location. Artillery fire has ceased at this time, being that a check fire was given as soon as the gunships arrived."

Since the direct threat of being overrun seemed past, our perimeter defense and three gunships would bring an adequate amount of fire power to pin the enemy down. This would allow the listening posts and ambush sites outside of our perimeter to get back to safety without fear of getting hit by backsplash from artillery rounds. As long as we were firing, they couldn't move safely.

"The gunships are now patrolling our area," I continued, "trying to get an accurate location of our infantry positions. Our elements have been popping star clusters or using strobe lights to reveal their positions. It's pretty quiet now. The gunships are just circling the area but they'll bring fire into Charlie's position as soon as they can tell who is the enemy and who is not."

The crew of the off shift began returning from where they had fled for overhead cover. One by one, they dropped down beside me. Helmets and bandoliers dropped in piles at their feet. As long as things were relatively secure, we could hang back and defend our own location. But the danger was far from over. We were still prepared to split for the perimeter at a moment's notice. I was really grateful for the infantry manning the perimeter. They were now laying their lives on the line. I was also thankful for those Hueys and Cheyennes. With their tremendous firepower, they had quickly reduced the enemy threat.

I flipped my microphone back on, thinking it would be fun to do some interviews.

"Outside the fire directions control bunker I have sitting with me Private First Class Mike Jensen. Also Specialist Fourth Class Leslie White."

I was cut short by a burst of machine gun fire.

"Now you can hear the action, as a stream of red tracers pour out from one of the gunships firing its automatic 79 grenade launchers and miniguns into Charlie's suspected location."

"Go . . . Go, man!" Mike said between clenched teeth.

"Go . . . Go . . . Go!" White chanted.

Vegetation and dust exploded in the wood line. The bamboo thicket that hemmed us in disintegrated. Puffs of smoke blossomed above the exploding grenades. Rockets, like miniature atomic explosions shattered the air. The noise was deafening.

Maybe now we'll get him, I thought. If he started to move, we'd be right on top of him. I wondered if we had them pinned down or if they were in tunnels by now. Now that the assault had been repulsed, I wanted vengeance!

Even with the gunship directly overhead, there was a lapse between the time we could see firing and hear it. Though the tracer rounds were five bullets apart, they formed an uninterrupted line that looked like someone urinating fluorescent red piss. That was how the expression developed that we were "raining pee" upon Charlie.

Artillery rounds began exploding on the southern end over our perimeter, and I wondered what was going on. But my attention quickly narrowed when the gunships began firing directly in front of us again.

"Again you can hear the M-79 grenades being launched from the gunship," I recorded. "The gunship has also just fired two of his rockets and is now firing his miniguns as he makes a pass over the area."

Grenades and rockets exploded like popcorn. Trees burst open, splintering the air. You could hardly see through the dust. It was amazing! No two infantry squads could have laid down as much firepower as this.

"I'm sure Charlie doesn't appreciate what's happening," I noted on the tape.

Flares began dropping. Gracelli pointed one out to me as it trailed, dropping just inside the perimeter wire.

"Olsen," he said, "run out to the perimeter and get that fucking parachute for me."

"Forget it," I laughed. I wished I could. They were a kind of status symbol the guys collected. A reminder that they had come through the kind of assault that had required sustained illumination. I spoke into the recorder mike: "Spooky is now flying over our area dropping flares."

Another burst of machine gun fire erupted from the gunship. Simultaneously, one of the infantry bunkers ten meters in front of us opened up, firing its M-60.

"Now you can hear mike 60s and M-79s going off. It's just like a carnival out here. It's really quite a show they're putting on." I had seen Fourth of July celebrations with fewer fireworks than this.

"Hey, what was that?" Mike said, pointing to an area to the east of our perimeter.

"A flare has just gone down to the east of our perimeter," I recorded, "leaving a long white column of smoke in the dark blue sky. Man, it's something else.

"You can now hear the mike 79s firing again from the gunships, along with sporadic fire from their miniguns. Uh . . . the rounds are impacting . . . whoops,

299

there they go . . . and after the M-79s come the rockets. The gunships are now firing to the northeast of our perimeter, approximately 300 meters out."

Thump-thump-thump-thump-thump—the grenades hit the ground like giant footsteps.

"Spooky is still on station, flying around dropping flares. He's really appreciated by the troops. The area is well lit now. The woodline is clearly visible, rising behind the clouds of smoke being created by the exploding grenades and rockets. These new Cheyennes are plenty pee bringers."

The tarp behind us lifted, and two more crew members crawled out of the bunker. Mitchell giggled nervously as he sat down next to us. His eyes glistened with excitement. Reaching over Gracelli, he made an attempt to grab my mike, but I pulled it away.

"Tell 'em what I'm doing here, man," he said.

"Now we have two more people outside to watch the fireworks," I began, "both part of fire direction control. One PFC Joe Gracelli, and PFC Elijah Mitchell. Elijah Mitchell, say hi."

"Hello y'all, y'all!"

"Hey Mitchell," said Gracelli, "get a football. There's plenty of daylight."

"Shee-it," Mitchell drawled, "give me a flashlight and I'll go find you a hole!"

"Before we could find Mitchell any place," I recorded, "he was crawling on the ground in a hole about three feet deep. It looked like he was a part of the undergrowth."

"I bet you look like you belonged in a gopher hole!" Mike added.

I looked up at the flare ship. The words from the tune "Spooky" by the Classics IV went through my mind. I always got a good feeling when I heard it.

"This is just like being at a football game," said Mike.

"Yeah, it reminds me of a lighted football field," I said. "Just like in high school when we played at nights. Cool like this, too."

KABOOM! Another set of artillery shells exploded in the tree line. The echo reverberated in our ears.

"Oh, oh!" exclaimed Mike softly.

Suddenly, the perimeter exploded in a flash of light.

"There they go," I said, recording again, "rocket fire is now coming out of the gunships. They are making another pass at the enemy locations. We are now unable to see the rounds impacting because of the quantity of smoke. The gunships are now firing their mike 79s. We seem to have pinned down Charlie and closed off his escape route. We're bringing one hell of a lot of pee on top of his location. There goes a stream of M-60 rounds from the gunships. The air above us is filled with long red banners of tracer rounds."

Whup! Whup! Whup! Whup! The chopper blades slapped the air above our heads. It was so dark that the chopper was hidden. Only the long burst of tracer rounds revealed its position.

Suddenly I heard the deadly clatter of an AK-47. I saw a single tracer round speed from the ground toward the hovering gunship.

"Those sound like AK rounds!" exclaimed Mitchell.

"The AK is shooting back at him," Gracelli added, astonished.

"Is 'at right," Mitchell replied, skeptically, moving to his knees and peering over the sandbag.

"Hell yeah!" said Gracelli.

"Real?" asked Mitchell again.

"Hell yeah, can't you hear him?" Gracelli replied, searching for his flashlight. "It goes klack-klack-klack-klack!"

"Oh man, numbah ten!" said Mitchell, apprehension creeping into his voice. "C'mon girls, c'mon girls," he chanted at the helicopters.

"They seem to be farther away than the ones I heard a bit back," I added.

Grenades began exploding on the perimeter again.

"Charlie was right in our back yard for awhile," I said.

"I thought he was knocking on the back door, man," said Mike.

"Shit, if I woulda known we were that close to Charlie I woulda been deedee-mowing boy, if I woulda knew what direction Charlie was coming from," exclaimed Mitchell.

"One of those PGs went off right over there, man!" shouted Gracelli.

"One of them landed about ten feet in front of Gun Three's parapet!" Mike added.

"Joe's gonna tell me one of them hit right there!" kidded Mitchell, pointing at his feet.

"One of 'em landed right out here in front, man!" Mike added seriously, but Mitchell kept right on talking. "Olsen," he said, pointing to a spot about thirty feet to our left, "when one of 'em hit right there, I went under the trailer, and by that time we had been under attack nearly fifteen minutes."

Rockets began exploding again on the perimeter and I resumed recording. "The gunship is now making another pass firing its M-60s and rockets."

Dangerfield and Vanous lifted the flap covering the bunker and crawled out.

"It seems as though nobody is running the fire direction control center," I recorded, "since everyone is out watching the sights."

"Olsen, is that your rifle next to the wall?" asked Gracelli.

"No, man," I said angrily, "the stock's busted on mine. They sent it back out and didn't fix it, so it doesn't work! I just grabbed the first one I could find."

"That's all right," said Gracelli. "I just wanted to know where mine was."

"Damn," I said in disgust, "they didn't even fix the son-of-a-bitch; they just sent it back out."

"Where your bullets?" said Mike.

Tapping the slings that covered my chest, I answered, "I got about thirty magazines. I think they're all ED's."

"Look at that shit, man!" exclaimed Gracelli, pointing to another stream of tracer rounds. The sound of gunfire followed.

"The gunships are now making a pass directly overhead," I recorded. "You can hear the deadly stream of mike 60 fire."

The tarp swung up again, and Dangerfield crawled back out, camera in hand. He began snapping photos of the gunship as it fired. I turned my recorder back on.

"Dangerfield, our photographer, is out taking pictures of the action. He wants to catch this on film as much as I want to on tape."

"Boy, I betcha ol' Charlie's just a-diggin' his ass off out there trying to get out from under that pee," said Gracelli.

"I'd dig too, man, if they were firing back this fucking way," I added.

"You ain't bull-shittin'!" Gracelli responded.

"Amen!" Mike added.

Another burst of machine gun fire exploded over our head.

"God-dang, boy, that's some fast fuckin' shootin'," said Mike.

"They must have Charlie pretty well pinpointed outside the wire," I said.

"Give me a light, Olsen," said Mitchell.

"Boy, I think I'd rather have those two gunships firing for me than anything else," Mike said.

"I have some mosquito lotion if you want to put some on," I said to Mitchell, noticing him swatting at a mosquito.

"I think I'd rather have gunships than artillery." Mike went on.

"You'd what, boy!" exclaimed Mitchell.

"Rather have gunships than artillery!"

"Hell, bring in the airstrikes," said Gracelli.

"They've got air strikes on call for this location," I said. "They're expecting us to get hit pretty hard here."

That seemed to sober everyone up. For a while, it became quiet. I took the opportunity to record some more.

"The action has cooled down quite a bit here since approximately one five to two zero minutes ago when all hell broke loose. The AK four-seven rounds were too close for comfort, and the numerous RPG-2s and 7s we received were so close they sounded like mortars. Some landed approximately ten feet in front of our bunk. . . ."

A burst of machine gun fire erupted from the infantry bunker directly in front.

"AK-47 fire," I shouted, as much in surprise as in warning.

"Here we go!" shouted Gracelli, diving for cover.

"Is that Mike 60?" I asked, looking at White for confirmation. "Shit, they must have Charlie spotted out there again."

"Look at the gunship, man!" warned Gracelli. Both gunships nosedived over our heads, hurling M-79 rounds and rockets into the woodline in front of us.

"Whew!" whistled Mike.

"Now one of the infantry patrols is opening up on Charlie," I said, clutching the microphone close to my face. "The VC must be out there trying to move out of their location. The infantry seems to have spotted them."

The gunships emptied their remaining stock of ammunition and left. Their slow retreat sounded like distant freeway traffic. Spooky began dropping a line of flares that quickly lit up the entire area. I flattened myself even closer to the earth. With the base lit up like daylight, I didn't want to be an easy target for any sniper who might have gained access to our perimeter. "The gunships have left our location at this time," I recorded. "They are probably refueling or getting more ammunition. The infantry is now firing M-79s into the woodline, along with machine gun fire and M-16s."

No sooner had I spoken than another gunship arrived. He circled the area, flying low, picking up on the infantry's location. He began laying down fire in the same location where the infantry had spotted movement. Another cloud of dust and smoke rose again from the woodline as heated gunfire shredded the earth. I wondered how anyone could possibly survive. Human flesh seemed much more frail than earth and trees, and I could see those things being vaporized.

"I hope we didn't get no damn flats," said Mike. "I don't wanna fix no fuckin' flats tomorrow." The last attack had blown out two of the tires on the three-quarter.

"They must have a Starlight Scope out at that bunker," I said.

"I didn't think anyone in Vietnam used a Starlight Scope," kidded Mitchell.

The miniguns from the gunship leaped into life again. "The gunships must have VC activity at the southern end of our perimeter," I recorded. "He is bringing fire into that location at this time."

"There he goes again," said Mike, pointing. This time the firing echoed even louder as the gunship passed directly overhead.

"Gimme a light, Mike!" said Mitchell, sticking another cigarette in his mouth.

"Keep that cigarette down, man," warned Mike.

"C'mon Mike," Mitchell repeated, and then added, "I'm hungry, man!"

I laughed.

The gunship flew over our heads again, this time firing into the barbed wire.

"That mother fucker's shooting entirely too close!" exclaimed Mitchell. "What's he doing?"

Gunfire rocked the area. Gracelli let out a whistle of amazement.

"I don't go for that shit at all," Mitchell said.

"The infantry's right over there, man," Mike said, "on the other side of the road."

"I don't give a fuck about the infantry," exclaimed Mitchell, "I'm talkin' about me!"

"Hey, they ain't firing at you!"

"I don't give a fuck! There's always the possibility of a short round!"

"A short round?"

"Boy, I betcha this scares the shit outta Charlie!" Mitchell said. "Charlie don't know what that is, those two lights running around up there."

I thought about it. Maybe he was right, but I doubted it. I was sure that by now there weren't any Vietnamese, regardless of how backwards, who hadn't seen a gunship.

I wasn't paying much attention to what was going on inside the FDC, but I caught the words "fire mission" being repeated over the radio, and I knew that meant the infantry had spotted movement again.

"They must have positive identification out there," I recorded. "They're getting up a fire mission inside." I felt around. "Has anyone moved my rifle?"

"Olsen," teased Mitchell, "you and Mike are gonna be sent out there."

"Has anyone seen my lighter?" I asked, ignoring Mitchell.

"Fire!" Mitchell said, repeating the command he had heard inside.

"Hey, Mitchell," asked Mike, "remember the night we fired for that new forward observer?"

"That fool!" Mitchell giggled. "He was talking about having fuckin' marking rounds!"

"Yeah."

"Marking rounds!" Mitchell squealed, mocking the FO that had called. "Yeah, every time he got lost . . . 'Gimme a marking over here!'"

Gracelli laughed.

The bunkers on the west side of our perimeter had opened fire. "Where in the fuck is Charlie hiding now?" Mitchell said.

"C'mon you son-of-a-bitch!" said Gracelli, shaking his fist in the air.

"Soon Charlie is gonna be all around this mutha-fucker," Mitchell added.

"C'mon man, be cool," said White, "maybe those mother fuckers took off by now."

"Hey Mitchell," said Gracelli, "where did they last spot Charlie?"

"Way on the outside, I guess, about sixty-five meters from us."

I heard someone inside giving the command to fire again. White got up.

"Hey Les, will you run and get me an orange, man, a couple of oranges? Get me a couple of oranges and you can suck on a lemon."

"Bring me one too," said Mitchell.

"Me too," said Mike.

"Mike said cancel his," Mitchell teased.

White's citizen band radio suddenly came to life. "Check fire," echoed a transmission.

I looked down. It was Dangerfield's voice. The radio had suddenly picked up part of the transmission from the PRC 25s inside. Shit, I thought, if this radio can monitor transmissions by accident, suppose that Charlie is out there with even more sophisticated equipment. He could be listening to everything that was going down.

"Everything seems to be pretty quiet at this time," I recorded. "I think we're gonna take a chow break."

"Hey, an' we'll come back in a minute!" Mitchell said, laughing, bending to the microphone.

"I don't think anything more will happen tonight," I went on, "unless we get into more contact. If anything should happen, I'm sure the artillery at this location will be able to handle it."

"I don't know!" Mitchell put in.

"Especially with this fire direction control," I added jokingly.

A little while later my tape recorder was running again, recording a steady stream of machine gun fire.

"The gunships are now back on location," I began, "firing at the southern end of our perimeter."

"Hey, tell them I'm back on station, too!" added Gracelli.

"O.K., Joe's back on station, too."

"Hey, man," Mitchell said to Joe, "turn your radio on."

"It's broke."

"Disregard," Mitchell said.

"The FDC is now working up another fire mission," I continued. "Artillery will probably be firing in about zero five."

My conversation broke as the gunship passed overhead. I stuck my microphone up in the air to get a clear recording.

"Hey Joe, who broke it?" asked Mitchell.

"I don't know."

"Who broke it, White?" demanded Mitchell. "Who broke the aerial?"

"No one!"

"Aw, man, Joe said it was broke! Boy, Joe, you're about a lying long ol' mother fucker!" He suddenly began brushing at his fatigues. "These big red ants are about to pull my ass away!" He brushed some more. "I got to write home and tell my sister we got hit tonight."

"Me too," said Mike. "That's the only time I have anything to say is when we get hit."

When Dangerfield's voice came over the radio again, I stuck my microphone next to it. "That's right. Roger. It'll be about zero three. Over."

"Ohhh, that's Dangerfield," said Mitchell, surprised as I was when I first heard it.

White and Gracelli looked over at me.

"Dangerfield!" I said, pointing down at the radio.

"We now have a radio sitting in front of our location," I said into the microphone. "Picking up on the FM radio, we can hear one of our pushes from inside the Fox-Delta-Charlie. They are now working up a mission so we might be able to pick up part of the transmission." Sure enough, we heard Dangerfield: "You're coming in very weak. Can you say again, over."

We sat quietly, listening, trying to pick up on the fire mission as helicopters droned over our location. There had not been any firing for nearly two minutes.

"Bengal Four Niner, I copy. You want one marking round from cigarette one, five, right six-two-five. Over?" came another transmission.

When I heard one of the guns fire, I knew a marking round was on the way. We watched as a white phosphorous round exploded in the air, illuminating the area below it.

"How the hell did that son-of-a-bitch get way over there?" Mitchell asked.

"He's not over there," I said, "no one but a dummy fires a marking round directly over his position. It would give him away. He's just fired it near enough so he can get his bearings and see if he's really where he thinks he is on his map."

"Say, you're gonna get busted in the head, Joe, if you don't get your head down," warned Mitchell as Gracelli stood up to get a better look.

Sitting back down, Gracelli continued his conversation with White. I could just get in on the tail end of it. "Yeah," he was saying angrily. "Four-five called us over the same push when we were in the middle of a fire mission, breaking into the infantry's transmission. I just said, 'Four-five, we have a fire mission on this push out!'"

"Yeah! Then he said, 'This is four-five; I know it!'" added Mike.

Those bastards in command always seemed to think this was some kind of game we were playing. They knew it was not only against regulation to break into a transmission, it also imperiled the lives of those in the middle of a fire fight where seconds could mean the difference between life and death. Four-five thought it didn't mean shit. Officers did as they pleased.

A burst of .50 caliber machine gun fire brought me back to the situation at hand. "Jesus Christ," I whispered, sliding down on my back. I knew that fire was coming from a bunker less than ten yards to our right. Grenades suddenly erupted around the bunker.

"Where the fuck . . . ?" I groped in the dark. "Hand me that helmet," I said to Mitchell, pointing to the one that lay at his feet.

"Hey Joe, throw me my rifle right there!" shouted Mitchell.

"Hand me my M-16," said Mike, "those mother fuckers are probably coming through!"

The .50 caliber opened up again, spraying the concertina wire that looped the perimeter. Four or five bursts of M-16 fire quickly followed.

"They ain't shootin' this-a-way!" Mike noted.

"How's that!" said Mitchell, crawling on his elbow. "They might start this way. If they do I'm gonna open up; I don't give a fuck who's in the way!"

"Shit! Take it easy, Mitchell," I whispered. I turned back to the tape: "The infantry element in the bunker right next to our location has spotted something out in the perimeter. They've opened up with M-79s and machine gun fire. The gunship is now proceeding to fire."

"79s . . . kill 'em . . . kill 'em!" shouted Gracelli.

An artillery round exploded in the treetops. Pieces of shrapnel whizzed over our heads.

"We're getting shrapnel back in here somewhere!" I whispered into the mike.

"Kill 'em . . . kill 'em . . . ," Joe continued to chant.

I kept my head close to the ground. "We now have M-60 fire, artillery fire and gunships going into the area of concentration."

Another explosion shook the woodline. "That ain't no out going right there, Olsen," Mitchell said.

306

"The infantry's just firing their 81 Mike-Mikes," I explained.

"Joe," Mitchell said, "gimme my helmet ... hey gimme my ah ... ah...."

"I don't know where your stuff is at! Where am I supposed to find your helmet?"

"I didn't say no helmet, man, my rifle's right over there!"

"Jesus Christ, that fucking artillery ... we're gonna get shrapnel back with that shit," I said.

The Viet Cong had to be out there. Otherwise they wouldn't be firing the artillery in so close. Rounds were exploding in the treetops less than 150 yards away. Nobody would have O.K.'d clearance for this kind of fire unless we really needed it.

My thoughts were confirmed as Dangerfield crawled out of the bunker.

"Hey you guys, the infantry is requesting all available personnel to the perimeter," he whispered urgently. "Charlie is coming on back in!" Shit, I thought, we were in for it now.

I dropped my microphone on the ground, not bothering to turn the recorder off. What the hell, I figured, it would shut off by itself. If the fighting got worse and I didn't make it back, well, it would just record the end.

Pulling on my flak jacket, I checked to make sure everyone was ready. As soon as we were set, I crouched and ran for the nearest berm. One by one, we slid over the top of the first berm and crawled across the rice paddy. We were now ten feet short of the grunts' bunker line. I rolled over on my back to check that everyone was there. Pressing my head tight against the earthen berm, I wondered what would happen now.

"Are we gonna go out any further?" whispered Mike.

"Fuck no, not me man!" answered Mitchell.

"Me neither," replied Gracelli.

"What do you say, White?" I said, smiling.

"What the fuck," he answered, "I'm game if you are."

I couldn't see his face in the dark, but I could tell he was grinning by the sound of his voice.

Well, what the hell, I thought. If we have to go down, it may as well be side by side. Those grunts were my brothers. It just wouldn't be right to hang back, even a little. If my time was up, I couldn't delay it, even if I wanted to.

"All right," I whispered, "I'm going over. You follow behind!"

I slid my M-16 over the berm and hugged the top as I crawled over. White soon followed. We crawled on our elbows, dragging ourselves to the bunker line. I turned slowly over on my back, breathing hard. White slid up next to me. For an instant our hands touched, and we let them linger.

I wasn't surprised when White nudged my arm and pointed back at the berm. The other guys were coming over!

That's all right, I said to myself. I drew a deep breath and turned over on my side.

21

6 November 1968
FSB Keene III
Xom Giong Dau

"We have been mortared twice since my last entry." I wrote in my diary. "We lost five men in the last attack two days ago. Enemy activity is on the increase everywhere. Like us, the 1st Brigade is now experiencing daily contact with enemy forces. The same with the 3rd. B-52 sorties are being flown daily, along with accompanying Air Force fighter bombings. The umbrella of cover fire we are providing has doubled. We are now providing support for the 2nd Battalion 12th US Infantry Division; the 4th Battalion 9th US Infantry; the 2nd Battalion 34th Armor; 2nd Battalion 27th US Infantry; 1st Battalion 5th Mech; 2nd Battalion 14th US Infantry; and the 2nd Battalion 22nd US Infantry. We are having to relay all their findings to Battalion Headquarters and what I am discovering isn't encouraging. It is a daily stream of gruesome tragedy; bodies dug up or found stuffed in tunnels; or counting the pieces after bombing missions. There is also the steady trickle of American dead and wounded. There is a growing arms count, but also the rising cost of tanks, APCs and helicopters. Rarely do the statistics balance out, one gun found for one life lost. Not much of an exchange. We seem to be firing incessantly, yet enemy losses cannot always be determined.

"What seems particularly ominous are the reports from the 25th Aviation Battalion helicopters which fly on border patrol near Cambodia. They are spotting increased Victor Charlie infiltrating into the 2nd Brigade area. Sampan activity on the canals has increased 100 percent."

I put my pencil down. As more Americans continued to die, I saw a rise in the frustration, anger, and hate the soldiers felt toward the Vietnamese. Also toward the brass! I had heard some pretty unnerving reports about how that frustration was being worked off in the bush. It was easy to understand, men flying off the handle and killing in rage. Burning and destroying everything in sight! Still, understanding didn't deaden my conscience. I was grateful that for the

308

next two days I would be back in the rear. I needed my teeth examined as a part of the Army's processing of my upcoming DEROS.

Standing in front of headquarters, I waited for orders with the rest of the men. There were only nine here today. Four of us were going to the field for sure, three other newbies and myself. We all had duffel bags packed, lying next to our feet.

I had filled a couple of bags with grass to resupply my stash in the field. That left nearly twelve pounds stashed in my locker.

I listened as the top went over the roster for the day, assigning duties and relaying the resupply schedule so we would know when we had to leave. I thought back to when I had first come in country and how I had despised latrine duty. Burning shit! If only I could do that now! What a small price to pay for a secure position in the rear.

"Johnson ... Mansfield ... Hill," Top grunted, "be right here at zero-nine-two-five hours. You'll catch the jeep to the chopper pad. Olsen! See me after we fall out."

What was going on? How come I wasn't on the list? I knew they were expecting me in the field. I was puzzled but it didn't override the sense of relief I felt. Still, having to go see the top left me guarded.

Shortly after the top finished, I made my way over to headquarters. I made an effort not to let my apprehension show. Who knew what was coming down.

Pirren was sitting at the reception desk and looked up when the door slammed behind me.

"Hey, what's happening?" I said. "I'm supposed to see the top. Is he ready to see me?"

"Yeah, I think he said you should go right in."

I wanted to ask him what the top wanted, to prepare myself, but Top's door was open. Pirren's face betrayed nothing except a small smirk I thought I saw on his lips.

"Olsen?" I heard the top snap. "Is that you?"

"Yes, sergeant."

"Then get your ass in here so I can take care of business!"

I deliberately walked slowly to the front of his desk. I wasn't going to let the bastard bully me around.

"Olsen," he snapped, "I'm giving you a break! I'm assigning you to guard the mess hall at the old battery location. Some of the other companies have been stealing the mess equipment we've got stored there. We've got to put someone on guard duty, so it may as well be you. Now there ain't going to be no one over there but you, but I'm sure you won't mind. Or would you rather go back to the field?" he added with a sneer.

I didn't say anything. I wanted to tell him to go fuck himself, but I was beginning to grasp what he had just said. I wasn't going to jeopardize what I had heard.

"Well ... what the fuck are you waiting for? Throw your gear into the back of the jeep. Pirren will take you over to pick up the rest of your stuff on the way to the area."

"Roger, sergeant."

I was elated. I nearly floated across the room. It was over! The war was over for me right now! I just couldn't believe it! I would be guarding the area until I DEROSed. Could this actually be happening? It was too good to be true.

I actually skipped over to my duffel bag and tossed it into the back of the jeep. I laid my rifle on the front seat, slipped my flak jacket off and threw it in the back. My heart was pounding. I couldn't keep from smiling. As I jumped into the front I looked sheepishly around to see if anyone had been watching. I looked back at headquarters, anxiously awaiting Pirren as if this reprieve would be cancelled if I waited around too long.

Finally, Pirren swung into the seat beside me, his clean, starched, freshly pressed fatigues in sharp contrast to my own.

"Man, I just can't believe this is happening!" I said. "It's hard to believe that the sergeant suddenly had a change of heart about me."

"Well, that's because he hasn't. I hate to burst your little bubble, but the top didn't pick you for this luxury job because he wanted to do you a favor. They created this position especially for you because they wanted to keep you out of the field."

"What do you mean? And who are 'they'?"

"They are Top and the brass. I was there when the order came in from the field. I handled it personally. The brass thinks you're having too much influence on the men and they wanted you out of the way. Apparently they think your insubordination and constant talk of peace has been subverting the morale of the men."

Shit! This I could not believe. I knew that I had earned the loyalty of my men, but I wasn't a fucking subversive! What the fuck were they thinking, that I was some kind of communist? Damn! But the more I thought about it, the more I understood where they were coming from. My anger soon passed and I began to feel a mixture of power and elation. It was the sweet sense of victory.

I had won! I had beaten the system. The Goliath that had threatened me and kept me bound in servitude had finally fallen. I felt a deep stirring as I rode silently to the area. It was a quiet, delicious, contained gratitude and an overwhelming sense of relief.

What quirk of fate or act of God had spared me the final ordeal I didn't know. It seemed insignificant now.

22

Padding across the bare concrete floor in my thongs, I made my way to the north side of the Mess Hall, clutching my M-16. I leaned it against the clapboard sliding that rose chest high around the building and rested my elbows on the ledge that separated the wall from the adjoining screened-in windows. It was bothersome to keep my helmet on so I hung it on the barrel of my rifle, within easy grasp. I didn't want to be caught out of uniform if some brass decided to come around for a surprise inspection. As it was, I would have to run for my boots and slip on my shirt if anyone came around. It was silly having to be in full uniform when on duty, but that was the way it was in the rear, and I was supposed to be on duty twenty-four hours a day. Those were the top's orders. Pirren had made it clear that I was to receive no visitors, allow no unauthorized personnel into the area and remain confined to the mess hall at all times. The only exception they made was to take a shower or go to the bathroom, but the showers didn't work. It was really solitary confinement for the remainder of my tour.

I stared out the screened-in window, watching a small group of Vietnamese peasants filling sandbags. They were all dressed alike in black pajamas, knees bent, sitting on their haunches, their butts inches from the ground. I had taken to sitting that way also.

I looked back at the neatly arranged furnishings which formed my new home. My cot, jungle blanket, footlocker and ammo can, all neatly tucked into the back corner wall which once separated the enlisted men's eating area from that of the officers'. I had set my cot against the south wall, the outside of which had been covered with sandbags, because it was the safest place I could find. I looked up at the tin roof wishing that it too was covered with sandbags. There was little protection if it was hit by a rocket.

Even here I could hear the sound of bombing most of the day, and I was frequently awakened by explosions from incoming rockets and outgoing artillery.

Flares and sirens illuminated the base camp after each attack. I always scanned the perimeter for any signs of a ground assault. At first I had run to the bunker line during the rocket attacks, seeking adequate shelter and scouting the perimeter, but now I did nothing. I was fairly sure I was in no immediate danger unless the rockets began landing in my area. In comparison to the field the days were quiet and unbothered.

I swung my attention to the Vietnamese work detail again. I counted them: fifteen, in two separate bunches. Picking up my M-16 and putting on my helmet, I walked over to the screen door, pushed it open, and stepped outside. I sat down against the wall, hugging the shade. I cradled my weapon across my lap and continued to study the peasants, looking for pretty girls. If there were any, the American soldier who supervised the crew would surely have them around his position. He was sitting a short distance away, talking with one of the baby-sans. It was too bad fraternization with them was against regulations. I wondered how close their supervisor stuck to his orders?

One of the older papa-sans stood up. His figure swayed slightly as if he might pass out. Waves of heat shimmered off the sand and he looked strangely like a shadowy silhouette swaying in the air. I envisioned him suspended from a rope like the dummie the Army had used in Basic for bayonet practice. I could hear myself running through the obstacle course screaming "kill . . . kill . . . kill!" With each yell I shoved a bayonet deep into the lifeless chest. "Louder!" my drill sergeant screamed, making me repeat the process again and again. "Louder! I want to hear you when you yell!"

Why hadn't I been bold enough to file for conscientious objector status then? Of course I knew why. There was one guy who did, and the way he had been treated by the DIs seemed worse than death itself! Of course at that time I had no real idea of what death was anyway. If only I had understood then what I did now!

The explosion rocked the mess hall! I instinctively rolled off my cot and pressed my face to the cold, hard concrete. Frozen in position, I listened frantically for the sound again. I could hear nothing. I shut out all other thoughts and strained again, listening. I searched my memory, trying to identify the explosion; it must have been a rocket.

I pulled my helmet on and slid my M-16 down from the wall, holding it close to my body. I wondered how they were getting along without me in the field.

Meditation and inactivity slowly replaced my once rigorous schedule, yet I was rarely bored. I worked on the exercises I had started nearly two months ago in the field, and I stayed stoned most of the time. Even though my quarters had been intended to be a kind of jail cell, they remained, for me, a refuge.

Occasionally Pirren dropped by, fulfilling his duties by inspecting my dress and making sure I was where I was supposed to be. Sometimes we talked, but not often. He generally warned me, though, when some major or captain was supposed to come around and inspect the area. Then I dutifully put on my boots, bloused my pants and dressed out in full uniform to await their arrival; otherwise, I rarely paid attention.

One day Pirren informed me that I had been recommended for a Bronze Star. He said he had typed up the orders himself, but I didn't believe him. It seemed rather inconsistent with the views that had led to this solitary confinement.

Occasionally Threet and Falcone came over to visit, even though it was prohibited. John was now in the middle of his court-martial trial and had acquired an attorney to represent him. Even so, it looked pretty bleak. He was trying not to let it get him down but I could always sense the bitterness he felt at being singled out. Seeds of bitterness were sprouting everywhere in Vietnam. Unrest was still on the rise and I wondered what it would be like after I left.

When Threet and Falcone visited they generally brought along a few cold beers and we would rap for hours, often late into the night. One night we even slipped out of the battery area to an adjoining infantry position to watch the movies that were being shown in a makeshift theatre. But mostly, the three of us talked about the war, brotherhood and peace. We had all come to the conclusion that if this war was between North and South Vietnam, it was much like our own Civil War, and we didn't need to be here. I didn't know why Vietnam was fighting a civil war—maybe it was to keep their country together, just like ours—but we had fought ours without outside interference and I had concluded that they should be allowed to fight theirs the same way.

Other than their occasional visits, or the late night visitations of a few rats, I was left entirely alone.

Slipping on my thongs, I walked out to the edge of the bunker line. The land stretching before me was flat and barren, lined with concertina wire crisscrossed with mines and trip flares and studded with claymores. Charlie would have a heck of a time getting in here if he ever tried. I wondered if my men in the field could feel as secure. I didn't like thinking about the guys but it was hard for me not to. I felt guilty as hell about not being out with them. I wondered if I would ever shake the feeling or if it would haunt me upon my return to the States.

Studying the distant woodline, I drew in deeply on a joint. Ten more days and it would all be behind me. The responsibility for the defense of the battery would be in someone else's hands. Someone else would be doing the computing and firing the guns. And someone else would have to bear the loss.

I heaved a sigh. I knew I was finally free but somehow it didn't make me feel any better. I was feeling extremely tired and I couldn't shake it, despite all the sleep I was getting. I wondered if this was what it felt like to be old and used up.

I wondered how many times had I sat like this, waiting and watching. Watching the sun slowly set, waiting for the sound of incoming mortars. Watching for the slightest hint of enemy movement, waiting for the attack that often as not didn't come.

Charlie's straw hat and black pajamas crossed the hairlines of my imagination

313

but I quickly shut them out. I didn't want to have to think about killing any more. The day I had visualized that peasant swinging in the air I had realized the enormity of what I had become: a trained killer. A person trained to look at people and see only faceless targets. How could I so lightly take the life I so desperately hoped no one would take from me? How easily I sometimes vacillated distressed me. I was glad I was no longer a part of the war.

I swung my feet out over the face of the bunker. It was odd! I had grown up with the constant reminder that killing was as commonplace as the common cold and no aspect of the media had ever made me think otherwise. There were rarely any alternatives presented. Even the Bible, what little I knew about it, was a grim chronicle of human behavior. Israelites killed Canaanites, Romans killed Jews. Even God seemed to condone killing and yet I remembered clearly that one of the Ten Commandments said "Thou shalt not kill"! It was confusing! I tried to remember if I had ever read any books or seen any movies or heard anyone talk about alternatives to violence. There were none. Jesus had made reference to turning the other cheek but that was all I could remember. I wondered if there was something in Jesus' teachings that I was missing. And what did Buddhism have to say about it?

This was unfamiliar ground. Fighting had been second nature to me. Violence was a way of life and it certainly wasn't just the military who believed it. The American people seemed as hell-bent on violence as the government. All, that is, but a handful of protestors. But I doubted that they would make any difference.

It was still hard for me to believe that as an American, I had turned out to be the bad guy . . . the one that seemed to be supporting a corrupt and apathetic regime rather than freeing people from one. I still didn't want to believe it was true. I tried to convince myself that what I had done was right, but I knew in my heart it wasn't so. I was just trying to shake the shadow of guilt that followed me around. I wondered again what my friends would think of me when I got back home.

Still, I was glad for the small stand I had taken. I had felt better about myself since coming to grips with some of the conflict I felt. Some of the decisions I had made would, I hoped, help me to salvage my soul.

My trust in the government and the American press had been completely shattered, but perhaps it was for the best! I wasn't sure.

I leapt down from the bunker, turned the cuffs in my fatigues down, and began my walk back to the mess hall. Shit, I thought, who cares about the war now anyway. I'm gonna forget it all as soon as I get back home. When I leave I'm gonna put it all behind me and I'm not looking back. I wanted to forget even now that some of my best friends were still out in the field.

I let the screen door slam shut behind me. I turned on the stereo that John and Frank had lent me and looked through their albums. Choosing a record out of a double set by Donovan, I put it on and slipped on a pair of headphones so as not to miss a word.

Donovan's gentle music had a kind of lightness and gaiety that reflected an innocence I wished were my own. His lyrics were richly spiced with a message of kindness and peace. They reflected a philosophy that I thought mirored my own.

I picked up the album cover and looked it over. Pink! It was mostly pink—the color for girls and sissies. How biased and narrow were the traditions of men. How blind I had been to have seen life from only an American perspective. How much of my life had been prejudiced and biased by the narrowness of my own culture. Being in the Army had opened my eyes to the rich diversity of culture in America; black, hispanic, southern, eastern. Each exposure had taken some adjustment, but as I had opened myself I had become richer for it. But it meant dropping some preconceived ideas of what was right, of what was normal.

Pink for girls, blue for boys! It didn't seem to make much sense. How limited we were in our imagination. I saw how by channeling each other in specific roles, humans close themselves off from a fuller life. Hadn't my limited view of manhood done that to me? Men were "supposed" to be aggressive, which I had equated with courage. If only men knew what true courage was! A gentle response in the face of violence took much more courage and discipline than simply lashing back. Laying down your life in preference to another's showed absolute freedom from the fear of death. Hadn't it been that fear that motivated me to strike back so heartily at the approaching "enemy"? At least Donovan had the courage to tear off the labels that paraded as symbols of manhood. He, in his own way, was freeing my mind. One thing for sure, I was sick of the garb of manhood that clothed itself in violence. I was more than ready to shake that image and to bury it with my past. When I got back home I would divest myself of anything that was even remotely connected to the military. If I didn't embrace a life of brotherhood and peace, how could I expect anyone else to? And if the world didn't find a way to live in peace, surely the end was in sight for the human race.

Lying down, I clasped my hands behind my head and started to do another round of sit-ups. No matter now anyway, I thought, trying to burn up my anger in a frenzy of exercise. I'm going home and that's all that matters. I've got to put Vietnam completely out of my mind. The less I say about it to anyone, the better off I'll be. Besides, nobody, no matter what I said, could really understand.

The squeal of tires caught my attention. I looked up out the window and saw a jeep. I immediately turned off the record player and slid off my cot. Sticking my bare feet into my boots, I turned my cuffs under and snapped on my blousing bands. I pulled my laces tight and stuck them into the top of my boots. Helmet on, M-16 shouldered, I headed for the door.

When I stepped outside, I saw only Pirren in the jeep. I quietly breathed a sigh of relief.

"Hey Olsen," Pirren yelled as he leapt from the jeep. "Get your equipment together! You got a drop in your DEROS! You're going home today!"

Epilogue

"In December the worn M101A1 howitzers of the battalion began to be replaced by the new M102. Battery A was first to be outfitted with the lightweight, longer range weapon capable of easy traverse to a full 6400 mils.

"This history has mentioned only the major engagements and operations. It does not mention the fact that almost daily some element of the battalion suffered attack by mortars or small arms, or encountered booby traps and mines. It does not list those howitzer sections sent on Fireball missions in which they stood their ground with small infantry units and augmented the defense of their perimeter with direct-fire Killer Junior and Beehive. The history does not show that for every time the artillery was called upon to suppress sniper fire, soften a landing zone, or engage a target of opportunity, artillerymen willingly stood exposed beside their guns in shallow parapets.

"But the history does show that the Automatic Eighth worked hard during 1968. It fired 289,687 rounds and was credited with 884 enemy dead by actual body count. Eighteen of its members were recommended for the Silver Star.

"On 31 December the battalion was still engaged in Operation Toan Thang II. Headquarters was located at Cu Chi, Battery A at FSB Reed II, Battery B at FSB Pershing, and Battery C at FSB Keene III."

From the Operational Report of the 25th Infantry Division for the Period Ending 31 January 1969, RCS ACSFOR-65 (R-1).

Military History of Howard Olsen

I volunteered for the draft and was inducted 3 May 1967 in Portland, Oregon. I attended Basic Training in Fort Lewis, Washington, graduating at the top of my class, and was promoted to E-2 at the end of my training. In Basic I qualified as an expert rifleman (M-14) and a sharpshooter (M-16) as well as qualifying on a pistol, M-60 and .50 caliber machine gun.

I was sent to the Leadership Preparation Academy for further training as a non-commissioned officer in Fort Sill, Oklahoma, where I graduated at the top of my class. While at Fort Sill I also received Advanced Infantry Training as an artilleryman, a gun operator for a 105mm howitzer. On 1 November 1967 I was promoted to Private First Class.

Attached to the 3rd Brigade 25th Infantry Division, in Vietnam, I was assigned to Charlie Battery, 1st Battalion 8th Field Artillery forces as an Operations and Intelligence Specialist. There, I served as Section Chief for the Fire Direction Control Center for a 105mm howitzer battery.

While in Vietnam, as part of a direct combat support unit, I participated in the following operations: Barking Sands, Atlanta, Camden, Saratoga, Quyet Thang, Toan Thang I & II, the Tet Offensive and Counter Offensives Phase II, III, IV, V and VI.

I was promoted to Specialist Fifth Class on 1 August 1968 and during my tour was awarded the Bronze Star, the Vietnamese Cross for Gallantry, the Vietnam Service Medal with a Silver Star, the Vietnam Campaign Medal, a Valorous Unit Award and two Meritorious Unit Commendations. After a short extension in Vietnam I completed my tour of duty on 7 December 1968 and was honorably discharged and separated from active duty the following day in Oakland, California.

Index

319

320

Phuoc Vinh 213
psychological operations (PSYOPS) 25, 26, 27
Purple Peanut 282

Quonset 8, 9, 32, 99

Rach Tra Canal 186
radio-telephone operator (RTO) 40, 88
reconnaissance-in-force (RIF) 37
rest and recuperation (R&R) 19, 106, 167, 277, 278
Roadrunners 11, 38, 97
Rome Plow 86, 107, 108, 138

S-2 82
Saigon 17, 26, 96, 126, 127, 130, 132, 164, 185, 189, 252
Saigon River 38, 41, 59, 86, 107, 138, 186, 201
search and destroy (S&D) 23, 37, 97
Second Battalion Fourteenth Infantry 80, 98, 159, 228, 241, 293, 308; A Company 295; B Company 296; D Company 295
Second Battalion Thirty-fourth Armor 87, 208
Second Battalion Twelfth Infantry 36, 153, 308
Second Battalion Twenty-second Infantry 59, 308
Second Battalion Twenty-seventh Infantry 56, 60, 75, 87, 98, 107, 109, 126, 131, 308; A Company 41, 73, 75; B Company 41, 64, 71, 75; C Company 41, 71, 75, 117, 234; D Company 41, 45, 46
Second Battalion Twenty-third Armor 82
Seventh Battalion Eleventh Artillery 80
Sixth Battalion Seventy-seventh Artillery 127
Sixty-fifth Engineers 80
South Vietnamese Army (ARVN) 15, 18, 25, 26, 36, 80, 86, 109, 118, 120, 127, 147, 154; 549th ARVN 78; Rangers 62, 118, 157; 2nd Battalion 7th ARVN Regiment 26, 48; 34th ARVN 81
Spooky 271
-stand tờ 59
starlight scope 90
Stars and Stripes 97, 124, 153
Suoio Ba Ca River 86

Tan Hoa 108, 133
Tan Son Nhut 7, 11, 36, 127, 132, 153, 189
Tay Ninh 25, 216, 240, 278, 294
Tet 24, 26, 123, 126, 130, 153, 189
Thanh An 81
Third Battalion Fourth Infantry 127
Third Battalion Seventeenth Cavalry: B Company 80
Third Squadron Fourth Cavalry 126, 240; A Comapny 80; B Company 80
Third Squadron Twenty-second Regulars 126, 133, 138, 153
Thu-Rung 82
Trai My 81
Trang Bang 79, 97, 109, 127
Trapezoid 36
Tri Tam 81
Trung Lap 82, 87
Truong Chua River 86
Tun Pho 82
tunnels 17, 20, 23, 24

Vinh Cu 108

War Zone C 17, 27, 131, 187, 278
Wolfhounds see First Battalion Twenty-seventh Infantry; Second Battalion Twenty-seventh Infantry

Xom Bao Cong 78
Xom Giong Dau 248, 293
Xuan Than 82